Philosophical Conversations

Drawing by Paul Niehaus.

Philosophical Conversations

Robert M. Martin

broadview press

Library and Archives Canada Cataloguing in Publication

Martin, Robert M.
   Philosophical conversations / Robert M. Martin

ISBN 1-55111-649-9

   1. Philosophy—Introductions.   I. Title.

BD21.M37   2005   100   C2005-905436-0

Broadview Press Ltd. is an independent, international publishing house, incorporated in 1985. Broadview believes in shared ownership, both with its employees and with the general public; since the year 2000 Broadview shares have traded publicly on the Toronto Venture Exchange under the symbol BDP.

North America
Post Office Box 1243, Peterborough, Ontario, Canada K9J 7H5
3576 California Road, Post Office Box 1015, Orchard Park, NY, USA 14127
Tel: (705) 743-8990; Fax: (705) 743-8353;
email: customerservice@broadviewpress.com

UK, Ireland, and continental Europe
NBN Plymbridge, Estover Road, Plymouth PL6 7PY UK
Tel: 44 (0) 1752 202301;   Fax: 44 (0) 1752 202331
Fax Order Line: 44 (0) 1752 202333
Customer Service: cservs@nbnplymbridge.com Orders: orders@nbnplymbridge.com

Australia and New Zealand
UNIREPS, University of New South Wales
Sydney, NSW, 2052 Australia
Tel: 61 2 9664 0999; Fax: 61 2 9664 5420
email: info.press@unsw.edu.au

www.broadviewpress.com

Broadview Press Ltd. gratefully acknowledges the financial support of the Government of Canada through the Book Publishing Industry Development Program for our publishing activities.

Consulting Editor for Philosophy: John Burbidge.

Typesetting and assembly: True to Type Inc., Mississauga, Canada.

PRINTED IN CANADA

Contents

Conversation III: Ethics

Participants: SCEPTIC • UTILITARIAN • DEONTOLOGIST • RIGHTS-THEORIST • KANTIAN • SUBJECTIVIST • RELATIVIST

Conversation IV: Mind and Body

Participants: SCEPTIC • DUALIST • IDENTITY THEORIST • ELIMINATIVIST • BEHAVIOURIST

Conversation V: Determinism, Free Will, and Punishment

Participants: IDENTITY THEORIST • SCEPTIC • DETERMINIST • FATALIST • MATHEMATICIAN • PHYSICIST • INDETERMINIST • HARD DETERMINIST • SOFT DETERMINIST • UTILITARIAN • RETRIBUTIVIST • PSYCHOLOGIST

Conversation VI: Knowledge

Participants: SCEPTIC • DEFINER • CARTESIAN • FALLIBILIST • EMPIRICIST • RATIONALIST

Conversation VII: Identity; Meaning

Participants: SCEPTIC • CARTESIAN • EMPIRICIST • RATIONALIST •
ANTIREALIST • INTERNALIST • REFERENTIALIST • SPEECH-ACT THEORIST

Epilogue: Quotations from Bertrand Russell / 335

Glossary Workbook / 337

Acknowledgements

Warm thanks to Janet Sisson and her class at Mount Royal College for having tried out a penultimate draft of this book; their extensive comments have resulted in many changes for the better. And to Paul Viminitz, John W. Burbidge, and an anonymous referee for their many very helpful suggestions. And to the students in the author's Philosophy 1000 classes at Dalhousie University over the past few years who were subjected to preliminary drafts of this textbook, for their valuable feedback about what they understood and didn't in those drafts, and for their enthusiasm about this project. And, as always, to the friendly and supportive folks at Broadview Press.

Introduction

This textbook is different from most others you'll see, so it's important that you pay attention to this Introduction: it will tell you what to expect, and how to cope with it.

1. Philosophy

Socrates—maybe the greatest philosopher of all time—grandly announced that "the unexamined life is not worth living." Do you think that's true? I mean, really? You're right, it isn't. It's an exaggeration. But stretching your mind and using your intelligence in abstract ways can be good for you; and many students find these activities interesting and amusing. Let's hope you're one of them.

To describe the subject to newcomers, textbooks often begin by reporting that the word 'philosophy' comes from Greek words meaning *love of wisdom*. This describes philosophy in a larger sense: philosophy is the search for some very general truths. But philosophy isn't in the business of providing "wisdom" in the form of vague but deep inspirational pronouncements on the meaning of life and the universe and everything. For that sort of thing, you should consult a guru, or start reading bumper stickers. Some philosophers have tried in the past to give advice about how to live, and sometimes that advice was good advice. Maybe you'll find some things in this book relevant in that way. Maybe not. A more modest claim for philosophy—one this book can make good on—is that it can give you practice in good critical abstract reasoning, some idea of how to spot reliable information, and an appreciation of the powers and limitation of rational thought. All this might help you become "wiser" in some sense.

Well then, you ask, what is it exactly that philosophers do? Well, ... um ... er.... Actually, it's not possible to give you a brief but accurate, informative and useful explanation of precisely what philosophers think and write about. Philosophy is a lot of little things, not one big thing. It's a large and miscellaneous collection of different problems and proposed answers. You'll find out what many of these are as you read this book.

2. How to Study Philosophy

Philosophy is unlike other things you study in university, and this book is to be approached differently from your other university textbooks. Before we get down to business, a few words on how things work around here.

The main way that philosophy differs from other subjects is that right at the beginning of an introductory philosophy class, you deal with questions whose answers are controversial. By contrast, in introductory chemistry, for example, the questions you start with have answers all chemists agree on; you're expected to accept and master these answers, and to be able to give them when asked. Of course, there are lots of chemistry questions whose answers are controversial—where the experts disagree on what the answers are. But you don't get to these questions until much later in your study, at a fairly advanced level. On the other hand, in philosophy, you get to contested matters right at the beginning.

So this book is different. Instead of presenting you with a lot of basic truths that you're expected to accept, here you'll find a variety of different answers to the same question; each answer will be accompanied by reasoning to try to make you accept it, and reject the alternatives.

Because several conflicting answers are presented to each question, these readings are written as if spoken by a variety of characters in a play, with the name of each character corresponding to the position the character holds. Pay close attention to who's saying what, so you can keep track of what's involved in the position each character represents.

What you'll read looks like a play, but it's pretty bad as drama: the characters are one-dimensional, and they happen, by unbelievable silly coincidence, to be around to talk about their positions at just the point when this becomes relevant. There's no plot and no dramatic tension. Well, this book doesn't try to be good theatre. The idea behind this format is simply to gather positions, arguments, and replies together, and to avoid having to say, over and over again, things like, "Someone who believes position A would claim that B but the adherent of the contrary position C would object that D and then the holder of position A would reply that E" and so on.

One of the characters you'll find in several of the discussions is named SCEPTIC. In philosophy, a sceptic is somebody who doubts the truth of some position, so when you hear somebody identified as a sceptic, you should ask, "A sceptic about what?" In this book, however, SCEPTIC appears in various places just to ask questions, raise doubts, and make criticisms of whatever position is being discussed at the time. You shouldn't conclude, however, that a philosophical sceptic about one position would necessarily be sceptical about something else.

None of the characters is referred to anywhere using gendered pronouns ('he' 'she' 'his' etc.) and you should resist the temptation—if you have it—to think of them as male. Most of the important work in philosophy in past centuries was done by men, but that's definitely not true any more.

In this book you'll find yourself presented with a variety of contrary answers, and you may find yourself wondering which one you're supposed to believe, and why it's not made clear to you which line is the official one. This unclarity is intentional: *none* of these conflicting views is being presented as the one you're supposed to accept. Don't try to guess which answers the author of this book really believes, or which answers he's trying to get you to accept (or to pretend you accept). There is no official doctrine that's being urged on you. Each of the contrary positions you'll be presented with is fully philosophically respectable (though they can't all be right!). For each one there are very good philosophers who believe it, and very good arguments in its favour and against its competitors. You probably will wind up believing some of the positions we look at. This is good: reading this book is judging a contest in which several contrary positions are vying for the prize, which is your acceptance. But it's all right also if, after careful consideration of all the competing positions, you don't know which to believe. The point is, you can achieve full success (and good grades) in a philosophy class no matter what positions—if any—you wind up believing. Some students find this uncertainty, these shifts in position, the lack of final answers, a bit confusing and troubling. Others find it exhilarating: everything is up for grabs!

Your job is first of all to get a thorough understanding and appreciation of a number of different competing answers to the same questions. If you think that any of the various answers proposed for a question is just stupid, then you've probably not understood it fully. Certainly you haven't appreciated it fully. Every one of the answers you'll find here has been accepted by some very smart philosophers. Every one of them is a live option today, and has something to be said for it. This is not to say that you should try to believe all of them—each contradicts other attempts to answer a particular question, so they can't all be right. Neither is it to say that you should try to remain undecided about who's right. Approach each position you'll read about open-mindedly, but after careful and sympathetic consideration of a position, feel free to decide it's definitely wrong.

Both the bad news and the good news about philosophy is that it's sometimes complicated and mind stretching. The concepts and the reasoning in philosophy are sometimes more complex and difficult than the simple stuff you'd run into in an introductory class in, for example, the censored Department. The author of this textbook is aware that introductory students can find philosophy a bit daunting, and has tried hard to explain everything in a clear, accessible, and friendly sort of way. But you'll still have to do some work. A good deal of what's in this book is simple, but at some points, things get more complicated and subtle. Re-read everything, and re-think it, several times. The more you do this, the more interesting ideas you'll find. Don't worry if, at the end of the day, some things are still not completely clear to you. In philosophy, there are always more depths to dig down to. And don't be discouraged by the prospect of a substantial intellectual workout. You might even find it enjoyable (like a good energetic exercise in the gym can be physically enjoyable—they tell me). You'll feel your brain getting stronger by the day.

Each section in these readings is quite short, and there's all together quite a small volume of reading to be done, in comparison to other classes. But that doesn't mean that you should do less work in this class. You'll have to read what's here very carefully, and think about it hard. Each reading must be done more than once. You should read each section before it is dealt with in class— that way, you'll be able to benefit from class lecture and discussion. Then you should read it at least one more time after class treatment.

After you've read a section, it's a very good idea to write down a summary of the positions and arguments, or try to explain it to a friend whom you're able to force to listen. You should also write down overall outlines of sections and of whole Conversations. Write these outlines in your own words—don't just copy what's said in the book. Just as memorizing and parroting back what's said is completely useless when it's done without understanding, taking notes by copying verbatim is also not helpful. Writing these little outlines for yourself in your own words is a much more effective studying technique than just reading and thinking, because it involves active processing of the ideas on your part. These outlines will also come in very handy when it's time for you to study for a test or write a paper.

Students who have read preliminary drafts of this book have sometimes suggested that this sort of outline be included. The reason that outlines have not been included is not that the author is lazy or disinclined to be helpful. The reason is that it's a very important part of the learning process for you to do this yourself.

Philosophical writing and talk include a lot of technical language—words which you may be unfamiliar with, or which are used with specialized meanings. The author of this book has tried to keep this sort of technical talk to a minimum, but sometimes technical jargon is useful and worth including as a shorthand way to refer to complicated concepts. When technical terms you're likely to be unfamiliar with are used, they are defined. Your job will be to make sure you understand and remember their meanings. These specialized terms will often be used in your classroom, and you'll be expected to show that you understand them on whatever written work is expected of you. So it's important that you master them. Most of these terms are italicized in the text. There is a Glossary Workbook at the back of this book where you'll find a list of the specialized philosophical terms in each section. While you're reading, or when you've finished, write a definition of each term in the Workbook, in your own words. Refer to your definitions if you've forgotten what a term means, or when preparing for a test or paper.

You've succeeded in studying this book when you've come to a good understanding of all the questions, of all the answers proposed to them, and of all the arguments back and forth. While you're reading, keep asking yourself exactly what the question under discussion is, what each answer to that question involves, and what the arguments in favour of that answer and against the contrary positions are. You should, at the end, be able to state in your own words exactly what the questions are, what each answer to a question is, how it agrees or disagrees with the other answers, and what the arguments are, pro and con.

3. Arguments

When philosophers use the word *argument*, they don't mean a disagreement involving yelling and slamming doors. An argument in philosophy is a set of considerations that attempt to give convincing reasons for some conclusion. They're vital to the philosophical endeavour. It's entirely insufficient, in philosophy, merely to express some opinion you believe. You have to give arguments in its defence.

You'll find lots of arguments in this book. Some students, thinking perhaps of "arguments" in the sense of *disagreements*, understand the phrase 'an argument for position X' to mean *an argument against position X*. That's not the way we'll be using that phrase. We'll be talking about (and presenting) arguments *for* (= *in favour of*) positions, and arguments *against* positions. Both are important in philosophy. What philosophers have to do is not only to think of good reasons in favour of their views, but also to survey the alternatives, and to say what's wrong with them.

An argument has two parts: the assumptions (sometimes called *premises*) and the conclusion: what the person presenting the argument is trying to give you reasons to believe. Here's a sample argument (though not a philosophical one): "Fred must have been here, because the peanut butter jar is out, and he's the only one who eats peanut butter." Here, the conclusion is that Fred was here; the assumptions—premises—are that the peanut butter is out, and that Fred is the only one who could be responsible for that. If the assumptions of the argument aren't true, then they don't lend any credence to the conclusion; so one important way to criticize an argument is to try to undermine its assumptions. In this case: is the peanut butter jar really out? (It's probably easy to check on this, just by looking.) And is Fred really the only one who eats peanut butter? (If Sally and Arnold do too, then they might have done it, and the strength with which the argument supports the conclusion—makes it believable—is greatly reduced.) Sometimes the assumptions behind an argument are unstated, just intended to be understood. ("Fred must have been here—the peanut butter jar is out.") So the evaluation and criticism of an argument very often involves making the assumptions of the argument explicit, and asking whether they are really true.

But even when the premises of an argument are very clearly true, it wouldn't make its conclusion believable if the premises do not give much logical support to the conclusion. So one might criticize the sample argument by claiming that, even were those assumptions true, they wouldn't necessarily mean that the conclusion is true. This is criticizing the *logic* of an argument, rather than its premises. We could agree that Fred's the only one who eats peanut butter, and that the peanut butter jar is in fact out, but imagine other plausible reasons why this is so. (Maybe it's a new jar that Sally just bought, and hasn't put away yet.)

A frequently used way to criticize the logic of an argument is the "that's-just-like-arguing" criticism. What you do is to produce a different argument with true premises and a clearly false conclusion, but in which the reasoning process is the same as in the one you're criticizing. Here's a very simple example. Suppose you were interested in showing that the logic was defective in this argument: "For centuries, every culture included a belief in God. Therefore, God really does exist." You might cast doubt on this argument by claiming that it was just like arguing that for centuries, every culture included the belief that the world is flat; therefore the world really is flat. The destructiveness of this sort of criticism depends on whether the logic of the clearly mistaken argument is the same as the logic of the argument you want to criticize. Be on the lookout for this sort of criticism in this book.

Both of these types of criticism—of the premises of an argument and of its logic—are ways to try to show that an argument does not establish its conclusion. If either of these criticisms is right, then potential support for that conclusion is removed, but it doesn't follow that the conclusion is false. It just shows that the conclusion is unsupported by that argument. There may be other arguments to support that conclusion; but even if nobody can provide a good argument to support a position, that still doesn't show that the position is false. But there is a more direct way to try to show the falsity of some view: to provide an argument *against* it. A very common way to do this—one you'll find often in this book—is to argue in this way: "Well, if that position were true, then it would follow that X. But X is obviously false." This sort of criticism of a position works provided that the X in question really does follow from the position, and that X is obviously false. Replies by defenders of the position will try to show either that X doesn't follow, or that X is not obviously false.

In this book you'll find a great number of arguments, and criticism of just about each one of them. Much of the fascination of philosophy comes from seeing ingenious arguments cooked up by the great philosophers, especially in favour of positions you think are implausible, and from discovering their unexpected criticisms of arguments you thought were good ones. But a good deal of the excitement in reading philosophy comes from the opportunity to create and criticize arguments yourself. When you come across a question in this book, stop and try to answer it yourself. Try to create persuasive arguments in favour of your answer. When you come across someone else's answer, stop and try to evaluate it, and the arguments provided to support it. Identify the conclusion of each argument, and its assumed premises, making any unstated assumptions explicit in your mind. Ask yourself whether these assumptions are really true, and whether the conclusion follows from them— that is, if those assumptions were true, would they really make the conclusion more believable. If you think that the argument fails for one of these reasons or another, can you see a way to fix it? Can you think of other ways to argue for the conclusion?

4. Notes on "Suggested Readings" Sections

The aim of the "Suggested Readings" section you'll find at the end of each conversation is to provide you with a list of readings (1) that are the best-known historical sources for most of the major positions discussed, and (2) that you might be able to read, profitably, with only the present book as philosophical background. These two aims are often in conflict, as you might imagine; and other philosophers will disagree about what's on this list, and what's been left off.

Years of birth and death are given for authors who aren't contemporary or close to it.

Sometimes what will be listed is a book of which only a part is relevant to the immediate topic. Sometimes this part is indicated on the lists; but when it isn't, you'll be able to figure out what to read when you look through the book. Only the titles of books have been provided—not the rest of the usual bibliographical information (publisher, location, date) because in almost every case many editions are available. Anyway, you don't really need all that bibliographical stuff to find the book in a library.

It will often be more useful for you, when looking for further readings, to find a good philosophical anthology, rather than to seek out the individual books listed in the "Suggested Readings" sections. Most anthologies designed for philosophy courses contain excerpts from books or articles by some of the authors mentioned in these sections; and substituting other readings from a good anthology will often be just as good. There are hundreds of good anthologies of philosophical readings available. You'll probably be able to find several in your university library, or in your university bookstore, or on the sagging bookshelves in your philosophy instructor's office. (Ask nicely and maybe you'll be allowed to borrow some.)

Among the Suggested Readings you'll find works by Descartes, Hobbes, Locke, Hume, Kant, and Mill. By far the best place for students to find these readings is on a website produced by Professor Jonathan Bennett: <http://www.earlymoderntexts.com>. The most famous works by these philosophers are on-line there, prepared by Bennett with students in mind— slightly shortened to eliminate repetitions, translated into modern English, with a style and vocabulary you can read, and with occasional clearly marked explanatory interpolations. You'll also find works on this website by Berkeley, Leibniz, Malebranche, Reid, and Spinoza. You're strongly advised to go to this extremely valuable website where these readings may be downloaded for free.

Okay, let's begin.

CONVERSATION I

Philosophy of Religion

Participants: RATIONALIST • ATHEIST • COSMOLOGIST • BIOLOGIST • PRAGMATIST • PSYCHOLOGIST • FIDEIST • SYMBOLIST • MYSTIC

1. The First-Cause Argument

RATIONALIST: I'm a religious person, but I also believe in rationality, logic, proof, evidence, and science. So I think that my religious beliefs ought to be reasonable, and that they should—at least—be compatible with what science and our ordinary experience tell us. But more than that—I think the truths of religion are actually provable by reasoning and evidence, the same way scientific truths are.

ATHEIST: Really! How's that supposed to work?

RATIONALIST: I'll give you two lines of reasoning that I think show that there's a God. The first one is called the *First Cause Argument*, sometimes also known as the *Cosmological Argument*. Here's how that one goes. It starts out with the idea that there are events happening in the natural world right now—something that nobody can deny—plus the reasonable idea that everything that happens has a cause.

ATHEIST: Well, of course, it's obvious that there are things going on in the world. And I'm inclined to agree with you that everything has a cause. I like the idea of being scientific, just as you do, and science seems to be based on the assumption that everything has a cause. So go on.

RATIONALIST: Okay, think of something that's happening right now, anything at all, call it Event A. We agree that everything has a cause, so Event A has a cause, whatever it is. So there must be some other event, call it Event B, that's the cause of Event A. Causes always happen before their effects; Event B happened earlier than Event A, at some time or other in the past. But Event B itself also had a cause, call it Event C, that happened before it did, and Event C had an earlier cause, Event D, and so on back in time.

ATHEIST: Okay, since we assume that everything has a cause, then we have to think that there are causes for causes, and so on, back further and further.

RATIONALIST: But this series of causes of causes, which we imagine going in a chain further and further back in time, can't have extended infinitely back into the past. There must have been a first item in this series, the *First Cause*. The First Cause is what religions call God. He's what caused the universe to start up, what some philosophers call the *Unmoved Mover*.

ATHEIST: Wait, aren't you contradicting yourself? I mean, you started with the assumption that everything has a cause. But now you're saying that there has to be a first event in a series of events, an event that doesn't have a cause. That shows that your assumptions can't both be true.

RATIONALIST: Why is that?

ATHEIST: Well, one assumption is that every event has a cause. The second assumption is that there can't be an infinite series. The second assumption means that there has to be a start to every series, but the first one means that there can't be a start to a series of causes, because that would be an event without a cause. You can't have it both ways. Either there's an event without a cause starting this series, in which case your first assumption is false, or else the series is infinite, in which case your second assumption is false.

RATIONALIST: Okay, then how about this. Suppose that there is a start to the series of causes, namely God, but this doesn't contradict the assumption that everything has a cause, because God causes himself.

ATHEIST: Causes *himself*? That doesn't make any sense to me. I mean, when something X causes something Y, then X has to exist first, before Y does, right? So how can God exist before himself?

RATIONALIST: God can do anything!

ATHEIST: Anything that isn't just nonsense.

RATIONALIST: Some religious thinkers haven't thought that's just nonsense. Anyway, maybe what I should have said is that God doesn't have a cause, but everything *natural* has a cause—that is, that everything in the universe of physical (and mental) events, everything of the sort science deals with—has a cause. So, if natural events were all there were, then there would have to be an infinite series running backward earlier and earlier without a start. But there can't be such a thing. So there must have been an event that wasn't natural, to start things off—a supernatural event, which doesn't need a cause.

ATHEIST: Okay, I suppose that takes care of that problem. But let's talk about your second assumption. Why do you think that there can't be an infinite series of events going back in time, with no first member of that series? What's wrong with that idea?

RATIONALIST: The whole idea of an infinite series of events, stretching back forever, without any start, makes no sense. There can't be genuinely infinite things in nature. Everything must have a start, or else it doesn't exist. So a series of events must have a first event.

ATHEIST: But I still don't see why there can't be an infinite series of natural events stretching back further and further forever.

RATIONALIST: I just told you. First of all, everything that exists has to have a start. If something doesn't have a starting point, then it doesn't exist.

ATHEIST: I don't accept that. I think that maybe there can be an infinite series of things stretching back in time, so I do think that there can be something that exists that doesn't have a start—that series of events we're talking about.

RATIONALIST: Do you really think that the universe has extended back infinitely in time?

ATHEIST: I don't know. But I don't see any reason to think it hasn't. Why do you think that assumption is true?

RATIONALIST: I don't think there can be infinities in nature. Look, the number of grains of sand on the beach is very large, but there aren't literally an infinite number of them. Everything in nature is finite: finite in number, like grains of sand on the beach, and finite in duration, with a beginning and an end. It doesn't even make sense to talk about an infinite number of grains of sand.

ATHEIST: How about the infinite number of points in a line?

RATIONALIST: That's just a mathematical abstraction—a consequence of the fact that you can think of a line being divided in half, then each half divided, and so on, without end. It doesn't correspond to any reality in nature. The fact that there can't be infinities in nature was known even to the ancient Greek philosophers who thought up this argument.

ATHEIST: The ancient Greeks had trouble in general thinking about infinity. But modern mathematics has made infinity a more manageable notion. For example, in algebra, we can do sums of infinite series, and in calculus we can manage infinitely small lengths. We now know that the ancient Greeks were too narrow-minded about what's possible and what isn't.

RATIONALIST: You're right in saying that modern mathematics has ways of dealing with infinities that earlier mathematicians didn't know about. But that doesn't mean that there really are infinities in the real world. There are lots of ideas in modern mathematics that don't correspond to things in the actual world. The idea of the square root of -1 makes mathematical sense, but that doesn't mean that you'll find any real-world object whose length is $\sqrt{-1}$ centimetres. But here's another reason why there can't be an infinite series of events stretching back in time. That series wouldn't have a start. But that can't be: if something doesn't have a start, it doesn't exist.

ATHEIST: I don't accept that line of reasoning. That's just repeating your assumption that there can't be an infinite series stretching back into the past, a series with no start. I'm looking for some reason to believe that.

COSMOLOGIST: Um, may I put in a few words here? You're talking about the *Cosmological Argument*, and I'm a cosmologist, so maybe I can tell you something about what scientists have to say about the matter.

ATHEIST: What's a cosmologist?

COSMOLOGIST: We're scientists specializing in studying the origin and general structure of the universe.

ATHEIST: Good. What do you think about causes and First Causes?

RATIONALIST: Yes, let's hear. I agree that science always should be considered where it's relevant.

COSMOLOGIST: Okay, I'll give you a simplified version of what we think. For decades we've known that the universe is expanding. Until a few years ago, there were three competing theories, each with its enthusiastic scientific advocates, about the history of the universe. The first theory can be called the *Steady State Theory*. This is the view that stuff is coming into existence at some central point in the universe right now, and has been doing that continuously, forever. After stuff comes into existence, it begins to stick together to make stars and so on, and to move outward from that point at which it originated. That would explain why we see all those stars and galaxies and dust clouds and whatnot moving away from each other wherever we look.

RATIONALIST: What causes all those new little bits of matter to come into existence?

COSMOLOGIST: Nothing, they just arrive, and that's all there is to it.

RATIONALIST: Hmm, I don't like that idea very much. Well, let's hear the other theories.

COSMOLOGIST: To understand the second theory, think of playing a movie of the history of the universe backwards, and imagine that we'd see things moving back to a central point where everything that exists now originated, all at once, in an unimaginably, infinitely dense and infinitely tiny point of stuff, which exploded, sending bits of matter that congealed into stars and gas clouds, and other things, moving outward. This theory is called the *Big Bang Theory*.

RATIONALIST: Wait a minute, what caused the Big Bang? What happened before that?

COSMOLOGIST: The answer supplied by the Big Bang Theory is: nothing. The Big Bang was the start of things.

RATIONALIST: Nothing? That's no good. I didn't like the Steady State Theory because it had little bits of stuff continually coming into existence out of nothing, with no cause. And the Big Bang Theory doesn't seem any better—it also has the material universe arising out of nothing, without cause. According to the Big Bang Theory, this all happened at once, but that doesn't make it any better. What's the third theory?

COSMOLOGIST: That one agrees with the Big Bang Theory that everything existing now originated at once, in a big explosion. But it doesn't think that this explosion was the first event. Before that, everything was moving inward—the universe was contracting—for a long time, until it reached that point and exploded. And before it began contracting, it was expanding. And another explosion started it expanding. And there was a contraction period before that explosion. And so on. So this theory, which we might call the *Cyclical Theory*, thinks of cycles of expansion-contraction-explosion, expansion-contraction-explosion, and so on, repeating over and over, infinitely back into the past, and infinitely forward into the future.

RATIONALIST: But there wasn't any first event?

COSMOLOGIST: No, this has just happened over and over.

RATIONALIST: At least this theory doesn't have any causeless events, as the other two did. But this one has a series that didn't start. That's no good either.

COSMOLOGIST: It's inevitable that any scientific story will contradict at least one of your assumptions. Science deals only in natural events. They all would have to have either a first causeless event—a natural first cause—or no first event, meaning a series without a start. That's just logic.

RATIONALIST: None of those theories is acceptable. The Cyclical Theory has a series without a start. The Big Bang Theory has a causeless natural event, and the Steady State Theory has lots of them. All of them are defective.

ATHEIST: Hey, I don't think it's up to us to tell scientists which scientific theories are acceptable and which aren't!

RATIONALIST: Well maybe we can, when a theory just doesn't make sense.

ATHEIST: But look. The Cosmological Argument was based on the assumptions that certain things—a series without a start, an event without a cause—were impossible, unthinkable. But these supposedly unthinkable ideas are built into those scientific theories, in one way or another. So these ideas are thinkable, after all, and what proves this is that they have been thought by reputable scientists.

RATIONALIST: Hmm, well, so scientists can accept the ideas of natural events happening without causes, or of an infinite series?

COSMOLOGIST: Well, yes, most of us can. There's another area of science, quantum physics, which also features uncaused events in its central theory. Here's a simple example of how that works. Imagine a bit of substance composed of a radioactive element. Each atom of that element will emit a certain particle at some point, and turn into another element. If the radioactive element has a half-life of, say, a year, that means that after a year, about half of the atoms will have emitted the particle. Some will do it much sooner, and some much later. The point is that there is no reason why one atom emits a particle at one time rather than another. Two atoms exactly the same in every relevant characteristic will emit particles after very different lengths of time, and there's no cause for this.

RATIONALIST: But there must be some difference that accounts for this! It's unthinkable that there is something like this with no cause whatsoever!

COSMOLOGIST: No, it's now a part of standard accepted physical theory that there is no cause.

ATHEIST: So it seems that it is thinkable after all.

RATIONALIST: And, if I understand them correctly, the Cyclical Theory and the Steady State Theory both agree that there was no first event, just things happening, over and over, infinitely back into the past. So according to the scientists who believe these theories, there would be an infinite series of events?

COSMOLOGIST: Right, but more recent observations have cast doubts on the cyclical theory.

RATIONALIST: Observations? Really?

COSMOLOGIST: Right. Observations have led to an estimate of the amount of stuff in the universe. It appears that there's not enough to produce the gravity necessary to make everything slow down and stop and start contracting. So the Cyclical Theory is unpopular at the moment. The Steady State Theory hasn't been a contender for years. So the Big Bang Theory is nowadays the only live option. But I have to admit that cosmology is in a state of rapid development and change. The prevailing view is highly subject to change!

ATHEIST: Okay, but the important point for us isn't which theory they believe at the moment. The important point is that neither the idea of events without cause nor the idea of a series of events stretching back in time is really unthinkable. Reputable scientists have thought them—I mean, they've included these ideas in their theories.

RATIONALIST: Well, I don't like either idea. There must be something wrong with the science that includes such absurd ideas. Didn't you agree with me earlier that every natural event must have a cause?

ATHEIST: Yes, that seemed to me to be right, at the time. I guess I was thinking that this was the basis of all science, and of rational clear-headed thinking about things in general. I mean, if some everyday ordinary event happened, like a doorbell ringing or a light going on, and you asked people why it happened, and they said that there was no reason at all, no cause whatsoever, you'd think that there was something wrong with their thinking. Imagine that your car was making a squeaky noise, and you took your car into the car repair shop, but the mechanic didn't fix it, and explained to you that there wasn't any cause at all for that squeak. That would be a good sign that you should find a different mechanic. You'd know that there must be a cause—it's just that the mechanic hasn't found it. And the same thing is usually true in science. When scientists haven't found a cause for something, they think that there must be one they haven't found yet, and keep looking. But I guess that isn't the case everywhere in science. The belief that everything has a cause is funny. We don't learn it from our experience, the way we learn, for example, that all dogs bark: we never experience a non-barking dog. But there are a really large number of things whose causes (if there are causes) we haven't experienced. I wonder why I think that everything must have a cause? Maybe that belief has to be dropped.[1]

RATIONALIST: Anyway, I just had an idea. Big-Bang scientists believe in a first cause, something that started everything off, but which itself has no cause; and so do the religious thinkers who see God as the causeless first cause. Maybe in some way they're talking about the same thing? Maybe the Big Bang is the Divine Creator?

ATHEIST: That's a cute thought, but it doesn't seem very religiously plausible. It's hard to think of worshipping and praying to a point with infinite mass that exploded, destroying itself, billions of years ago. Doesn't sound like any religion I've ever heard of! Hey, maybe I should start one with ...

---

1 More discussion of the idea that everything has a cause will occur in Conversation V; and of how (if it's true) we might know it, in Conversation VI.

RATIONALIST: Okay, okay, but seriously, here's a version of the First Cause Argument that maybe doesn't run into the difficulties we've just talked about. No matter how science tells us the universe came about, there's still one question that no science could ever answer. That question is: Why is there something rather than nothing? This question doesn't ask for the causes of any particular item: maybe science is the only way to answer this question, or else to tell us that one or more very peculiar items don't have causes. The question considers the whole enormous series of events that make up the history of the universe, and the whole collection of things that have inhabited it, and will into the future. Why all of this, rather than nothing at all? Isn't something outside the natural series, something supernatural rather than natural, the only way to answer this question?

ATHEIST: Well, maybe there isn't any answer.

RATIONALIST: That's not a particularly satisfying response!

ATHEIST: Well, if you can explain each individual thing on the basis of the earlier thing that caused it, then what's missing? Isn't that an explanation of everything? And if you take the whole pile of things, all together— everything there is—and asked what explained *that*, then there can't be any answer. I mean, X can explain Y only if X is a different thing from Y, not part of Y. But if you ask what explained the whole universe, then there can't be anything else to explain it.

RATIONALIST: I'm taking the whole *natural* universe and asking what explains it. You're right—you can't explain it by anything in the natural universe. That's why you have to give it a supernatural explanation—a religious one.

ATHEIST: I think that the real issue here is whether a scientific cosmological theory gives a full, satisfactory explanation all by itself. You suppose that natural cosmological theories, which rely only on natural events and caus- es, must always be incomplete, and God must always be brought in to fill a gap. But it seems that the scientific theories can do a good job without having to rely on anything supernatural. It reminds me of a famous story involving Napoleon and the astronomer and mathematician Pierre Laplace. Napoleon said to Laplace, "You have written this huge book on the system of the world without once mentioning the author of the uni- verse." Laplace replied, "Sire, I had no need of that hypothesis."

2. The Argument from Design

RATIONALIST: Anyway, here's the second argument I mentioned earlier. This one starts off with the fact that many things in the observable natural world are very complex and highly adapted to their function. For instance, think about woodpeckers. They eat insects that live under the bark of trees, and they have to peck holes in the bark to get at them. And they're beautifully engineered to do this. Their beaks are very sharp, and fairly short, because a long pointy beak wouldn't be as strong and would tend to break more often under the enormous pressure exerted on it when the bird pecks on a tree. Their tails are short, blunt, and very muscular—built just right to brace against the tree to give the bird more leverage as it pecks. Their toes are curved to give a really strong grip on the tree, so they don't fall off when pecking really hard. The enormous force exerted by their fast strong pecking would jiggle around and injure any other bird's brain, but woodpeckers' brains are specially cushioned so as to remain undamaged. Other such examples of complex adaptation of a plant or animal to its needs are everywhere in nature.

ATHEIST: Okay, so what?

RATIONALIST: So all this is evidence that things have been *designed* to suit their environment. And design implies that there's a designer.

ATHEIST: Oops, hold on! Where do you get that?

RATIONALIST: Here's a familiar analogy. Suppose you were walking along a beach and found a watch lying on the sand. Even if you weren't familiar with things like this, you would still be able to figure out what it was for, once you noticed that the hands moved regularly and pointed in exactly the same direction at the same time every day. If you opened it up, you'd see a complicated and precise mechanism, exactly suited for that time-keeping function. It would be clear to you that this thing was not a random result of natural processes—of the action of the waves on the sand, or the wind. It's clear that this thing was designed to suit its function by an intelligent designer. You'd be right, of course: human intelligent designers, hired by the watch manufacturer, were responsible. But now consider all those things we see around us—like the woodpecker—that show just as much or more evidence of ingenious intelligent design to suit their functions. No people designed them. So there must be an intelligent designer who created natural objects, one superior in power to even the finest human watchmaker. And that super designer is, of course, God. We don't encounter God directly, but we see evidence of his intelligent design everywhere.

ATHEIST: Hmm, well. What did you say that argument was called?

RATIONALIST: It's usually called the *Argument From Design*, but it's also called the *Teleological Argument*. The word 'teleological' means *having to do with ends*. The argument is called that because it's based on the idea that things are set up to suit their ends. The woodpecker's engineering suits its aim of catching bugs.

ATHEIST: That's sort of like the First Cause Argument, in some ways, isn't it?

RATIONALIST: Yes, they both claim that something that we can obviously see in the natural world is evidence for the existence of an unseen God, because God provides the only explanation for what we see.

ATHEIST: But is that sort of argument—that pattern of reasoning—a good one in general? I mean, do the premises of that sort of argument support the conclusion? Do they make the conclusion more believable?

RATIONALIST: Yes they do. These arguments are a perfectly acceptable form of reasoning, sometimes called an *argument to the best explanation*. Some premises are presented which, presumably, everyone can agree upon; and if there's only one explanation for those premises, or if one explanation is much more plausible than any other, then we have a good reason to accept that explanation as conclusion to the argument. Here's a really simple example. You go outside in the morning and see the pavement is wet. The best explanation of that is that it rained overnight. So you conclude that it rained.

ATHEIST: Unless there's another plausible explanation. Maybe the guy next door had his lawn sprinkler out overnight, spraying water all over the place.

RATIONALIST: Right, the argument works when the conclusion is the only explanation, or at least, the only plausible one. It's a useful sort of argument for establishing a conclusion whose truth isn't known by direct observation. (You wouldn't need that argument, for example, if you *saw* it raining overnight.) The argument to the best explanation is also a familiar pattern of scientific reasoning. Nobody's ever seen electrons, but their existence is accepted, because it's the best explanation for all sorts of observations.

ATHEIST: Okay, that sort of argument pattern sounds all right to me in general. So what's at issue with both the First Cause Argument and the Argument from Design is whether God provides the only explanation for what we observe. That's really the basis for the central criticism of the First Cause Argument: the Cosmologist's scientific accounts of what might have happened far back in the history of the universe provide other sorts of explanations for why things eventuated in their current observed state, so the existence of God turned out not to be the only possible explanation: there are scientific explanations that are plausible—at least to the scientists who know about such things—and the argument loses its force.

RATIONALIST: Okay, but my argument was that the scientific explanations are not plausible.

ATHEIST: So what we have to do in this case, for the Argument from Design, is to ask the same question: whether there's any other sort of possible plausible explanation for the adaptations that living things show, other than being designed by a designer.

RATIONALIST: Yes, I agree.

BIOLOGIST: Can I say something here? We biologists have what almost all of us think is a successful scientific explanation for the fact that living organisms are suited to their environment. The explanation was given in broad outline by Darwin in the mid-1800s. It's the *Theory of Evolution Through Natural Selection.*

RATIONALIST: Of course we've all heard of that, but I'd appreciate it if you would summarize what that theory says.

BIOLOGIST: Okay. Darwin's Theory of Evolution basically says that the current adaptations of living things can be accounted for by two factors, called *Random Variation* and *Natural Selection.* Random Variation means that living things don't always produce offspring that are exactly like themselves; occasionally there will be a genetic mutation, or a genetic recombination. These change around the genes in the organism in a way that produces changes in the organism's characteristics—changes that may be passed on to that organism's own offspring. These variations are random as far as adaptation to the environment is concerned; most of them will alter the organism in ways that are either irrelevant for its adaptation, or are harmful. Occasionally, however, just by accident, a variation will be beneficial—that is, it will result in an organism better able to deal with its environment than the rest. For example, it will be better at competing for food in scarce supply, or at avoiding predators, or at attracting the opposite sex for mating. This fortunate organism, and its offspring to which it passes on that new adaptive trait, will live longer and reproduce more, and the population of that kind of plant or animal will, over the years, contain a larger and larger proportion of individual organisms with that new advantageous trait. This process, by which those random variations that are advantageous replace others in the population, is called *natural selection.*

RATIONALIST: Hang on, are you saying that all the complex and intricate features of living things, so beautifully suitable for their needs, really came about by a random mindless process, by a series of accidents? That's crazy. That's like imagining that you take a bunch of scrap metal and plastic from the dump and put it in a trashcan and shake it up for a while and it rearranges itself into a fully operational computer.

BIOLOGIST: I am saying that all those adaptations really are the result of random processes, but they don't happen all at once, or anywhere near as quickly as in your trashcan example. Evolution takes a very long time, and occurs in small cumulative steps. Starting with primitive organisms millions of years ago, organisms gradually developed, bit by bit, into more and more complicated, differentiated, and adapted forms, till you get what we have today. You're right that you don't suddenly, by accident, get animals with complicated adaptive features like eyes, where their ancestors didn't have anything like that, by accident. The way it works is that long ago some animal developed a very simple light-sensitive organ, which could tell the difference only between light and dark. This wouldn't be a big step; and it might give the animal an adaptive advantage to be able to sense this. Then very gradually, very slowly, this simple light-sensitive organ evolved through a long series of stages of gradually increasing complexity.

ATHEIST: Well, that kind of evolutionary story explains your woodpecker, without needing to bring in God.

RATIONALIST: Not so fast. Darwin's "Theory" of Evolution—isn't it just a theory, not a real proven fact?

BIOLOGIST: When scientists call something a *theory* they don't mean that it's just a guess, or an unsubstantiated hypothesis. A theory is a systematic collection of concepts and generalizations, suitable for explaining a broad range of phenomena. Some theories are extremely well-confirmed by the evidence, strongly enough to be taken as fact by everyone, like for instance the Atomic Theory of matter, or the Sun-centred Theory of the solar system, or the Germ Theory of the cause of certain diseases. The Theory of Evolution, in broad outline anyway, is one of those: there's so much evidence in its favour that almost all biologists believe it. They think that there's no *scientific* reason to doubt it at all. The only reason that anyone objects to it is because of their view of religion: the Bible gives a different story of the origin of species, and some religious people—creationists—prefer to understand the Bible literally, and to take it as more reliable than science. Lots of religions fully accept Darwin, however.

RATIONALIST: But isn't there a scientific theory that rejects evolution, and that thinks that the Bible has the basic story right?

BIOLOGIST: A few biologists are working in that area, called *Creation Science*, but most biologists think that this is religiously, not scientifically motivated, and think it's pretty bad—*as science*, that is. Maybe it's just fine *as religion*.

RATIONALIST: Okay, maybe there are two competing ways to explain design in nature: the scientific way and the religious way. Why prefer one to the other?

ATHEIST: Well, here's one way that the scientific theory beats the religious theory. If nature were created by a perfect all-powerful designer, then everything in nature would be perfectly designed. But it's not. For example, I was reading an article the other day that pointed out the bad design of people's sinuses—the eight little hollow spaces inside the bones of the head and the face. They're U-shaped, and drain at the side, not the bottom. This means that they don't drain effectively, and so lots of people get sinus infections. Imagine you were an engineer designing a way to drain an industrial site: you wouldn't do it that way, unless you had to work with a site that was already constructed, and could only be modified in small ways. That's just the sort of less-than-ideal design, the result of small cumulative modification, that we find in nature. So it's much better explained on the basis of small improvements on existing setups—the way evolution explains things—than on the basis of design by an all-powerful, all-wise designer, all at once. But anyway, look, didn't you say earlier that you respect science? Doesn't that mean that you accept what science claims has been well-established?

RATIONALIST: Well, yes, I don't like the idea of religion and science being in competition. In its own realm, science is the best tool for knowledge we've got.

ATHEIST: But the Bible very clearly says that God created all the plants and animals we know, all at once. So do you agree that religion gets this wrong?

RATIONALIST: Maybe we should take the Bible as a sort of symbolic version of the story, not exactly as literal truth. But evolution doesn't show that there isn't any God, does it?

BIOLOGIST: I don't think so. Actually, I'm a religious believer myself, and I know some other scientists who are (as well as others who aren't). It seems clear to me that evolution is just part of the complexity that reveals the wonderful divine design of things.

RATIONALIST: Yes, and there are lots of examples of design in the universe that are not accounted for by the blind forces of evolution—order in things other than living things. Think of how such a wonderful diversity of stuff is made out of just a small number of naturally-occurring elements, fewer than 100 of them. Think of how everything is connected, how all of nature is interrelated, not just the living things in it. Think of how there are patterns all over the place, how everything is regular and cyclical. And how things fit together. The universe is just like an expertly designed machine, much more beautiful, complex and huge than anything any human could possibly create. All this precision and harmony couldn't possibly occur merely by chance, from blind random collections and interactions.

ATHEIST: I agree that the universe is marvellous and awe-inspiring, but the question remains whether there are any regularities in it, any "designer" features, that couldn't be accounted for merely on the basis of natural causes—the sorts of mindless mechanical processes science talks about. Whenever scientists encounter some sort of regularity or interconnection, they try to find a natural explanation for it. They never assume that anything couldn't possibly be explained by natural factors, or that a divine designer would have to be brought in to complete the scientific story.

BIOLOGIST: I guess that's true. But doesn't the fact that some very good scientists are nevertheless deeply religious show that science is compatible with religion—that accepting a scientific explanation for something doesn't mean rejecting God?

ATHEIST: Maybe it does, maybe it doesn't. Anyway, that's not the issue we're discussing right now. What we're wondering about right now is whether there's anything unexplainable by science, for which God is the only possible (or only plausible) explanation. The claim that some things are like that is the basis of both of those arguments we've been looking at. If there were, that would give evidence for God's existence. But we still haven't found anything like that. It appears that neither argument is much good.

BIOLOGIST: But that doesn't show that God doesn't exist.

ATHEIST: True enough. Showing that an argument for the truth of X is faulty doesn't show that X is false. But before we leave this topic, I want to add something. I've been arguing that neither of the two arguments we've been looking at proves what it's supposed to. The First Cause Argument doesn't prove that there has to be something outside the natural order that started things up, and the Argument from Design doesn't prove that there's a supernatural designer. But even if they did work, neither would prove the existence of what believers understand as God. God is supposed to be all-powerful, and all-knowing. He's supposed to care for humans, and to respond to our prayers. Even if you've proven the existence of a First Cause or of a Designer, you've got some distance to go still to establish that that thing is God, in any full sense.

3. The Ontological Argument

RATIONALIST: Anyway, here's a third argument. It's called the *Ontological Argument*.

ATHEIST: What does 'ontological' mean?

RATIONALIST: It means *having to do with existence*. It's not a particularly descriptive name. Anyway, this argument is based on the idea that God is perfect, by definition.

ATHEIST: I don't accept that. I don't think that there is any such thing as God.

RATIONALIST: No, no, you don't have to believe that God exists in order to accept a proposed definition for 'God.' That's just saying what's involved in the idea of God, or what's meant by the word. Look, unicorns have one horn, by definition, right? Truths by definition don't depend on existence.

ATHEIST: Okay, I can accept that. The word means something, and people do have an idea corresponding to that word, and I guess the idea of God does include perfection—so God is perfect by definition.

RATIONALIST: That means that, by definition, it wouldn't be possible to think of anything better than God in any way. So for example, God would have to have infinite perfect knowledge, because any being that fell short of this—whose knowledge was finite, only partial, couldn't be God, by definition.

ATHEIST: Okay. Hey, didn't you say a while back that there are no infinite things?

RATIONALIST: No infinite *natural* things.

ATHEIST: Oh, okay.

RATIONALIST: And God would have to be completely good, completely powerful, and so on, right?

ATHEIST: Right, if there were any such thing.

RATIONALIST: Okay, consider an imaginary being that has perfect knowledge, that is perfectly good and powerful, but doesn't exist. Non-existence is a defect in that being: it would be more perfect if, in addition to all its other attributes, it existed. But God, by definition, is perfect, so God couldn't be merely imaginary. God, by definition, exists in reality.

ATHEIST: Wait a minute. You were saying that something that exists is more perfect than something that doesn't, but that doesn't make any sense to me.

RATIONALIST: Well, look at it this way. If you said, "I have a male sister," that would have to be false by definition, because it's part of the definition of the word 'sister' that the person be female, right? If somebody was male, he couldn't be anyone's sister, right?

ATHEIST: Sure.

RATIONALIST: And we agree that it's part of the definition of the word 'God' that it has to be the most perfect thing conceivable, that it would be impossible to conceive of anything better, right?

ATHEIST: Okay.

RATIONALIST: So if somebody said, "God has imperfect knowledge" that would have to be false by definition, right?

ATHEIST: Right. Something that has imperfect knowledge couldn't be God, by definition.

RATIONALIST: But if somebody said, "God doesn't exist" this is also attributing a characteristic that's less than perfect, so that has to be false by definition also.

ATHEIST: Yes. Wait, no, nothing exists by definition.

RATIONALIST: Why not?

ATHEIST: Well, suppose it made sense to include existence in the definition of something. Consider this. I like those ATMs, those Automated Teller Machines that banks have outside. They're very convenient. But they do have one defect, which is that they only give you money already in your account. What I'd like to see in front of my bank is an IATM.

RATIONALIST: Which is....

ATHEIST: An Ideal Automated Teller Machine. It's ideal—the best it could be—much better than the ones they have now. For one thing, it gives you free money without having to take anything out of your account.

RATIONALIST: Right, that would be great.

ATHEIST: One of these has existed in my imagination for years, but I'm not rich because that one has another defect: it doesn't exist in reality, so it's not what I'd call ideal either. By definition, my ideal machine would have to exist in reality, not just in imagination. So it's contradictory to say that my IATM doesn't exist. There! I've just proven that it exists.

RATIONALIST: No you haven't.

ATHEIST: Of course I haven't. But that's just like your argument about God.

RATIONALIST: No, look, that's not the same thing at all. It's in God's very nature to exist, whereas it isn't in the very nature of the IATM to exist. So it's a factual matter whether an IATM exists (and actually, unfortunately, there aren't any in existence).

ATHEIST: I don't get what the difference is supposed to be here. Anyway, this is a really weird argument. Is it really important to religion?

RATIONALIST: Well, it is different from the first two arguments, which lots of religious people who have never taken philosophy have heard of. I'd guess that only philosophers have ever heard of the Ontological Argument, and I'd also guess that (in contrast to the other two arguments) almost nobody has ever been turned into a believer by this one. But it's certainly worth thinking about anyway. I mean, if it's right, then mere logic proves the existence of God!

ATHEIST: But you also have to admit that none of these three arguments would convince anybody who wasn't already a believer. And I wouldn't think they're even very important for believers. Look, tell the truth: it's not as though you became convinced of the existence of God when you came across one or the other of those arguments, is it?

RATIONALIST: No, I guess that it wasn't any of those arguments that convinced me.

ATHEIST: Well, then, what are your real reasons for thinking that God exists? I mean, are there any arguments that might actually convince someone, and that really are the basis for some religious believers' belief?

4. The Argument from Morality

RATIONALIST: Okay, how about this. Think about morality: the fact that there are morally right or wrong actions. If there weren't any God—if the claims of religion weren't true—there wouldn't be any basis for morality. You can't have real ethics without a religious basis. That's why people who want to take morality seriously have to be religious believers.

ATHEIST: Why's that?

RATIONALIST: Well, for one thing, suppose that what religion said was false. In that case, there would be no reason for anybody to act morally. The only real reason people have for doing what's right is that God punishes wrongdoers after death, and rewards good people.

ATHEIST: But there are also punishments and rewards on earth, aren't there? I mean, there are the police and the courts enforcing the moral rules of society, and there are more informal social pressures to be moral, aren't there?

RATIONALIST: Right, but it's obvious that these don't provide anywhere near enough motivation to produce moral behaviour, because there are a whole lot of immoral acts you can get away with, unpunished. If that were the only reason anybody had to act morally, then there'd be chaos: everybody would be doing immoral things all the time. But religious people have an additional motivation, and a very strong one, to do good things and avoid evil. Unlike the police, God knows what everyone does, all the time; and the punishments and rewards offered by religion in the next life—eternal damnation or salvation—are unavoidable, and much more important than any punishments and rewards administered on earth.

ATHEIST: There are a couple of things I think are wonky about your reasoning here. First of all, while I agree that the threat of punishment and the promise of reward offered by religion can be motivating to some people— much more motivating, sometimes, than what can happen on earth—but those threats and promises don't seem to me to be a good basis for morality at all.

RATIONALIST: Why's that?

ATHEIST: Well, a moral person does what's right because it's right, not because of a promised reward. And a moral person avoids doing what's wrong because it's wrong, not because of the threat of punishment. So while religious promises and threats about the afterlife might motivate people to do what's in fact right, and to avoid what's in fact wrong, these promises and threats aren't making those people moral. People who are motivated by future reward or punishment are only looking out for themselves. So I don't think that religion actually encourages morality—moral thinking or truly moral motivation. Threats of punishment and promises of reward are just ways of keeping people under control—they're not ways of encouraging them to be ethical.

RATIONALIST: Well, maybe. But you have to admit that it's a good thing that religion does get people acting morally, and that without it we'd be in a big mess, with everyone doing nasty things all over the place. And threats and promises aren't the only way religion gets people to be moral. There's also more substantial moral teaching, which gets people to think and act in genuinely moral ways.

ATHEIST: Okay, I guess that's possible. But look, what we were wondering about was whether there was any good reason to believe in God, or in the other claims of religion. The facts that religious belief makes for a better society, and teaches morality—if those are facts!—don't show that religion is true. I think in fact that the rewards and punishments offered after death by religion, and the stories religion tells to illustrate and reinforce morality, are all false. Whether society is better off when people believe in them has nothing at all to do with their truth.

RATIONALIST: If you don't like that reasoning, here's another sort of consideration about religion and morality. It's famously expressed in Dostoevsky's novel *The Brothers Karamazov*, where there's the argument that if there were no God, then everything would be lawful or permitted. God provides the basis for morality. There has to be a God, because otherwise all morality would be nonsense.

ATHEIST: I don't get that.

RATIONALIST: Look, it's clear that there are facts about right and wrong actions. But without God, there couldn't be any such facts. I mean, scientists discover facts about the material world, about molecules and comets and genes and earthquakes and all the other material things. But what they never discover is the moral facts. Those aren't physical facts, discovered by observation and experiment. They're facts about another sort of reality altogether. They're about what's desirable and what's not, but they're not about any particular human desires; those are subjective, variable and culture-bound. For there to be *objective* morality, these have to be thought of as the desires of God—what God decides we should do.

ATHEIST: Well, I agree that it's an interesting question what, if anything, makes morality a matter of objective fact. But in any case, I don't think this argument works. First of all, even if God would provide the only basis for ethical fact, that doesn't show that God exists. Maybe there aren't any ethical facts.

RATIONALIST: That's ridiculous. Do you really mean that it's possible that everything is really permissible?

ATHEIST: Maybe it is.

RATIONALIST: But isn't it just obvious that ethics must have some objective underpinning?

ATHEIST: I don't find that obvious at all, but we can talk about it later.[2] Anyway, I think that even if ethics does have some objective basis, God wouldn't provide it.

RATIONALIST: Well that's a weird thing to say. Isn't it central to religion to see God's will as the source of right and wrong?

ATHEIST: I don't think so, and I'll try to show you why. Is there a Bible around here?

RATIONALIST: Here's one.

ATHEIST: Okay, I'm looking for something in the book of Leviticus. That book is mostly composed of God telling the moral law to Moses. Hmm ... Here it is. Leviticus, Chapter 20, verse 13: God tells Moses, "If a man also lie with mankind, as he lieth with a woman, both of them have committed an abomination: they shall surely be put to death; their blood shall be upon them."

RATIONALIST: What's that about? "Lie with mankind"?

ATHEIST: God's telling Moses that male homosexuality is horribly immoral, and that both participants should be put to death. What do you think about that?

RATIONALIST: Well, I don't know. Lots of cultures have thought that homosexuality is morally wrong. Some people around here think so right now.

ATHEIST: Come on now, you don't really think that homosexuality is an abomination, do you? I didn't think you were homophobic! And anyway, even people who think that homosexuality is wrong don't think that it deserves the death penalty! But in Leviticus God gives Moses all sorts of other horrible moral rules, and ones that are just silly or crazy. Here's one, Chapter 19, verse 19: "Thou shalt not sow thy field with mingled seed: neither shall a garment mingled of linen and woollen come upon thee." God's laying down the law against wearing clothes made of two different fibres. You'd better get rid of your cotton/polyester blend shirt right away!

RATIONALIST: Okay, I have to admit that what you've read is a little peculiar.

ATHEIST: But the Bible is supposed to be the word of God!

RATIONALIST: Well, it's really the word of God as interpreted—filtered, modified, and applied—by people and cultures long ago, and some of what it says there reflects cultural views we don't share. So what's your point? Is it just that the Bible was written by fallible people, that it contains some silly rules, and some morally objectionable ones?

---

2 This is discussed in Conversation III.

ATHEIST: No, my point is about your reasoning. When you read the Bible, you pick and choose. You accept some of the moral rules indicated in there, and reject others. The ones you reject you consider not to be the genuine will of God.

RATIONALIST: Right, so?

ATHEIST: So your morality is not really based, at bottom, on God's will. When you run across something that's supposed to be Divine law, you *first* decide whether that rule tells you to do what's genuinely right or forbids what's really wrong. *Then*, the ones you approve of, you count as the genuine will of God; the rest you decide are merely somebody's or some culture's opinions. So it's not as if you base your ethical views on what God wills: it's rather the other way around. You have some other way of deciding what's right and what's wrong, and then, having decided this first, on that basis you sort out religious claims into those that genuinely reflect God's will and those that don't. So you're actually basing your morality, when it comes right down to it, on something else, not on God.

RATIONALIST: Well, look, I think the issue of interpreting the Bible is not really central here. My point, basically, is that religion makes ethics objective, makes it make sense. Without it, ethics would be just a matter of opinion. Without God, ethics would have no grounding in reality.

ATHEIST: Maybe so. But even if that's right, it doesn't prove that God exists. Maybe there isn't any objective basis for morality!

RATIONALIST: That's unthinkable. I couldn't even contemplate that possibility.

ATHEIST: The fact that you can't contemplate that possibility doesn't show that it's not true.

5. The Pragmatic Argument

PRAGMATIST: There's one sort of argument you've given a couple of times that I want to question. At a couple of points, you've said that the fact that some belief is good for us doesn't have anything to do with its truth.

ATHEIST: Well, isn't that obvious?

PRAGMATIST: No, it isn't. Actually, there's a famous twentieth-century American philosopher William James who famously argued in favour of the truth of religion on exactly that basis—that religion is good for you. James was just as well known for his work in psychology as for his philosophical writings, and he did a far-reaching study of what happens to peo-ple psychologically when they have a religious conversion. He concluded that there were all sorts of psychological benefits.

ATHEIST: Maybe, maybe not; but the question is, what does that have to do with truth?

RATIONALIST: Right, that's the real question. James argued that the truth of religious claims was to be decided the same way the truth of any other claim was to be decided: by the value to the believer of believing it, in terms of the practical consequences to the person's life. James was a cen-tral figure in the philosophical movement called *pragmatism*. The word 'pragmatic' means having to do with practical matters. He thought that the meaning of a claim had to do with what sort of change believing it would make on a person, in terms of that person's actions and state of mind. Desirable beliefs—the ones it's a good thing to hold—are the beliefs that make people act in beneficial ways, that make them better off. And he had lots of evidence that religious beliefs were of this sort.

ATHEIST: Maybe they were, but, again, what does this have to do with truth?

PRAGMATIST: Well, I guess the argument here is that calling some beliefs 'true' is just a way of saying that those beliefs are the ones that it's good to have—that make people better off. This is the *Pragmatic Theory of Truth*.

ATHEIST: Wait a minute, you're saying that the usefulness of a belief is evi-dence that it's true? If it's useful, then it's probably true?

PRAGMATIST: No, what I'm saying is that this usefulness is all that truth amounts to. That's all there is to it. Truth is nothing but usefulness. This is a theory of what truth is.

ATHEIST: Hmm, that doesn't sound right to me. Truth seems to me to be cor-respondence with the way things are. Aren't the truth of a particular belief, and its possible beneficial consequences, two different matters?

PRAGMATIST: I don't think so. Having true beliefs is an advantage in practical matters, isn't it?

ATHEIST: Sometimes but not always. I mean, aren't there true beliefs that actually make us worse off? And false beliefs that make us better off?

PRAGMATIST: Like what?

ATHEIST: Well, to take an extreme case, imagine that your grandfather, who's really fond of you, is old and dying, and would be very upset if he knew the horrible things you've been up to these days.

PRAGMATIST: Hey, wait a minute!

ATHEIST: Only imagining!

PRAGMATIST: Okay, so?

ATHEIST: In that case knowing the truth about you would make him very unhappy, and might even hasten his death. I mean, it's not as if he could do anything about what's wrong with you, if he knew. It would just make him miserable. He'd be better off thinking that everything was fine.

PRAGMATIST: Well, maybe.

ATHEIST: So there's an example in which a true belief makes him worse off, and a false belief makes him better off. And there are true beliefs that are neither helpful nor harmful—completely irrelevant either way. For example, I read the other day that the TV program "Leave it to Beaver" and the Russian satellite Sputnik 1 were launched on the same day in October 1957. I believe this—I suppose it's true—but this belief is clearly completely useless!

6. Pascal's Wager

PRAGMATIST: Well, here's another argument based on the practical consequences of belief. It's called *Pascal's Wager* after the man who invented it, Blaise Pascal, a seventeenth-century French mathematician and philosopher. Like James, Pascal thought we ought to consider the consequences of believing in God vs. disbelief, but he wanted us to consider possible results after death. God offers eternal salvation after death to believers, something of huge, maybe infinite value, but unbelievers will get sent to hell for eternal torture and damnation.

ATHEIST: Right, that's if God exists, but what if God doesn't exist?

PRAGMATIST: Well in that case, both reward and penalty would be trivially small. If God didn't exist, if what religion tells us were false, then there would be no afterlife, and neither reward nor punishment. Believers would turn out to have held a false belief, but that's no big deal. And atheists would turn out to have been right, but that's not a great benefit. So it's a very good idea to be a believer: if you're right, you get a huge prize, and not much penalty if you're wrong. On the other hand, if you're a nonbeliever, there's a huge penalty if you're wrong, and not much benefit if you're right.

ATHEIST: This sounds like placing a bet.

PRAGMATIST: Right, that's why it's called Pascal's Wager. He's saying it's a very good bet.

ATHEIST: So Pascal is arguing that believing in God is like buying a ticket in a lottery, where you get an enormous prize if you win, but no great cost if you lose.

PRAGMATIST: Yes, but with the added extra incentive that the alternative, non-belief, has an enormous cost if you lose, but hardly any benefit if you win.

ATHEIST: Okay, but to decide if it's a smart idea to buy a lottery ticket you have to know what the odds are. If the odds of winning are really really low (and they almost always are, in real lotteries), then it's not even worth the small price of the ticket to bet on an enormous win. Don't we have to know what the odds are that God exists, before we can tell whether this is a good bet? What are those odds anyway?

PRAGMATIST: Well, in this case it doesn't matter what the odds are. Even if the odds are really really small that God exists, belief is still a good bet, because the prize is so enormously, maybe infinitely, high, and the cost is so low, maybe nothing at all. It's like betting on a lottery where the ticket is free, and the prize is infinitely large. It doesn't matter how small the odds are: you should get a ticket.

ATHEIST: Maybe that's right. It could be a really good bet to believe in God, just in case he exists, and you'd get a huge post-mortem reward for belief, or a punishment for disbelief. But here's what I really think is wrong with this line of reasoning. It assumes that believing is something you can do intentionally, when you think that believing would be advantageous to you (or at least a very good bet to be). But I don't think belief is like that. I don't think that showing someone the potential advantages of having a belief would result in that person's believing it.

PRAGMATIST: No? Why not?

ATHEIST: Okay, I'll show you. Let's try an experiment. I'll give you $10 if you can get yourself to believe that pigs fly. Let me know when you've succeeded.

PRAGMATIST: Right! I've done it! Pay up!

ATHEIST: You're joking. You haven't succeeded, have you?

PRAGMATIST: No, I admit I haven't. I don't even know how to go about trying to believe that pigs fly. It's so obviously false.

ATHEIST: Okay so I'll give you $10 if you can get yourself to believe something not obviously false: that exactly 10 years from today, it will be cloudy in Chicago.

PRAGMATIST: Well, I don't believe it *won't be* cloudy, but I can't get myself to believe it *will be* cloudy either. Other than the fact that you've just saved yourself $10, what's the point?

ATHEIST: The point is that believing is not an intentional action—not something you can do on purpose. And that's why, by the way, the whole religious idea of rewarding believers and punishing unbelievers makes no sense. It's not something that anybody can do on purpose, intentionally, and it makes sense to punish or reward somebody only for what they do on purpose. That's what was stupid about the Inquisition, by the way, when they went around torturing people and burning them at the stake for believing the wrong thing. Aside from the horrible immorality of the whole procedure, it was useless, because that's not how belief works. Belief is not an intentional action that can be induced by reward or punishment.

PRAGMATIST: I'm not too fond of the Inquisition myself, but at least maybe it wasn't stupid: maybe what it was interested in forcing people to do was religious practice, not religious belief. But anyway, back to the main issue. Maybe ordinary belief can't be induced by reward or punishment, but belief in God is not like other beliefs. Other beliefs just happen to you, but belief in God is something you do intentionally, on purpose.

ATHEIST: Hmm, I don't understand what kind of "belief" that's supposed to be, or how that could work. But here's a second problem I see with Pascal's Wager. Religions suppose that belief in God is a supremely important part of what makes a good person, and would result in a reward of infinite worth. But somebody who believed in God just for the chance of that reward, and to escape risk of an infinitely horrible punishment for disbelief, wouldn't really be doing something religions would count as virtuous, would he? I mean, his faith is just a practical way to look after his own future. It's not a religiously virtuous act at all: it's merely selfish.

PRAGMATIST: That's the same sort of objection you raised to the idea that religious belief provides motivation for morality, isn't it?

ATHEIST: Right. And here's a third objection to the way of thinking behind Pascal's Wager, the idea that God (if he existed!) would punish atheists and reward believers. Bertrand Russell, the twentieth-century English philosopher, thought that there's no evidence for God's existence at all. Russell argued that if God did exist, he'd presumably reward people for being good, and punish them for vice; but as far as belief is concerned, it's a virtue to suspend belief when there's hardly any evidence for something, and a vice to believe something in the absence of evidence for it.

So God could be expected to punish people who believed in him, and reward atheists!

PRAGMATIST: That's a cute joke, but of course it's contrary to the whole spirit of religion. Maybe there is very little evidence for God, but some religious thinkers hold that that's just the point of faith: to believe in the absence of good evidence.

ATHEIST: I can't see why that could be a good thing.

RATIONALIST: Well, there's lots about religion you don't see. Anyway, I don't accept the idea that there's no evidence for God's existence. I think that there's plenty of convincing reason to believe, in any case, sufficient evidence to justify belief.

ATHEIST: Well if there was, then it would also be peculiar to think of God rewarding belief and punishing disbelief. If there was plenty of good evidence, then just ordinary rationality would lead anybody to belief in God, and it wouldn't be the sort of thing that justifies a huge reward. For example, if your doorbell rings, that's very good evidence that there's somebody at your door, and anybody with a shred of common-sense knowledge and the minimum of reasoning ability would come to that conclusion. So reaching that conclusion when you hear your doorbell is hardly something that merits any praise at all. And anyone who didn't reach that conclusion must have some sort of peculiar mental defect, but punishment for that intellectual vice is a very weird idea. My point is that when there's sufficient reason to believe something, it's no great virtuous act to believe it; and when there isn't, we shouldn't believe it. So either way, it wouldn't make sense for God to reward belief in him, or punish disbelief.

7. The Burden of Proof

RATIONALIST: You're quite sure there is no God, aren't you?

ATHEIST: Yes, I'm an *atheist*.

RATIONALIST: By the way, what exactly does that word mean? Is being an atheist the same as being an agnostic?

ATHEIST: It comes from a Greek word combining the prefix '*a*,' meaning *without* (as in 'apolitical' or 'asymmetrical'), and the word '*theos*,' meaning *god*. So it means someone who is without a god—someone who believes there is no such thing. The word *agnostic* derives from the same prefix '*a*,' plus '*gnosis*,' meaning *knowledge*; so an agnostic is someone who is without knowledge, in this case of whether God exists or not. The difference is that an atheist believes that God doesn't exist, while an agnostic doesn't believe that there is a God, but doesn't believe that there isn't either. Agnostics just withhold belief one way or the other.

RATIONALIST: Sounds like a pretty wishy-washy position to me.

ATHEIST: I think so too.

RATIONALIST: But agnostics would agree with you that those two proofs of God's existence don't work, and I guess they'd also agree with you that there isn't any good argument or evidence for God.

ATHEIST: Right.

RATIONALIST: Well, suppose you're right, and none of the arguments in favour of God's existence are any good. You admit that this wouldn't show that God doesn't exist, don't you?

ATHEIST: Right, the failure of arguments for X doesn't show that X is false. But I should point out here that it's up to you to give evidence for God's existence—it's not up to me to show that God doesn't exist. As the philosophers say, the *burden of proof* in this case is on you.

RATIONALIST: Why do you say that?

ATHEIST: Well, when it comes to a controversy about something's existence, the default view, so to speak, is that the controversial thing doesn't exist, and it's up to believers to prove that they do. If you claimed, for example that Sasquatch existed ...

RATIONALIST: Who?

ATHEIST: You know, Bigfoot, the giant ape-man who some people suppose lives in the woods in the Pacific Northwest. It's up to them to prove he exists. It's not up to nonbelievers to prove he doesn't. The default view is non-existence, so the burden of proof is on believers.

RATIONALIST: But that's not the way it works in the case of God's existence. I think that the default view, throughout history as well as now, is that God exists. That's the mainstream view in just about every society throughout history. If just about everybody believes something, then what they believe is the default view.

ATHEIST: I admit that religion has been pretty widespread, historically speaking, but that doesn't necessarily mean that belief in God has been.

RATIONALIST: Really? Can there be religion without belief in God?

ATHEIST: Well, historically speaking, the idea that there is only one God is a fairly recent invention. Lots of major religions in history, and even some today, believe in several supernatural beings or spirits of various kinds. And Buddhism, which is certainly a major religion, doesn't really involve belief in supernatural beings at all. Anyway, I don't think that the question of how widespread a belief is has much to do with whether that belief is true.

RATIONALIST: All I was claiming was that the widespread belief makes it the default view, and puts the burden of proof on you. Do you think that there are any really good arguments against the existence of God? How could you possibly have an argument like that? It's often clear how you can prove that something exists—you observe it, or you find some good evidence for it. But proving something doesn't exist is another story. How could anyone prove, for example, that Sasquatch doesn't exist?

8. The Argument from History

ATHEIST: I think I have some good arguments. One of the reasons I have for being an atheist, and not just an agnostic, has to do with the picture I have of the history and function of religious belief.

RATIONALIST: Let's hear about that.

ATHEIST: As I mentioned, primitive societies have a very large number of major and minor deities and spirits inhabiting everything in nature. In the primitive mind, these spirits provide something like an explanation of why things happen. If there's a thunderstorm, some spirits are angry with us. If the crops do well, the spirits of that crop are feeling kind. Bread nourishes, fire burns, poison kills, all because of the actions and intentions of the spirits that inhabit them. Explaining why things happen in this way of thinking is applying the kind of explanation we give for people's actions to natural events. They're thought to happen because of spirits' or gods' anger, envy, jealousy, love, benevolence, and so on. Primitive people thought they could influence nature the same way people are influenced: by begging, doing favours, offering gifts, promising service, and the like. But as civilization developed, the number of spirits people believed in decreased. The ancient Greek religion, for example, had only a dozen or so gods who were responsible for important natural occurrences, plus some lesser spirits; but the Greeks also developed the idea of natural processes occurring merely naturally, without anyone's intentions, emotions, or desires being involved. In Judaism, and in the religions that developed from it, Christianity and Islam, the number of divine spirits decreased further to one, and whereas the Greek gods meddled in earthly matters quite a bit—causing a storm here, deflecting a spear there—as time went on the unique deity was thought to manage things on earth less and less. You can see this change between the Old Testament God, who meddled in earthly affairs quite a lot, and the New Testament God, who stayed pretty much aloof. Around 1600, the Scientific Revolution began, which vastly increased the power of scientific—natural—explanation; and the part played by God's desires and actions in explaining things correspondingly decreased. People increasingly thought of things as happening because of natural causes, explainable through scientific laws, rather than because of divine will. And this process continues to this day. Nowadays science is the main way to explain things, though it hasn't yet fully replaced religion. Religious people still see things, to some extent, as the result of God's emotions, loves, hates, and desires. They still try to influence events by praying to God, making pleas and promises. But all this is just a primitive leftover. Atheists are the thinkers of the future.

RATIONALIST: Well, I agree that history has shown a contraction of the explanatory power of religion in favour of naturalistic explanation, and a contraction of the relevance and influence of the ideas of spirits and of God. But what makes you think this is progress? Why is this a good thing?

ATHEIST: Because primitive spiritualism didn't work, but the naturalistic science that replaced it does. Praying to the spirits or to God to improve your crop yield simply does not work. Scientific farming techniques do.

RATIONALIST: Science doesn't always work better than spirituality. Sometimes it makes us much worse off.

ATHEIST: Yes, but on the whole it works a whole lot better. In the middle ages, when prayer was the only remedy for disease and famine, the average life expectancy was somewhere around 35, partly because of a high rate of infant mortality. But now, in developed countries where they use natural science to understand and change things, it's close to 80. Science works; religion doesn't. Everyone knows that primitive religious beliefs are just superstition. But modern religion is just more sophisticated superstition.

RATIONALIST: You know that I have respect for science, and that I think that it does its own jobs, such as curing disease or making crops grow, much better than religion could. Still, I can't help thinking that there are other sorts of jobs that religion is suited for, and science is not. Anyway, if it's true that science works better than religion does for practical purposes, that doesn't show that the claims of religion are false. You yourself argued just earlier that practical usefulness is different from truth.

ATHEIST: Yes, but usefulness in terms of prediction, explanation, and control are the tests for the truth of a theory. They show that scientific theories are true, and religious ones aren't. Anyway, the idea that religion isn't designed for the same jobs as science is an interesting idea, and one I'd like to get back to later. But still, you have to admit that a great deal of religion is just a leftover of primitive superstition.

RATIONALIST: Well, maybe, though I feel uncomfortable calling some ways of thinking, and the people who think that way, "primitive." That word is offensive—it shows disrespect. It devalues those ways of thinking.

ATHEIST: Hmm, well, I think there's much to be admired about the cultures that held those beliefs, but I do intend to "devalue" their beliefs. They're false! They don't work!

RATIONALIST: Anyway, your story might show that we now know better than to try to understand or manipulate the natural world by appealing to spirits; but it doesn't show at all that this is what the idea of God is really about, or that there's no longer any function for religious belief, or that the religious idea that God exists is false.

9. The Argument from Psychology

PSYCHOLOGIST: I've been listening to your discussion of what function religious belief might have, and I'd like to tell you the view of the great early twentieth-century Viennese psychologist Sigmund Freud. He started from the obvious point that the way people see God is similar to the way small children see their fathers: as all-powerful and all-knowing, the person who provides aid and protection, and who punishes for wrongdoing. As they grow up, children stop seeing their fathers this way because of sexual repressions I won't go into here, and the original father-image is transferred to an imaginary god. The conflicts and guilt-feelings one unconsciously has about one's father are transferred into religion, where one feels penitent and seeks absolution, regressing, as it were, to our childhood.

RATIONALIST: If you'll pardon my saying so, all that sounds sort of implausible to me.

PSYCHOLOGIST: A Freudian might say that that's just your unconscious repressed fear talking!

ATHEIST: There are much simpler and more common-sense accounts of why people are believers. The idea that God watches over us provides us with security and reassurance that things won't really go badly wrong. Religious belief in immortality is a response to our fear of death.

PSYCHOLOGIST: I just read about a psychological study that claims that the fear of death motivation is not all that important. I've got the article here, let's see. The author claims that the appeal of religion can be explained on the basis of sixteen different desires: power, independence, curiosity, acceptance, order, saving, honour, idealism, social contact, family, status, vengeance, romance, eating, physical exercise, and tranquility.

ATHEIST: *Eating*? People become religious because of the *food*?

RATIONALIST: Well, that list sounds to me like the list of motives for anything. I don't doubt that there are psychological motives for having any belief system. So what? The fact that your belief has psychological motives doesn't show that the belief is false.

ATHEIST: Not necessarily. But it does raise real doubts. I mean, when having a belief fills some deep psychological need, you have to suspect that that's the real reason why people have that belief, not because that belief is true, or because there's any rational basis for it. You have to admit that religious belief looks an awful lot like irrational wishful thinking.

RATIONALIST: Right, but that wouldn't show that it is false. Your argument is an interesting contrast to James's view, by the way. He argued that, because religion served various psychological functions, it was true. You're arguing that, because it serves various psychological functions, it's false!

10. The Argument from the Existence of Evil

ATHEIST: There is a line of reasoning that I think does directly show that God, as usually conceived of, doesn't exist.

RATIONALIST: Okay, let's hear it.

ATHEIST: First of all, let's get clear on what God is supposed to be like, at least as understood by many mainstream religions. The religions that have only one God think of him as the Supreme Being, as perfect in every way. (You already acknowledged this, as the premise in your Ontological Argument.) So for one thing, God's perfection would mean complete knowledge of every past, present, and future fact.

RATIONALIST: Right. The word they use for this state of complete knowledge is *omniscience*—the 'omni' part means *everything*, and the 'science' part means knowledge; so an omniscient being knows everything.

ATHEIST: For another, he'd have to have infinite power: he can do anything he wants.

RATIONALIST: Agreed. The word for this is *omnipotence*—'omni' again, plus 'potence' meaning power.

ATHEIST: And third, he'd have to be perfectly benevolent—that is, as wishing us well, without any mean streak.

RATIONALIST: Right again. Maybe we can call this *omnibenevolence*, though this is not exactly a real word.

ATHEIST: Okay. The question is whether there is such a being—one that is omniscient, omnipotent, and omnibenevolent. Now, imagine what it would be like if there were. Being omnibenevolent, God would want the world to be the best it could be for us. Being omniscient, he would know every detail about the way things were: nothing that was less than perfectly suited to us would escape his attention. And being omnipotent, he could make the world any way he liked. So, of course, the world we inhabit would be absolutely the best possible place for us: our situation would be absolutely ideal. It would be the best of all possible worlds. It couldn't be any less. How could there be any flaw in it? If there were, then God, being omniscient, would know about it; being omnibenevolent, he would want it fixed; and since he's omnipotent, he could fix it. But it's clear that the actual world is not the best of all possible worlds. There are some good things and some bad things—it's not perfect. So it follows that God does not exist.

RATIONALIST: Wait a minute, not so fast. One of your assumptions is that this is not the best of all possible worlds. What makes you so sure it isn't?

ATHEIST: Well, there are bad, even horrible, things in it. There are diseases that cause suffering that we can't do anything about. Natural disasters sometimes kill or injure thousands of people. Evil human beings cause all sorts of misery.

RATIONALIST: But maybe from a religious perspective, all these are actually good things in disguise.

ATHEIST: What? How could that be?

RATIONALIST: Maybe it's punishment for misbehaviour. There's the religious story of Adam and Eve, in which Eve ate the forbidden apple and brought evil and pain into the world.

ATHEIST: That's clearly just mythology though. I mean, a talking serpent? It's a fairy tale.

RATIONALIST: Many religious believers think it's literally true. But lots of other religious people think that this story symbolically gives an answer to the pain and suffering we face. It's punishment by a just God for human sinfulness in general.

ATHEIST: But that doesn't make any sense. Look, when loving and responsible parents feel that they must punish their children, they make sure that it's done right. That means that the punishment should be inflicted only where it's deserved, and in proportion to the bad act that is being punished—so children who haven't done something wrong shouldn't be punished, and they shouldn't be punished a lot for small misbehaviours. And they should know exactly why they're being punished. But the pain and suffering from disease, for example, is distributed all wrong. Good people—even completely innocent little babies—get some of it; it appears to be distributed randomly, rather than on the basis of what's deserved. And the connection between this "punishment" and what we've done wrong is never clear. Parents who punish their children with this kind of massive unfairness and disproportionality have their children taken away by Children's Aid! The horrible things like disease that sometimes happen to people are obviously far from fair, humane, and effective as punishment.

RATIONALIST: How about this way of looking at it. Maybe some of these things may be put on earth to test us, to give us the opportunity to struggle to overcome a really bad situation. Humans are often at their best when they're faced with horrible situations, like for instance when they have a long-term painful disease, and they have to find the courage to bear it.

ATHEIST: It doesn't sound very loving to me to give somebody a horrible disease just to give them a chance to bear up under it.

RATIONALIST: The struggle can make them and their friends and relatives who love them better people. I remember a sermon in which my minister called this *soul-building*. Pain and suffering builds souls.

ATHEIST: Sometimes it does and sometimes it doesn't. I'll tell you the story of my grandfather. He was, up till the last year of his life, a really good guy—everyone liked him a lot. But then he got a particularly horrible form of incurable cancer. This sort of cancer lasts a long time before it kills you, a time filled with increasing pain, which becomes really terrible for a few months before the end—pain that medical science can't do anything about. If anyone could bear this with grace and courage, it would have been my grandfather, but even he couldn't manage. Toward the end he became selfish and nasty, and no wonder. He didn't turn into a better person—just the reverse: a really good person was slowly destroyed. And my grandmother's personality also suffered from the experience. She survived him by decades, but she was never the same. Before that, she was loving and cheerful; afterwards, she was gloomy, depressed, and inward-turning. She was psychologically destroyed by his horrible illness and death. The whole family suffered. Everyone became worse, not better. This wasn't soul-building, it was soul-destroying.

RATIONALIST: Look, I don't want to trivialize how painful that was for everyone, but let me give you an analogy of how it might be seen from a different perspective. Think about how a little child feels when her mom tells her she can't have another cookie, or when her dad takes her to the dentist, or when her mom punishes her for doing something she shouldn't. She thinks that her parents are being mean to her, that they don't love her. But this is only because she doesn't really understand what's good for her. She doesn't know, for example, that some minor pain in the dentist's office now will prevent a whole lot more pain later. If she knew better, she'd realize that her parents are actually looking out for her well-being— they're doing what's good for her.

ATHEIST: But God is supposed to be omnipotent, so he could look out for our well-being without all that pain, couldn't he? I mean, he's got the ability to be a completely painless dentist!

RATIONALIST: My point is that when you have limited understanding, you can misinterpret things. We adults understand things a whole lot better than that little girl, but we still have only limited finite understanding. Religions always say that God works in mysterious ways—ways that surpass understanding—but that we should trust as being for our good in the long run.

ATHEIST: I don't find that convincing at all. It's obvious to me that my grandfather's experience was really bad for everyone involved, and it doesn't change my mind when you point out that it might really have been good for everyone in ways that nobody can understand. You might as well claim that it could be that snow is really hot, that dogs really climb trees, that pebbles are bigger than mountains, but all in ways that we can't understand. If we can't even understand how my grandfather's illness was a good thing, then how can we believe it?

RATIONALIST: Okay, look at things this way. If you think that a world with pain and suffering in it is imperfect, imagine a world without any. You could hurl yourself off a cliff, and you'd float harmlessly down. You could put your hand on a lit stove burner, and it would feel pleasant. If I shot you, the bullets would just pass harmlessly through your body. Nothing anyone did would really make any difference; our actions wouldn't matter. We'd never have to think about anything. Our lives would be meaningless and empty.

ATHEIST: Well, that's true, but it doesn't follow that the way the world really is *now* is the best of all possible worlds. I easily imagine a world that would have been a good deal better: a world in which people had discovered how to alleviate my grandfather's pain, and he didn't have to suffer quite so much. I mean, after all, people are trying to figure out how to alleviate pain. If you're right, and if pain actually is a *good* thing, then they're doing something bad by trying to eliminate it. Come to think of it, if this world is perfect exactly as it is, then isn't *any* attempt to change it a mistake?

RATIONALIST: No, part of the perfection of this world is that there are tasks for us to do to improve its imperfections!

ATHEIST: Well, that sounds pretty strange to me. It couldn't be that an omnipotent God would need our help in improving things.

RATIONALIST: Right, but maybe an omnipotent God would leave some imperfections in the world so that we'd have tasks to do. Think of loving parents again. They don't do everything for their children. They leave their kids some things to do for themselves. When the kids are learning how to ride a bike, loving parents don't keep running along behind them to catch them if they start to fall, but at a certain point, the parents just let them try on their own. They have to—otherwise kids would never learn how to ride a bike. If parents prevented their kids from coming to any harm in life, then the kids wouldn't learn to be responsible and capable people.

ATHEIST: Yes, but loving parents wouldn't allow their kids to try something really dangerous, or something the kids would be incapable of doing. But people are often faced with danger they can't control, and with tasks they can't manage; can you really imagine that God does this for our benefit?

RATIONALIST: Well, it's better if we keep trying, even if we can't succeed.

ATHEIST: And the existence of pain and suffering is only one of the problems for the idea of a perfect God. For example, given that sort of God, prayer would be useless. It wouldn't inform God of what you want, because he's omniscient and would already know it. It wouldn't get him to do anything, because he would do what's best even without your asking. And how about omnipotence: the idea of a perfect, infinite power doesn't even make sense. Could God, for example, make a stone too heavy for him to lift? If he couldn't, then he couldn't do everything. If he could, then he wouldn't be able to lift that stone, so he couldn't do everything. Either way, he couldn't be omnipotent. Come to think of it, maybe the Ancient Greeks had a more sensible religious view. They had many gods, all with certain limitations on their powers; they were sometimes on your side and sometimes against you; they didn't always know everything that was going on. All that seems to me to be at least more consistent with an imperfect world and the necessity of human effort.

RATIONALIST: A religion with a multitude of imperfect gods is not the kind of religion I believe in. All these difficulties you raise just go to show that we're a long way from understanding the mysteries of the nature of God.

ATHEIST: Hmm. As I said before, I don't go around believing things I can't understand.

11. Life After Death

ATHEIST: But look, there are big difficulties with all the main religious dogmas. Take the idea of life after death, for example. It's a preposterous idea.

RATIONALIST: But isn't there evidence for the survival of bodily death? Some people actually seem to have communicated with the spirits of dead people, and there are reports of the experiences people have had who have died during medical operations and then have been revived.

ATHEIST: That evidence is no good at all. When people who claim to communicate with the dead actually allow scientific investigation of what they're doing, the result is, in almost every case, that they are shown to be fakes. And those reports about experiences people have when their hearts have stopped during operations for a few minutes are easily explainable as hallucinations caused by oxygen deprivation to their brains. The belief in life after death is just like all those other religious beliefs: wishful thinking, not hard fact.

RATIONALIST: I admit that some legitimate doubts have been raised about some of this evidence, but you have to admit that there are some scientifically-minded investigators who think they have turned up good evidence for life after death.

ATHEIST: I don't think so, but never mind; there are some pretty good philosophical reasons to doubt the possibility of survival of death.

RATIONALIST: Really? Like what?

ATHEIST: I think that the idea that a person can still exist after bodily death is just nonsense, some sort of contradiction. It's just like thinking that a car might still exist after it's been totally wrecked and turned into scrap metal—for a car to survive its "bodily death" so to speak. Nobody can even get a clear idea of what that would be like: talking about it is as nonsensical as talking about a circle with four right angles.

RATIONALIST: I agree with you about the car, but that's because a car is nothing but a physical object. When the physical object is destroyed, the car is gone. But people aren't just bodies.

ATHEIST: I disagree. I think that the only things that exist are physical things. A human being is a body. Destruction of the body is the destruction of the human.

RATIONALIST: That's a view that most people find very implausible. Anyway, it certainly needs some support. Another time we should go into the matter further.[3] In any case, for the moment, just let me point out that there doesn't seem to be anything self-contradictory, or unthinkable, or inconsistent about the idea that a person has survived bodily death. These difficulties do arise when we're talking about physical things. But we can imagine a person surviving bodily death—we imagine the continuance of a non-physical thing, a soul or spirit. It's at least not nonsense, not self-contradictory. So it's hard to see how there can be merely philosophical reasons to doubt the existence of life after death.

ATHEIST: But even if there is something—a non-physical thing that continues after physical death (which I doubt!)—there's another problem. That non-physical thing couldn't be a person who used to be alive. Think of the wrecked car again. What constituted it still exists—there's still a pile of scrap metal around—but that doesn't mean the car still exists. That pile of scrap metal isn't the car.

RATIONALIST: What makes you say that a surviving mind or soul couldn't be a person who used to be alive?

ATHEIST: To start off with, I don't think a surviving spirit, whatever that might be, could even be counted as a person at all. It would be missing all of the characteristics we associate with persons. It couldn't talk, or breathe, or walk around, or read a book. It couldn't see or hear. It couldn't do anything that requires a body. That means that there's just about nothing it could do. What makes that thing a person at all?

---

3 It's gone into a lot further in Conversation IV.

RATIONALIST: I agree that it would be missing the physical organs we use for these tasks, but maybe it could accomplish these things in some other non-physical way.

ATHEIST: But they're all physical activities, which require interaction with the physical world. How can something non-physical do any of that?

RATIONALIST: Even if it can't, it still might be a person. Those characteristics you mention aren't the really important ones that make for a person. The important ones are consciousness, ability to communicate, self-awareness, and other characteristics that you wouldn't need a body for.

ATHEIST: But here's an even worse difficulty. Everyone knows that a person's memories are stored in the physical brain, and that brain damage can erase those memories. There's no worse brain damage than the complete destruction that happens at death! So it's certain that a person's memories get erased at death. Now let's just suppose that you're right, and that there are disembodied persons—spirits or something. None of them would remember anything that happened to any embodied earthly person. Why identify any of those spirits with any person who has died? What would make a particular spirit count as the same person as Fred or Sally who died earlier? The spirit couldn't remember any of the lives of either of them.

RATIONALIST: I think, first, that maybe there's a way that a disembodied spirit might have memories even though there's no physical brain left. And I also think that spirit could count as the same person as the one who earlier was alive on earth even if the spirit has no memories of earthly existence. But look, we're again getting into big issues here: what makes something count as a person at all, and what does it take to be the same person as an earlier one. These need a lot of discussion, and we don't have time right now. Some other time,[4] agreed?

ATHEIST: Right.

12. Fideism

FIDEIST: I've been listening to your discussion, and I'd like to inject a different point of view. I'm religious, so I disagree with ATHEIST, but I also disagree with RATIONALIST. I think you've both got religion all wrong. Earlier I heard you debating about evidence for the existence of God, as if

---

4 Conversation VII.

belief in God were something there had to be evidence for. And then you were wondering about the consistency of belief in God with facts about the world like pain and suffering.

RATIONALIST: Well, what's wrong with all of that?

FIDEIST: It treats religious beliefs just like any other beliefs. For regular everyday beliefs, you need the support of observation or evidence, and you need to worry about consistency with other facts you believe. For instance, take the belief that your friend Sally was in your apartment while you were out. Since you didn't see her there, you should have some evidence if you're going to believe that she was there. And you need to worry about consistency: if you believe that Sally was there, but you believe she always tells the truth, and she tells you that she wasn't there, then you've got a problem because of inconsistency. But religious beliefs are entirely different. I mean, evidence and observations and proof and consistency all are completely out of place when it comes to religion.

ATHEIST: You're right in saying that religion is often inconsistent, and that it does a terrible job of giving evidence. But doesn't that show that it's doing a bad job?

RATIONALIST: If I thought that religion fell short in the departments of evidence and consistency, then I'd agree that it should be fixed or rejected.

FIDEIST: I disagree with both of you. I think religion has its own totally different ways of going about discovering its truths. It doesn't look for evidence. Instead, it uses faith and trust and feeling.

ATHEIST: Is that position called *fideism*?

FIDEIST: Yes, that word comes from the Latin word '*fides*,' meaning *faith*. A fideist is somebody who thinks that religious knowledge comes from faith or revelation—in any case, that reasoning and evidence are out of place in religion.

ATHEIST: Faith is nothing but wishful thinking—believing what you'd like to be true, in spite of the fact that there's no evidence, or that there's evidence to the contrary. It's just the sort of procedure that's likely to give you false beliefs.

FIDEIST: I agree it's a bad procedure if you use it to get beliefs about ordinary matters like whether Sally was in your apartment earlier, or if you use it to answer scientific questions. But faith is entirely appropriate as a methodology to get answers to religious questions.

ATHEIST: How can it be the wrong procedure in science, but the right procedure in religion? I mean, isn't a procedure for arriving at belief either a reliable one or not, period?

FIDEIST: I don't think so. I think that whether or not some belief-getting procedure is a good one depends on what game you're playing, so to speak. Look, here's an analogy. Answer this question for me. During a game, is it legitimate to pick up the ball and run with it?

ATHEIST: Well, that depends. If you're playing American football, and somebody on the other team has fumbled, then it's legitimate. But if you're playing soccer, then it isn't.

FIDEIST: That's just like the situation I'm talking about here, with religion and every-day knowledge. They're different games altogether. They have their own rules for proper and appropriate procedure. Judging the procedures of one by the rules of the other is totally mistaken.

ATHEIST: No, I think that truth is truth, and the only way to get it reliably is to look for evidence and consistency.

FIDEIST: I guess that's the core of our disagreement. I think that religion provides a totally different kind of truth from science and everyday common sense.

ATHEIST: I have no idea what that means. There's only one kind of truth.

13. Symbolism

SYMBOLIST: I agree with FIDEIST that the way religious thinking works is appropriate in religion, though not for finding things out in everyday or scientific contexts. But I think that talking about a different kind of truth is a misleading way to put it. Look at things this way. You might say that what's in a novel, in a work of fiction, is true in some sense, true-to-life maybe, but strictly speaking, almost every sentence in the novel is *false*. The characters in a novel never existed, and the events in it never happened. If a newspaper article contained literal falsehoods like that, that would be a bad defect; but it's no problem at all in a novel. Novels aren't supposed to give literal truth. The writing there serves other purposes altogether. Just about every statement in a novel is false, but that doesn't matter. Novels are not about telling you what's actually true.

RATIONALIST: Okay, that's the way novels work. And there are other things we write or say that aren't concerned with literal truth. There's writing poetry or song lyrics for instance.

ATHEIST: Right, lots of what's said in poetry or song is false, and that doesn't matter there either. What matters is something else, but it's hard to say exactly what.

SYMBOLIST: Maybe novels can *symbolically* represent some general types of things that really happen. A good novel can teach us important things about life, can represent a meaningful valuable outlook on things. Maybe reading a good novel can even change us personally, for the better. So even though what's said in a novel is strictly speaking literally false, it can be valuable for what it says symbolically—true-to-life, and meaningful.

ATHEIST: All of that sounds right to me. Maybe we should get together some other day and talk about what fiction and poetry are for, and come to think of it what other art, like painting and music, are about. That's an interesting question.[5] So you think that religious "truth" is like this?

SYMBOLIST: Right. I think that symbolic truth is what religion is after. So lack of evidence, inconsistency, and falsehood are all irrelevant in religion.

ATHEIST: Aha! You admit that what it says in the Bible is false! So you agree with me!

SYMBOLIST: Right, I agree with that much, but I think the Bible is a really important book, maybe, for us anyway, the most important book there is.

ATHEIST: Are you saying it's just a great novel? I think it's a terrible novel—some parts of it are so boring!

SYMBOLIST: I don't think it's great as a novel, exactly. I think it's a great work of mythology.

ATHEIST: Mythology! I prefer truth. What's so good about mythology?

SYMBOLIST: Every culture has a mythology which gives people stories they use to express their central values, fictional stories about what they think is most important. Think of Greek mythology, with all those gods and so on. We know that none of that is literally true—it's all perfectly false—but can appreciate it anyway because of what it represents symbolically. But of course it's not *our* mythology. Think of how much more those stories meant to the Greeks. Those stories were a really familiar and basic and central part of their lives. They heard these stories over and over from the time they were very young, and the stories took on enormous significance for them, expressing what they found most meaningful and important. The Bible is *our* mythology.

ATHEIST: Well it's not my mythology!

---

5   Unfortunately, there's no Conversation in this book dealing with these and other questions in philosophical aesthetics. Sorry!

SYMBOLIST: I think even you react differently to those stories than you do to the mythology of some other culture.

RATIONALIST: So you're saying that it's not literally true that God exists?

SYMBOLIST: Right, but I think that you're missing all the important things if all you see in that statement 'God exists' is that it's false. Of course it's false! But who cares? You don't dismiss what it says in a poem or a novel because it's false. Religious statements are poetic expressions of feelings and attitudes that matter to us. Looking at it that way reveals how inappropriate proof and evidence are. Proof and evidence are appropriate when the truth of a statement is at issue. But we don't look for proof or evidence of statements in fiction or poetry or mythology. Here's another thing. I heard you talking about prayer earlier on. The problem about prayer arises when you think of it as a way of getting something, like for instance when someone tries to get water for the crops by praying for rain. Asking God for rain superficially resembles asking Dad for the car keys. But prayer does not work, at least as a way of increasing the probability of getting what you pray for. It doesn't increase the likelihood of rain.

ATHEIST: I'd certainly agree with that, but I guess you think that prayer is effective for some other purpose.

SYMBOLIST: I think what it's really for, and what it does a good job at, is expressing our desires. You know how when you really want something, you have an almost irresistible tendency to state that desire out loud? Like when you're waiting anxiously for an important phone call, you might say out loud "Oh *come on*! Ring, telephone!" It's clear that what you said wouldn't actually make the telephone ring, but it's a natural way of expressing your strong desire and your powerlessness, and of releasing the tension you feel.

ATHEIST: But what makes you think that your interpretation really describes what's going on in religious practice? Don't religious people think their beliefs are really *true*, and that prayer really *works*?

SYMBOLIST: For one thing, look at the big differences between religion on the one hand, and literal-truth-producing activities like history and science on the other. Religion gets its stories from tradition, but history and science use observation or experiment. There are no laboratories for discovering religious truths. Religious stories are told in church, while historical and scientific stories are told in universities. People chant their religious beliefs (for example, in the Nicene Creed: "I believe in one God, the Father almighty, maker of heaven and earth ..."), but nobody chants literal facts. And look at the big differences between prayer and practical ways of bringing things about. If prayer were just another way of making things happen, then it would be just another industry; but look at the difference between a church, where we pray for things, and a factory, where we produce them. Factories never have the awe-producing architecture of the great cathedrals. They never have incense, or stained-glass windows, or music. The whole apparatus of religion is designed around symbolic representation that expresses and elicits feelings, not around literal truth and industrial production.

ATHEIST: Let me get clear on this. You're not saying that it's a good thing to believe something that's clearly false, because it expresses and elicits good feelings, and so on, are you?

SYMBOLIST: No, I'm not saying that. I agree that when you're considering what to believe, truth is the only relevant matter. I don't think that religion is concerned with believing in that sense. Religious people appreciate and resonate with the stories in their religion.

ATHEIST: Well, interpreted that way, religion maybe isn't a bad thing. It might be useful or enjoyable or uplifting or something—to some people anyway, people who respond to that sort of thing. Anyway, it wouldn't matter that everything it says is false! But is that really what religion is about?

RATIONALIST: Yes, that's the problem I see. I mean, most religious people I know think that what religion says is true, and they don't mean that it's merely symbolically or poetically true. They mean, just plain true, at least in its main beliefs.

SYMBOLIST: How about those really implausible Bible stories, like the talking snake in Genesis, or when Lot's Wife was turned into a pillar of salt, or when Moses parted the Red Sea. Do your religious friends believe they really happened as reported?

RATIONALIST: Some do, but many of them doubt the details of the stranger stories in the Bible. They might agree that these things aren't literally true, and that a symbolic interpretation is more appropriate there. But I think that very few religious people think that the main statements their religions make—about the existence of a loving God, for example—are to be taken only poetically. We think that God really, literally, exists. This isn't poetry—it's literal truth. So your interpretation of what religion is really about can't be right, because you can find hardly any religious people who think that way.

SYMBOLIST: Maybe you're misled by superficial similarity of how religious and ordinary beliefs are expressed. People say, "I believe God loves me" and "I believe that Brazil is in South America." Those two sentences have the same general form—"I believe X"—and it's tempting to think that both sentences should be treated in the same way, by judging, for example, whether the X is true or not. But I'm suggesting that they really mean very different sorts of things. Religious "belief" might actually be not much like ordinary belief. Notice, by the way, that there are even differences in the languages of religious and ordinary belief: you say that you believe *that* when it's an ordinary truth, but you say you believe *in* God.

14. Mysticism

RATIONALIST: Anyway, I just noticed that MYSTIC has been sitting in the corner over there quietly this whole time. Can we invite you into the conversation?

MYSTIC: Religion for a mystic doesn't really include much talking, as a rule. Anyway, I might as well tell you, RATIONALIST, where I disagree with you most centrally. I gather that you were talking about evidence and arguments for the existence of God because you thought that his existence couldn't be established by direct experience, in the way, for example, that you can find out that it's a sunny day just by looking. But I think that God can be experienced. In fact, I have had such experiences myself.

ATHEIST: Really! What's that like?

MYSTIC: Well I really can't say. These experiences can't really be described, at least in any literal way. Other mystics sometimes use poetic, figurative language to describe the mystical experience of God, but it's not really a description at all. It's rather a sort of expressive poem about it. Mystics believe that there is a spiritual reality that can be experienced, but it's a reality different from what can be perceived by the physical senses. You can't think about it intellectually, or say anything about it that's very clear or enlightening. You just have to be there.

ATHEIST: Hmm, that's not much help to us!

MYSTIC: Yes, I know. That's why I wasn't eager to enter into your discussion.

RATIONALIST: I've never had experiences like that.

MYSTIC: Some people just seem to get these experiences, but in many mystical traditions, it's thought that you can prepare for them, and develop the capacity for having them. In most religions there are at least some people who seek mystical experience, and who use traditional exercises that will tend to bring those experiences on. These often involve some sort of deep meditation, or fasting, or trance, or even some kinds of natural drugs.

ATHEIST: It sounds to me like those exercises and drugs and so on are all just the sort of thing to bring on hallucinations in people who have a tendency in that direction. How do you know that those experiences are really of God, and not just hallucinations?

MYSTIC: I guess I don't. I certainly can't prove that I really do experience God. But I do know that these experiences are so vivid and important to me that I don't need any further convincing of the reality of God.

ATHEIST: But that doesn't count as any reason for *me* to accept that God exists. I mean, I'm sure you've had some sort of weird experience all right, but you've brought it on by exercises that are known to tend to produce hallucinations.

MYSTIC: I agree that it certainly shouldn't convince you. I really have no evidence or argument for you at all. Again, that's why intellectual discussions and arguments usually aren't important for mystics. All I can tell you is that if you wholeheartedly practised the exercises we prescribe, then you might experience the Divine too.

ATHEIST: Well, thanks for the invitation! Maybe another time!

Suggested Readings

(See the Notes on "Suggested Readings" sections, p. 17-18.)

The most famous attempted proofs of God's existence are by St. Thomas Aquinas (1225-74). He provides "Five Ways" in his *Summa Theologiae* (Part I, Question 2, Article 3).

William Paley (1743-1805) gives a version of the Argument from Design in his *Natural Theology* that includes the famous finding-a-watch analogy.

The originator of the Ontological Argument is St. Anselm (1033-1109). There's a very brief presentation of the argument in his *Proslogion*, Chapters II-V.

René Descartes (1596-1650) also presents influential versions of several proofs, in his *Meditations,* 5. By far the best edition of this for students is on-line at <http://www.earlymoderntexts.com>.

Dialogues Concerning Natural Religion by David Hume (1711-76) is an extremely interesting treatment of a variety of different points of view on religion, including Hume's sceptical doubts. By far the best edition of this for students is on-line at <http://www.earlymoderntexts.com>.

The most famous modern sceptic about religion is Bertrand Russell (1872-1970). Many essays of his on the subject are available in several of his books; *Religion and Science* and *Why I am Not A Christian* are especially good places to look.

Blaise Pascal (1623-62) presents the Wager in his *Thoughts*.

William James (1842-1910) gives his psychological findings on religion, and his pragmatic justification of belief, in an essay called "The Will to Believe" and in his book *The Varieties of Religious Experience*.

In *Candide*, Voltaire (1694-1778) compellingly raises the Argument from the Existence of Evil.

John Hick is widely known for his defence of religion against the Argument from the Existence of Evil. This and a wide-ranging discussion of other issues, including arguments from science and psychology, are found in *The Philosophy of Religion*.

Karen Armstrong's *A History of God* tells the complicated and interesting story of historical changes in how religious people understand God.

The symbolist position is presented by George Santayana (1863-1952) in *Reason in Religion*.

Sigmund Freud (1856-1939) gave his views on the psychology of religion in *The Future of an Illusion*.

That article PSYCHOLOGIST referred to is by Steven Reiss, in his book, *Who Am I? The 16 Basic Desires that Motivate Our Action and Define Our Personalities*.

CONVERSATION II

Social Philosophy

Participants: SCEPTIC • LEGALIST • CONTRACTARIAN • MORALIST •
BIOLOGIST • COMMUNITARIAN • INDIVIDUALIST • COMMUNIST •
LIBERTARIAN • INTERVENTIONIST • FEMINIST • EGALITARIAN

1. The Question

SCEPTIC: A few weeks ago I was in a situation that started me thinking about some things I'd like to discuss with you. Here's what happened. I was driving my car out in the country, in an area where it's very flat farmland, and there was almost no traffic. It was midday, in bright sunshine. Visibility was perfect and I could see what must have been a couple of miles in every direction. I was coming to a crossroad, and it was clear that there was nothing on the road I was on, behind me or coming the other way, and nothing on the crossroad in either direction. As I got closer to the crossroad, I saw a stop sign there. I could see that there was absolutely no danger in driving right through the intersection without stopping, and because I was in a bit of a hurry, I didn't stop. But as I continued my drive I started to wonder whether I had actually made a mistake by driving right through. It's not that I was running the risk of being caught by the police and fined for running the stop sign. I could see that there was nobody around for miles in any direction. If there was any risk at all of getting into an accident when I sailed through the intersection, I wouldn't have done it. I certainly would have stopped if there were a chance of damaging my car and injuring or killing myself, and it would have been immoral to put other drivers at risk. But again I could see that there was no chance of any of that. The only reason what I did could be called wrong was that there was a law against it—failing to stop was breaking a law. But (and here's where the philosophy comes in), since I could get away with breaking the law, with no risk of harming anybody, was it wrong for me to do it? If it was, then why?

LEGALIST: Look, isn't there an obvious answer to your questions? Yes, it's always wrong to break the law, because we're all members of society, and society has the right to make laws, and when it does, we must obey them.

SCEPTIC: Well, that doesn't answer my questions. What I'm asking is why society has the right to make laws, and why laws produced by society have binding force on me.

LEGALIST: They've got binding force because you'll get caught and punished if you disobey.

SCEPTIC: Yes, I know that, but in the case I'm talking about, there wasn't any chance I'd get caught. I could see there were no police anywhere around.

LEGALIST: Well, you can't really be perfectly sure you won't get caught, and in lots of other situations, you do run that risk.

SCEPTIC: In this particular situation, I was perfectly sure that I wouldn't get caught. It's true that in other situations, I'd run that risk, but I'm talking about this situation.

LEGALIST: But it's a good idea to get into the habit of obeying laws like this one, because then you'll do it without thinking, and you'll stay out of trouble. If you think about each case, and wonder if you'll be caught or not, you'll make a mistake sooner or later.

SCEPTIC: No, look, what I'm asking is this: is there any reason for me to obey beyond the purely practical selfish one that I'll regret breaking a law if I get caught and punished?

2. The Tragedy of the Commons and the Prisoner's Dilemma

CONTRACTARIAN: Okay, maybe I can answer your questions. Here's a little fable called *The Tragedy of the Commons* that I think is relevant. Once upon a time there was a village in which several farmers raised cattle. None of the farmers owned enough land to provide sufficient grazing for their cattle, but the village had a "commons" which was land owned by nobody, on which anyone could put their cattle to graze. This arrangement worked out well for a while, but then, as farmers increased their herds, it became clear that the commons was becoming over-grazed, and the grass didn't have enough chance to grow back, so that by the following year, if things kept going on the same way, there wouldn't be any grass left on the commons at all. So the farmers got together to talk about the matter, and those who knew about such things told them that the commons could support a restricted level of grazing—that is, that if each farmer restricted his cattle to a half day on the commons, the grass would be able to recover and the farmers could continue to use this resource year after year. Each farmer would have preferred a longer grazing time for his cattle—that would reduce the amount the farmer had to pay for supplemental feed. But one farmer argued that if they all did this, there wouldn't be any grass left on the commons by next year, so they'd better agree to restrict themselves to a half-day's grazing. Each farmer saw the wisdom of this, so they each spoke up in turn, saying that they agreed to the restriction. From then on, no farmer grazed his cattle longer than half a day, and the commons continued to provide feed for everyone's animals.

SCEPTIC: Okay, but what does that have to do with my question?

CONTRACTARIAN: The idea is that there are certain dangers that arise if everyone is out for him or herself. But if we all agree to certain restrictions, then we'd all be better off in the long run. Some philosophers think that this is the basic idea behind the origin and function of society, and that this explains why we have an obligation to obey society's rules.

SCEPTIC: Hmm, well, we'll have to talk about that.

CONTRACTARIAN: First, let me tell you a second story, with a different situation that has something like the same point. It's called the *Prisoner's Dilemma*. Here's how it goes. Imagine that you and your buddy have just committed a crime together, and the police bring both of you in for questioning.

SCEPTIC: Is the point here that we're both immoral criminals, and society should defend itself against us?

CONTRACTARIAN: No, that's not it. Hold on till you've heard the whole story. So the police separate you from your buddy, and they tell you that right now they have enough evidence to convict you (and your buddy) of conspiracy to commit a crime—and this would put each of you in jail for a short time. But they don't have enough evidence to convict either of you of the crime itself, which carries a larger penalty. So they're going to offer you a deal. If you confess to the crime, and implicate your buddy, but he keeps quiet, then you'll only get 1 year in jail. If you confess and he does too, then you'll get three years. But if you keep quiet and he talks, then you'll get four years.

SCEPTIC: Wait a minute, this is hard to follow.

CONTRACTARIAN: Okay, here's a table summarizing what you're being offered.

	Buddy Confesses	Buddy Keeps Quiet
You Confess	You get 3 years	You get 1 year
You Keep Quiet	You get 4 years	You get 2 years

On this table, your choices are to the left, and Buddy's choices across the top. What happens to you, given each choice of yours, depends on what Buddy does. So for example if you keep quiet, that puts you on the bottom row; and if Buddy keeps quiet what happens to you can be read off the right column. So if you both keep quiet, the situation is represented by the lower-right square: you get 2 years.

SCEPTIC: Okay, I think I understand.

CONTRACTARIAN: One more thing: the police are giving Buddy the same deal, at the same time.

SCEPTIC: Okay.

CONTRACTARIAN: Now, let's assume that your only desire here is that you minimize the time you're going to spend in jail: you don't care what happens to Buddy. Then what should you do?

SCEPTIC: Well, that depends on what Buddy decides to do, doesn't it? Am I told what Buddy is going to do? Do I have any reason to expect him to confess or to keep quiet?

CONTRACTARIAN: No, you're not told, and have no idea what he's likely to do. But actually, that doesn't make any difference.

SCEPTIC: Really? Why not?

CONTRACTARIAN: You don't know what Buddy is going to do, but you can reason like this: If Buddy confesses, then I get 3 years if I confess, or 4 years if I keep quiet. So if Buddy confesses, I'm better off confessing too. Now, if Buddy keeps quiet, I get 1 year if I confess, or 2 years if I keep quiet. So if Buddy keeps quiet, I'm better off confessing.

SCEPTIC: Hold on, let me go over that on the table. Okay, if Buddy confesses, then that means that the left-hand column tells what happens to me. So I'd get 3 years if I confess (in the top left box), or 4 years if I keep quiet (in the bottom left box). So, if Buddy confesses, I'd be better off confessing.

Now, if Buddy keeps quiet, that means the right-hand column tells what happens to me. So I'd get 1 year if I confess (in the top right box), or 2 years if I keep quiet (in the bottom right box). So, if Buddy keeps quiet, I'd be better off confessing. Either way, if Buddy confesses or keeps quiet, I'm better off confessing. So you're right. Even though it matters to me what he does, because that would affect how many years in jail I'd get, I'd be better off if I confessed no matter what Buddy did. So it's clear I should confess—provided that I'm only looking out for myself.

CONTRACTARIAN: Right. Now, remember, Buddy is being offered the same deal at the same time. He reasons exactly as you do, and concludes that whatever you do, he's better off if he confesses.

SCEPTIC: Wait a minute.

CONTRACTARIAN: Here's the whole thing laid out in a different sort of table:

	Buddy Confesses	Buddy Keeps Quiet
You Confess	3 3	4 1
Buddy Confesses	1 4	2 2

This table summarizes what happens to you and what happens to Buddy. The numbers all represent years in jail. Your sentence is the number in the lower left of each box. Buddy's sentence is in the upper right of each box. If you work your way through this, you'll see that each of you is being given the same deal, the one we've been describing. Now, because of the reasoning we've been looking at, both of you, reasoning on the basis of your own self-interest, confess. So the real outcome is in the upper-left box, and you both get three years.

SCEPTIC: Right. But I can see now that this is less than ideal for me. It's almost the worst possible outcome. It would have been possible for me to get only one year, if I told on Buddy. (Of course, then he would have been screwed, but I don't care about that.) Or if we had both kept quiet, we'd both have gotten only 2 years. And the same thing's true for Buddy. If I had kept quiet, he could have gotten only 1 year by confessing (and screwing me). But again, we'd both have been better off if we had both kept quiet.

CONTRACTARIAN: Exactly. So there's a possibility here that would have made both of you better off: both keeping quiet. So suppose, somehow, that you and Buddy knew in advance about the deal you would each be offered by the police, and you both made an agreement to keep quiet. If you both kept that deal after you were arrested, then you'd both wind up in the lower-right box of your table, with only two years in jail. That's why this case is like the Tragedy of the Commons. Given that people are all out for themselves, everyone winds up badly off in the long-run; and everyone would be better off if they somehow could make an effective agreement to restrain their pursuit of their own advantage.

3. The Social Contract

SCEPTIC: Okay, I see what you're driving at. In both cases, a binding agreement would have made everyone better off. So this is all supposed to have something to do with society's rules?

CONTRACTARIAN: Yes. Here's why. Imagine that there was a time long ago, before recorded history, when society hadn't yet been invented; everybody was just out for themselves. Philosophers have called this situation the *state of nature*. In the state of nature, if you had food and I was hungry, then I'd just pick up my club, walk over to your cave, bash you over the head, and grab your food. Of course, then when you regained consciousness, you'd take your club over to my cave, or someone else's, bash them, and grab their food.

SCEPTIC: Doesn't sound very nice.

CONTRACTARIAN: Right. Everyone would spend a lot of time bashing other people, or protecting themselves from getting bashed, and there would be a lot of people killed or injured. Nobody would plant crops, because they knew that they couldn't guard them sufficiently, and somebody else would grab what was being grown. Nobody would have much time or energy to gather plants, or go hunting, because of the constant warfare. In the words of the seventeenth-century English philosopher Thomas Hobbes, in the state of nature, there'd be a "war of every one against every one," with the result that each person's life would be "solitary, poor, nasty, brutish, and short." But at some point, people realized that they'd all be better off if they ended all this warfare, and stopped all that bashing and grabbing. Then they'd have the security and time necessary to provide for themselves, and be free from those destructive conflicts. So for everyone's advantage, they all agreed—as if by signing a contract—to respect each other's possessions, and to refrain from aggression. This is what's called the *social contract*. It establishes society and makes us all better off.

SCEPTIC: So the idea is that society's rules make everyone better off in the long run, and so we've all agreed to abide by them?

CONTRACTARIAN: Yes, that's basically it.

SCEPTIC: Okay, now I see the similarity between this idea and what's going on in the Tragedy of the Commons and in the Prisoner's Dilemma. In all three cases, if people are able to agree to restrict the pursuit of their own self-interest, and to abide by rules for cooperation, then everyone would be better off in the long run.

CONTRACTARIAN: Right. The state of nature is a state where people are out for themselves, when they're considering only their own self-interest. On the commons, that means that farmers graze their cattle all day long and the grass dies. In the Prisoner's Dilemma, it means that each prisoner confesses, and both get 3 years. In the state of nature, life is solitary, poor, nasty, brutish, and short. But if there's an agreement that works, then the farmers restrict their grazing and the grass continues to grow on the commons. The prisoners both keep quiet, and spend a year less in jail each. And in society in general, all of us, when we abide by the social contract, have much better lives than we would have had in the state of nature.

SCEPTIC: I can see what you're saying, but maybe that doesn't answer my question about why to obey society's laws. Look, first of all, unlike the farmers living around the commons, and the prisoners who reach an agreement to keep quiet, I never agreed to participate in society. I never agreed to society's laws. I didn't sign anything, or give a verbal okay, and I was never asked to. And, really, probably nobody ever agreed. I mean, philosophers who use this "social contract" idea don't think that all those cave people got together one day and wrote up a contract and signed it, do they? We're not talking about history here. I doubt that the invention of society really involved any kind of agreement like that at all. I've got a quotation here—let me see if I can find it—oh, here it is. It's by the eighteenth-century Scots philosophical sceptic David Hume: he says, "Almost all the governments which exist at present, or of which there remains any record in history, have been founded originally either on usurpation or conquest or both, without any pretence of a fair consent or voluntary subjection of the people." (Hume, "Of the Original Contract," 1748.)

CONTRACTARIAN: But when Hume wrote that in 1748, there were hardly any democratic governments in existence, then, or in all of preceding history.

Just about every country was ruled by an absolute hereditary monarchy. The American and French revolutions were still in the future.

SCEPTIC: Yes, that's right, but I don't think that the growth of democracies in the world since then changes his point. Despite all that talk in modern democracies about "government of the people, by the people," despite the fact that we get to vote on who rules us, we still haven't agreed to the government that we have. I never made any promises to my democratic government—never signed any social contract—and neither did anybody earlier. I suppose it might be a different story if I had agreed to a contract (though I'll have to think about that), but if I haven't agreed to it, then I wonder why I should obey society's rules. It sounds to me like you're trying to produce some sort of automatic justification of at least the kind of democratic society we've got here and now, and I don't accept that. When it's not clear to me that it's to my advantage to follow a particular rule of society, this business about a fake contract doesn't make me any more inclined to follow the rules.

CONTRACTARIAN: Well, you're right that there wasn't a historical event involving an explicit agreement to a social contract. That sort of thing probably evolved gradually, unconsciously, without anyone's ever really thinking about it, and without formal agreement. The point of telling the social-contract story isn't to speculate about pre-historical events. It's rather to give a justification for the existence of society. The point is that having a society which restricts us in some ways is much better than having no society at all—than being in the state of nature. Society is advantageous to everyone, and we *would* all agree to its restrictions, once we realized its advantages.

SCEPTIC: Okay, maybe the current society is one I *would* agree to; but I didn't. How can a contract bind me if I didn't actually agree to it?

CONTRACTARIAN: In a sense, we all do give silent agreement, to the restrictions of society, just by living in it and participating in its institutions and enjoying its advantages.

SCEPTIC: Well, I don't know about that silent agreement business. When I agree to something, I like to know what I'm agreeing to—and that I'm agreeing!

CONTRACTARIAN: But silent agreement does make sense. Imagine for example that you're standing around in the park watching some people play basketball, and they motion you to join in, and you do. Somebody throws the ball to you, and you stick it under your shirt. Then you run to the sidelines and grab a big box, which you drag under the net. You stand on the box, and drop the ball into the basketball hoop. They all say to you, "You can't do that!" and you say, "Why not? I can do what I want in the park, can't I?" But they say that what you did is forbidden by ordinary basic rules of casual basketball—rules that apply to anyone who's playing. But you reply, "Why do those rules apply to me? I never agreed to them. I never promised to obey them. I never told you I was going to play basketball!" But they're right. Just by participating in the activity, you in effect agree to be governed by the rules.

SCEPTIC: Well, maybe, but here's a worse problem. Let's go back to the Tragedy of the Commons. Suppose I'm one of the farmers, and it's noon on the day after we've agreed to restricting our cattle to a half-day's grazing. My cattle have been on the commons all morning, and I think to myself: My cattle will get more to eat if I keep them here all day. Why not do it?

CONTRACTARIAN: But you agreed the day before to do it. You've got a contract, so to speak.

SCEPTIC: Right, but the question I'm asking now is, Why should I obey the terms of the contract? It's to my advantage not to.

CONTRACTARIAN: Okay, but breaking the agreement is screwing the other farmers. Don't you care about them?

SCEPTIC: Suppose I do, but suppose that the grass wouldn't be harmed if I left my cattle to graze all day. It would be harmed only if several people allowed their cattle to graze all day. So I'm not going to do them any damage by breaking the agreement. Provided they keep their end of the agreement, the grass will do fine.

CONTRACTARIAN: But what if the other farmers broke the agreement too? What if everyone did that?

SCEPTIC: If everyone else was going to break the agreement, then the grass would die by next year whether I kept the agreement or not. We'll all be in trouble pretty soon, when the grass was all gone. But if this was going to happen, then I might as well make the best of a bad situation, and get the most for my cattle while I can. See, either way it's better for me to break the agreement. If all the rest of them are going to honour our agreement, then it won't harm the grass if I break it and feed my cattle all day, so I should. If the rest of them are going to break our agreement, I also should break it and feed my cattle all day. Either way I should break the agreement. My actions don't make a real difference in either case.

CONTRACTARIAN: But your actions might make a difference in some cases.

SCEPTIC: Right, for example, if the grass was in real trouble, near the edge of extinction, and if I grazed my cattle a little longer than permitted that would do it. But that's really unlikely. I'm supposing that my actions alone won't have any significant bad result for anyone.

CONTRACTARIAN: Well, here's a realistic possibility. Suppose that the other farmers are all set to honour the agreement, but then when they found out that you're breaking the agreement, they'd start doing that too. They'd say, "If that jerk can graze his stock all day, well then, dammit, so can I!" Your breaking the agreement would *make* them break it. So the choices you face then are either honour the agreement, in which case they will too, and everyone would be better off, or else break it, which will result in their doing the same, and everyone would be worse off. So you should honour the agreement.

SCEPTIC: But remember, they're not going to find out I've done it, so my breaking the agreement wouldn't make them break the agreement also.

CONTRACTARIAN: But what if they broke the agreement just because they were thinking in the same way you are?

SCEPTIC: Well we're imagining now that the way they think doesn't *depend* on the way I think (because they don't know what I'm thinking). So if by coincidence, they were all thinking that they ought to break the agreement, then the grass doesn't stand a chance, and I might as well break the agreement too. But if enough of them honour the agreement, then when I overgraze it won't damage the grass beyond recovery, and I might as well overgraze my cattle. Either way there's no reason why I should take my cattle home after half a day. The point here is that it always seems to pay me to break this sort of social contract, as long as I can get away with it. That was my original question. It's the same situation in the Prisoner's Dilemma. Suppose that Buddy and I, anticipating the deal offered by the police, agreed in advance to keep quiet. Suppose then we were offered the deal; the self-interested reasoning we were talking about earlier would still be correct. Despite that deal, I'd be better off if I confessed, and ratted on Buddy.

4. Enforcement of the Contract

CONTRACTARIAN: Well, how about this. If you broke the agreement, wouldn't you get in trouble with the other farmers? They'd be mad if they found out that you broke the agreement. They might do you some harm. Maybe they'd come around and burn down your barn or something. And the same sort of thing might happen in the Prisoner's Dilemma. When the two of you got out of jail, Buddy might be expected to do some pretty nasty things to you, if you broke the agreement you made to keep quiet.

SCEPTIC: That's true. Those possibilities would give me good reasons to keep the agreements, but that doesn't really answer my question. It's just like the response we just talked about, in which we imagined that my breaking the agreement would result in the other farmers' breaking the agreement too. Both responses add additional consequences to my actions beyond those I specified in the original story. If they'd burn down my barn when they found out, then of course it would be in my self-interest to keep the agreement. But again that doesn't really answer my question, which was why I should keep the agreement, if there's nothing in it for me. Suppose I add to my story the additional condition that the other farmers won't ever find out.

CONTRACTARIAN: Okay, but I think that this sort of response to the Tragedy of the Commons and the Prisoners' Dilemma, and other situations like that, actually does reveal something important about the Social Contract in general, which is that we normally add enforcement to make it in people's self-interest to keep the agreement. We could expect that the farmers would set things up so that they could find out if anyone was breaking the agreement, and maybe even provide some regular procedure for penalizing any farmer who did.

That's the way it works in real society as a whole. The social contract restricts us from certain actions which would be to our individual advantage, like stealing somebody else's goods. Realizing that stealing and so on would be to their advantage, some people would try to break the contract, and do what it forbids. To guard against this, society establishes a police force to find out who's breaking the rules, and courts and jails to punish them. If you think that you stand a good chance of being punished, then it's not in your interest to break the terms of the contract after all.

That, by the way, was Hobbes's answer to the problem of how to get a Social Contract to work. People realize that the only way to enforce the contract is to have a system of enforceable penalties for contract-breakers, so they set up a great big powerful state with unlimited powers to enforce the social rules.

SCEPTIC: Right, that's again where enforcement comes in. But by the way, I just remembered an interesting puzzle that I think has something to do with what we're talking about. It's called the *Voter's Paradox*. Often, when there's an election, you have some sort of preference among the candidates—suppose, for example, that you really want Candidate X to win. Now, it's going to take some effort for you to get out to the polling place and cast your ballot—not very much effort. The question is, is it worth even that small effort to go vote?

CONTRACTARIAN: Of course, you really want X to win!

SCEPTIC: No, here's the problem. In order for your vote to have any influence on who wins, it would have to break or create a tie. Given (we suppose) that there are a large number of voters, the chance that your vote would break or create a tie is close enough to zero to be negligible. With such overwhelming odds against your vote making a difference, it's not worth expending any effort at all to go to vote, no matter how much you want X to win.

CONTRACTARIAN: I get it. Obviously, however, you ought to go vote for X anyway: this way of thinking has some flaw in it.

SCEPTIC: That's what seems obvious to everyone. The problem here is to explain what's wrong with the reasoning that proves the opposite!

CONTRACTARIAN: What does this have to do with what we were talking about?

SCEPTIC: It's like the Tragedy of the Commons, in that both are cases in which an individual action is extremely unlikely to make any difference, but in which, if everyone thought that way, there'd be important consequences; and in which one person's action doesn't cause other people to act that way.

5. A Moral Answer

MORALIST: Can I join your conversation for a moment? What you just said reminded me of a way some people try to answer your basic question here, and I'd like to hear your response to this answer. Let's get back to the Commons, and imagine that you're the farmer thinking about breaking the agreement. We've agreed that if everyone broke the agreement, then everyone, including you, would be in deep trouble. But then, doesn't the question "What if everyone did that?" influence you, in any way, when you're wondering whether you should do it?

SCEPTIC: I've agreed that this question would be relevant if my doing it *made* everyone else do it. But if it didn't, then why would this be relevant?

MORALIST: Well, look, we're assuming that all the other farmers are in basically the same boat as you are. They're reasoning the same way you are. If you decide to break the agreement, then they would probably decide to break it too. Then you're all in a mess.

SCEPTIC: That's probably right, but it doesn't follow that therefore I should keep the agreement, because that wouldn't make them keep it too.

MORALIST: Okay, but doesn't the question have some force with you anyway? I mean, when we're wondering what to do, isn't the question "What if everyone acted that way?" a relevant consideration, even when we assume that your actions would have no effect on others? The fact that it would be a disaster if everyone did something often seems to be a good reason, just in itself, for me not to do something. That's the basis of moral thinking, isn't it?

SCEPTIC: I guess that the question you mentioned is what people generally ask when they're thinking morally, so I suppose that there would be a moral reason for keeping the contract in this case. If that's the case, and if we can assume that these farmers have got moral motivation, then the problem I've been talking about wouldn't come up. I guess I raised the problem thinking that we couldn't assume morality in the participants to begin with. I mean, when Hobbes and other philosophers thought about these matters, they began by assuming that the farmer on the commons, the prisoners in the Dilemma, the people in the State of Nature were motivated only by self-interest, not by morality, so the question "What if everyone did that?" wouldn't have any relevance to them. The philosophers didn't start off by assuming a social conscience: they wanted to see if social action could be motivated just on the basis of self-interest.

CONTRACTARIAN: Well, maybe there is an interesting answer here anyway. Maybe consideration of the Social Contract and the Tragedy of the Commons and so on give a clue to the origin and function of moral thinking. Look at it this way. Earlier, I was talking about the necessity for enforcement, in order to get people to keep the agreement. The obvious way to do this is to get a public enforcement institution: the police and courts and so on, as well as more informal social pressure. But there are a couple of severe limitations on the power of these institutions. For one thing, the police can't be everywhere, and the courts don't always convict the guilty. And for another, you can't have the police and the courts enforcing every sort of cooperation. I mean, they might enforce laws and formal legal contracts, but they couldn't be expected to enforce just any informal promise. What would be a very useful supplement to this external enforcement would be an "internal" enforcement, and I think that this may be where morality comes in. It's as if society has placed little police officers and judges inside us, that tell us to keep our agreements and punish us when we don't. Maybe that's what moral training and socialization is supposed to do to children: brainwash them into keeping their contractual agreements to society, making them their own enforcers of the social contract. So if the farmers are motivated by the question, "What if everyone did that?" and by consequence remove their cattle from the Commons after half a day, that shows the success of this social brainwashing.

SCEPTIC: Okay, that makes sense, but it still doesn't really get at the heart of my question. I agree, if I've been successfully brainwashed by society into moral thinking, I'd ask myself, What if everyone kept their cattle in the Commons all day? What if everyone jumped stop signs? And so on. But what if I don't see the relevance of these questions? If society hasn't managed to brainwash me? Are there any considerations to convince me that I should be doing so?

MORALIST: Well, I think that there is a good, objective basis for morality. But this is a big question, and one I suppose we should get into later.[1]

6. A Biological Answer

BIOLOGIST: I've been listening to all of you, and I'd like to suggest another possibility. I think that SCEPTIC and CONTRACTARIAN are both making a mistake. SCEPTIC was asking, "What's in it for me to obey society's rules?" and CONTRACTARIAN was trying to answer that question on the basis of the Social Contract. But then the same question arose again: why obey the terms of the contract? Most recently, you both seemed willing to agree that there was social training—"brainwashing"—to produce internal enforcement of social rules, but then there was a question of motivation to obey these rules if this sort of training didn't take. So the question still arose about how contract keeping could be motivated by self-interest. When you talk about a state of nature in which people are all out for themselves, you assume that this is the way people naturally are, and that any other way of looking at things would have to be justified by appealing to this sort of selfish interest. The basic motivation assumed all along, here, is selfish.

SCEPTIC: Well, isn't that the way people naturally are?

---

1 Conversation III deals with this question.

BIOLOGIST: I don't think so. Of course, we're not on very solid ground when we try to speculate on how human beings might be just because of their inborn nature, rather than because of what they learn through their culture and society, but there's some pretty good reason to think that lots of animals, and so probably human beings too, have automatic instincts which are social and unselfish, not just individualistic and self-regarding.

SCEPTIC: Really? I've seen plenty of examples of animals that seem to be just out for themselves. You can watch birds at the bird-feeder, for example, pushing each other out of the way to get at the bird-seed. I thought that the basic principle of nature was competition of each animal against all the rest, survival of the fittest, nature red in tooth and claw. Isn't that right?

CONTRACTARIAN: Yes, that's how I've been assuming that humans are by nature. I think that social restrictions, including the internal motivation of morality that MORALIST was talking about, come from invented culture.

BIOLOGIST: Well, I guess that there is a lot of competition visible in nature, but there's also a lot of cooperation, especially between organisms that are closely related. Many organisms live in elaborate social organizations, in which individuals look out for the benefit of others in their society, even at their own expense. And they do this instinctively—they have cooperation built right into their instincts. That's where the Prisoner's Dilemma comes into biological thinking.

CONTRACTARIAN: How does that work?

BIOLOGIST: Evolution will tend to produce instincts in organisms that further the survival and reproduction of that genetic type. In Prisoner's Dilemma type situations, the organisms in general will be better off, as far as survival and reproduction are concerned, when they tend to cooperate with each other. Individual animals with the genetic tendency to choose "generous" behaviour would then wind up in the upper left-hand box—providing that they were playing the game with others similarly inclined; and they'd all be better off. So evolution will very often produce cooperative, "generous" behaviour, rather than "selfish," just looking out for number-one. That's why the "state of nature" involving "war of each against all," as Hobbes imagined it, is not the natural state of many organisms. We believe that there's an evolutionary reason for "generous" instinctive behaviour: an animal mother will give up some of her food for her children; some animals may give up their lives defending the colony; and so on. We might even imagine an instinct in animals grazing on a commons, ·restricting their grazing time when the grass is in danger of dying!

SCEPTIC: Okay, maybe that happens in nature, but how about in humans?

BIOLOGIST: As I said, it's not easy to find out what contribution human biological nature makes to our behaviour. But it is reasonable to suppose that
some sort of altruistic motivation is built right into us, as it is in many
other animals, to help us solve our Prisoner's Dilemmas.

SCEPTIC: All right, just suppose that some sort of altruistic motivation, some
impulse to generosity and to social cooperation, is built right into people.
You wouldn't have to justify obeying the rules of the Social Contract to
them. But this sort of thing doesn't occur everywhere in animal nature:
there's plenty of competition too. And you have to admit that there are
some people who really are only out for themselves, and that even nice
people like me think that it's a serious question why we should act coop-
eratively, in accord with social agreements and rules. So it doesn't seem
that we're all automatically motivated to act that way all the time: the fact
that my question is a serious one shows that.

7. Communitarianism

COMMUNITARIAN: Okay, let me try to answer SCEPTIC's question. I agree with
BIOLOGIST that you two, SCEPTIC and CONTRACTARIAN, have been
approaching this question from entirely the wrong point of view. I agree
with BIOLOGIST that the picture you start with is mistaken—the view that
people are, basically, independent and self-interested. You're imagining
that each human being is completely independent, interested only in him-
or herself. And I agree with BIOLOGIST that this is a mistake.

SCEPTIC: Well, then, is your position the same as BIOLOGIST?

COMMUNITARIAN: Not exactly. BIOLOGIST wanted to convince you that people
in fact have instinctual cooperative, social desires and motivation, not just
the self-interested ones you've been thinking about. I agree that this is certainly possible, but I agree with you two that sometimes, at least, some
people seem not to have any social motivations, and there seems to be
only selfish motivation. And I agree that it's a serious question why people *ought* to think socially.

SCEPTIC: Good. What's your answer?

COMMUNITARIAN: Let me put it this way. You're assuming that society is
nothing more than a combination of individual people, nothing more than
the sum total of all the people that make it up. Your view could be called

atomistic, because it's like the way physicists and chemists think about material lumps of stuff, as nothing but a collection of atoms, the building blocks of the lump. Its atoms have individual characteristics, which exist independently of their combination with other ones, and the characteristics of the lump they compose are only a matter of the characteristics and arrangement and interaction of the individual atoms. Your view of society and the individual is atomistic like this. According to your view, society can be judged only on the basis of whether it serves the individual needs of the people that make it up, the needs these people would have if that society didn't exist, and which might be served better or worse by any given society.

INDIVIDUALIST: That's exactly how I think about matters.

CONTRACTARIAN: Me too. But what's wrong with that?

COMMUNITARIAN: What's wrong is the idea that people's needs exist, and can be understood, independently of the society they belong to. This is backwards. People have no important characteristics, no nature, no needs or desires, independently of the society they're part of.

INDIVIDUALIST: What do you mean, exactly?

COMMUNITARIAN: Look, when you try to think of your most important characteristics, I'll bet they all have to do with your place in society, with your relations with other people—your friends, your family, your local community, your country, and so on. For example, there are the characteristics you see in yourself, the obligations you have, insofar as you are somebody's parent or child, sister or brother, lover or friend. There are your rights and duties as worker, boss, or student. You think of yourself as friendly, or loving, or a leader or follower. All of these things involve your relations—how you connect—with others. Even thinking of yourself as a loner is defining yourself in terms of how you relate to others. What you really are, what you need and want, what you should and shouldn't do, are all tied up with how you fit into a society. So your identity—I mean, how you think about yourself, how you really are, basically—is entirely tied up with your social relations. Human beings are social animals, and that means that the real basic nature of each individual person depends on that person's relations with other people in society, on the way that person fits into the whole. Society makes us the way we are. It's the society that's basic for understanding and evaluating individual people, not the other way around. So what that means is that you can't judge the worth of a society by how well it fits the needs of individuals, because there are no real important needs of individuals apart from their social nature, apart from the society they fit into. What you want is really defined and determined by your place in society, so it doesn't make sense to say that you could choose a society on the basis of what you want. This assumes that you have wants independent of the society you're in.

SCEPTIC: So what you're claiming is that my identity is wholly a matter of how I fit into society, of my relations with other people?

COMMUNITARIAN: Right.

INDIVIDUALIST: But I don't see people's identity that way. I admit that when I think about my own identity, about what I really am like, I think of some things that have to do with my relationships with other people, but lots of other things are just individual facts about me. For example, there's my taste in music and food, the fact that I enjoy tennis and hate watching football on TV, that I'd prefer an outdoor to an indoor job, that I like reading mystery novels, that I'm grumpy when I wake up in the morning, and that too much beer makes me giggle. These are all individual facts about me, not facts about my relations with other people or groups.

COMMUNITARIAN: Okay, but even these have a social component. I mean, your individual characteristics, your personality, your likes and dislikes, all are learned from other people, all are created by social forces. You'd be completely different if you were raised in a very different sort of society. If you grew up entirely in isolation from society you'd—well—you wouldn't even exist. People can't survive alone.

INDIVIDUALIST: I admit that there's a good deal of the way I am that's a result of social conditioning, of learning from others, of training by my parents and peer group and society as a whole. But there's also a whole lot about me that's just a matter of my own individual nature. Some of that I have chosen, out of my own free will—I've just decided how I want to be. Some of it just happens, not really in my control, but isn't caused by society either. Some of it is just a matter of human nature.

COMMUNITARIAN: I think that our human nature is a social nature: humans are social animals. I also think that this idea of independent free choice is a mistake. Like what we want, what we choose is also a matter of our social relations, of our place in society. Our social relations make us choose what we do.

INDIVIDUALIST: Hmph. Well, I can choose for myself.

COMMUNITARIAN: I don't want to be insulting, but I suggest that you only think you can. Everything you are, everything you want and don't want, every way you think about yourself and about everything else, all these are products of the society you've grown up in. For instance, all the ways you think about anything—the ways you categorize them—are social constructs.

INDIVIDUALIST: Wait a minute. What's a *social construct*?

COMMUNITARIAN: Well, think of the ways you divide things up into kinds: male/female, green/red/blue/etc., delicious/yucky, animal/vegetable/mineral; all of these categorizations are arbitrary divisions of things developed by your society, and taught to everyone as they grow up, when they learn language. All of our basic concepts and patterns of thinking, all the significance anything has for us, all of this is socially invented, taught to us by our society.

INDIVIDUALIST: Well, I'd be willing to grant that all our concepts and thought-patterns are taught to us, though I'd like to see this discussed further.[2] But it doesn't follow that these are not real divisions, in the objective external world. For example, isn't the distinction between male and female humans an objective biological fact?

COMMUNITARIAN: I don't think so. I think that the way we make that division, and how it's significant to us, is a social construction. We don't learn it from nature—it's not an objective fact of biology. It's a human invention. The distinction comes from our socially-learned values, not from a real division in the way things objectively are. We didn't discover this division: we invented it.

INDIVIDUALIST: I doubt it. Where exactly we draw the line in this division, and what the significance of it is taken to be, are maybe social inventions, consequences of our society's values, but I don't think that the distinction between male and female is just a fiction we invented! In any case, we clearly disagree about the extent to which human beings are products of their society. I'm much more individualistically-minded than you are.

CONTRACTARIAN: But let's suppose you're right, and the basic facts about everyone, and the causes of their characteristics, are all social. Why exactly is this a criticism of the Social Contract Theory?

COMMUNITARIAN: The social-contractarian picture thinks of a bunch of individuals, with individual natures, wants and needs, able to decide what they want and how to get it, all independent of society. Then it imagines a society which gets its legitimacy from how well it suits all these independent freely-choosing individuals—from how well it provides for their individual needs. But if I'm right, you can't think of society as resulting

---

2 It is discussed further, in Conversation VI.

from a contract between freely-choosing independent cave people, or even as what we, as freely-choosing independent agents, would choose. Because nobody really is a freely-choosing independent agent. We're caused by society to choose as we do. Our whole nature is a matter of our society: how we think of ourselves, and what we are. All the important things about you, what you want, how you see yourself, how you think about anything, are all products of society. That's why the idea that a social arrangement is justified by how well it fits the original needs of the people that make it up is foolish. There aren't any such original needs. Society makes your needs first, and then it satisfies them—or doesn't.

CONTRACTARIAN: Well, according to you, then, where does society get the right to govern, to make decisions about what laws there should be, and about what people have to do, or are prohibited from doing?

COMMUNITARIAN: I think that society has its own rules, its own needs and wants, its own natural laws of development. We don't create it: it creates us. We find our meaning and significance from it, not the other way around. So when somebody asks "What's in it for me?" that person is asking the wrong question. In a way, President Kennedy's famous statement sums it up: "Ask not what your country can do for you; ask what you can do for your country."

INDIVIDUALIST: Well, first of all, even supposing that it is a fact that my needs are created by society, I don't see how it's supposed to follow that I'm wrong to expect society to try to fill those needs, and that I ought to be thinking instead about what I can do for society. But secondly, I find the whole idea that we get our meaning from our place in society pretty awful. Your picture sees human beings like ants in an ant colony. Each ant's life is entirely a matter of its job inside the colony; it would be nothing without its place in the ant community. Ants exist only to serve the colony. No ant ever asked "What can the colony do for me?" No individual ant is responsible for anything, or has any individuality, or any value as an individual.

COMMUNITARIAN: In a sense, that's something like my picture of human society. I've heard it proposed that the ant colony should be thought of as the basic organism, and that each ant should be thought of as organs whose significance and function is in serving the whole organism in some way. That's not far from the view I'm arguing for about human society: the society is the basic organism, not the individual.

CONTRACTARIAN: That sounds awful to me. To see us as ants in a colony denies all of our individuality.

COMMUNITARIAN: That's not much of a deprivation, since that individuality was really an illusion to start off with.

SCEPTIC: I'm bothered by the way *communitarianism* rules out the question of whether society is doing people inside the society any good. That looks like an attempt to justify society in general—just whatever sort of government and social arrangement happens to exist. But there are lots of cases in history when individuals noticed that their society was not organized for their benefit, and they worked to change it, to overthrow their government if necessary, and they should have. Isn't communitarianism a really conservative position, then, if it won't allow this?

COMMUNITARIAN: Well, some communitarians certainly did have this conservative aim in mind for their theory, but not all.

8. Communism

COMMUNIST: I'm glad that question was raised. We communists are communitarians, but we do ask for whose benefit a society is organized. Our political position is designed exactly to deal with those objections to both communitarianism and contractarianism that SCEPTIC raised: that both of those views seem to be aimed at justifying, making legitimate, the status quo—the sort of society we have now, despite the fact that our current society is controlled by the rich and the powerful, and exists for their benefit, not ours.

INDIVIDUALIST: Gee, I didn't know there were any communists left, now that the Soviet Union has crumbled. I mean, doesn't just about everyone think that communism is a social experiment that failed?

COMMUNIST: A lot of the old communist regimes don't exist any more, but there still are people who think that communist social theory has a lot to offer. We still have what I think is a convincing story about how to think about social arrangements and their value.

INDIVIDUALIST: Okay, let's hear.

COMMUNIST: Well, first, as COMMUNITARIAN has been saying, we think that the idea of an individual apart from society is an illusion. Insofar as individuals have beliefs or desires or needs, that's all a product of—created by—their position in society. So it's wrong to think of society as a contractual arrangement between individuals. We agree with other communitarians that society is an organism with its own laws of behaviour and development. The specific communist emphasis, however, is that these laws are *economic* ones, having to do with production and wages, prices and costs, buying and selling. We think that the basic units that operate in society and interact economically are not individual "atomic" people, but social classes—groups defined on the basis of their economic position. So we see society as the power struggle between the *capitalist* class—the privileged group who own the land and the big corporations—and the *proletariat* class, meaning the workers—the rest of us, who do the actual labour. Individuals get their desires, their views of themselves and the world, their very significance, identity, and meaning, from the class they belong to.

INDIVIDUALIST: But if you're not interested in how well a society fits individual needs, then how do you judge its worth and its legitimacy?

COMMUNIST: We think that the only legitimate and worthwhile society is the one that embodies the interests of the proletariat—the one that's ruled by the proletariat, and that arranges things for their economic benefit.

INDIVIDUALIST: So after all you are judging the worth of a particular society on the basis of its success in giving individuals what they want—but not all individuals, just the proletariat?

COMMUNIST: Not exactly. We do value the interests of the proletariat, but we are communitarians, and don't conceive of this the way individualists do, as a sort of sum totalling of the subjective desires of individuals. Instead, we consider the objective interests of the proletariat as a class, insofar as they are determined by the place of that economic class inside past, present, and future society. This is important, because the subjective desires of individual workers can be different from their objective needs as a class. Right now, in fact, in advanced capitalist societies, most workers identify with capitalist values. They're interested in furthering the capitalist system, because they think that's the way they can improve their own well-being, but their subjective idea of their own well-being is mistaken— they have false values, different from those appropriate for their economic class. These false values have been created by the brainwashing techniques of capitalism: the ideals portrayed in advertising, Hollywood movies, and so on.

INDIVIDUALIST: I don't understand how you can claim that the real values of a bunch of people are different from what those people in fact desire.

COMMUNIST: Well, even though many workers under capitalism might feel that they are on their way to getting what's really in their interest, they're wrong. They're not getting what they really need from capitalist society.

It's the workers in a society who make up the vast majority of people, and who actually contribute by working. The capitalists—landlords, factory owners, investors—are oppressors, parasites living for free off the labour of their workers. Under Capitalism, factory owners and stockholders don't actually produce anything. They just skim their unearned profits from the production of the workers they hire. So capitalist society is unjust.

INDIVIDUALIST: Wait, a minute, why do you think that a factory owner is a parasite? Isn't the owner's profit legitimate? What if the owner pays the worker a fair wage?

COMMUNIST: Well, consider the economics of a factory under capitalism. Suppose the factory is manufacturing widgets, and each worker can turn out one widget per hour. Suppose each worker makes $10 per hour. In order to make a profit, the factory owner has to sell each widget for more than $10, say, for $12, to make a profit of $2 per widget. But that means that in one hour the worker does not make enough to buy what that worker's labour has produced during that hour. The worker produces a widget that sells for $12, but is paid only $10 for it. This is unfair.

INDIVIDUALIST: But what's the alternative?

COMMUNIST: If the widget factory were owned by the workers themselves, then the workers would get full value for their labour. Or if the factory were owned by every worker in society—that is, by a communist government that represented their interest—they could be paid a salary that gave them full value for their production.

INDIVIDUALIST: But what makes you say $12 isn't a fair price for that widget? Maybe they're very good widgets—beautiful, really fast-widging—and people are happy to pay $12 for them.

COMMUNIST: The idea that the real worth of something is determined by what people are willing to pay for it is basic to capitalist economics, and we reject it. In capitalism, the price of a thing and the amount workers are paid are determined by market considerations, not by justice.

INDIVIDUALIST: What do you mean, *market considerations*?

COMMUNIST: Under capitalism, manufacturers can set prices at the maximum they can get—that is, at the maximum price people are willing to pay for what's manufactured. And their workers' wages can be set at the minimum that can be paid while still managing to hire workers. So the two figures have nothing do with each other. Prices for a widget can be much higher than what workers are paid to make it; in fact, for a manufacturer to make a profit, they must be.

INDIVIDUALIST: But why do you say that the manufacturer is charging too much for that widget? Maybe it's really worth $12.

COMMUNIST: No, according to our theory of value (called the *Labour Theory of Value*) the real value of something is not determined by the market, but rather by the amount of labour put in to make it.

INDIVIDUALIST: Well, how could you get the widget manufacturer to pay workers what you call a fair wage, and to sell those widgets for what you call a fair price? It seems that there wouldn't be any profit for the manufacturer then. Why would they go into business in the first place?

COMMUNIST: Right, they wouldn't! That's why an unregulated market economy—one in which investors determine what factories are built and how they're run—wouldn't work if they had to pay fair wages and charge fair prices. Letting individual owners (or corporations) own things, with the right to set wages and prices, would never produce economic justice for the workers. That's why we think that the means of production can't be owned and managed by private entrepreneurs. They have to be owned and managed by the government, which has the workers' interests—economic justice—as its guiding principle.

INDIVIDUALIST: So you'd advocate abolishing private ownership?

COMMUNIST: Right. What we think is needed is the creation of a society in which the proletariat is boss, and gets what it deserves—a society which embodies their values, not like the current western societies which embody false capitalistic values. In capitalist society, as we've seen all over the place nowadays, wealth and power get concentrated in a few people, because of the dynamics of the free-enterprise system. But under communism, there will be no private ownership. Everything will be owned in common, and what's given to people for consumption and enjoyment, and what they have to contribute to society in the form of work, will all be centrally decided on the basis of efficiency and justice, rather than on the basis of the unjust but free capitalist market.

INDIVIDUALIST: Well, you certainly wouldn't get a capitalist to agree to that social contract.

COMMUNIST: Sure wouldn't! We're not claiming that this sort of system serves *everybody's* interests. It's designed to serve the interests of the working class only. The capitalists may have their property removed, may even suffer a worse fate, so that there can at last be a just society.

INDIVIDUALIST: Seems to me you're talking about a society in which some people are treated very badly, and in which nobody is allowed a great deal of freedom. People aren't going to be allowed to bargain freely for their wages, or to charge what they can get when they produce something. Their property would be taken from them. There's going to be state control of a lot of what people do.

COMMUNIST: I admit that. If you give people freedom to do what they please, politically and economically, pretty soon you have accumulation of wealth and power among the few, and the workers they hire don't get their fair share. This is not just a matter of money income: it's a matter of power. Anyone who owns a lot of private property determines the economic arrangements, and takes power away from where it belongs—with the people in general. When one group is rich and powerful and the other group poor and powerless, they can't freely bargain for a social contract— fair bargaining can take place only on a level playing field. That's why we don't allow people freedom to amass personal wealth, property, and power. That's also why communist countries tend not to allow political opposition—that would open the door to the oppression of the proletariat all over again. So, at least while there are people who would destroy the justice set up under pure communism, we must have very powerful and effective internal regulation, to make sure these people don't succeed. So you're right—communist states don't permit much freedom—but we think that trading freedom for justice and equality is a good deal. Freedom in the capitalist countries just means allowing the rich to get richer, and to keep the poor in poverty and oppression.

CONTRACTARIAN: So you don't see a fair and just society being created on the basis of a bargain—a social contract—for everyone's advantage?

COMMUNIST: I certainly don't. As long as the capitalists have all the power and wealth, they'd never reach a fair contract with the workers. The only way a just society can be established is by a revolution, in which the capitalists are forced to give up their power. They'd never agree to it, never do it freely—it's not in their interests.

9. Socialism, Fascism, Nazism

SCEPTIC: There's another political theory that also goes quite far in denying the rights of the individual and repressing freedom in order to further what it takes to be the aims embodied in a certain group, and that's the fascists, the Nazis.

COMMUNIST: We're very strongly opposed to them, but I admit that we do share a certain basic view. Fascism and communism are two (among several) versions of communitarianism. That's where the similarity ends, however.

SCEPTIC: Before we go any further, could you clarify all those labels for me? Communitarian, communist, socialist, Marxist, fascist, Nazi. I'm not at all sure what each of these positions believe, and what the differences are.

COMMUNIST: Okay. *Socialism* is a political theory that advocates government ownership of at least the most important means of production—that is, ownership by the people as a whole. So for example under socialism there might be government-run medicine, communications, and big industry. Socialism is thus the competition for capitalism, which works on the basis of individual ownership and control. Socialists believe that when the means of production are publicly owned and operated, they can be made to further everyone's benefit, not just the benefit of the owner under the capitalist system. They think this will produce a more equal and just society, in which benefits are equally spread around, instead of being concentrated on rich people, or those with special talents or abilities. A familiar socialist slogan is, "From each according to his abilities; to each according to his needs." Socialists emphasize cooperation over competition. They think that elimination of the profit motive and group decision-making (or, at least, decision making with general benefit in mind) will result in a society that's more just.

SCEPTIC: That sounds like what you were advocating. Is socialism the same thing as communism?

COMMUNIST: 'Communism' and 'socialism' are sometimes words used interchangeably, though *communism* usually refers to a more extreme and rigorous form of socialism, the kind practised during part of the last century in the Soviet countries and China. Some socialists advocate government ownership and management of only some of the institutions in a society, and would allow sometimes a large degree of private ownership and private profit; whereas communism, in its classical form anyway, advocated doing away with private ownership altogether. So, for example, Sweden can be considered a moderate socialist country; and the "left wings" of the New Democratic Party in Canada, and the Labour Party in Britain, at times have advocated a very mild form of socialism, and have succeeded in introducing some very mildly socialistic features into their societies, like universal free medical care. Because central planning and control are much more ferocious under communism than under most other socialist systems, the communist countries also characteristically have a single-party political system, a far greater degree of restriction on individual freedoms, and a considerable degree of violation of what people in the Western democracies (including the somewhat socialist democracies) consider to be individual rights. The most important theorist of socialism was the nineteenth-century German economist and philosopher Karl Marx, so *Marxism* is more or less synonymous with 'socialism.'

SCEPTIC: Okay, where do fascism and the Nazi form of government fit in here?

COMMUNIST: *Fascism* is a communitarian form of government also. Like other communitarianisms, it considers the interests of a group to override the interests and rights of any individual. Like communism, fascism favours a rather rigorous form of political and economic control, with an extremely powerful central government, a single political party, a powerful dictator, and forcible suppression of political opposition. But there are certainly important differences. While socialism directs its policies toward the interests of the working class, or of society as a whole, fascism often designates a supposedly superior race as the beneficiary of its policies. The Nazis, who were the fascist ruling party in Germany during the 30s and 40s, under Hitler, instituted an extremely harsh communitarian regime in the service of what was supposed to be the "master race" of so-called Aryans, who were supposed to be the tall blond blue-eyed northern Europeans (though Hitler was short and dark). They supposed it was the destiny of the Aryan race to dominate—even to exterminate—the "inferior races"—Jews, Catholics, Gypsies, and others. Fascists see society as a cold, cruel organism, ruthlessly exploiting or exterminating some "inferior" people for the sake of the "superior" ones. But we see society as friendly, dedicated to promoting equality and humanitarian values.

SCEPTIC: People who know about the horrors of Stalin's regime in Russia might be hard to convince of this.

COMMUNIST: Well, some communists think that Stalinism was a horrible mistake—that it was a perversion of their humanitarian ideals. Others think that extreme measures like Stalin's are sometimes justified—when they're necessary for the initial revolution, which transfers power to the proletariat, and for keeping the development of the post-revolutionary communist state on track.

10. Libertarianism

LIBERTARIAN: The discussion you've been having has clarified for me what I have against all communitarianism. Every kind of communitarian government restricts individual liberty. The most obvious way the communists do this is by eliminating economic freedom. A free market is the economic expression of individual liberty. Your economic status depends on your own initiative—your own energy, intelligence, and good luck.

COMMUNIST: What use is that to someone who is poor and powerless?

LIBERTARIAN: A free market means that everyone has a chance at wealth and power. COMMUNIST was talking a lot about justice, but it's not justice when the communist revolution takes away the property of land and factory owners by force. Anyway, the communist regimes have promised economic benefits for the poor, but they didn't deliver. All they managed was to restrict individual liberty in ferocious ways, just like the fascists. Even the mild socialist measures in Canada or Sweden or the other democracies interfere with individual liberties.

SCEPTIC: Lots of people object to the harsh repressive dictatorships of the communists and fascists, but what do you have against Sweden? Or Canada?

LIBERTARIAN: It's only a matter of degree. The best government is the one that interferes with people, restricts their individual liberty, the least. The Nazi and Soviet societies were extreme examples of repression, but Sweden and Canada do it too. Even in those countries there's a pretty substantial degree of government ownership and management, and there are lots of laws that restrict individuals and private companies in all sorts of ways.

SCEPTIC: But you must admit that there are some justified restrictions on anybody's doing just whatever they want! I mean, you wouldn't want to live in the State of Nature, of War of Each Against All, would you?

LIBERTARIAN: No, of course, I'd accept some government restrictions on liberty. I'd agree with the basic idea of CONTRACTARIAN, that some restrictions are justified. People shouldn't have the liberty to go around bashing others, or grabbing each others' property. I'd accept laws against murder, for example, even though that would restrict my individual freedom to murder someone.

SCEPTIC: Well, I'd hope so!

LIBERTARIAN: What I have in mind is sort of an extension of the idea of the free market into other social matters. In economic matters, we libertarians believe that people can accept economic restrictions—can be forced to do some work, or to give up some of their property—when they've freely contracted to do this. So if you and I have a contract that says that you'll pave my driveway and I'll give you $1000, then I've bargained away my freedom to do what I like with that $1000, after you've done the job. And if I refuse to pay after the work is done, the government should step in and force me to. I'd accept the same sort of justification for other restrictions in a free society: when people would freely bargain certain freedoms away, in exchange for benefits that make this bargain worth it. So, for example, those farmers freely exchange their freedom to graze their cattle as long as they like, in exchange for a reliable continuing supply of grass on the commons. But when you don't (or wouldn't) accept a bargain like that, you should be free to do what you like. The problem with lots of governments and societies in the world today and historically is that they interfere in individual freedom much more than that.

SCEPTIC: So what sort of bargains for governmental restriction on individual freedom do you think are good ones, in general?

LIBERTARIAN: For one thing, I'd think that it would be rational for everyone to accept a bargain in which people are restricted from doing some things that substantially harm others. In the state of nature, everyone was in constant danger of being clobbered by someone else. It's obvious that what's needed is a social contract in which individuals give away their freedom to go around clobbering their neighbours, in exchange for their own safety. Another main function of society everyone would agree to is to establish and protect private property. Most of us would agree to give up our freedom to take what we wanted from anyone else, in order to have our own property safeguarded.

SCEPTIC: The kind of society you'd prefer sounds more or less like the one we're living in.

LIBERTARIAN: No, not really. I think that the laws in my country go way beyond this, and interfere with my liberty in all sorts of ways I would never agree to. Take the driving laws for example. I can accept the existence of laws prohibiting and punishing drunk driving. Drunk drivers are much more likely than others to kill or injure other drivers or pedestrians, and to damage other people's property. But compare that to the seatbelt laws that governments have added to the driving rules during the last few years. That's an unjustified interference with our freedom.

SCEPTIC: But isn't that beneficial? I mean, hasn't it been definitely proven that wearing a seatbelt considerably reduces the risk of death or bad injury in car accidents?

LIBERTARIAN: Yes it has. I'm not arguing with that. But I don't think that government has any business preventing you from doing things that might harm only you. If you choose not to wear a seatbelt, then you think that the annoyance of having to remember to put the damn thing on, and the discomfort of wearing it, aren't worth the possible gains, because it's so unlikely that you'll have an accident. This is a bargain you wouldn't make.

SCEPTIC: Well, I know that your chances of getting into a fatal car accident are pretty small, but given that they're there at all, and that a seatbelt really improves your likelihood of survival, isn't it a little like suicide to ride in a car without wearing one?

LIBERTARIAN: That's a little far-fetched, but I accept the analogy! Suicide is another case where the main effect—the only significant one—is on the person who does it, not on anyone else. So I think that suicide is another area that government has no business regulating.

SCEPTIC: Does government regulate suicide now? I mean, you're not going to throw a person who has committed suicide in jail! And people who try to kill themselves and fail are given psychiatric help, not jail sentences.

LIBERTARIAN: Right, but suicide is still counted as a crime. The real effect of this is on people who help others to kill themselves. That's being an accessory to a crime. Legal punishment is enforced there, and does make a difference.

SCEPTIC: But let's get back to the seatbelt question. A person who decides that wearing a seatbelt is more annoyance than it's worth—isn't that person making a big mistake? Wouldn't anyone with sense think that the small annoyance of wearing a seatbelt is worth it?

LIBERTARIAN: Maybe. If you get yourself injured or killed because you've decided that wearing a seatbelt wasn't worth it, maybe you've been foolish, but that's your choice. I think that it's up to each of us to decide what's worth it and what's not worth it, when it comes to our own possible benefit or harm. When the government acts to force me to look after myself, it's interfering in my liberty.

SCEPTIC: But wouldn't there be harm to other people if you were injured in an accident because you weren't wearing a seatbelt?

LIBERTARIAN: How's that?

SCEPTIC: Well, maybe you're the source of income for your family, and they'd suffer a drastically reduced standard of living, and maybe they'd have to take care of you for a long time if you were paralysed or something. And, of course, there's their grief if you were injured or killed (assuming they cared about you!). And maybe there would have to be public money spent on your health-care and rehabilitation. There might be lots of harm to others.

LIBERTARIAN: No, look, first of all, I don't think that government should take care of families who have their income reduced, or cover the medical expenses of people who get injured. But all that is irrelevant to the seatbelt case. The main harm that wearing a seatbelt is meant to prevent is the potential harm to the person who's wearing it, right?

SCEPTIC: Well, maybe. I guess we have to investigate the facts further here.

LIBERTARIAN: Agreed, but whatever the real facts about seatbelts, my main point is that it's maybe okay for laws to force me not to act in ways that might significantly harm other people, but that's the limit on legitimate government interference.

SCEPTIC: Wait a minute, why do you say "maybe okay"? Don't you agree at least that it's always justified for government to prevent people from harming others?

LIBERTARIAN: Not always. For example, it's now actually illegal to insult people in certain ways, for example, on the basis of their race, and I don't think that punishing people for producing racial insults is acceptable.

SCEPTIC: I can't believe you said that! Are you really saying that it's okay to insult members of minority groups? That's awful! Are you some sort of bigot?

LIBERTARIAN: No, no, look, I think racial insults are degrading and horrible. I'd never produce a racial insult, and I wouldn't be friends with anyone who did. I very strongly disapprove of them, really!

SCEPTIC: But doesn't that imply that the government should act to prevent people from doing that, by making it illegal?

LIBERTARIAN: No it doesn't imply that. This is an important point: there are some things that are bad, that harm other people, but that government has no business interfering with. For example, suppose you want to break off a relationship with somebody who's in love with you. That would inflict psychological pain on that person, and it can have other psychologically harmful results. But it shouldn't be illegal. Or suppose you're lying to your spouse, and having a secret affair on the side. Everyone will agree that what you're doing is bad, but it doesn't follow at all that there should be laws against what you're doing.

SCEPTIC: But you'd agree that in some cases government is justified in preventing people from harming others. What makes the difference in these cases?

LIBERTARIAN: That's a difficult question. I think that one consideration is that government shouldn't interfere when the harm to others isn't very great. In addition to that, there are some activities (like speech, for example) where freedom is so important that they shouldn't be restricted, even when quite harmful. And there are other things to think about too.

11. Interventionism

INTERVENTIONIST: I agree that preventing harm to the wearer is the real motive for seatbelt legislation, but I think that that's a good justification for it. It's a legitimate function of government to prevent people from harming themselves. There are all sorts of ways in which government does this, and I approve of them. They really ought to do more. My government, for example, has put very high taxes on cigarettes. This is a way of pressuring people into not smoking, for the good of their own health.

SCEPTIC: But there's all that talk about the dangers of second-hand smoke too. Isn't it really a matter of harm to others too?

INTERVENTIONIST: I don't really think so. I think that there's really no very good evidence that second-hand smoke is a significant harm. But this is a scientific matter that we can't really decide here! My suspicion, anyway, is that the real motive people have for trying to discourage smoking is that smoking is definitely very harmful to the smoker. This business about second-hand smoke is just a way of getting people with libertarian sympathies on side, because those people might agree to government interference if they thought that smoking was seriously harmful to someone other than the smoker.

LIBERTARIAN: That's very sneaky. I agree that the smoking issue is like the seatbelt issue: both are really about whether it's legitimate for governments to intervene when the only significant effect of people's actions is on themselves.

SCEPTIC: Why do you, INTERVENTIONIST, think that government is justified in legislating actions for people's own good?

INTERVENTIONIST: I think it's obvious that the justification for government action is that it makes our lives better. This means not only preventing people from harming other people, but also from harming themselves.

LIBERTARIAN: But a really important part of a good life, as far as I'm concerned, is having the freedom to do what you want. High smoking taxes and seatbelt laws limit my personal freedom. Don't you value freedom?

INTERVENTIONIST: Well, maybe, but I guess I don't value it as much as you do. I'd much rather see a reduction of the pain and suffering and death that result from cigarette smoking and driving without seatbelts. I guess freedom just means a lot more to you than it does to me.

LIBERTARIAN: But there's more to it than that. Look, you just said that you think that lowering the risk of pain and suffering is worth a reduction of freedom. That's what you'd prefer, for yourself. But notice that you're urging that governments make that decision for everyone. Other people want to take that risk. Don't you think that everybody should decide for themselves?

INTERVENTIONIST: No, I don't, really. I think that some people's values are mistaken, and that their reasoning is foolish, and that they can't be trusted to make the right decision. I think that for their own good, choices ought to be made for them, by people who are more rational, who have the right values, who can think straight. For example, I've heard people object to seatbelt laws because, they say, seatbelts actually increase the danger of injury in an accident. But they're just wrong about the facts. If it was up to them to decide whether to wear their seatbelt or not, they'd make the wrong decision. I've also heard people claim that they're such good drivers that they run no risk of getting into accidents, so it's pointless for them to wear seatbelts. The other day a friend of mine said that she's not going to try to stop smoking because it's really not all that dangerous, and her total evidence for this was that her Uncle Fred smoked two packs a day and lived to be 103. All this is just bad reasoning about probabilities and evidence. You can't let people who reason that badly look after themselves—they'd cause themselves damage. It's like allowing a small child to decide whether to play around with sharp knives. When people don't have reasoning ability or the knowledge of facts necessary for looking after themselves, you have to step in and make their decisions for them.

LIBERTARIAN: I agree about children, but we're talking about adults here.

INTERVENTIONIST: Right, but lots of adults reason as badly as little children about matters involving their own good. Take smoking for example. People don't start smoking because of a rational decision, based on reliable knowledge and clear thinking. They do it because they imitate people they admire, or because of the irrational pressures of advertising. They stupidly ignore really big long-term health dangers, because they're more interested in doing something they think is cool. A lot of our decisions are made that way, because of social pressure, or because of unexamined assumptions or false values. Even sensible thoughtful people like you and me make a large number of our decisions irrationally.

COMMUNITARIAN: Yes, I agree. Almost all of our values and decisions are created by external factors. The idea that we're all independent rational decision makers is just wrong. I see this mistake behind the views of CON-TRACTARIAN and INDIVIDUALIST and LIBERTARIAN, all three of you.

LIBERTARIAN: I'm not assuming that everyone knows the facts, or makes rational decisions about them. I agree that lots of people make bad decisions based on false beliefs, irrational thinking, brainwashing by others, emotional factors, social conditioning, and so on. All I'm saying is that when you make a bad decision that harms only yourself, then that's your problem. Freedom means that you're allowed to make mistakes that harm only you. I think that freedom is a really valuable thing. In a really free society some people would be stupid and harm themselves, but that's the kind of society I want, for the sake of freedom.

INTERVENTIONIST: I'd prefer restrictions to protect people from their own stupidity.

LIBERTARIAN: And here's something else. In our society, where there's so much intervention at the cost of our freedom, people get out of the habit of thinking for themselves, and looking out for their own good. They just assume that if something was potentially harmful for them, the government would make it illegal. So they stop thinking about their own actions. In a truly free society, in which people were allowed to make decisions about themselves, even harmful ones, people would instead have the habit of thinking about what they're doing.

SCEPTIC: So, if I have it right, you think that the freedom you're talking about might really not be all that harmful?

LIBERTARIAN: That's right. People would start looking after themselves, thinking about what they're doing, and being careful. But that's not the main reason I'm in favour of personal liberty. I just think it's an enormous value, all by itself. Even if a libertarian society did result in more harm for some people, we'd still be better off, because liberty is a really important good thing. It's necessary for human dignity.

SCEPTIC: Why do you say that?

LIBERTARIAN: Because people's lives are really what they should be only when those people are taking responsibility for what they're doing: when they're allowed to determine the basic contents of their own lives, instead of having somebody else restrict and direct them, just in case they might not make the right decisions.

But look, anyway, here's a very basic problem I see with INTERVEN-TIONIST's position. It's based on the idea that sometimes people make decisions because of false values. But does the idea of a "false value" make any sense? The way I see it, each of us has our own values, and sometimes they differ from other peoples' values, but nobody can say which values are really true and which are false. We're all entitled to our own values, aren't we?

INTERVENTIONIST: I think it does make sense to think of some values as false ones. Here's an important example of that. Suppose a woman was raised in a conventional, old-fashioned household, where she was brought up to think that her duty is to serve her husband, and to neglect her own personal development or fulfillment. This woman is likely to make some bad decisions: for example, she might agree to marry a man who will expect her only to serve his needs, and who might become abusive if he detects signs of independence in her. Maybe she'll feel like things are okay if they turn out this way, because they're the way her false values say they should be. But she's wrong.

LIBERTARIAN: That woman's values don't match mine, but I think it's dangerous to think that some values are false values. I mean, where do we get an objective standard for what values are right? Isn't it just a matter of what people happen to prefer?

INTERVENTIONIST: I don't think that's right. I think that some people's values are false, so they have to be regulated for their own good.

FEMINIST: I was just listening in to what you were talking about, and I want to add that that example of the woman with conventional false values is just the sort of thing that we feminists take very seriously. We believe that women in our society are oppressed, and kept in an inferior position in lots of different ways. But up until recently a large number of women didn't feel oppressed by their condition. They so strongly identified with the dominant male-oriented values of their society that they didn't feel anything was wrong. They often might even be opposed to various sorts of feminist reform to improve their situation. So sometimes one of the first jobs for feminism is to be to make women dissatisfied with their current state.

LIBERTARIAN: But this isn't a job for government, is it?

FEMINIST: Hardly! Government often represents and furthers the dominant values in a society, the false values that we're interested in correcting.

SCEPTIC: So is *feminism* a kind of communitarianism and interventionism?

FEMINIST: Some feminists are communitarians and interventionists when it comes to social philosophy. But some aren't—some are actually libertarians, aiming at the removal of restrictions on women's liberty. Feminism is actually an extremely diverse collection of positions on social matters, and on many other philosophical questions also. It has become important all over philosophy. It would be nice if there were time to go into it more deeply.

SCEPTIC: Agreed!

12. Equality

LIBERTARIAN: Here's another thing about my society that I find objectionable. I pay really high taxes, and a lot of that goes to help out people on welfare.

SCEPTIC: It certainly does. Don't you think that you ought to be helping out people in need?

LIBERTARIAN: I do, but I think I ought to be given the freedom to decide when I want to do this. If I want to help out needy people, I can voluntarily donate to charities that help them. I object to the idea that I should be forced to give my money to improve the lives of people who have less than I do.

SCEPTIC: But didn't you agree, earlier, that government can step in to prevent harm to people? And aren't really poor people in for a good deal of harm?

LIBERTARIAN: I agreed that there were some cases in which government would be justified in preventing people from harming others. But now this is a different question: whether government should force us to help others.

INTERVENTIONIST: You've just got no sympathy for people in need.

LIBERTARIAN: You're wrong, I do. I think it's a good thing to help others in need. I have a lot of sympathy with people who are badly off, and I give a lot of money to charities that help them. All I'm saying is that government has no business forcing people to help. I think that just as there are some bad things government shouldn't step in to prevent, there are good things that government shouldn't force us to do.

EGALITARIAN: I'd like to say something here about your positions. LIBERTARIAN has been concentrating on the value of individual liberty, which can be removed only in order to prevent people from harming others; and INTERVENTIONIST has been arguing that in addition government should prevent us from harming ourselves; but you're both ignoring something else that's very important: the value of equality.

LIBERTARIAN: But usually the only way the government can do anything about that is at the expense of people who are better off.

EGALITARIAN: I agree. That's one of the things a government should do, and one of the most important.

LIBERTARIAN: So you think that government should be like Robin Hood, robbing the rich to give to the poor?

EGALITARIAN: Yes, essentially that's right—except I don't like to call it robbery! The best societies are not necessarily the ones with the greatest total wealth. Sometimes a society with a huge total wealth is one in which the wealth is very unequally distributed, in which the rich are very rich and the poor are very poor. The measure of a good society is its equality.

LIBERTARIAN: So you think that a society that's really very poor, but in which there's no inequality because everyone is equally poor, is better than a society in which a lot of people are very rich, and the rest of the people are only fairly well off, because there's a fair degree of inequality here? That's crazy.

EGALITARIAN: Well, no, obviously equality is not all there is. But it's very important, so I'd think that a society in which everyone is fairly well off is better than one in which there are super-rich and super-poor, even if the unequal society contains more total wealth than the equal one.

SCEPTIC: So how do you propose that we weigh the value of equality against other values that you think are important?

EGALITARIAN: I'm not sure, but I am sure that it's fairly obvious to most people that the equality of a society is an important thing. Almost every society has some Robin Hood features intended to decrease inequality, to help the poor at the expense of the rich. In our society, for example, there's income tax, which (in theory anyway) forces very rich people to pay quite a high percentage of their income, and a lot of this money is redistributed in the form of welfare payments and other provisions for the poor and for people in need.

LIBERTARIAN: That's slave labour.

EGALITARIAN: Oh, come on. You're exaggerating.

LIBERTARIAN: No, really, I'm serious. A society that forces some people to work for others is a slave society. And that's precisely what goes on here: in essence I have to work for free, without getting paid, for a good proportion of the year, to benefit other people.

EGALITARIAN: You're getting paid.

LIBERTARIAN: Yes, but the government is taking away my pay by taxation. People should be free to keep what they earn!

EGALITARIAN: Well, remember that a lot of wealth isn't earned: often wealth, and poverty for that matter, are the result of things you have little or no control over. Sometimes it's just a matter of luck. For example, lots of wealth is inherited, so it's just a matter of how lucky you happen to be about getting rich parents. Poverty is to a large extent inherited too: people growing up in poor families rarely have the education and other advantages necessary to advance themselves. And look at the example of a basketball player for the NBA, who is making several millions of dollars a year, and that's largely the result of his being born with the genetics that made him super-tall. It's like discovering oil underground in your backyard: you'll become rich, but it's just luck. It's not deserved. We ought not to let these sorts of inequalities persist.

LIBERTARIAN: Hold on there. What makes you think that that basketball player doesn't deserve to have that enormous salary? Is it just that he was lucky enough to be super-tall? I agree that that's just luck, but now that he is super-tall, he's got something that other people really want: he can (given some natural coordination, and a good deal of practice, of course) play basketball in a way that people will pay a lot to come and see.

EGALITARIAN: But what he's got to offer doesn't make him deserving of all that money.

LIBERTARIAN: Yes it does. The only way we can determine how much something is worth is to see how much other people will pay for it. The fact that people will pay a lot to see this guy play basketball means that what he's got is worth a lot. The same thing for somebody who discovers oil in his backyard.

EGALITARIAN: But you have to admit that some people who have a whole lot don't deserve what they have. And some people who have very little don't deserve that.

LIBERTARIAN: Well, I think that a good deal of the inequality that exists is deserved. But even when it isn't—when it's just the result of good or bad luck—the government shouldn't come around and steal your property to give it to someone else. I agree with CONTRACTARIAN that one of the main jobs of government, one of the reasons people are willing to enter into a social contract, is for the protection of private property. You've worked for it, or inherited it, or had the genetic makeup to grow up really tall, or found it in your backyard, so it's yours. Justice requires that nobody else be allowed to steal it from you, that you keep what's yours.

EGALITARIAN: Well, I think that a society with a good deal of inequality isn't just.

SCEPTIC: You two can't agree on what's justice and what isn't. I wonder how that question could be settled. I mean, is there any good way to really decide what sort of arrangement is just?

13. Justice

CONTRACTARIAN: An important twentieth-century American philosopher named John Rawls proposed a way of deciding what's just and what isn't, based on an extension of the idea of the Social Contract. Here's roughly what Rawls had to say. Imagine, as in the story I told earlier, that we're all in the state of nature—Rawls calls that the *original position.* In this position, everyone's interested only in looking out for him or herself, but it becomes clear to all of us that we need a Social Contract to restrain everyone, so that we'd all be better off. Now, some of the things that should be in that contract are pretty clear: there should be laws to prevent violence, and to establish secure ownership of property, at least to some extent.

SCEPTIC: Why do you say "at least to some extent"?

CONTRACTARIAN: Here's why. Suppose that you were considering various arrangements of society, weighing which set-up would be the best contractual arrangement for you to sign on to. Now imagine that one set-up included slavery and the other one didn't. In the first, the slave owners are rich, richer in fact than anyone in the second set-up. Which set-up would you prefer?

EGALITARIAN: I'd prefer the one without slavery. Slavery is obviously a horrible injustice!

CONTRACTARIAN: No, that's just what we're trying to establish. You can't start off assuming that. All we assume, in this thought-experiment, is that you start off, in the original position, with no interests except selfish ones—that all you care about is getting the best for yourself. Justice means nothing to you.

SCEPTIC: Okay, then my answer is that the set-up I pick depends on where I wind up in the society set up that way. If I would wind up as a slave in the first society, that would obviously be terrible. But if I were to wind up as a slave owner, then as far as my selfish interests were concerned, that would make that set-up superior to the second. Until you tell me what position in society I'm to hold, I can't decide.

CONTRACTARIAN: That's just where things get interesting in this story. You're not given this vital information on purpose, and we'll see why in a minute. The way Rawls puts it is that you're to choose what sort of contract you want under the *veil of ignorance*—a picturesque way of saying that you're to think about a proposed society without knowing what position in that society you'd hold.

SCEPTIC: Ah, hmm. Well, under those conditions, I'd choose the second society. I wouldn't be as rich in that society as a slave owner would be in the first, but I would be guaranteed to be better off than a slave in the first. I guess that the risk of winding up worse in the first society means that I should choose the second. The worst position in the second is not as bad as the worst position in the first.

CONTRACTARIAN: That's what Rawls thinks you'd say. The principle of choice you're using here is sometimes called the *maximin principle*. That means, when you have alternatives, you should choose the one which maximizes the minimum possibility—that is, which has the least-bad way you could possibly wind up. Here's another illustration, a very trivial one, of how this might work. Suppose somebody was going to cut up a cake into eight pieces, and you and seven others were each going to get one piece of it. You can't decide which piece you'll get, but it's up to you to say how that person should cut the cake up: should they be of even size, or should there be some slices that are bigger, and some smaller? You'd prefer the biggest piece from an uneven cut, but if it were cut unevenly, you might get the smallest. If the pieces were cut evenly, the piece you'd get wouldn't be very big, but it's guaranteed not to be very small. So you'd pick the even cutting method.

EGALITARIAN: Aha, in this case the fair solution is the one that's the most equal. That's exactly what I was claiming. So is Rawls really an egalitarian?

CONTRACTARIAN: No, not exactly. In the cake example, the arrangement that satisfies the maximin principle is also the most equal one, but that's not always the case. Sometimes there will be big inequalities in the best arrangement: it's best because the worst off there is better off than the worst off in the alternatives.

SCEPTIC: For example?

CONTRACTARIAN: Well, compare two societies, one of which has equal pay for everyone, and the other of which gives higher pay to certain professions, like doctors for example. The second one is less equal, of course. But in the second one, people might be inclined to go through all the work and expense of medical school, and work the long hours that doctors do, to get the higher pay, so the first society might have a big shortage of doctors, and some ill people would be very badly off. So the maximin principle might tell us to choose the second society, despite its inequality.

SCEPTIC: Okay, I think I see that. But what does all this, the maximin principle and the veil of ignorance, this have to do with *justice*?

CONTRACTARIAN: Well, in the cake example, the choice you make using this method of choosing, under the veil of ignorance, is in fact the way that's most just for everyone who's going to get a piece. So the idea is that what justice is can be explained as what people would choose under these circumstances.

SCEPTIC: But what's the connection? Why exactly does choice behind the veil of ignorance produce justice?

CONTRACTARIAN: The idea is that justice means equal consideration for everyone, choices not based on one's particular position in a situation. Rawls thinks it's inevitable that people in any society will differ from each other with regard to natural abilities and assets, and simply in how lucky they are, and that there will be differences between groups, in gender, race, culture, and so on. Given all this, the fairest societal arrangements would be the one chosen by people who didn't know whether they'd be the advantaged or the disadvantaged people—people who imagined that they might be lucky or unlucky, tall enough to be a basketball player or short, the finder of a backyard oil well or not, male or female, black or white, and so on. Here's an example I heard about recently. A woman trying to immigrate into my country was having an interview with an immigration official who was being nasty and giving her a hard time. She objected, and said to the official, "How would you feel if you were in my shoes, if you were being treated this way?" That's the right question, because she's asking him to look at matters as if from behind the veil of ignorance, not knowing—in this case, ignoring—what position he held. That way he can notice the injustice.

SCEPTIC: So what happened in that case?

CONTRACTARIAN: The official replied something like, "Well I'm not in your shoes, and I never will be."

SCEPTIC: Immigration officials aren't known for sensitivity to justice. But look: it's not clear at all that what you're calling the maximin situation is always the rational one to choose. Maybe I'd choose an arrangement with the worst off person very badly off by comparison, if there were only very few people that badly off, and I thought that my chances of ending up that way were very small.

LIBERTARIAN: Yes, and here's another problem. Where does personal liberty come into any of this?

CONTRACTARIAN: Well I haven't talked about that yet, but Rawls agrees that freedom is a good thing. (He doesn't think that it's the only good thing, or the most important good thing, however.) Anyway, he thinks that rational self-interested people in the original position, under the veil of ignorance, would choose a society in which each person would have an equal right to the most extensive basic liberty possible, provided that it's compatible with similar liberty for others.

LIBERTARIAN: Why is there that provision about compatibility?

CONTRACTARIAN: The idea here is that it might be that a society might give one person a whole lot of liberty only because it denies that amount of liberty to other people. For instance, in a society that permits slavery, slave owners have a lot of liberty to do exactly what they please, just because their slaves don't. And that of course is hugely unjust. So the principle of liberty Rawls argues for has the provision that liberty must be distributed fairly. Anyway, I haven't answered the problem that SCEPTIC raised a minute ago, and there's a whole lot more about Rawls's theory that we should talk about. But I suppose we'll have to do that another time.

Suggested Readings

(See the Notes on "Suggested Readings" sections, p. 17-18.)

Thomas Hobbes (1588-1679) presented his early and influential version of contractarian social philosophy in *Leviathan*. By far the best edition of this for students is on-line at <http://www.earlymoderntexts.com>.

John Locke (1632-1704) was also a Contractarian. See his *Second Treatise on Civil Government*.

An influential theorist of communitarianism was the sociologist Emile Durkheim (1858-1917): In Chapter I of *The Rules of Sociological Method* he argues that social facts are not reducible to individual facts.

A recent communitarian critique of individualist ethics and social philosophy is *After Virtue*, by Alasdair MacIntyre.

John Stuart Mill (1806-73) issued a famous defence of individual freedom of thought and speech in *On Liberty*. By far the best edition of this for students is on-line at <http://www.earlymoderntexts.com>.

Edmund Burke (1729-97) criticized the ideals of the French Revolution—liberty and equality—and argued for the importance of custom and tradition in *Reflections on the Revolution in France*.

Republic by Plato (427-347 BC) is the classic work in social philosophy. Plato considered the nature of justice at length. He argued against democracy, in favour of a dictatorship ruled by the wisest people (who are, of course, philosophers).

Utopia by Thomas More (ca. 1478-1535) is an interesting and far-reaching treatment of philosophical issues concerning society.

Adam Smith (1723-90), economist and philosopher, was an early and influential theorist of capitalism. See his *The Wealth of Nations*, especially Chapter 10.

Karl Marx (1818-83) is of course the paradigm defender of socialism. His most famous work, *Capital*, is long, technical, and difficult. Start instead with his much briefer and clearer *The Communist Manifesto*.

John Rawls' book *A Theory of Justice* is arguably the most important work on social philosophy of the twentieth century.

CONVERSATION III

Ethics

Participants: SCEPTIC • UTILITARIAN • DEONTOLOGIST •
RIGHTS-THEORIST • KANTIAN • SUBJECTIVIST • RELATIVIST

1. A Question

SCEPTIC: A friend of mine recently told me about a moral problem she had.
  She was visiting her rich uncle Fred in the hospital. He told her that he
  was dying, but that he'd die happy if she promised to do him a favour.
  There was a million dollars in a bag in the closet in the hospital room, and
  Fred asked her to give it to his girlfriend Sally after he died. He had to
  keep it a secret, and not mention it in his will, because the family would
  try to prevent Sally from getting it. My friend wanted to ease Uncle Fred's
  last moments, so she got the million out of the closet and promised to give
  it to Sally after he had died. He died later that day, and a few days later,
  my friend put the million in her car, and started to drive to the casino
  where she knew that Fred's girlfriend Sally spent every day, drinking, carrying on with various low-life men, and spending vast amounts of money
  at the gambling tables. She'd been doing that behind Fred's back for
  months.

  But on her way to the casino, my friend started wondering about
  whether she was doing the right thing. Fred's girlfriend was very rich, and
  the million wouldn't have meant much to her, even if she noticed the gift
  through the alcoholic haze she was always in. Anyway, it would be gone
  in short order, gambled away. Maybe, my friend thought, she should keep
  it for herself! She could certainly use it more than Sally. Or maybe she
  should give it to Fred's wife and children. They probably were legally
  entitled to it, because of the usual rules involving property not mentioned
  in a will, but it wouldn't have brought them much benefit either, because
  they were all rich too. So, my friend thought, maybe she should give it all
  to a worthy charity, where it would do the most good. So she drove home,
  and phoned me to ask me what I would do in her position—what I
  thought she should do.

UTILITARIAN: So, what did you say?

SCEPTIC: I told her that there really wasn't anything helpful I could tell her. I mean, what I would do in that position doesn't have any relevance to her problem. She's trying to determine the right answer here, but I don't know there is one. You just wind up doing what you most feel like doing, and that's about all there is to the matter. You really can't say more than that.

2. Hedonism

UTILITARIAN: I think there's a right answer to your friend's question, and I think that there's a good clear way to figure out what the right answer is.

SCEPTIC: Okay, let's hear.

UTILITARIAN: First of all, Uncle Fred is dead, so he's out of the picture here—he can't be harmed or benefited—he's beyond all that. So there isn't anything morally relevant about Fred's involvement. Giving Sally the money might please her a little, but she'd really hardly notice, because she spends her days in a drunken stupor, she's already very rich, and the money would be gone in a few days of gambling anyway. If your friend kept the money herself, it would make a big difference to her, right?

SCEPTIC: Yes, she's on a really tight budget now, working while trying to get through school. Because she has to work long hours, she has no time to do anything enjoyable, and anyway she couldn't afford to take a vacation or have some fun even if she had the time. That cash Uncle Fred entrusted her with would make her life much more enjoyable.

UTILITARIAN: It would benefit her much more than it would benefit Fred's immediate family?

SCEPTIC: Yes, much more. His family is rich too.

UTILITARIAN: But if she gave it to a good charity like Oxfam, it would produce the most benefit—even more than it would do if she kept it for herself. Organizations like that are very efficient in saving lives, preventing and curing diseases, and lessening the miseries of horrible poverty in the worst areas of the world. Because the people they help are so needy, a little money can produce an enormous amount of benefit. I mean, $10 could save the life of someone starving in the third world, but it wouldn't even be enough to give your friend a night at the movies.

SCEPTIC: Okay, but so what?

UTILITARIAN: So that answers the question. What she should do is give the money to Oxfam.

SCEPTIC: Really! That's an interesting conclusion. How do you figure that?

UTILITARIAN: That's where the money would do the most good, in terms of producing human happiness or preventing human misery. That's the only thing that's morally relevant here.

SCEPTIC: But there are all sorts of facts about this case that you haven't mentioned. There's the fact that Uncle Fred wanted the money to go to Sally. There's the fact that she promised Uncle Fred to give Sally the money. And the fact that Sally had been cheating on Uncle Fred for a long time. And the fact that legally speaking, his wife and children are probably entitled to the inheritance.

UTILITARIAN: Right, I think those facts aren't relevant.

SCEPTIC: What sort of reasoning tells you that?

UTILITARIAN: The ethical theory I'm using to figure out what's right here, the one I believe in, is called *utilitarianism*. It has a long history, though a famous version of it was put together during the nineteenth century by the English philosopher John Stuart Mill. The idea behind utilitarianism is very simple: it's that the only thing that makes any action morally good or bad is that it leads to human happiness or unhappiness. The right action—the best one among possible alternatives—is the action that produces the greatest *net happiness* for the greatest number of people.

SCEPTIC: What do you mean, "net happiness"?

UTILITARIAN: Actions sometimes produce some happiness for some people, and some unhappiness, for other people (or the same people). The idea here is roughly that you add up all the happiness produced, and subtract all the unhappiness, and what you get is a measure of the net happiness (which might be negative, if the total of unhappiness outweighs the total of happiness).

SCEPTIC: So according to this theory, you just figure out what the results would be of various possible actions you could do, and you see how the happiness of various people is affected?

UTILITARIAN: Right, and in this case, based on what you tell me, I think that the best action would be for your friend to give that money to a good charity: that would produce the greatest benefit for the greatest number of people.

SCEPTIC: Okay, wait a minute, just before you were talking about happiness, but now you've switched to *benefit*. Which?

UTILITARIAN: Well, some utilitarians think that increasing happiness (or decreasing unhappiness) is the only real benefit—the only morally relevant result. Mill thought that, but an earlier version of utilitarianism held that pleasure was the only good thing (and pain the only bad thing), so that what made actions good or bad was how much they increased pleasure and/or decreased pain.

SCEPTIC: But why would anyone think that pleasure/pain production is even relevant to ethics? What does pleasure or pain have to do with ethics? Sounds implausible to me.

UTILITARIAN: Well, these utilitarians thought that the whole basis of ethics should be what people really found desirable—what they really wanted—and they thought that pleasure-seeking was the basis of all human motivation. Pleasure-seeking, that is, and pain-avoidance.

SCEPTIC: There are two questions here. The basic question is whether what people actually desire is the basis of morality—I doubt it—but we can talk about that in a minute. But even assuming that what people find desirable is the basis of morality, aren't those utilitarians wrong about what people really desire? I mean, of course people desire pleasure, and want to avoid pain, but there are lots of other things people desire and want to avoid, aren't there?

UTILITARIAN: Well, the position called *psychological hedonism* claims that the only motivations for anything are seeking pleasure or avoiding pain. The word *hedonism* means a position that makes pleasure and pain central; this is *psychological* hedonism because it's a psychological theory—a theory about how human motivation works. It's called *psychological* hedonism to distinguish it from *ethical* hedonism, which is the position that what makes an action ethically good is merely that it increases pleasure or decreases pain. The full name is *egoistic psychological hedonism*; it's called *egoistic* because that word means *pertaining to me*—it's supposed that it's only *one's own* pleasure or pain that motivates a person.

SCEPTIC: Whew. Let me see if I have all this straight. First of all, there's the idea that what in fact motivates humans—what they desire to get and to avoid—is the only basis for moral goodness and badness.

UTILITARIAN: Right.

SCEPTIC: And there's the psychological theory, egoistic psychological hedonism, which says that the only human motivation is pleasure-seeking or pain-avoiding.

UTILITARIAN: Correct.

SCEPTIC: So you put these two assumptions together, and they give you the idea that an action is morally good if it increases pleasure or decreases pain. And an action is morally bad if it decreases pleasure or increases pain. That view is ethical hedonism.

UTILITARIAN: Right.

SCEPTIC: Okay, neither of those assumptions seems to me to be right. First of all, egoistic psychological hedonism is obviously wrong. It's true that *sometimes* your motivation is to produce your own pleasure, or avoid your own pain. For example, in the winter, when I'm cold, I really like to take a nice hot bath, because the warmth feels so good. It's the pleasurable feeling that motivates me. And when I feel a headache coming on, I get an aspirin. It's the pain-prevention that is my motive here. But it's clear that a whole lot of my motivation has nothing to do with my own pain or pleasure. I like to climb mountains, but pleasure isn't involved here at all. It's actually sort of painful when it's a steep and difficult climb. I do it because I like energetic activity, and it's satisfying to reach the top.

UTILITARIAN: Well, don't you get physical pleasure from the activity?

SCEPTIC: No, it's painful!

UTILITARIAN: Right, but it's the sort of pain you like, right? It's a kind of physical pleasure for you, isn't it?

SCEPTIC: I enjoy it, all right, but that doesn't mean it's pleasure.

UTILITARIAN: And isn't the satisfaction you get when you reach the top a psychological pleasure?

SCEPTIC: I think that that's a misleading way of putting it. I do get satisfaction from a good climb, but I don't think that's exactly pleasure. And here's something else. Egoistic psychological hedonism says that the only motivations are *one's own* pleasure and pain. I mean, even if I granted that pleasure and pain are the only relevant things, it's not just *my own* pleasure that motivates me. I'm also concerned about some *other* people, like my friends and family. I want good things to happen to them, and I want them to avoid bad things.

UTILITARIAN: So imagine that you care about your baby sister. So for example, you'd feel bad if she fell down and scraped her knee, and you'd want to prevent this if you could, right?

SCEPTIC: Right.

UTILITARIAN: So what's motivating you is that *you'd* feel bad if she scraped her knee. Once again, it's *your own* pleasure and pain that's relevant.

SCEPTIC: No, that's just the same mistake again. You're just reinterpreting anything I desire as being desirable to me because it's my own pleasure, and anything I'm motivated to avoid as my own pain. That's not the way it works at all. There are plenty of things that motivate me that have nothing to do with me, and nothing to do with pleasure or pain.

UTILITARIAN: Well, okay, I have to admit that some utilitarians have been impressed by your objection, and have rejected egoistic psychological hedonism. They agree that people can have all sorts of aims—that a lot of things that have nothing to do with pleasure and pain, and involve other people, not just one's self, can make one happy. But they insist that people's own happiness and unhappiness are the only motivating aims. So, for example, climbing mountains makes you happy, and your baby sister's knee-scrape makes you unhappy. That's why you're motivated to do mountain-climbing, and to try to prevent your sister from falling.

SCEPTIC: But what's happiness? That's a very vague term. Is that really what people are always after? I know some people who don't seem to be interested in their own happiness at all.

UTILITARIAN: Maybe not. So sometimes the hedonistic view is made even broader, saying that *satisfaction*—getting what you want—is the source of all motivation—that people in fact desire all sorts of things, and that it's the achievement of what they want, whatever it is, that's the central principle.

SCEPTIC: You said "the hedonistic view." Are psychological theories which claim that one's own happiness or satisfaction are the basic motivators also called egoistic psychological hedonism?

UTILITARIAN: They sometimes are considered versions of that theory. That's what makes things confusing. Maybe we're better off restricting the term 'hedonism' to refer only to the view that bases things on pleasure and pain. We can call the other theories the *happiness psychological theory* and the *satisfaction psychological theory*.

SCEPTIC: The satisfaction psychological theory doesn't seem to me to be much good as a theory of motivation. It just says people want whatever they want, doesn't it? But it does seem reasonable to say that people desire all sorts of things.

3. Utilitarianism

SCEPTIC: Anyway, now, let's get to the main question: whether what people actually desire is really the basis for ethics.

UTILITARIAN: Good. In order not to get bogged down in what the basic nature is of what people actually desire (pleasure, happiness, or satisfaction), let's just use a technical term for whatever it is that's the basis of human motivation: *utility*. So now we can speak of whatever it is that's desired as an increase of utility, or a decrease in disutility, whatever that really amounts to. This allows for the wide variety of different sorts of things that people want. In those terms, the basic utilitarian ethical claim is that utility production (and disutility avoidance) is the only factor that makes things good. In those terms, utilitarianism is the position that an action is morally good just insofar as it brings about net utility. The best action is the one that brings about the greatest net utility for the greatest number of people. And the reverse: that an action is bad insofar as it brings about net disutility. (So, depending on what psychological theory utilitarians accept, they might count the source of ethical value as production of pleasure, or happiness, or satisfaction.)

SCEPTIC: This may seem just a small point, but why restrict this just to people? Don't utilitarians think that pleasure and pain, happiness and unhappiness, satisfaction and dissatisfaction—utility and disutility—of *animals* is also relevant?

UTILITARIAN: Yes, some utilitarians have rejected the restriction to people. They thought that the happiness and pleasure, unhappiness and pain, of any creature capable of experiencing these things are relevant. So animals get counted in here too. But to keep things simple, let's keep talking about people's utility.

SCEPTIC: Okay, anyway, let me see if I have this straight. What you're supposed to do, according to the utilitarian, to judge the moral worth of any action, is to consider what will happen as a result of it—how it will affect people's utility (and disutility). So, everybody considered, the action which increases the utility most to the greatest number of people is the best one.

UTILITARIAN: That's right.

SCEPTIC: So this isn't an *egoistic* ethical position: it's not just one's own utility that's relevant to the morality of an action—it's everyone's.

UTILITARIAN: Right, and everyone counts equally with one's self. Here, I'll show you a simplified example of how a utilitarian would think. Imagine that you had a choice of doing nothing at all, or doing ACTION A or ACTION B. Imagine that there are only four people who would be affected, call them p, q, r, and s. Then what you do is total up the effects on everyone, like this:

	DO NOTHING	ACTION A	ACTION B
person p	0	+2	-1
person q	0	+3	+4
person r	0	+1	+2
person s	0	+3	+5
TOTAL	0	+9	+10

This shows that ACTION B is the best of the three alternatives. DO NOTHING leaves things as they are, with a sum total difference of 0. ACTION A makes everyone better off. ACTION B makes person p slightly worse off, but everyone else benefits, and the total is better than that of the other two alternatives. So B is the best thing to do. Now suppose person p is you. Even though you'd be worse off if you did ACTION B, it's still the morally right thing for you to do.

SCEPTIC: What do those numbers mean, exactly?

UTILITARIAN: They're supposed to measure what the utilitarian counts as relevant effects on people—the amount of increase or decrease in each person's utility. Utilitarians call the units of utility *utiles*. So for instance ACTION A causes person p to gain 2 utiles, and ACTION B causes that person to lose 1 utile.

SCEPTIC: But is that a reasonable way to think about things? As if there's some sort of scale that you can use to measure the good that will result for somebody? I can't even imagine how to assign sensible numbers here. For example, I like pistachio ice cream, so how many utiles do I get from eating a pistachio ice cream cone?

UTILITARIAN: Well, of course, the utile scale is arbitrary—it doesn't matter how numbers are assigned here, as long as the things you're comparing are rated on the same scale. So suppose that eating a pistachio ice cream cone gets you 5 utiles.

SCEPTIC: Okay, now I also like going to the movies. So on the same scale, should I assign going to one movie a gain of 5 utiles, or 1, or 10?

UTILITARIAN: Which one do you like better: going to a movie or eating a pistachio ice cream cone?

SCEPTIC: Well, I don't know.

UTILITARIAN: Suppose I offered you a choice of one of the two; which one would you pick?

SCEPTIC: It depends on the movie, but I guess, on average, I'd prefer going to a movie.

UTILITARIAN: Good, there's some progress. Now, suppose I offered you the choice of going to a movie or having three pistachio ice cream cones.

SCEPTIC: Well, I suppose the ice cream.

UTILITARIAN: So between the movie and two ice cream cones?

SCEPTIC: I guess they're about the same. It wouldn't matter which I'd get.

UTILITARIAN: Good, so the number of utiles we'd assign to going to the movie should be double the number we'd assign to eating a pistachio ice cream cone. On the scale which counts the pistachio ice cream cone as giving you 5 utiles, going to the movie would give you 10. So just maybe, after considering a large number of trades of this sort, we could come up with something like a sensible list of utiles for the things you like and don't like.

SCEPTIC: Maybe, but I have some doubts. For example, I have no idea how many ice cream cones I'd trade for world peace! Isn't that sort of a nonsense question?

UTILITARIAN: Difficult to answer, but not nonsense. Imagine doing a very careful and wide-ranging comparison of all the things you want and don't want. Sometimes the answers aren't really clear, but we can give answers anyway. Think of practical choices you have to make in real life, for example, whether a more expensive car is worth the additional money to you—that is, whether getting the more expensive car should be traded for what else that additional money could get you. People do make comparative decisions like that all the time.

SCEPTIC: Well, here's a problem that I think might be worse. You're going to have to assign utilities to several people at once, aren't you? For example, on that table you've shown me above, you've got utilities for four people. But how are you going to produce numbers that relate one person's utilities to someone else's? For example, suppose that ACTION A on your table involves everyone's getting a candy bar. What would make you think that person q and person s should both get the same utiles from this—3 each?

UTILITARIAN: Yes, this is a problem that utilitarians (and also economists) have faced. A lot of assumptions need to be made here. For example, if q and s would both go to the same expense in terms of money or effort to get that candy bar, then we assume they'd get the same numbers of utiles from it.

SCEPTIC: But that assumption might be wrong. Maybe we like candy bars equally much, but I'm lazy, so I wouldn't go to as much effort as you would.

UTILITARIAN: You're right. We have to make a lot of assumptions in applying the theory.

SCEPTIC: Anyway, here's a different sort of problem I think your theory runs into. You say that *all* the consequences of an action need to be considered for utility production or reduction, and the change in utility of *everyone* affected, right?

UTILITARIAN: Right.

SCEPTIC: So this means that you can't consider just the immediate effects of some action, but you also have to weigh in effects in the future, even the far distant future?

UTILITARIAN: Of course. Considering only the short-term effects of some action is a mistake. For example, imagine building a factory that will improve the economy for a few years and help out some people now, but that will produce long-term pollution affecting people in more subtle ways, but for generations to come. It's easy to think only about short-term gain, but it's a mistake.

SCEPTIC: Okay, but that means that you'll sometimes have to include effects into the very far future, a lot of which are certainly unknown. For example, imagine trying to evaluate the eventual results of the death of one child. It's possible that, if that child lived, the child's great-great-granddaughter would finally find a cure for cancer. Of course, there's no way of knowing this!

UTILITARIAN: Agreed.

SCEPTIC: And if you have to consider effects on *everyone*, then that again introduces all sorts of unknowns. For example, an apparently harmless act like catching a bus might slow the bus down a few seconds, causing somebody to miss a really important appointment, with the result that their life is ruined! You can't consider all these possibilities, right? But your theory counts all of them as relevant.

UTILITARIAN: Right, but this effect would certainly be relevant to the morality of your action. I think it's obvious that all the effects on everyone affected, into the indefinite future, should be counted when considering the morality of an action. Sometimes we can predict and consider all relevant effects with confidence, but I agree that it's very often impossible to know what these effects will be. What might be, in all these respects, is limitless and unknowable, and there's always at least some degree of doubt attached to utilitarian conclusions. But this surely can't be a reason to think that utilitarianism is not the correct theory of moral reasoning.

Everyone knows that ethics is an inexact science, and that any theory of how we get ethical conclusions where everything is supposed to be definite, simple, and clear is an incorrect theory.

4. Objections to Utilitarianism

DEONTOLOGIST: May I butt in here? I think the problem you've just been considering, about calculating utiles, is merely a technical one in applying utilitarianism, and doesn't get at what's really wrong with that position. You've already brought up a case that shows this, and just let it go by. It was the one where the utilitarian advocated lowering one person's utility in order to increase that of others.

UTILITARIAN: Well, if the total amount of utility was increased in this case, what's wrong with it?

DEONTOLOGIST: In the case you were looking at, the numbers seemed to indicate that gains and losses were small, so maybe this didn't seem so bad, but consider a case in which there are really big gains and losses. Here's an imaginary example—the Case of the Evil Surgeon—that works like this. A doctor in a hospital transplant unit is worrying about three patients. Each of the patients is about to die, but each could be saved by an organ transplant. Alice needs a heart, Betty needs a kidney, and Carl needs liver tissue; but none of these organs is available. While worrying, the doctor glances out the window and sees Fred, an apparently healthy person walking past the hospital. An idea strikes him: all he has to do is to grab Fred (with the aid of a couple of burly orderlies), kill him quickly and cleanly, and cut him up for parts—there will be enough to save all three patients. Let's assume that people's lives are worth 1000 utiles each, so a death amounts to a loss of 1000 utiles, compared to continuing to live, which just leaves them were they are and counts for 0 utile change.

	DO NOTHING	KILL FRED
Fred	0	-1000
Alice	-1000	0
Betty	-1000	0
Carl	-1000	0
TOTAL	-3000	-1000

Okay, UTILITARIAN, what should we do?

UTILITARIAN: Er, I guess I'd have to say that we should kill Fred.

DEONTOLOGIST: That's what your theory says you should do, but that answer is crazy. It's obviously completely wrong for the doctor to do this, and everybody knows that.

UTILITARIAN: No, look, here's my reply. Just as far as those four people are concerned, it's better that only one die than that three die. But in real life, many more people would be affected by an action like this. People would notice Fred's mysterious disappearance, and the mysterious sudden availability of the needed transplant organs. People would start to suspect that they might be the next victim of this sudden disappearance, and they'd suffer from anxiety, stay home more, try not to walk around alone, and so on. If ten thousand people lose only one utile each because of these things, then −10,000 should be added to the −1000 for the death, and the total for the kill-Fred option is −11,000, much worse than the do-nothing, which remains at −3000. So a Utilitarian calculation that is more adequate to the situation comes out with what you think everyone agrees is the right answer.

DEONTOLOGIST: But suppose that this sort of general anxiety and so on would not result from the action, because Fred wouldn't be missed—he's a homeless person without friends or relatives. In that case, if we stipulate that the table above really does give all the relevant effects, then the utilitarian clearly advocates the wrong action. The problem is that there really are cases in which the total utility is raised by unfairly victimizing some people, and this sort of action is always wrong.

UTILITARIAN: Well, I guess I have to admit that we have a basic moral difference here. But here's another example of the same kind of situation. It's called the *Case of the Innocent Cave Explorer*. Marvin is leading a group of three other people out of a cave when he gets hopelessly stuck in the opening. There is a rising tide that will cause everyone inside the cave to drown unless they can get out. The only option for removing Marvin is to blast him out with dynamite that someone happens to have.

	DO NOTHING	BLAST
Fred	-1000	-1000
Alice	-1000	0
Betty	-1000	0
Carl	-1000	0
TOTAL	-4000	-1000

In this case, isn't BLAST the right alternative?

DEONTOLOGIST: Killing an innocent person is always wrong, even when that person would have died anyway.

UTILITARIAN: Now you're the one who sounds crazy.

SCEPTIC: By the way, what's the word 'deontologist' mean?

DEONTOLOGIST: It's a philosophy jargon term, deriving from a Greek word *deon*, meaning that which is obligatory. So *deontology* would mean simply the science of what you must do, or, in other words, ethical theory. But philosophers nowadays use that word to mean, more particularly, the ethical theory which rejects the idea that the ethical goodness or badness of an act is a matter of its consequences, its results. *Consequentialism* is the name of any theory which holds that the ethical evaluation of an act depends on its consequences. Utilitarianism is one sort of consequentialist view, because it evaluates actions via their consequences—in terms of increasing or reducing human happiness, pleasure, pain, satisfaction, or the like. We deontologists think it's never right to maximize the total benefit by lowering one person's benefit in order to raise that of others.

UTILITARIAN: but don't you think that it's a good idea to convict a habitual criminal to a good long jail sentence, in order to stop him from committing crimes? Throwing the criminal in jail would certainly mean a substantial lowering of his utiles, and a raise in everyone else's. So this is a case of maximizing the total benefit by lowering one person's benefit in order to raise that of others. But you just claimed that's never right.

DEONTOLOGIST: Okay, what I really meant is that you can never lower somebody's benefit to maximize the total well-being, the utility of others, *unfairly*, or *unjustly*. The habitual criminal deserves punishment.[1] But the random person walking down the street outside the hospital obviously doesn't! Here's another example of something the utilitarian would approve of, but is clearly wrong. Suppose that an economic system involving slavery would be overall quite beneficial—to everyone except the slaves, of course. It's possible that slavery would increase the total utility in society a good deal, in comparison to societies without slavery. But a slave society is clearly immoral, because the slave-group is being unfairly victimized for everyone else's benefit.

UTILITARIAN: But how about this: suppose the total well-being, everyone included, would be higher if some money were taken away from the rich, who don't need it much anyway, and used for services for the poor. That's

---

1 The justification of punishment is discussed at much greater length in Conversation V.

a proposal in which the total benefit rises, at the expense of lowering the benefit enjoyed by a few. What do you think about that?

DEONTOLOGIST: I think that would be unfairly penalizing the rich. I mean, assuming they earned their wealth fairly, you can't just take it away from them to benefit other people.

UTILITARIAN: But that's exactly how the income tax works in every country.

DEONTOLOGIST: Yes, well, maybe there's something wrong with income tax in that case.

UTILITARIAN: No, that's ridiculous. You can't get off that easily! There are countless examples in which we all think that lowering some people's utility, for the sake of benefiting others, and raising the sum total, is justified. It's not difficult to think of a whole lot of them. For example, suppose that building a big highway, or establishing a national park, would be very beneficial to a lot of people, but you'd have to force a few people to move in order to do it. You'd want to minimize the harm to these people, of course, by paying them for the property they'd have to give up, but still they'd suffer harm, if they were, for example, sentimentally attached to the house where their family had lived for generations. The victims, who have to move, don't deserve this misfortune: they didn't do anything wrong. It's just their bad luck. But your theory seems to say that this is never justified! That has to be wrong.

5. Doing and Not Doing

DEONTOLOGIST: Here's another way in which I think that utilitarianism gets things badly wrong. You don't distinguish between harming somebody else failing to prevent somebody else's harm.

UTILITARIAN: Right. Do you think there's a distinction there?

DEONTOLOGIST: Well, think about this example. I'm going to give you two scenarios to compare. Suppose that Evil Harold has decided to kill his loveable old grandpa, in order to inherit his fortune. So he goes to his house at the time he knows grandpa takes a bath, lets himself in, and walks upstairs to the bathroom, intending to murder grandpa in the bath where it will look like an accident. Okay, now consider these two conclusions to the story: *Scenario 1*: Evil Harold enters the bathroom and pushes grandpa over so that he knocks his head on the side of the bathtub and falls unconscious into the filling tub. Then Evil Harold leaves, knowing that when the tub fills up, grandpa will drown. *Scenario 2*: Just by strange coincidence, the second before Evil Harold enters the bathroom, grandpa slips and falls, hitting his head on the side of the bathtub. When Harold enters, grandpa is lying unconscious in the filling tub. All Harold has to do to save him is to turn off the water, so that grandpa won't drown, and when he regains consciousness, he'll be okay. But Harold wishes him dead, so he does nothing, and leaves the bathroom, knowing that when the tub fills up, grandpa will drown. Okay, my question is, compare the evil that Evil Harold does under each Scenario.

UTILITARIAN: In both cases, the way Evil Harold acted resulted in grandpa's death. He did the wrong thing in both cases, and the two scenarios are morally identical. He acted just as badly in both cases.

DEONTOLOGIST: I think that's completely wrong. In Scenario 1, Evil Harold kills grandpa. In Scenario 2, Evil Harold merely lets grandpa die. Evil Harold does evil in both Scenarios, but killing is worse than letting die, so he does worse in Scenario 1.

UTILITARIAN: Wait a minute. You're not suggesting that it would be okay for Harold to let grandpa die, are you? Isn't it obvious that it can't be right for him not to take the obvious steps to save a life?

DEONTOLOGIST: Of course it's not right. I agree that Harold would be wrong to let grandpa die. What I'm saying is that it's worse for Harold to kill grandpa than for him to let Grandpa die.

UTILITARIAN: But there's absolutely no difference in results.

DEONTOLOGIST: That's right. That shows that results aren't the only thing that matters. But here's another way you have things wrong. You think that it's a good thing to help other people, and nobody could disagree with that, but according to you, we're *morally required* to help others. Somebody who fails to help others in need is *evil*.

UTILITARIAN: That's right. Doesn't morality require us to help others to the extent we're able?

DEONTOLOGIST: No, that's not really required. Look, remember that earlier example that came up when we were talking about your friend and the million dollars, and you mentioned that giving something to a very needy person would produce more benefit—more utility—than giving that same thing to somebody better off?

UTILITARIAN: Right, I think that's true.

DEONTOLOGIST: Okay, so suppose you now own four pairs of shoes, but there's this guy Abebe in poverty-stricken Ethiopia who owns no shoes. If you gave Abebe one of your four pairs, then you'd lose some utility, but it would mean a tremendous amount to you. Here's a chart, with a stab at plausible utilities:

	DO NOTHING	GIVE AWAY PAIR #4
You	0	-1
Abebe	0	+20
TOTAL	0	+19

UTILITARIAN: Okay, so that proves I should give Abebe a pair of my shoes.

DEONTOLOGIST: Okay, that leaves you with three pairs. Maybe it's a bit more of a loss to you to give away another pair—perhaps –2 for this pair of shoes—because that would leave you with only two, but that's still outweighed by the gain for Bogalech, another shoeless Ethiopian:

	DO NOTHING	GIVE AWAY PAIR #3
You	0	-2
Bogalech	0	+20
TOTAL	0	+18

UTILITARIAN: Hmm, okay.

DEONTOLOGIST: You can see where this is going. The loss of every pair of shoes except your last would be outweighed by the benefit of giving that pair to a shoeless person. (Not the last because that would leave you shoeless.) So you should give away pair # 2 to Zema, but you can keep one pair! It's in general true that something is worth less to a person who has a lot of that sort of thing than to a person who has only a little; so by the same reasoning, you should also give almost all of your other clothes to poverty-stricken people, and almost all of your food, and almost all of your bank account, and so on. In fact, just as long as you're better off than anyone else in the world, you should give away what you have till you're equal. So the result of utilitarian thinking is that everyone is required morally to be charitable to an absurd extent. This is crazy.

UTILITARIAN: Well, maybe it's not crazy. Maybe we really are all required to be that charitable.

DEONTOLOGIST: Oh, come on. You really don't think so, do you? If you accept that line of reasoning, why aren't you acting on it?

UTILITARIAN: Maybe it's because I'm not as good a person as I'd like to be.

DEONTOLOGIST: Don't be silly. Any moral theory that says that we're required to be that ridiculously saintly has got to be wrong. Look, I think there are at least two things wrong with the way you're thinking about this example. The first is that you don't distinguish between actions which are obligatory, and those that are good but not required. Even if giving away all but one of your pairs of shoes to the needy were a good thing to do, surely it's not required. I mean, we might count somebody who did it as an extraordinary good person—a sort of saint—but we wouldn't count somebody who didn't as a bad person, failing to do what's morally obligatory. You've got no way to make this distinction. As far as your way of calculating morality goes, the action that produces the greatest net utility is the only right one, and is obligatory, and everything else is wrong. But here's the second thing I think is misguided about your theory. All you consider when you're thinking about the shoes example is the total net utility, but there are lots of other things to think about when considering whether you should give away your shoes, that you're ignoring. Like, for example, the fact that they're *your* shoes, and nobody else has a claim on them. You earned them, you have legal title to them, others have no right to claim them. So there's nothing wrong with your hanging on to them if you like. Your theory doesn't take account of any of these things.

6. Admiral Byng

SCEPTIC: Okay, here's a real historical case I've heard philosophers debate about, and I think it would be interesting to hear your reactions, which I'll bet will be different. In the middle of the eighteenth century, the French fleet defeated the English, taking Minorca. The English took out their frustration not by punishing the ministry who had given the English fleet orders impossible to carry out, but by charging Admiral Byng, the commander of the fleet, with treason. Byng, who hadn't actually done anything wrong, was convicted and executed. In his famous work *Candide*, Voltaire, who was dismayed by this event, remarked that in England they "put an admiral to death now and then, to encourage the others." What do you think of what they did?

DEONTOLOGIST: I think it's terrible. Maybe they were acting out of frustration, or maybe, as Voltaire said, they were intending to get the other admirals to try harder in the future; but in either case, they were acting very immorally. Everyone knows that it's immoral to kill an innocent person.

UTILITARIAN: Not so fast. Suppose that the English were just angry and frustrated, and took out their feelings on Admiral Byng. This sounds bad, but very often, anyway, what's really going on when you act out of anger about something that somebody has done, what you're really trying to do, maybe only unconsciously, is to influence people in the future. So maybe Voltaire's wisecrack about encouraging the other admirals was pretty accurate. Anyway, whatever the real motives of the command, let's think about the effects of their action. I'd think it would certainly encourage their armed forces to take what they're doing more seriously. Maybe it really did get admirals to try harder. If it did, (and presuming that future English sea victories were a good thing) then maybe it was the right action after all.

DEONTOLOGIST: Oh, come on! First of all, it's really implausible to think that their action might have encouraged the other admirals in the long run. I think it would have resulted in disaster, a huge crisis in morale.

UTILITARIAN: Well, I'm not arguing that the execution really would encourage the others. I'm just saying that it's possible that it did, and that if it did, then this might just make that execution a good thing. Anyway, if they thought it would, then their motives were moral.

DEONTOLOGIST: I agree that we don't have to worry about what the real-life effects of that action actually were. The real question is: supposing that it did have those desired effects, would that morally justify the action? I gather you're saying it would, and that's ridiculous.

UTILITARIAN: War is hell. You've got to do some pretty nasty things to prevent greater disasters.

DEONTOLOGIST: No, killing an innocent man is always wrong, no matter what good effects it might have in the long run.

UTILITARIAN: *No matter what*? You can't really mean that. In the case of Admiral Byng, maybe you can't imagine results so good as to make the execution worth it, but can't you imagine cases, maybe other ones, in which a great deal of good arises from a fake conviction, so much that it's worth the harm caused to the guy who's the unlucky victim? Imagine, for example, that we could really prevent a whole lot of future terrorism, and save thousands of lives, by convicting somebody falsely of a past terrorist act, in order to make future terrorists think that they can't get away with it? Or, to take a more extreme and unrealistic example, suppose that you could prevent hundreds of deaths by inflicting some small harm on an innocent child, like sending her to her room without dinner, even though she hadn't done anything wrong?

DEONTOLOGIST: Well, that would be wrong.

UTILITARIAN: Hmph.

SCEPTIC: That's what I thought you both would say! Well, we haven't reached any agreement, that's for sure, but at least there's a very clear and vivid choice.

7. Rights

SCEPTIC: Well, I've heard lots of objections to utilitarianism from DEONTOLOGIST, but I still don't have much of an idea of what kind of moral theory is available as an alternative. If the greatest happiness for the greatest number isn't the basis for morally right action, then what is?

RIGHTS-THEORIST: Here's my view on that. I think that the basis of morality is respecting the *rights* of other people. This principle would also show what's wrong with the way the English treated poor old Admiral Byng. Clearly they violated his rights.

SCEPTIC: What, exactly, is a right?

RIGHTS-THEORIST: When you say that people have a right, you're talking about what others are morally required to do for them, or morally prohibited from doing to them. For example, when people have the right to vote, that means that others are morally prohibited from preventing them from voting: that it's wrong to stop them from voting. When you've got the right to a basic education, that means that society is morally required to provide you with the opportunity for this: that it would be morally wrong if society failed to provide basic educational facilities.

SCEPTIC: So the right to do something can mean that nobody is morally permitted to prevent you from doing it?

RIGHTS-THEORIST: That's it. For example, the right to free speech means that you can say what you want, and nobody is permitted to stop you.

UTILITARIAN: Not even if what you're going to say is nasty, or hurtful?

RIGHTS-THEORIST: That's correct. Morality doesn't have anything to do with harm or benefit.

SCEPTIC: It's clear that you're a deontologist, not a utilitarian.

RIGHTS-THEORIST: Correct.

SCEPTIC: If rights are what you say they are, then I doubt that anyone has any of them.

RIGHTS-THEORIST: Why do you say that?

SCEPTIC: Because I doubt that there's anything that people are morally required to allow me to do no matter what. For example, I clearly don't have the right to freedom of speech. One reason for this is a conflict of rights.

RIGHTS-THEORIST: What do you mean?

SCEPTIC: I assume you'd believe that people have the right not to be demeaned by racist slurs?

RIGHTS-THEORIST: Yes, that's another right.

UTILITARIAN: But doesn't that right restrict the freedom of people to say just anything they want? If I had the right to say whatever I liked, then it would be wrong for others ever to prohibit me from saying anything, and then I'd be free to make verbal racist slurs. But if others have the right not to be racially harassed, then I'm not free to make verbal racist slurs.

RIGHTS-THEORIST: Okay, yes, I guess I have to say that when rights conflict, one might limit the scope of another. The right to freedom of speech means that you can say what you want provided it doesn't interfere with another person's rights.

UTILITARIAN: But how about the classic case of someone's yelling "FIRE!" in a crowded theatre (I mean, just as a prank—there isn't any fire). There will be panic, and people will be injured or killed in the rush for the doors. Nobody thinks that people should be allowed that sort of speech.

RIGHTS-THEORIST: Well, isn't this just another limitation of the right to free speech, that you've got that right except when it interferes with another person's rights?

UTILITARIAN: I don't think so. I can't see how this is a conflict of rights at all. I think that in this case you shouldn't be allowed to yell "FIRE!" because that would cause an enormous amount of *harm*.

RIGHTS-THEORIST: Okay, I guess that shows that our right to free speech isn't absolute. In certain cases we can legitimately be prevented from saying certain things, when a lot of harm results. So I guess what should be said here is that I haven't described the right correctly: it's not to say just anything, but to a certain kind of speech.

UTILITARIAN: Speech which isn't harmful? What's left of your claim that there's a "right" here? I mean, aren't you just saying that people can say whatever they want, except when what they do is harmful? That makes your position just the same as mine!

RIGHTS-THEORIST: Well, I do think that there are certain cases in which rights really do override considerations of harm or benefit. For example, everyone in our society with a valid driver's licence has the right to drive, even though we can identify some of them who are likely to wind up having accidents that will harm themselves and others. For example, it's well known that teenagers and elderly people have a higher frequency of accidents than the rest of the population, but, with a valid license, they still have the right to drive. When you say that somebody has a right to do something, harms and benefits are not considered, unless they are really drastic.

UTILITARIAN: Well, then I think that there aren't any genuine rights at all, because potential harms and benefits are always to be considered.

RIGHTS-THEORIST: Okay, maybe there are problems here about how far rights extend, and about what to do about conflict of rights. But I still think that there is a valid notion of *basic* rights, which are more important than other rights, and which overrule consideration of at least some harms and benefits. At least everyone agrees what the basic rights are, don't they?

SCEPTIC: I don't think so. The United Nations Charter of Rights is an important document signed by most of the countries in the world. It lists a whole lot of supposedly basic rights that people have, including the right to form trade unions, the right to practise their religion, and the right to a higher education.

RIGHTS-THEORIST: Well, I'd agree with all that. All those are good things. What's your point?

SCEPTIC: The point is that even though all those countries agreed to that charter, none of them really thinks these things are basic rights.

RIGHTS-THEORIST: What makes you say that?

SCEPTIC: If we were genuinely to count those things as basic rights, then they'd allow or grant them despite harm that might result. So, for example, workers would be allowed to form a trade union under any circumstances whatever. But just about everywhere governments count certain occupations as so vital that the employees are not allowed to form unions.

RIGHTS-THEORIST: Well, maybe the workers' rights are being violated by the very government that claims to respect them. Or maybe there really isn't a right to form trade unions, but rather a more specific right to do so in certain situations.

UTILITARIAN: What you're really saying is that it's okay to allow trade unions unless they really interfere with the general welfare. You don't need to invoke the notion of "rights" at all for that position.

RIGHTS-THEORIST: Maybe.

SCEPTIC: And about those other supposedly basic rights: nobody thinks that people should be allowed to perform any practice of any religion, no matter what, do they? For example, one feature of some religions is that they think that blood transfusions are immoral, so parents who seriously practise that religion refuse permission for their children to receive blood, even when that would save the child's life. But routinely governments interfere, and prevent those parents from practising that aspect of their religion, and arrange for the child's life to be saved anyway.

RIGHTS-THEORIST: Hmm. Well, maybe there are some religious practices that people don't have a right to perform.

SCEPTIC: The same thing goes for the so-called right to a higher education. Nobody thinks that all human beings have this right.

RIGHTS-THEORIST: No?

SCEPTIC: No. If we really thought so, we'd have to provide free higher education for everyone, and allow anybody in, no matter what their previous educational background and achievement was. If this was really a right, then dropouts from the third grade could claim it, and we'd have to let them in to universities.

RIGHTS-THEORIST: Okay maybe that's not really a right either.

SCEPTIC: Here's another example. John Locke, the seventeenth-century English philosopher who was very influential in developing the idea of rights said that it was obvious that everyone had the right to life, liberty, and property. Does that phrase sound familiar?

RIGHTS-THEORIST: It reminds me of the phrase in the United States Declaration of Independence, "life, liberty, and the pursuit of happiness."

SCEPTIC: Exactly! Thomas Jefferson, who wrote the Declaration of Independence, was strongly influenced by Locke, but he changed Locke's phrase by eliminating the right to property and introducing the right to the pursuit of happiness. Jefferson thought that *his* list of rights was obvious: he said that it was "self-evident" that human beings had those rights. Well, is there a right to property or isn't there? How in the world would we figure that out? Isn't it really just that Locke felt that allowing ownership or property was extremely important, but Jefferson didn't?

RIGHTS-THEORIST: Well, I'm not sure whether there really is a right to property or not. That's something I'd have to think about.

SCEPTIC: Okay, but I'm not sure how you'd go about finding out!

8. Using People

KANTIAN: The most influential deontologist philosopher of modern times was the eighteenth-century German philosopher Immanuel Kant, and I'd like to tell you about what he thought. Like all deontologists, Kant thought that morality has nothing to do with increasing human pleasure or satisfaction or anything like that. We Kantians, like all deontologists, think that when you're considering the morality of an action, those results are irrelevant.

SCEPTIC: So you agree with RIGHTS-THEORIST that an act with really undesirable results might actually be the morally right one to do?

KANTIAN: That's correct.

UTILITARIAN: That's why your theory is all wrong, from the word go. Human desires—for happiness, well-being, pleasure, satisfaction, and so on—are the only things worth considering. Any morality which thinks that there are other considerations is perverted.

KANTIAN: Well, look, we don't ignore humans altogether! Kant argued that the morality of an action depends on whether that action shows respect for persons as persons. That means that you're not allowed to *use* people for others' benefit. They were using Admiral Byng to send a message to other admirals, to have an effect on their future performance. That was a case of horrible disrespect for Admiral Byng as a person. It's all right, of course, to use *things*—inanimate objects—for people's benefit. You can use your car to take you to where you want to go. But using people is always wrong. Another way of putting this is, in Kant's words, that people aren't to be considered as means to an end—yours or anyone else's. People must always be treated instead as *ends in themselves*.

UTILITARIAN: Even when the person you're using as a means isn't harmed?

KANTIAN: Harm and benefit have nothing to do with the morality of an action. That's utilitarian thinking, looking out for harm and benefit. What's wrong with using someone is not that the person is harmed. It would be wrong even if the person isn't harmed.

UTILITARIAN: You can't mean that.

KANTIAN: I do.

UTILITARIAN: Okay, how about the other day when I was lost and I asked somebody for directions. I was using that person for my benefit, as a means to my end.

KANTIAN: Well, I agree that you're considering the other person as a means to an end in that case, and that it isn't bad. I should have said that it's bad to treat someone as a means *only*. That's actually Kant's position, and I should have made that clearer earlier.

UTILITARIAN: So you'd say that when you ask people for directions you're not treating them as a means only? You're also treating them as ends-in-themselves?

KANTIAN: Right.

UTILITARIAN: How does that come in?

KANTIAN: Well, you're respecting them as people, by asking them politely, and thanking them afterwards, and so on.

UTILITARIAN: I agree that this is a good thing to do, but I can't see how this is necessary for morally permissible action. Look, how about this example. The other day, I went to the bank to deposit a cheque, and there was a big lineup of customers. I gave the teller my endorsed cheque and my deposit slip, and she typed some stuff into her computer, gave me a receipt, and I left. There wasn't any chit-chat, not even those little please-and-thank-you politenesses. We were both in a rush, and very businesslike. I wasn't impolite, but there wasn't any sort of special respect in my behaviour either. I dealt with her in just the sort of way that I would have dealt with an automatic teller machine. In other words, I was using her entirely as a means to my end of making a deposit, and there was absolutely nothing in my actions that could be considered treating her as an end-in-herself.

KANTIAN: It doesn't sound like a very nice encounter.

UTILITARIAN: It wasn't nice, but it wasn't nasty either. It was just businesslike. The point is, that although I was using her entirely as a means, there was absolutely nothing wrong with my actions.

SCEPTIC: By the way, what do you think my friend should do with her uncle's money?

KANTIAN: She should give the money to her uncle's girlfriend Sally.

UTILITARIAN: What? Really? But that's the least beneficial outcome of all! Why should she do that?

KANTIAN: Because she promised him she'd do that. Morality requires that you keep your promises, no matter what the consequences.

UTILITARIAN: That's ridiculous too. Anyway, I don't see how that answer follows from the moral principles you were just describing, involving respect for persons, and never using them as a means.

KANTIAN: Well, promise-keeping could be interpreted as a case of respect for persons. Imagine that you're buying a used car from someone, but you're $100 short of the price; the seller agrees to let you have the car now, if you promise to pay the remaining $100 when your paycheque arrives later in the month. You promise, but you haven't the slightest intention of paying up later. You're leaving town, and the seller won't have any way to find you, so you'll just ignore your promise. That's clearly a case of using the seller as a means to your ends, of failure to respect him as a person.

UTILITARIAN: I don't see that at all. I agree that it's wrong not to keep your part of the deal, but I don't think that has anything to do with using people as means or respecting them. I think it's wrong because it's harming the person. That example you just used illustrates the second basic problem I see with your position. It's not just that the moral judgements that follow from your theory are sometimes silly or crazy. It's also that perfectly reasonable moral judgements don't follow from them.

9. The Categorical Imperative

KANTIAN: Well, I do have to admit that it's sometimes a little difficult to see exactly what moral advice follows from Kant's theory, and what doesn't. He's a difficult writer, and there is some disagreement about how to interpret him. Maybe anticipating the difficulty, Kant provided more than one way to understand his basic ethical principle, which he called the *categorical imperative*.

SCEPTIC: What's that mean?

KANTIAN: An imperative is a command. *Categorical* means without any conditions; this is opposed to *hypothetical* which means conditional. So for example 'If you want to impress your boss, work hard' is a *hypothetical imperative*. It tells you what to do *if* you want something. But 'Work hard!' is a categorical imperative: it just tells you what to do, period. Obviously a hypothetical imperative, while it might give you good advice, isn't binding; in the example I just gave, if you don't care about impressing your boss, you can ignore it. But when something is your duty—when it's a moral obligation—then that's expressed as a categorical imperative. It's just something you have to do. For Kant, there are many hypothetical imperatives, but there's just one basic categorical imperative—with a couple of different ways of understanding it. We've already talked about one of the ways Kant gives for understanding the categorical imperative. It is "Act in such a way that you always treat humanity, whether in your own person or in the person of any other, never simply as a means, but always at the same time as an end." Another way of expressing the same idea is this: "Act as if the maxim of your action was to become through your will a universal law of nature."

SCEPTIC: You're right: it's not easy to understand Kant! Please explain.

KANTIAN: A *maxim* is a general principle, a rule of conduct. So Kant is saying that, when you're thinking about the morality of an action, you should imagine that there is a general rule telling people to act the way you're considering doing. And imagine that this general principle were "a universal law of nature"—that is, binding on everyone. So, for example, suppose you're thinking of breaking a promise in order to benefit the needy. Now consider the rule: "Always break your promises when people stand to benefit." Now imagine that this rule were binding on everyone. Then everyone would go around breaking promises when people stood to benefit from it. Kant argues that you couldn't will that this be a universal law. So that means that breaking your promise would be immoral.

SCEPTIC: I don't get it. Why couldn't I will that this be a universal law? Is it because I wouldn't want others to break their promises to me?

KANTIAN: Some people think that that's what Kant meant. In that case, the categorical imperative would turn out to be a lot like the "Golden Rule" in Christianity: "Do unto others as you would have them do unto you." But most Kant scholars think that this misinterprets Kant. The reason you can't will that to be a universal law is not that you wouldn't like the results. Remember that Kant is very clear that likes and dislikes, and consideration of consequences, are totally irrelevant to moral thinking. What Kant meant is more like this: The reason you couldn't will that everyone should break promises when that would bring benefits is that if everyone did that, then the whole concept of promising would become meaningless.

SCEPTIC: Why's that? Because people would stop trusting anyone who promised? I thought you said that for Kant, the results of actions were irrelevant to their morality.

KANTIAN: Well, here's what I mean. The very idea of promising involves the obligation to keep the promise, even when breaking it might be beneficial. Saying that it's okay to break a promise any time it's beneficial is a contradiction. So Kant isn't considering what would result if I broke my promise, or even what would result if everyone did. Kant is saying that thinking about the morality of an action is thinking about it as if it were to become a general moral rule for everyone. But promise-breaking couldn't be a general moral rule for everyone, because the whole idea is a contradiction: it says that everyone can continue to make promises—that is, to commit themselves to doing something whatever the consequences—but also that they can break those promises if the consequences are no good. That's a self-contradictory general moral rule. It's saying, you always have to do X, and you don't always have to do X.

SCEPTIC: I have several problems with this. First, I don't see what any of that has to do with treating other people as ends not means.

KANTIAN: Well, the idea here is that when you're thinking morally you're not supposed to think just about your own ends, but you have to consider everyone's. That's why you're required to consider your action as if it were a general moral rule, applicable to everyone.

SCEPTIC: But second, more importantly, it doesn't seem to me that Kant's reasoning about promising has any relevance to what I should or shouldn't do. Suppose that, were it a universal law that promises could be broken, the practice of promising would disappear, or that the whole concept would become inapplicable. I don't know why it's supposed to follow that I should keep my promise right now. I mean, even if there's something sort of contradictory about this becoming a universal law, that's not what we're worrying about. I'm just thinking about my action right now. If my doing that was going to somehow contribute to it being adopted as a general rule, then maybe that would be relevant. But my own little action won't make that happen.

KANTIAN: Right, it won't. But remember, Kant isn't interested in the consequences of your action. He's saying that, to think morally about an action, you have to think about your action as if it were a general rule for everyone's action—even though your action won't make it become a general moral rule.

SCEPTIC: I still don't see why we're supposed to think that way. Anyway, my third problem with this principle is that I can't see how it rules out all sorts of actions that everyone would think are immoral. I mean, how, for example, is this supposed to show that torturing little babies is wrong? Is it supposed to be *contradictory* to will that it be a general rule that everyone torture little babies?

KANTIAN: I admit that it's hard to see how willing this as a general rule is exactly self-contradictory. Maybe what's wrong here is that torturing little children to suit your own ends is ignoring their ends; it's making an exception of yourself, rather than thinking of a general moral rule. So it's inconsistent in that sense. Anyway, I think it's clear that what makes an action morally good is not that it contributes to happiness or pleasure. Our moral heroes, the people we admire because of their ethical actions, are often not much interested in anyone's pleasure or happiness at all. And the people who produce a lot of pleasure and happiness are often not our moral heroes.

UTILITARIAN: For example?

KANTIAN: Well, think about Nelson Mandela. He's one of my moral heroes because he worked so hard and so effectively to provide dignity and equality for black people in South Africa. But along the way, he produced a whole lot of conflict and unhappiness.

UTILITARIAN: Yes, but his actions were good because in the long run he increased the happiness of so many South Africans.

KANTIAN: Maybe, maybe not, but happiness isn't the issue here. He worked to restore human dignity, and that's what matters, not anyone's happiness or pleasure. And look at people who produced a whole lot of happiness, like famous movie actors or singers. Mick Jagger's singing produced an enormous amount of pleasure and happiness, but nobody counts him among their moral heroes, for sure! Jonas Salk's discovery of the polio vaccine prevented a great deal of suffering, and we're all very grateful for that, and he's a hero of a sort, but not a *moral* hero.

10. The Motivation Question

SCEPTIC: I'd like to hear how you respond to a different question. UTILITARIAN and DEONTOLOGIST agreed that my friend shouldn't keep the million dollars for herself, but should do something you consider morally right instead (though DEONTOLOGIST didn't say what). But I'd like to ask about motivation. It's clear to me why someone would be motivated to keep the million, but what would lead anyone to do something else with it? Why would anyone want to do anything but keep it, when there would be nothing in it for him or her?

UTILITARIAN: If your friend is asking, "What's in it for me if I give the money to Oxfam?" I'd say, "Nothing." If she doesn't care about the misery of starving people—if she cares only about herself—then there's nothing in the morally right action to motivate her.

KANTIAN: I agree.

UTILITARIAN: But I think, and I'm sure KANTIAN agrees, that there are other motivations beside the anticipation of more utility for oneself.

SCEPTIC: Wait a minute. Weren't you agreeing earlier with the egoistic psychological hedonists that the only thing that motivates people is their own pleasure or happiness or satisfaction—their own utility?

UTILITARIAN: Right.

SCEPTIC: But if that's true, how can anyone ever have moral motivation, which is the desire for everyone's utility, not just one's own—and sometimes at the expense of one's own.

UTILITARIAN: Well, a morally motivated person is somebody who gets pleasure or happiness or satisfaction—utility—out of seeing the general utility increased.

SCEPTIC: Hmm.

UTILITARIAN: I think that the morally right action is the one that increases utility for everyone, not just the person doing the action. So the moral person is the person who cares about—gets pleasure from—the happiness and pleasure, unhappiness and pain, satisfaction and dissatisfaction, of others. Not everyone feels this way. Very young children, for example, care very much about themselves, but not at all about other people. Toddlers are quite happy to clobber other kids to take away something they want. They don't seem to care about pain or pleasure in other people. Maybe you can get them not to clobber their friends by punishing them when they do, or rewarding them when they play nice, but that's because they're motivated by avoiding punishment or getting reward, not by other people's pain or pleasure. But sooner or later, most people mature past this stage, and start desiring other people's satisfactions. First it's their close family and friends they start caring about, and then later maybe this broadens out to include others whom they don't even know.

SCEPTIC: But some people never develop out of the initial selfish stage, right?

UTILITARIAN: Right. I know somebody like that, and I wish I didn't. That sort of person doesn't act morally. They're motivated to do only what they think might eventually work out to their own advantage. Sometimes, of course, they'll do something nice for you, but that's only because they think that someday they'll get something good in return from you. Moral motivation, however, is not self-serving. People who react morally are people who care about others' utilities in something like the same way they care about their own: they just want others to have pleasures, and to avoid pains, to be happy and satisfied, not for the sake of their own eventual benefit, but just because they get pleasure out of other people's pleasure; other people's unhappiness makes them unhappy. Some philosophers have called this sort of care about others the feeling of *sympathy*, though that's maybe a little too narrow a term, since it usually suggests only that someone has a compassionate reaction to somebody else's pain. This sort of sympathy also means that one participates, so to speak, in other people's pleasures as well.

SCEPTIC: But what about people who don't have that sort of sympathy, like your selfish friend? Could you give that person any reason to do what a utilitarian would count as the morally right thing?

UTILITARIAN: Of course you might effectively motivate them, the way you would a child, by offering reward or threatening punishment. That might get them to do the right thing, and that's what really matters.

SCEPTIC: But according to you they wouldn't have the proper sort of motivation?

UTILITARIAN: Well, it doesn't matter what motivates someone, as long as they do the right thing—that's what I care about. Maybe they do it because of unselfish sympathy, or maybe they selfishly think they might get rewarded, or get punished if they don't do it. But on the whole, I think that sympathy is a more reliable moral motivation than the anticipation of punishment or reward. I wouldn't trust somebody motivated by the prospect of punishment or reward. Lots of times—most of the time— there's no system of rewards for doing the right thing, or punishments for doing wrong. And even when there is, it doesn't always work: people think they can get away without being punished—and they're often right. It's preferable—much more reliable—to have people motivated by sympathy. They'll do the right thing even when there's nothing in it for them.

SCEPTIC: That reminds me of the account of the internal policeman, discussed earlier.[2] But how do you get people to have this kind of sympathy?

UTILITARIAN: I suppose there are ways of encouraging it in people, like when you try to talk to little Shawn about how he shouldn't poke little Shawna in the nose, because it hurts Shawna, just like getting poked in his nose would hurt him. But basically I think that if a person doesn't feel that

---

2 In Conversation II.

sympathetic response with others, then there's nothing much you can do to convince him. I think it's just a kind of response that normally develops as you mature, but not always. Either you get it or you don't. Some people don't, and that's why we need jails and police.

SCEPTIC: So, in effect, you're just saying that some people just happen to develop sympathy, and some don't, and that's all you can say about it? I mean, there's no way you could demonstrate to somebody that they're making a mistake if they aren't inclined to act morally?

UTILITARIAN: I guess that's right. Imagine, for example, that we've managed to make little Shawn fully aware of little Shawna's pain that he causes when he pokes her, but little Shawn just doesn't care. We remind little Shawn just how much he dislikes getting poked in the nose, and, we suppose, he fully appreciates this, and cares very much about future pokes to himself. But he still might have no aversion at all to producing a similar pain in Shawna.

SCEPTIC: Do you think you could motivate my friend to give the million to Oxfam?

UTILITARIAN: Maybe I could get her to care about the utility of needy people in the third world by telling her what's really going on there. It could be made vivid to her by showing her films of what life is like there, or she could even be taken there to see for herself. Then maybe she'd be motivated to help out.

SCEPTIC: This would work if she's already the sort of person who'd feel sympathy for their suffering, and in this case the reason she doesn't give to Oxfam is merely that she doesn't really know about the extent of suffering there is out there. But what if she did find out what's going on, I mean, fully and vividly, but still didn't care? Or what if she was somewhat moved, but still she was so strongly motivated to keep the money, because she needed it so badly, that her motivation to keep it outweighed her charitable motives?

UTILITARIAN: Well, in those cases, (and assuming that I couldn't convince her she'd get into trouble if she kept the money) I guess she couldn't be motivated to do the right thing.

SCEPTIC: Well, that's a little disappointing. I was hoping to find some convincing reason for being motivated to do right things. You're telling me only that some people care about doing it, and some people don't, the end.

KANTIAN: Excuse me, but maybe I can give a more satisfying response.
I agree with UTILITARIAN that there's a difference between being self-

interested and being motivated by sympathy, and I agree that some people develop sympathy for others, and some other people don't, and that there might be nothing you could do to get people who don't to feel differently. I guess that might be just as impossible as trying to talk somebody into liking pistachio ice cream. But I think that all of that is irrelevant to the question you're raising, because I don't think that motivation by sympathy is moral motivation.

SCEPTIC: Really! Well, why not?

KANTIAN: I think that being motivated by sympathy is one thing, but moral motivation is something different altogether. Suppose, for instance, that you see some old lady struggling to reach something heavy on a high shelf in the supermarket. The moral thing to do is to help her. Now maybe she's your poor old granny whom you love and really care about, and you have this burst of sympathy for the poor old soul. But maybe she's your nasty fifth-grade teacher who used to torture and humiliate you, and you feel a certain glee at her present disabled condition, and no sympathy at all. But both of these feelings are irrelevant to moral motivation. It's your duty to give her a hand, whether you feel sympathy or antipathy or nothing at all. Moral action is doing something because it's right, not because of your feelings. Sometimes doing what's right goes against your feelings, and sometimes it's in accord with them, but that's irrelevant. The only thing that makes an action morally good is that it's motivated solely by the desire to do what's right. Any other motivation is beside the point.

UTILITARIAN: That's crazy. Do you really think that moral motivation has nothing to do with caring about the well-being, the happiness and pleasure and satisfaction of others?

KANTIAN: That is what I think. Acting correctly is acting with the right moral motivation, and this is merely wanting to act in accord with your duty—to do X because X is right. This has nothing to do with the consequences of that act for anyone's well-being or pleasure or happiness or satisfaction. That's why feelings of sympathy are irrelevant. Look, here are some examples. Suppose that your friend has just spent a whole lot of money on some new clothes, and shows them to you very proudly, asking you how you like them. You think they're terrible. Should you lie to your friend, saying they're beautiful? Nothing good will come out of telling the truth: your friend will be hurt and insulted, and nobody will ever benefit. Sympathy and goodwill, the desire not to hurt, are all on the side of lying. But lying is wrong. Everybody knows that. And the wrongness has absolutely nothing to do with hurting people or benefiting them or anything else.

SCEPTIC: So if caring about other people's pain and pleasure and satisfaction and happiness and so on isn't moral motivation, then what is?

KANTIAN: The moral person is the person who's motivated to do something not because of any effects that thing will have on anyone, but rather simply because it's right. Immanuel Kant put it this way: the only thing of value in the world was a *good will*, by which he meant the desire to do what's right just because it's right, and for no other reason. Kant thought that people who act out of sympathy for others, or any other feeling, are not necessarily evil people, but their motivations aren't moral motives. Somebody who has a whole lot of sympathy for the sufferings of others is no more moral than somebody who doesn't. Sympathy is beside the point. Moral motivation is simply to do what's right because it's right. It's a matter of knowledge, not feeling. You know that something is right, and that's your motivation. Good people give to charity because they know that it's the right thing to do, and that's it. You'll need to motivate them by playing on their sympathies only when they have insufficient moral motivation.

UTILITARIAN: I don't see how your picture of moral motivation can work. I mean, knowledge can't motivate all by itself. There has to be some feeling, some desire, some pro or con emotional state. For example, knowing that there's pistachio ice cream in the freezer doesn't motivate anyone to go there unless they like pistachio ice cream.

KANTIAN: I don't think that's right. Knowledge can motivate just as feelings can. But they're different kinds of motivation. Feelings just push you around, but knowledge is a higher form of motivation, appropriate for moral action.

11. Ethical Knowledge

SCEPTIC: Here's what bothers me about all of your positions. All of you are *ethical objectivists*—you believe that there are real objective facts about what's right and wrong, don't you? And that knowledge of these facts is possible?

UTILITARIAN: Sure, I do. I think that right and wrong are a matter of what action will result in the greatest utility, and that's purely a factual matter. Of course, sometimes you don't know what will have this result, but often you do.

DEONTOLOGIST: I don't think this is what ethical facts amount to, but I agree that right and wrong is a matter of objective fact, which can be known. All of us deontologists think so. KANTIAN and RIGHTS-THEORIST agree, don't you?

KANTIAN: Yes.

RIGHTS-THEORIST: I agree.

SCEPTIC: I think there are problems with all of your positions, and with ethical objectivism in general. I wonder whether there is such a thing as an ethical fact at all, but let's put aside that question for a moment, and let's talk about the possibility of ethical knowledge. You can find out whether something is green, or bigger than a breadbox, or whether it smells or tastes like a peach, just by using your senses. But do your senses tell you that an action is right or wrong?

KANTIAN: Rightness and wrongness aren't visible, or smellable, or detectable by any of the physical senses. I've already told you about Kant's view on moral knowledge, which is that the basic ethical principle, the categorical imperative, can be discovered just through the operations of reason. And when you apply this, you find out about the rightness or wrongness of any particular action.

SCEPTIC: Well, we've already talked about the problems I see with his view.

DEONTOLOGIST: Some philosophers think that there's a way of finding out moral facts called *moral intuition*. It's not a matter of perceiving things with your senses. It's a totally different way of finding out facts directly. It doesn't use your senses, or your reasoning power, or inference from evidence.

SCEPTIC: You mean, you just know that something is bad?

DEONTOLOGIST: That's right. You just think about it, using your moral intelligence, and you can discover its moral characteristics.

SCEPTIC: That's weird. Does that way of finding things out really exist?

DEONTOLOGIST: It's not actually all that bizarre. Just think about some obviously bad action, like torturing little kittens. It becomes immediately clear to you that this is wrong, doesn't it? You don't see it with your senses, or reason about it. You just know it.

SCEPTIC: Suppose that somebody doesn't know that torturing little kittens is wrong. How could you get them to see this?

DEONTOLOGIST: I suppose that there are some people who are just incapable of moral intuition. Maybe it's not really possible to teach somebody morality who doesn't already have these intuitions, in the same way that you couldn't get someone who is completely colour-blind to understand that an apple is red.

SCEPTIC: Hmm, I'm not really sure there is this kind of way of getting knowledge without any sense input, merely by intuition. That would be a really strange way to find things out. And I also have my doubts about KANTIAN's proposal, that you can find out about ethical facts just by using reasoning power. I mean, is there any knowledge of facts that doesn't involve sense perception of the external world?[3]

DEONTOLOGIST: I admit that on my view ethical facts, and the ways we have of knowing them, are very different from the usual sorts of facts and ways of knowing them. But why expect them to be like other facts?

UTILITARIAN: Well, this is where my position has the advantage over yours. I've got a clear account of exactly how you find out that something is right or wrong, and it doesn't involve any mysterious non-sensory way of finding things out. All you have to do is find out what the results of an action would be on people's utility.

SCEPTIC: But sometimes that's something that's very hard to tell. Sometimes we're quite wrong about what we think the results of an action might be, and sometimes we don't have any idea at all.

UTILITARIAN: I agree, but that's really not an objection to my position. I never claimed you can always tell whether an action is right or wrong. Sometimes we're mistaken about consequences, and sometimes there's just no way to know. But sometimes you can have a pretty good idea, as in the examples we've been considering, and I think I've got the right idea about how we find out in those cases.

SCEPTIC: Okay, I agree that in some cases we can find out pretty well what the effects of an action will be on people's happiness and pleasure and so on, and that this is something we find out in the ordinary ways we find out anything about the real world. When you find that out, however, you're not finding out the moral worth of that action.

UTILITARIAN: Why not?

SCEPTIC: You claim that ethical rightness of an action is the same thing as that action's maximizing utility; but I don't think that's right. If that were right, then it wouldn't make any sense for someone to agree that some action maximizes utility, but to still wonder whether it was the right action. Here's an analogy. To be somebody's sister is exactly the same

---

3 This question is discussed at length in Conversation VI.

thing as being somebody's female sibling. So knowing that Zelda is (or isn't) Sam's female sibling settles the question whether Zelda is (or isn't) Sam's sister. But knowing that something will maximize utility doesn't settle the question whether or not something is morally right. It leaves that question still open. Somebody might agree that an action would maximize utility, but still sensibly wonder whether the action was right or wrong. The fact that that question is still open means that maximizing utility and being morally right aren't the same thing. (This argument is what philosophers call the *Open Question Argument*.)

UTILITARIAN: Well, I don't buy that argument. I think that once you've settled the question whether or not an action maximizes utility, at that point the question whether or not that's the right action is no longer open. You've closed that question, answered it. The answers to the two questions are the same, because they're the same question!

SCEPTIC: I don't think so. Anyway, to sum up what I'm saying here: All three of you think that there are ethical facts. DEONTOLOGIST offers a mysterious implausible non-sensory intuition for finding out these facts and KANTIAN equally implausibly thinks you can find them out by reasoning alone. UTILITARIAN offers an unmysterious methodology, involving use of the ordinary senses, but what's found out here is something different from these facts.

12. Ethical Subjectivism

SUBJECTIVIST: I agree with your objections here, and I've got what I think is a diagnosis of the problem all these positions face. Their problem is that they all think there are such things as ethical facts. But there aren't.

DEONTOLOGIST: No, look, that can't be right.

UTILITARIAN: I agree with DEONTOLOGIST on that matter anyway. Everyone knows that certain things are right and certain things are wrong. There are ethical facts.

SUBJECTIVIST: Like what?

DEONTOLOGIST: Well, for example, torturing innocent little children is certainly wrong, isn't it? I mean, you do disapprove of that, don't you?

SUBJECTIVIST: Yes, I disapprove of that, but that's a different question. What we disagree about was whether there's an objective characteristic of something called moral wrongness, or rightness for that matter, and I'm saying there isn't.

DEONTOLOGIST: But then what are you saying when you say that torturing little children is wrong? That certainly looks like a statement of fact, just like when you say that there are penguins in Antarctica, or that salt dissolves in water.

SUBJECTIVIST: The statement about torture looks like the others, and the others say (or try to say) the way things are, the sort of thing that's true or false depending on the characteristics of the objective outside world. But this resemblance is misleading; I don't think that the torture statement makes a claim about real-world facts at all.

DEONTOLOGIST: But doesn't everything people say make a claim about real-world facts? Isn't everything people say either true or false?

SUBJECTIVIST: No. Here's another case in which what looks like a statement of fact is actually not: when someone says, "Pistachio ice cream is delicious." Deliciousness isn't an objective characteristic of things. What the person's statement is doing is not making a claim about facts. It's just expressing the person's feelings about pistachio ice cream. It's just like saying "Yum!" when eating it. An expression of feelings doesn't say anything about objective external characteristics, so it can't be true or false. A true statement is one that says that something has a characteristic, when that thing really does have that characteristic. A false statement is one that says that something has a characteristic, when the thing doesn't. But when what's said doesn't attribute any characteristic to what's talked about, but merely expresses a feeling about it, it's neither true nor false. Clearly "Yum!" is neither true nor false. And neither is "Pistachio ice cream is delicious."

DEONTOLOGIST: So you're saying that "Torturing little children is wrong" isn't true?

SUBJECTIVIST: Right, but it isn't false either. And don't get me wrong: I'm as opposed to torturing little children as you are! This opposition is a negative attitude I have toward torturing little children—it isn't a belief about what the moral facts are. There aren't any moral facts. Look, there are all sorts of different attitudes we have about things, which we can express in words. You might for example love the feeling when you get into a warm bath when you're tired and cold, and you express that feeling by saying "Ahh" or "That's wonderful!" When you're watching a football game and the team you're rooting for scores a touchdown, and you say "Yay!" or something like that.

DEONTOLOGIST: *"Yay"*?

SUBJECTIVIST: Okay, "Awesome!" And there are also negative expressions:

when you groan when you stub your toe, or when you say "Oh no!" (or something less polite) when the team you're rooting for is scored against.

DEONTOLOGIST: What do you mean by 'attitude'?

SUBJECTIVIST: Well, it's basically a pro or con feeling.

DEONTOLOGIST: But when you say "Pistachio ice cream is delicious," aren't you telling people a fact, which is that you like pistachio ice cream? So isn't that sort of statement true or false, depending on whether or not you really like pistachio ice cream? And isn't "Awesome!" like telling people that you're happy your team scored, and "Oh no!" that you're unhappy the other one did? All these things are facts—facts, that is, about you. So these are true if the facts about you are as you say they are, and false if they aren't.

SUBJECTIVIST: I don't think so. Saying "Awesome!" is different from informing people that you're happy your team scored. The first one *expresses* an attitude, and the second one *informs people* that you have that attitude. It's complicated, though, because expressing an attitude can inform people too. Let me see if I can explain what I mean. You simply inform people that you like some ice cream by saying "I like this ice cream." Then what you say is true or false. It's true if you like that ice cream, but it's false if you're lying and you really don't like that ice cream. Its truth or falsity depends on the facts, in this case, the facts about what you like and don't, ice cream-wise. But when you say "Yum!" there's no question of truth or falsity. You're expressing your attitude, not stating that you have it. So when you say "Yum!" and you really do like that ice cream, then that doesn't make what you say true. It makes it, I guess, appropriate. If you say "Yum!" but you dislike that ice cream, then that doesn't make what you say false. It makes it insincere, like a fake smile. "Yum!" doesn't state a fact about the speaker.

DEONTOLOGIST: But doesn't "Yum!" state a fact about the ice cream? Isn't it the same thing as stating that the ice cream is delicious?

SUBJECTIVIST: In a way you might want to say that they're the same, because saying "This ice cream is delicious" can be another way to express one's approval of the taste. But there's no question of truth or falsity here as far as facts about the ice cream are concerned either. If I say, "Yum!" about, say, pistachio ice cream, and you say "Yuck!" expressing your dislike, it's not as if one of us is correct and one incorrect. There are no facts about pistachio ice cream that make what one of us said true, and what the other one said false. Pistachio ice cream in itself is neither really delicious nor yucky. It's just that some people like it and some people don't. People who like it appropriately say "Yum!" (or, what amounts to the same thing, "This ice cream is delicious!") and people who don't appropriately say "Yuck" (or "This ice cream tastes terrible!") and that's all there is to it. Nobody's said anything true or false. They're just expressing their approval or disapproval of the taste of pistachio ice cream.

DEONTOLOGIST: Okay, I think I get what you mean by an expression of an attitude, as opposed to a statement that might be true or false. Where do you think that morality fits into this?

SUBJECTIVIST: I think that when somebody says, "Giving money to charity is a morally good thing to do," or "Torturing little children is wrong," what they're doing is expressing attitudes, positive in the first case and negative in the second. It's just like saying "Giving money to charity: awesome!" and "Torturing little children: oh no!" This idea—that when you're talking ethical value you're expressing an attitude, not making a factual claim—is called *emotivism*.

DEONTOLOGIST: So according to you, when somebody says that something is morally right or wrong, they're merely expressing an attitude toward it, they're not stating any facts?

SUBJECTIVIST: That's right.

DEONTOLOGIST: But look, here's an important difference between moral statements and expressions of attitude. Suppose I say "Pistachio ice cream is yucky" and you say "Pistachio ice cream is not yucky." I agree that we're doing nothing but stating our own attitudes toward pistachio ice cream ...

SUBJECTIVIST: No, *expressing* our own attitudes.

DEONTOLOGIST: Okay, okay. It's just like saying "Yum!" and "Yuck!" But you think that moral statements are also nothing but the expression of the speaker's attitudes. So if I say "Abortion is wrong" and you say "Abortion is not wrong," then according to you we're just expressing our attitudes. But I think there's a difference between the two cases. In the ice cream case there's no conflict. I've got my tastes, and you've got yours, and that's all there is to it. But in the abortion case, there's genuine *disagreement*—there's a question about which of us is correct, and both of us can't be. It's just like if I said, "Baltimore is south of Philadelphia," and you said "No it isn't."

SUBJECTIVIST: You're right that expression of contrary moral feelings involves a certain sort of disagreement in a way that expression of different tastes in ice cream doesn't. But I don't think it's disagreement about the facts. The difference between moral attitudes and tastes is that when we have moral attitudes, we're not content with the idea that I've got my feelings and you've got yours, and that's all there is to it. I hate pistachio ice cream, and you don't, and neither of us is bothered that the other person feels different about the stuff—that's the end of the matter. But when I feel moral disapproval toward something, it's important for me that you feel that way too—that everyone feel that way. It's important because moral attitudes result in actions. For example, if I feel moral disapproval for abortion, then I don't want to have any part in any abortion myself, of course, but I don't want anyone else to either. So when I express my moral disapproval of abortion, and you say that you feel it's okay, we're advocating incompatible policies: you're advocating that abortions be performed, and I'm advocating that they not be. It's like the case in which we're trying to decide on what movie we should both go to. If you like the idea of one movie, and I like another, you say, "Let's go to *this* movie!" and I say, "No, let's go to *that* movie!" We're urging incompatible policies for action, but we're not disagreeing about the facts.

DEONTOLOGIST: So you think that making a moral statement is a combination of expressing an attitude and inviting other people to feel the same way, or at least, to act the way you approve of?

SUBJECTIVIST: Yes, something like that. I've been advocating not just emotivism, which emphasizes the attitude-expression function of ethical talk, but also *prescriptivism*, which emphasizes the function of prescribing feelings or actions to others. So if I say, "Abortion is wrong" I'm not only expressing my attitude, but I'm encouraging you to feel that way too, urging a general policy that abortion be prohibited, contrary to your wishes. That's where the conflict can come in.

DEONTOLOGIST: But you think that, just as in a matter of taste, it's not the case that one of us has the correct attitude, or a true moral belief, and the other one the incorrect attitude, or a false moral belief?

SUBJECTIVIST: Right, I think there's no truth or falsity, correctness or incorrectness, when it comes to morality.

DEONTOLOGIST: I have a real problem with your position. It seems really obvious to me that there are moral truths—that some moral views are mistaken, and some correct.

SUBJECTIVIST: Your view is called *ethical objectivism*, because it thinks that there are objective ethical facts that you can say correct or incorrect things about. UTILITARIAN over there is also an ethical objectivist. My view is called *ethical subjectivism*.

DEONTOLOGIST: Look, here's an objection to subjectivism. If ethics were all just a matter of taste, then there'd be no possibility of rational discussion where there's a disagreement. If you like pistachio ice cream and I don't, there's nothing to be said about it. But when people have moral disagreements, there can be genuine debate. And sometimes new evidence can give you a good reason to think that your moral view was mistaken.

SUBJECTIVIST: I agree that some moral views can be mistaken, in the sense that they're based on false factual beliefs. Here is an example. Some people used to think that it was morally wrong to put fluoridation into the public water supply, because they thought that the fluorides would cause big health problems. They were wrong about the facts, and so they had mistaken moral beliefs in that sense. But it's possible for two people to disagree morally even though they both agree about all the relevant facts. I think the abortion debate is an example of this. In that case, I'd say that the moral views are "mistaken" which disagree with mine, but I wouldn't say that what they say is *false*.

DEONTOLOGIST: So when do you think that rational debate about ethics is possible?

SUBJECTIVIST: When there are relevant facts that there's disagreement about. Maybe one person doesn't know the real facts about the act they're talking about. For example, suppose Jane spent the afternoon with Jim in the park, breaking a promise to pick someone up at the airport. Jim doesn't know that she had made that promise, so he thought there was nothing wrong with Jane's spending the afternoon with him, even though he thinks that promises should be kept. So you can convince Jim that he was mistaken in thinking that Jane did nothing wrong by spending the afternoon in the park, by revealing a fact to him: that she had promised to pick someone up at the airport that afternoon. In this case, factual information changes Jim's evaluation, because it shows him the real factual nature of what he's reacting to. In this case, you and Jim have a rational discussion about your initial ethical disagreement, and you rationally convince Jim that his initial reaction was a mistake. But that's only because there was a difference in the relevant factual beliefs that you could settle. Notice, however, that this depended on underlying moral principles that are not subject to debate. Jim disapproves of breaking promises, and this is never debated. In just the same way as this, rational debate might be useful about an ice cream reaction. Jim's served a plate of ice cream, and says, "Yuck!" thinking that it's pistachio ice cream in the plate. You inform him that it's actually mint ice cream, and Jim, who loves mint ice cream, says, "I was wrong. Yum!" But there's no real debate about tastes in ice cream here. Basic subjective preferences can't be debated.

DEONTOLOGIST: Well, I agree one person might be wrong about an ethical view because of a mistake about ordinary factual matters, or because of incomplete information about those matters, but I also think that someone might be wrong because they have the *ethical* facts wrong. I mean, two people might agree on all the ordinary facts, but one of them might think that there's nothing wrong with lying, and that person is mistaken, but not about ordinary factual matters. That person has a false *ethical* belief.

UTILITARIAN: I agree with DEONTOLOGIST that there are ethical facts, and that somebody might have a false ethical belief.

13. The Weirdness of Ethical Characteristics

SUBJECTIVIST: One of the main reasons I doubt that there are ethical facts is that, for this to be true, there would have to be real, external ethical characteristics that things have.

DEONTOLOGIST: So what's wrong with that?

SUBJECTIVIST: That sort of characteristic would be really weird, like no other sort of characteristic we can think of. For one thing, when something X had the possession of the characteristic *goodness*, that would automatically tell everyone to pursue X, and would automatically motivate anyone who knew this fact to try to seek X. That's weird, isn't it? I mean, some fact about X is supposed to automatically motivate everyone to try to get X, no matter what that person's particular likes and dislikes happen to be. X would have you-gotta-get-this-ness built right into it.

DEONTOLOGIST: I agree that moral characteristics are different from other ones, in that they automatically motivate. That's what makes them *moral* characteristics. So what's the problem? I mean, every different type of characteristic has its own peculiarities. Visible characteristics alone can be seen. So what?

SUBJECTIVIST: Another way that ethical characteristics are weird has already been mentioned by SCEPTIC. How are we supposed to be aware that X has this characteristic? Our ordinary senses detect only physical characteristics: colour, shape, odour, smoothness, the fact that something is a chair and that something else is a cabbage. But goodness isn't something detected by the senses. So how in the world are we supposed to find out it's there? For these two reasons, it seems much better to think that there is no such external characteristic.

DEONTOLOGIST: Okay again—the presence of moral characteristics is not sensed in the usual way. But this again isn't so weird that it's impossible. Consider how we know mathematical truths, for example: we don't discover them using our senses either.

SUBJECTIVIST: Well how *do* we discover ethical truths? Or mathematical ones for that matter?

DEONTOLOGIST: As I said before, it's not through sense experience—it's by a kind of moral or intellectual intuition.[4]

SUBJECTIVIST: My third argument comes from the well-known fact that different people, especially from different cultures, have different ethical views. You wouldn't have such widespread disagreement if there were ethical facts there to be found out. We'd sooner or later discover these facts, and disagreement would gradually decrease.

DEONTOLOGIST: But there are disagreements that haven't gone away in all kinds of other areas, where we all admit that there are objective facts to be known about real external characteristics. For example, historians of the French Revolution disagree about what some of the historical facts were, but nobody doubts that there are facts there. Disagreement doesn't show that there are no objective facts to disagree about.

SUBJECTIVIST: Yes, but when historians or biologists or psychologists disagree, this is because they have inadequate evidence, and they've only got speculative hypotheses. But in the case of moral disagreement, that's not what's going on. Lack of evidence or inadequate or distorted perception doesn't seem to be the problem when there's moral disagreement. I think that the disagreement instead stems from people's different attitudes.

14. Relativism

RELATIVIST: I agree with SUBJECTIVIST that there aren't any objective moral facts, and that it follows that no moral view is either true or false. That is, true or false *period*. I'd prefer to say that a moral view might be *true for me*, but *false for you*. It's true or false relative to different people. It's just like this analogy: it doesn't make any sense to say that a certain pair of shoes is too small, *period*. It's too small relative to Fred, who has big feet, but it's not too small relative to Shawn, who has small feet.

---

4 In Conversation VI there will be a discussion of the claim that all knowledge comes from sense experience, and a consideration of the source of mathematical knowledge.

SUBJECTIVIST: I'm not sure about that way of speaking. "True for me but not for you" sounds odd to me. I'd think that if something is true, it would have to be true *period*. I think that a better way to express the position I guess we share is to say that moral statements are neither true nor false; and instead of saying that a moral statement is true for me but not for you, we could say that it expresses my feelings but not yours.

RELATIVIST: Maybe this is just disagreement about ways of speaking. But here's what I think is a genuine disagreement between us. I think that everyone's moral views deserve respect, and I don't think that you feel that way. As I see it, because there's nothing correct or incorrect about moral views, we're all entitled to our own moral views, and we all should do what we individually think is right, even when it disagrees with what other people think; nobody should go around forcing their own moral views on other people. Here's an example of the sort of thing I object to. Earlier on, when there were lots of colonial states in Africa and elsewhere, European missionaries tried to stamp out the customs and views of the local people. They tried to make them believe that some of their customs were immoral, and tried to stop them from doing things that were part of their native cultural traditions. These missionaries were not just being nasty: they really thought that they were doing the locals a favour, by getting them to change their views and practices into ones that were morally acceptable. The missionaries believed that they had the moral truth, so they were doing a good thing in eliminating mistaken moral beliefs. But now we see that sort of practice as a very bad thing. It's merely the imperialistic enforcement of the customs and preferences of the powerful on the cultures of the oppressed. Now that we know that there is no such thing as moral fact—and therefore no such thing as being correct or incorrect in one's moral beliefs—we wouldn't do that sort of thing.

DEONTOLOGIST: So, in other words, you think that we're entitled to our own moral views, and that we all should act on the basis of our own individual, personal morality?

RELATIVIST: Correct. Nobody has the right to try to force moral views on anybody else.

DEONTOLOGIST: So we don't have the right to try to make somebody else stop doing what we think is immoral but they don't?

RELATIVIST: That's right.

DEONTOLOGIST: So let's look at a really extreme example of this. This is a real-life, very troubling example. In certain non-western Islamic cultures, it's a long-standing tradition to perform a certain surgical operation on the external sexual organs of young girls. I won't go into the details here, beyond mentioning that the purpose of this is to make it unlikely for these girls to be sexually active before they're married, and to prevent them from enjoying sexual relations after marriage. So it prevents pre-marital sexual activity, and post-marital infidelity. Now, I think everyone here would agree that this custom treats women as mere possessions, denies them their rights, mutilates them, and removes a potential important source of gratification. It's really horrible. We're right to do what we can to make them stop doing it. This operation is illegal in my country, and when people from these cultures come to live here, they're forced not to practise this custom by law. I also think that it would be a good idea for pressure to be exerted on the countries that allow this practice, to make them prohibit it.

RELATIVIST: You should respect cultural differences.

DEONTOLOGIST: I do respect cultural differences. I mean, the Chinese think cheese is disgusting, and the Canadians think it's delicious. That's fine—nobody's inclined to force their views on the other group. But it's different when it's a matter of morality.

RELATIVIST: I don't think so. Even though I personally find that custom of operating on girls really abhorrent, I respect their acting on their own moral views. Nobody should enforce his or her own moral views on others.

SCEPTIC: But that's a moral view you just expressed, right?

RELATIVIST: When?

SCEPTIC: When you said that nobody should enforce his or her own views on others.

RELATIVIST: Okay, so?

SCEPTIC: So imagine that others think they *should* enforce their own views on others. (This isn't so hard to imagine: there are lots of people like this.) So do you think they're entitled to that view, and entitled to act according to it?

RELATIVIST: Um ...

SCEPTIC: Gotcha!

DEONTOLOGIST: Anyway, I think what's really wrong with your view is that according to you, moral commitments are merely a matter of individual taste, like preference for pistachio ice cream. That's absurd.

SUBJECTIVIST: I agree with DEONTOLOGIST that moral commitments aren't like taste in ice cream (although I disagree with DEONTOLOGIST's position that they are true or false judgements about external facts). I think that the difference between mere tastes and moral commitments is that there's no conflict when somebody has a different taste in ice cream from mine, but it's in the very nature of moral commitments that somebody who has a real moral feeling wants to get everyone else to feel that way too, and to act in accord with that feeling. How can you feel that somebody else is doing something genuinely wrong, but at the same time still not care that they're doing it?

DEONTOLOGIST: Wait a minute. I agree that RELATIVIST can't account for genuine moral disagreement, but I can't see how you, SUBJECTIVIST, can allow it in your theory either. If you don't think that there are moral facts, then how can you make sense of moral disagreement? If there aren't facts to get right or wrong, then wouldn't it all boil down to a matter of individual taste? Where do you come off trying to change somebody else's attitudes, if there's no question of correct or incorrect?

SUBJECTIVIST: Well, that's just the way things are. Sometimes we're perfectly happy to allow for different attitudes, and sometimes we aren't, when it's important to us that everyone feel and act the same way.

DEONTOLOGIST: Anyway, we both agree that RELATIVIST is mistaken. If you're unwilling to apply your preferences on what should and what shouldn't be done to others, if you're happy for others to act in any way they like, then those preferences are not really moral preferences at all. They're much more like taste in ice cream.

RELATIVIST: Okay, I agree that I understand moral preferences differently from you two, and that on my view they're more like matters of etiquette or taste. You appear to be taking morality a lot more seriously than I am, but maybe that's not the right thing to do. The advantage of my view is that it doesn't lead to forcing your own moral tastes on someone else, so it respects everyone's views. And it doesn't lead to imperialistic forcing of one culture's preferences on another. I'm the one who has genuine respect for other cultures.

Suggested Readings

(See the Notes on "Suggested Readings" sections, p. 17-18.)

The ancient philosopher most closely associated with Hedonism was Epicurus (c. 341-271 BC). There's no big book by him—just collections of smaller writings.

John Stuart Mill (1806-73) presents his views in *Utilitarianism*.

The Case of the Innocent Cave Explorer and other interesting examples are produced by Kai Nielsen in his article defending utilitarianism, "Traditional Morality and Utilitarianism." The article can be found in *Ethics: The Big Questions* edited by James Sterba.

Plato (427-347 BC) was certainly no relativist, but he presents a very good explanation and defence of that position (for later refutation) in the early chapters of *Republic*.

The place to look for the ethics of Immanuel Kant (1724-1804) is his *Foundations of the Metaphysics of Morals*. It's not an easy read.

A.J. Ayer (1910-89) was the champion of an extremely influential (for a while) form of ethical subjectivism. Read about his emotivism in *Language, Truth and Logic*.

CONVERSATION IV

Mind and Body

Participants: SCEPTIC • DUALIST • IDENTITY THEORIST •
ELIMINATIVIST • BEHAVIOURIST

1. Materialism

SCEPTIC: I think that the discussion about ethics we've just been having[1] is nonsense. There really isn't any such thing as ethics at all in the first place. Ethics tells you what you should or shouldn't do, but nobody has any real choice in anything, because we're all just really machines.[2]

DUALIST: Wait, hold on! There's an awful lot of debatable stuff built into what you just said, and it needs a great deal of explanation. First of all, why do you think we're really just machines?

SCEPTIC: Well ...

IDENTITY THEORIST: Okay, this is where I can help out. I'm a materialist, and we materialists think that human beings are machines, in the sense that all we are is physical objects: biological entities, which are made up of chemical substances, subject to all the laws of physics and chemistry as is everything else in the universe. So everything we do has regular material causes—physical and chemical ones.

SCEPTIC: I thought that that word 'materialist' meant someone who cares only about making money and owning things.

IDENTITY THEORIST: That's what the word means in ordinary talk, but philosophically speaking, it's the position that everything there is, including human beings, is material—that is, is made out of the same sort of physical stuff, and subject to the same sort of laws of cause and effect. We're also sometimes called *physicalists*.

DUALIST: So you really deny the existence of non-physical things, like minds, thoughts, and feelings, memories and desires and decisions?

---

1 Conversation III.
2 This Conversation considers the claim that we're "machines" in some sense. Conversation V discusses whether this has any implications for the possibility of real choice.

IDENTITY THEORIST: Well, some materialists go so far as to deny the existence of all of these things, but I think that all of them exist.

DUALIST: But you just said that you think that physical things are all that there is.

IDENTITY THEORIST: Right, I think that minds, thoughts, and feelings are all physical. I think that the mind is just the brain, and that thoughts and feelings and the rest of those "mental" items are just physical things happening in the physical brain.

DUALIST: Well, that sounds completely wrong to me, and I have all sorts of objections to it that you'll have to answer. But first, do you have any arguments in favour of that position?

2. The Science Argument

IDENTITY THEORIST: Okay, first of all, consider the general direction that our understanding of the world has taken through history. Primitive people thought of the world as governed by spirits, gods, ghosts, and other non-material entities, who made things happen because of their desires or feelings. They thought that volcanoes erupted because the gods were angry, for example. But by the time of the ancient Greeks, a different way of seeing the world was emerging, in terms of physical objects, pushes and pulls, things hooking together or falling apart. This sort of material science took off during the scientific revolution, starting around the second half of the 1500s, and advancing with great strides by lots of scientists including Galileo, in the late 1600s and Newton in the early 1700s. Of course, science has continued to develop, at an ever-increasing rate. The progress of science consists in its discovery of material explanations for what goes on.

DUALIST: I remember in an earlier discussion ATHEIST mentioned this historical trend.[3] I didn't think that this historical trend showed that atheism is correct, and I don't think that the truth of materialism follows either. I agree that, historically, materialism has gained a good deal of ground, but I don't think that shows that it gets us closer to the true nature of everything in the world.

IDENTITY THEORIST: I think it does, and what shows this is that materialist—physical—science has been successful where earlier views failed. Physical

---

3 Conversation I.

science really does explain the world successfully. Once geologists understand the physical causes of volcanoes, for example, they're much better able to predict eruptions. Earlier primitive explanations involving angry gods were hopeless—completely useless at prediction. People used to think of comets as some sort of divine sign in the heavens, and hadn't any notion at all about when a particular comet would reappear, but Newton's way of thinking, involving paths of bodies with various masses through gravitational fields, produced good predictions of comets, for the first time, and eventually vastly improved predictive ability all over astronomy and in many other areas. Physical science also for the first time allowed real control over nature—not over volcanoes and comets, but to a very large extent over diseases, crop failures, and all sorts of other things. So the scientific revolution—the *materialist* revolution—wasn't just a different way of thinking about things. It was a better way of thinking about them. And whenever we have a more successful way of thinking, better in terms of prediction, control, and explanation, then we're justified in thinking that we're getting closer in touch with the way the world really is.

DUALIST: Okay, again I can agree that physical science is an improvement when it comes to volcanoes and crop failures and so on, but that doesn't necessarily mean that it applies as well to human minds, decisions, thoughts, memories, and feelings. I mean, isn't it true that materialistic science hasn't had anywhere near the success you talk about when it comes to explaining human beings?

IDENTITY THEORIST: Right, I agree it hasn't. That's because human mental goings-on are more complicated than the eruptions of volcanoes or the paths of comets.

DUALIST: Well, I think it's because human mental goings-on aren't physical at all, so materialistic science can never really explain, predict, or control it! I guess we've reached a stalemate here, haven't we?

IDENTITY THEORIST: No, not really. While materialistic science hasn't done very well yet in the realm of human mental phenomena, it nevertheless has made some real progress. What's going on in the brain is not a total mystery. Some of the broad outlines of the physical nature of mental processes have been known for a long time.

DUALIST: Really? For example?

IDENTITY THEORIST: Everyone has known for centuries, for instance, that getting banged hard on your head can give you amnesia. This shows that memories are somehow stored in a physical configuration inside your head, so that hitting your head can jiggle things around inside there sufficiently to destroy them. It's also been known for a long time that various sorts of brain injury or brain tumour or blood clot on the brain can result, in systematic ways, in various mental disabilities. Some really important twentieth-century work on the physical nature of the mental was done by a brain surgeon, Wilder Penfield, working at the Montréal Neurological Institute during the 1950s. Penfield was trying to locate places in the brain where surgery could cure or improve epilepsy. He was partly successful in doing this, but more importantly, he also found brain locations where electrical stimulation produced distinct memories. Stimulation in a different area of the brain caused the patient to hear a familiar song so clearly that the patient thought it was being played in the operating room. And in another area, the patient experienced the smell of burnt toast. A different area produced a strong emotion. From this data, Penfield gradually produced a detailed mapping of many of the mental functions of the brain. (By the way, I think it's interesting that Penfield's personal motivation here, in addition to his desire to advance medical science and neurophysiology, was that he wanted to discover a physical basis for the human soul!)

DUALIST: How did he know what brain areas connected with what memories or smells or whatnot?

IDENTITY THEORIST: He stuck a little wire in some area, and gave it a tiny electrical shock, and the patient reported what he or she experienced.

DUALIST: You mean, the patient was *awake* during the brain surgery?

IDENTITY THEORIST: Right! There are no pain receptors in the brain. All you need for brain surgery is local anaesthetic, so you can cut through the scalp and the skull bone.

DUALIST: Ugh, I don't want to think about that!

IDENTITY THEORIST: Me neither! Anyway, lots more has been done since then. They now have ways of measuring electrical activity in the brain without surgery, and they can see in general terms what's going on when the person has various thoughts, emotions, memories, decisions, and so on. What they're discovering is the real physical nature of all these mental goings-on.

DUALIST: But there's still a great deal they don't know, isn't there?

IDENTITY THEORIST: Yes there is, but we materialists believe that science will continue to progress, and that some day the materialistic science of the mind will be as thoroughly successful as the other materialistic sciences.

DUALIST: Well, look, I don't want to quarrel with the idea that science has made some progress, and it seems reasonable to think that the progress will continue. But I don't think that those facts really support your position. Suppose, for example, that some day they get a really clear idea of exactly what's happening in the brain whenever people remember their last birthday, or feel thirsty or angry, or believe that Moose Jaw is in Saskatchewan, or whatever. What they'd have discovered is just what *goes along* with all these mental items, not what these mental items really *are*. It's just a correlation.

IDENTITY THEORIST: Wait, what exactly do you mean by 'correlation'?

DUALIST: I mean that they always go together. For example, thunder and lightning are correlated: when you get one, you get the other. Similarly, I wouldn't be surprised if it turned out that whenever you get a mental event of a certain sort, you also get a physical brain event of a particular kind. But two things that are correlated are *two* things, not one. Thunder isn't lightning: it just accompanies it. I'd say that what Penfield and others discovered, and what future brain physiologists will continue to find out, is that particular kinds of mental event are always *accompanied by* particular kinds of brain event. So, for example, what you were just talking about—the association of brain damage and memory loss—is just that: an association, a correlation. And what Penfield discovered was that a certain sort of brain activity is correlated with a particular mental event like having a sensation or remembering something. But the brain activity is one thing, the mental event is another.

IDENTITY THEORIST: No, I think that scientific progress of this sort really would show that we've just got one thing here, and that the physical brain event is really what the mental event *is*. In philosophical talk, we'd have discovered that the brain event and the mental event are *identical*.

DUALIST: "Identical" in what sense?

IDENTITY THEORIST: In the sense that when two things are identical, then there's actually just one thing, referred to in two different ways. For example, Chicago is identical to the largest city in the Midwest. There's only one thing here, referred to in two different ways. In that sense, I think that what brain science is on its way toward showing is that mental events are identical with brain events. That's why the materialist view I've been arguing for is sometimes called the *mind-body identity theory*.

DUALIST: Okay, but what makes you say that brain science gives evidence for this identity theory? I think what it shows is just what kinds of correlations there are between distinct, non-identical things.

IDENTITY THEORIST: Well, your mentioning of lightning just before reminded me of a good example of the discovery of identity. Lightning is a case in which scientific information gave the real physical nature of an observed phenomenon—discovered a physical event that was identical with lightning, not just correlated with it. For a long time, nobody knew what lightning was, although everyone could see it. Ben Franklin suspected that lightning was actually electrical discharge, just a much bigger version of the spark you get when you shuffle across a rug and touch a doorknob. So he proposed an experiment of flying a kite into a cloud, with an electricity-detector at the bottom of the kite string. The experiment would show that his suspicion was right. (Some historians now doubt that he really did this experiment, but never mind.) The point here is that what scientists soon came to accept was not that lightning and electrical discharge were correlated—that whenever you get one you also get the other. Rather their observations and experiments showed that lightning *is* electrical discharge: that lightning and this sort of large-scale electrical discharge are identical. That's what science discovers: the real nature of things: what ordinary things are identical with.

DUALIST: Okay, that's what they discovered in this case, but consider another scientific discovery. Louis Pasteur studied the process of fermentation that converted grape juice into wine, and found that micro-organisms were always present when fermentation was taking place. But this isn't the discovery of an identity. Micro-organisms are correlated with fermentation: whenever there's fermentation, there are micro-organisms. But they aren't identical. Micro-organisms cause fermentation. They're two different things. This is analogous to what I think is happening in the brain or the mind. There are causal connections, but not identity. What Penfield showed was that a small electrical current in a particular part of the brain *caused* the person to have a memory. He didn't show that the electrical event in the brain *was* the memory.

IDENTITY THEORIST: Okay, sometimes correlation and causal connection, rather than identity, is what's discovered, but what science is really after is simplicity. When one kind of thing, or one set of laws, can do, there's no reason to have two sorts of things, or two sets of laws. This is an old principle of science, even of rational thought. It's sometimes called *Ockham's Razor*, named after William of Ockham, the medieval English philosopher who made it an important part of his philosophical technique. It tells us not to multiply the kinds of things we believe in, when it's not necessary. It is necessary to think of micro-organisms and fermentation as two different things, but it's not in the case of lightning and electrical discharge.

DUALIST: Well, I think it is necessary to have two different kinds of things in our theory of mind and body.

SCEPTIC: Your belief that there are two different kinds of things is what's behind the name 'DUALIST'?

DUALIST: Right, *dualism* means *two-ism*. My position is called that because it holds that there are two basically different kinds of stuff making up reality: the physical, and the mental. Materialism holds that there is only one kind of stuff, the physical (although certain varieties of physical things and goings-on are designated as mental). The version of dualism I'm talking about is sometimes called *Cartesian dualism*. 'Cartesian' is the adjective form of the name 'Descartes.' René Descartes was a very famous and influential French philosopher, mathematician and natural scientist, who died in 1650. He's considered the first important philosopher of the Modern era—the period that begins at the end of Medieval times. Descartes didn't invent dualism, but he presented his version of it clearly, convincingly, and systematically.

IDENTITY THEORIST: But wasn't it also Descartes who said that there's no position so absurd that you won't find some philosopher who took it?

DUALIST: No, it was Cicero.

IDENTITY THEORIST: Anyway, I guess that materialism could be thought of as *monism*—"one-ism."

DUALIST: Right again. There's another kind of monism, which agrees that there is only one kind of thing and process, but thinks that it's mental. Mental monism is sometimes also called *idealism* though here again the names are confusing, because 'idealism' means something quite different in ordinary talk. Anyway, that kind of idealism isn't a very popular position nowadays, so let's just ignore that one and talk about the differences between our views.

IDENTITY THEORIST: Okay, let's hear your arguments for dualism then.

3. Is Dualism Obvious?

DUALIST: Well, first of all, I think that the truth of dualism is just obvious. It's something that most philosophers, and most people in general, have believed throughout history.

IDENTITY THEORIST: Is that supposed to be an argument in its favour?

DUALIST: Yes, when something is obvious to everyone, that really does create a strong presumption of its truth, doesn't it? Dualism is really a common-sense position. People who have never studied philosophy, who have never heard a word about the debate, think it's true. You'll hear people talk about their mind on the one hand, and their body on the other. All ordinary people—I mean non-philosophers!—think that the mind is different from the body, and that each can influence the other—that they're related to one another by cause and effect.

IDENTITY THEORIST: That argument doesn't seem to me to be much good. Look, I agree that it makes sense to talk about the mental on the one hand, and the physical on the other, because I think that there are some things that are mental, like thoughts and feelings, and some things that are (purely) physical, like ships and shoes. But I think that mental things are a variety of physical thing.

DUALIST: Well, I think that's where you'd find ordinary people disagreeing with you.

IDENTITY THEORIST: I don't know about that. For example, imagine asking people to point to the place where they just had a thought. I'd bet that almost everyone would point to their head. What they're pointing at is their brain. That's where people think thoughts happen. And, of course, what's going on in a brain is a physical process, involving electricity and chemicals.

DUALIST: But on the other hand, lots of people think that there's a mind that can survive death, when all the physical parts of a human have stopped working. So they must be thinking about the mind as non-physical.

IDENTITY THEORIST: Anyway, I don't see what relevance any of this has. Even if it were the case that ordinary people who have had no philosophical training are dualists, that doesn't provide any good argument in favour of that position. Lots of ordinary people believe all sorts of false unscientific things, like astrology, "alternative" medicine, visitations of aliens from outer space, and on and on. What we need is some good arguments.

4. The Differences Between the Mental and the Physical

DUALIST: All right. A good reason why we should think of mind and body—the mental and the physical—as two separate things is this: there are certain kinds of characteristics that might be true of one sort of thing but cannot be true of the other. Take size, for example. Every physical object has some size or other—it's got physical dimensions. We know in advance that if anything is physical, it has to have some dimensions. If something has no dimensions, then it can't be physical. Now consider some memory you have—for example, your memory of what you had for breakfast this morning. What size is that memory? Is it 10 centimetres wide, or bigger or smaller? It's none of the above. That thing has no physical size at all. Another physical characteristic—something every physical thing has, and has to have, is location. Think about what you had for breakfast this morning. Now where is that thought?

IDENTITY THEORIST: I agree that every physical thing has to have dimensions and a location, but I think that a memory does in fact have dimensions and a location. It's a process going on in your brain, so it must be about 15 centimetres wide or less. And it does have a location, as I've already mentioned: it's inside your head.

DUALIST: That can't be right.

IDENTITY THEORIST: Why not? How do you know?

DUALIST: The reason why not is because I know that it doesn't make any sense to assign a mental event any size or location. Asking about this is just like asking where last Thursday is located now, or how many centimetres wide it was. It's not that we don't know the answers to those questions: it's that we know that there can't be any answers, that they're nonsense questions to start off with.

IDENTITY THEORIST: I don't think so. I think it makes good sense to ask about the physical location of mental events, and about their size. But suppose you're right, and people don't even know what you're asking—they think that it's nonsense to ask. That might just be because they don't know enough about science; they're still stuck in primitive thought, and the idea that there might be a physical nature to the mental is so foreign to them that they think that it's nonsense to ask about the physical characteristics of a mental event, or to suggest an answer.

DUALIST: Every physical object has some colour or other. What colour is your mind?

IDENTITY THEORIST: My mind is my brain. My brain is coloured a sort of greyish-white. So that's what colour my mind is.

DUALIST: No, that can't be. Minds don't have colours.

IDENTITY THEORIST: Well, I don't think it's nonsense.

DUALIST: I know what mental things like memories and desires and beliefs and hopes and emotions are like, and I can tell that they're not physical things. I mean, for example, if you ask me what my last birthday party was like, and I try to remember, I don't go searching around in my brain for some sort of electrical circuit.

IDENTITY THEORIST: I think that's exactly what you do.

DUALIST: To find an electrical circuit you'd need one of those meters electricians use, or something like that. I really don't know exactly how to go about searching for an electrical circuit. But I have a perfectly good idea how to search for a memory. And I know that it doesn't involve any electrical apparatus.

IDENTITY THEORIST: I think that there might be two ways of searching for a memory. One would be the way you do it. Another way would be the way Dr. Penfield might have done it, with electrical apparatus.

DUALIST: But even if I could get access to my brain somehow and measure the electric circuits there, I wouldn't have any idea which one of them was a representation of my last birthday party.

IDENTITY THEORIST: But when you discover that you do remember your last birthday party, what makes you so sure that what you've discovered wasn't really a brain circuit?

DUALIST: I can just tell it isn't. I'm perfectly clearly aware of what a memory is like.

IDENTITY THEORIST: But science often discovers that the real nature of something is nothing at all like what it seems to people. For example, it was once obvious to everyone that the earth was flat and unmoving, but science tells us otherwise. Rocks are obviously dense, solid, and stable, but science has discovered that they're really composed almost entirely of empty space, with a lot of very tiny particles in it—electrons and protons and so on, either jiggling rapidly in place or whizzing around in tiny circles at incredible speed.

5. Introspection and Infallibility

DUALIST: I know what the real nature of my mental items is. It's perfectly clear to me that they're not physical.

IDENTITY THEORIST: What makes you so sure? Maybe you're wrong. I mean, it took scientists centuries to begin to have any notion of the physical basis of the mental, so it's not obvious at all what this physical basis is.

And they're just beginning to find out the complicated and deeply hidden facts about this. So what makes you so confident about these matters?

DUALIST: Because mental things are clearly available for my inspection, and I'm able to find out about them perfectly easily, and without any possibility of mistake. So whatever those scientists are just beginning to find out, it can't be the facts about mental things.

IDENTITY THEORIST: How do you think you find out what mental things are like?

DUALIST: Well, it's completely obvious, though hard to describe. When I have a memory or desire or belief or hope or emotion, all I have to do is to pay attention to it, and I can see exactly what it's like.

IDENTITY THEORIST: You don't literally see what it's like, with your eyes.

DUALIST: No, not with my eyes. I only see physical things with my eyes. That's why it's hard to describe mental self-awareness. I'm just aware of what it's like, without having to use any of my physical senses. It's as if there were some sort of inner sense, giving me awareness of what's going on in my mind. Philosophers call this sort of inward sense *introspection*, which means, *looking inward*, but of course it's not literally looking. So for instance I can tell instantly and without possibility of error whether or not I'm remembering now what I had for breakfast, or I'm desiring some lunch, or I believe that it's past noon, or I hope that there's something in the fridge to eat, or I have a headache, or I'm angry or happy or sad or whatever. All these mental things are available for my awareness by introspection.

IDENTITY THEORIST: Hmm, I don't know about that. It's not clear to me that all mental things are available for instant knowledge by the person who has them. For example, when you think that you remember having Sugar-ohs for breakfast yesterday, you might be mistaken. Maybe you had Sugar-ohs the day before yesterday, and you just remember wrong. Or maybe I ask you what you had for breakfast yesterday, and you try to remember, but you draw a blank, and you think you just can't remember, but then when you go into the kitchen, it suddenly comes back to you. It turns out that that memory was actually stored in your mind all along— it's just that you couldn't get at it just then when you were asked.

DUALIST: Sure, of course I agree that memory is imperfect in both of those ways, and more. When I claim that introspection reveals things fully and infallibly I'm not saying that the memories we introspect are always correct. What I'm saying is that if you have a memory image—whether it's accurate or inaccurate—of having Sugar-ohs for breakfast yesterday, then you must be aware that you have that image, and of what that image is like.

IDENTITY THEORIST: But suppose that it's not an image of having Sugar-ohs, but rather in fact an image of having Shreadlets?

DUALIST: I already agreed that you might have a memory image that's mistaken, in this case because you seem to remember having Sugar-ohs but in fact you had Shreadlets.

IDENTITY THEORIST: No, that's not what I'm saying. I'm saying you might be wrong about the memory image you're having *now*. Never mind what you actually had for breakfast: maybe you now have what you think is a memory image of having Sugar-ohs, but in fact that image now represents your having Shreadlets.

DUALIST: Well, whatever I in fact had this morning that's responsible for the memory image I have now, at least it's perfectly clear to me what this image is like. Look, here's an analogy. Think of a memory image as a photograph. If it's a blurry faded photograph, then you might be mistaken about what it's a photograph of. But if you're looking at it under good light, when you're wearing your reading glasses you can very clearly see what the photograph itself is like.

IDENTITY THEORIST: Okay, never mind memory; let's look at a different example. Suppose I think that something has made you angry, and I ask you if you are. Your introspection does not discover any anger, but in fact you are angry—you just don't recognize it in yourself. Or else, your introspection tells you that you're feeling sad, but you're mistaken about that: you're actually feeling angry.

DUALIST: I don't think that's possible.

IDENTITY THEORIST: I do. Suppose I see you striding around frowning, muttering to yourself, and slamming doors. It's absolutely clear that you're angry. But you don't think you are.

DUALIST: If I don't think I am, then I'm not, despite my behaviour. If I'm really angry, then I know it. If my introspection doesn't reveal anger, then there can't be any there.

IDENTITY THEORIST: Well, I guess we just have to disagree about that.

DUALIST: But that's an important point, because it's connected to a central argument for dualism, against materialism. Imagine that brain science progresses to the point that they've discovered what they take to be the exact physical basis of anger in the brain—that is, which brain states are associated with which mental states. And suppose that they've got a simple way of telling from the outside what's going on in brains without having to cut them open—imagine that there's a brainometer, a data-collecting thing worn on the head like a hat, wired to a computer which analyzes the data and tells scientists exactly what's happening. Now suppose that the computer screen says that Fred's having the brain event that scientists have associated with anger, but Fred's introspection doesn't reveal any anger to him. According to you, when that brain event is there, Fred really is angry—because anger just is that brain event. But what this really would show is that what the scientists thought was wrong: that brain state wasn't in fact always associated with anger. Whatever the scientists have discovered, and whatever the brainometer shows on this occasion, Fred's not angry. It wouldn't matter what's going on in his brain. If he doesn't have that inner anger experience, which he discovers through introspection, he's not angry, and that's all there is to it. That's because anger is an inner experience, it's not a brain event. Even if it happens to be associated 100 per cent of the time with a particular brain event, and the brainometer reveals that anger-brain-event when and only when people introspect anger, still that brain event is only associated with anger—it isn't the anger itself.

IDENTITY THEORIST: You're right at least in seeing that this is an important difference between our positions. I think that if scientists find an extremely high correlation between a reading on the brainometer and reported anger, then that would show that the brain event is anger, and at that point, if Fred had that brain event but didn't introspect anger, or did introspect anger when the brainometer didn't show that brain event, then we'd think that Fred's introspection was mistaken.

6. Recognizing the Mental vs. Recognizing the Physical

DUALIST: Look, here's an argument in favour of dualism. I know perfectly well when I'm feeling tired, or experiencing the smell of burnt toast, or remembering my last birthday party, or wishing it were the weekend, or doing any other sort of mental activity. But I haven't any idea at all of what's going on in my brain. How could any of these mental events actually be brain activity? But to the extent that I can picture brain activity, it's clear to me that it's completely different from my mental states.

IDENTITY THEORIST: So your argument is: I can recognize X perfectly well, but I haven't any idea about Y; so X can't be Y.

DUALIST: Right.

IDENTITY THEORIST: Okay, let me ask you a question. Have you eaten any of this chemical today: CH_3COOH?

DUALIST: Jeez, I hope not. I try to avoid eating chemicals. I really don't know.

IDENTITY THEORIST: Maybe it would help you answer my question if you knew that this is the chemical formula for acetic acid.

DUALIST: That doesn't help. I wouldn't know a bathtub full of acetic acid if I fell right into it.

IDENTITY THEORIST: Yes you would. Acetic acid, CH_3COOH, is just pure vinegar. You have no trouble recognizing vinegar. In fact, when we were at lunch earlier, I saw you pick up a bottle of it and put some on your French fries. So this is an example in which you have no trouble recognizing X—vinegar—but haven't the faintest idea about Y—CH_3COOH— even though vinegar is identical with CH_3COOH.

DUALIST: But how about the fact that insofar as I can understand or picture brain states, they seem to me to be completely different from mental states? I mean, if somebody showed me the inside of a brain, I wouldn't have the slightest tendency to think I was seeing a mental state. If they were really identical, wouldn't I know it?

IDENTITY THEORIST: No, not necessarily. The identity of X and Y doesn't imply that someone who recognized something as X would also recognize it as Y. Here's a story to illustrate that. Imagine that somebody's favourite singer is Snoop Dogg. She wishes that some day she might meet the guy. She discusses this with her next-door neighbour, a guy named Calvin Broadus. What she doesn't know is that 'Snoop Dogg' is Calvin Broadus's stage name; her neighbour *is* Mr. Dogg. She thinks of Broadus and Dogg entirely differently. She recognizes him next door as Broadus, and on movie videos as Dogg. She would of course deny that they are the same guy. And yet, they're identical.

DUALIST: Well, here's another slant on my argument, a clever version produced by Thomas Nagel, a contemporary American philosopher. Nagel invites readers to try to imagine what it's like to be a bat. This task involves special difficulties, much more than in trying to imagine what it's like to be your mother, or the President of the US, or an Ancient Greek, or a cave man or your pet dog for that matter. Most bats experience the world almost entirely by echo location: they emit very high-pitched shrieks, and the echoes of these noises are very subtly modified by the location, speed, size, shape, and even texture of the objects they bounce off. Their brains analyze these echoes, and they're able to get information about the world comparable to what we get by seeing. Bats, being mammals, no doubt have conscious experiences, but Nagel invites us to try to imagine what these experiences are like—what it's like for a bat to be a bat. He argues that their form of life is so alien to ours that we can't even begin to imagine what their inner experience is like.

IDENTITY THEORIST: Okay, what if I agree so far?

DUALIST: But scientists have already gone a good distance in finding out the physical facts about bats. Some day they'll no doubt have a pretty thorough picture of how their brains and sensory apparatus work. But all this information gives us absolutely no information about what the inner life of the bat is like, which would remain a mystery.

IDENTITY THEORIST: Aha, I see where this is leading. So we're supposed to conclude that inner experience is something quite distinct from physical goings-on.

DUALIST: Right.

IDENTITY THEORIST: Well, I don't accept that conclusion. I agree that scientific information may never give us insight into what it's like for a bat to be a bat—that is, into how it feels to be a bat when you are a bat—the view of batness from the inside. It's obvious that the only way you can get information about how something seems from the inside is to *be* inside. But it doesn't follow at all that what is being observed from the inside is something different from what is being observed from the outside. Look, here's an analogy. Suppose one person looks at a strawberry, and then somebody else eats it without looking at it. One person senses the way the strawberry looks, while the other person senses the strawberry's taste. They're in contact with exactly the same thing—the strawberry—but in very different ways. This means that their experience of the same thing will be very different. It doesn't mean that there are two different strawberries. There's only one. Similarly, what's going on in a bat must seem extremely different when experienced from the inside, by the bat itself, and from the outside, by the bat scientist. It doesn't follow that they're different things. In the same way, what anger feels like to the angry person is really quite different from how it is revealed from the outside, by the brainometer. But it doesn't follow that the anger experienced by the person, and the brain state revealed to scientists by the brainometer, are two different things.

7. Interaction

IDENTITY THEORIST: Here's a reason why I think dualism is scientifically defective. You believe that mental states and body events are causally related, don't you?

DUALIST: What do you mean?

IDENTITY THEORIST: You believe that physical events sometimes cause mental events, and that mental events sometimes cause physical events?

DUALIST: Sure. An example of the first kind is when somebody physically steps on your physical toe. This causes a chain of physical events: the nerves in your toe give off electrical/chemical impulses that travel up your foot, your leg, and your spinal column, up to your brain. Some sort of brain state is set up as a result. And this eventuates in your mental feeling of pain.

IDENTITY THEORIST: So somewhere along the line, a physical event, maybe some sort of event in your brain, *causes* a mental event, a feeling, right?

DUALIST: Right. And it can go in the opposite direction too, when a mental event causes a physical event. For example, when I mentally decide to go get a drink of water, this mental event causes nerve impulses to travel through my brain, and that in turn causes other nerves to fire down my spine and into my legs, where they cause my leg muscles to contract to lift me up off my chair and walk into the kitchen, and so on.

IDENTITY THEORIST: But isn't the idea of mind/body causal interaction unscientific?

DUALIST: No, why?

IDENTITY THEORIST: We know now what causes electrical activity in neurons: they may be stimulated by physical pressure (the sensing neurons on the skin) or by light energy (the receptors in your eye), or by little bits of chemical released by other neurons or sensed by the receptors in your mouth or nose, and so on. These physical processes all need a physical cause.

DUALIST: I agree that there can be physical causes for activity in neurons, but what makes you think that every electrical change in a neuron has to have a physical cause? Why can't some of them have non-physical, mental causes?

IDENTITY THEORIST: Because there has to be some sort of physical change— application of physical energy—to start up any physical process. But in your view, sometimes electrical activity in neurons is caused by something entirely non-physical: a decision in your mind. This sort of non-physical causation is entirely rejected by science. I mean, you know from science what kinds of things are capable of causing an electric current to flow: you need a moving magnetic field, or a chemical reaction like what happens in a battery, or the application of an external charge, or some other input of physical energy. In general, for any sort of physical change to happen you have to have an input of physical energy. You can't have a physical change without a physical cause. This is a basic idea behind all science. You can't get those electrons moving in a neural circuit without some sort of physical energy input. And there's the same sort of problem the other way around. You imagine that, for example, physical brain activity can in certain cases result in non-physical mental activity, but how is that supposed to happen? Physical activity has effect only on things in certain locations, but mental events, you suppose, aren't located anywhere. And how is electrical activity (what scientists suppose is going on in activated brain cells) supposed to produce a change in something spiritual, non-material? We know how electrical activity can result in heat (in an electric heater) or light (in a light bulb) or motion (in an electric motor) or magnetism (in an electromagnet) or sound (in a speaker) and so on, but it's a complete mystery how it can result in changes in a non-material thing. This idea violates the basic principle of science called the *conservation of energy*. Whenever an energetic physical process causes something to happen, some of its energy is lost, because it's transformed into another physical form, as when electrical energy is transformed into heat or light, and so on. But it would violate the principle of conservation of energy if it disappeared from the physical world altogether.

DUALIST: Okay, I agree that the notion of mind/body interaction is a mystery as far as physical science is concerned. But that doesn't bother me. Physical science only deals with the realm of the physical. When it comes to the non-physical, it draws a blank. This is the way things should be. I mean, you wouldn't expect microbiology to explain economics, would you? They're interested in two very different things. Yet they do interact. For example, in the middle ages, the Black Plague—an event that had microbiological causes—had big economic effects. But that doesn't mean that we should expect microbiology to deal with this interaction.

IDENTITY THEORIST: But the Plague and its economic effects were both *physical* events!

DUALIST: Look, first of all, you're missing my point, which is that it's not a problem for dualism that physical science can't explain mind/body interaction. A science deals only with what's in its own realm, and can't explain interactions with phenomena outside its consideration. But secondly, I think the example of economics raises another important point. Economic changes are *social* phenomena, not physical ones. That shows that there are perfectly acceptable and ordinary examples of things that are not physical. Anyway, that principle you announced earlier, that every physical event has to have a physical cause, is just part of the materialist credo. You're supposed to prove it, not just announce that it's a principle. Scientists who believe it ought to be more open-minded—ought to have their beliefs formed by experience, not dictated by prejudice.

8. Eliminative Materialism

ELIMINATIVIST: I'd like to pose another difficulty for the identity theory. You're very sure that some day science will discover the physical nature of each kind of mental state. But suppose that scientists really get very thorough knowledge of our brains some day, but they find out that there's no one type of brain state corresponding to what we call a particular kind of mental state. Maybe there are two or more very different brain states corresponding to one kind of mental state.

IDENTITY THEORIST: How could this happen?

ELIMINATIVIST: Well, things like that have happened in scientific history. For example, at one time, they classified whales and dolphins together with mackerel and cod—all were considered fish. But some advances in biology showed that these were really two different kinds of thing—that the whales and dolphins should be classified with giraffes and cats instead, as mammals, and that the things they used to call fish were actually not one kind of thing at all. Their category of fish has no scientific basis. The same thing happened with the ordinary concept of sore throat: science has discovered that this is not one sort of thing, but rather two: a viral disease, and a bacterial, with different causes, different dangers, different treatments, and so on. What makes you so sure that the categories of mental things we all believe in now will correspond to the categories of some future brain science?

IDENTITY THEORIST: Well, I'm not sure. Maybe they won't.

ELIMINATIVIST: But if they discovered that there were two very different sorts of brain states associated with what we now call anger, wouldn't you have to conclude that anger doesn't exist?

IDENTITY THEORIST: I'm not sure about that either. Maybe the right conclusion would be that anger comes in two varieties, or as in the "fish" example, that some of the things we earlier called anger actually aren't anger.

ELIMINATIVIST: Okay, sometimes this happens, but sometimes what science shows is that an earlier categorization just has to be dropped.

DUALIST: I don't think that science could possibly show this about mental states. Whatever they discovered about correlations or lack of correlations between mental states and brain states, that wouldn't show anything about the reality of mental states or categories.

IDENTITY THEORIST: Do you, ELIMINATIVIST, really think that it's likely that advance in brain science will result in our dropping mental categories altogether?

ELIMINATIVIST: Yes, I think so. I think that current concepts—beliefs, desires, memories, emotions, pains, and so on—are really old-fashioned, pre-scientific ways of thinking about things, and the sorts of explanations of how people work that involve these concepts are pretty useless. When we do psychology using these concepts, we're essentially in the position they were in other areas before the Scientific Revolution. I believe that a revolution in psychology, which will be necessary to make it scientifically respectable, will involve throwing away all these useless concepts.

DUALIST: What a bizarre idea!

ELIMINATIVIST: Maybe it's not so bizarre. Some concepts that people used to think were useful in describing and explaining the world have been scientifically discredited, when they were shown not really to correspond to real categories. For example, people used to talk about witches, categorizing women who behaved in certain sorts of ways. But nowadays we know that this doesn't correspond to a category at all. Some of the people called witches were mentally ill; and some of the others were just unconventional or eccentric. So we don't now have an identity theory for witches: we haven't discovered the real basis for that sort of thing. It's rather that we've discovered that there isn't any such thing. The concept has disappeared because of the growth of knowledge. That's what eliminativists think will happen with mental concepts.

IDENTITY THEORIST: But you are a materialist, aren't you?

ELIMINATIVIST: Right, I agree with you that everything that exists is physical—that there is no separate category of things that are purely mental. (Philosophers often call my position *eliminative materialism*, indicating that it's a form of materialism too.) But I disagree with you about the status of the so-called mental objects: thoughts, feelings, memories, desires, beliefs, and so on. You think each of these things exist, and their real nature is physical. I think that none of these things exist.

IDENTITY THEORIST: Hah! It's interesting for me to find myself agreeing with DUALIST for a change! Okay, so suppose that science discovers that there are two very different sorts of brain states associated with what we now call 'anger.'

ELIMINATIVIST: Then I think that we'd decide that the word 'anger' didn't name one unified sort of thing at all, and that there was therefore no scientific basis for that concept; so the idea would just be discarded—people would stop believing that there was such a thing.

DUALIST: Well, my reaction would be quite different. I'd say that this discovery would show that neither sort of brain state was identical with anger, but that's no surprise, because I don't think *any* brain state is identical with anger.

ELIMINATIVIST: Consider what went on when science eliminated the concept of witches. One motivation for eliminating that concept was that the general theory the concept played a part in had almost no scientific value. I mean, nobody could predict who was going to be a witch, or what witches were likely to do, or how to prevent people from becoming witches, or how to stop them from being witches. The idea, and the general story that the idea was part of, had no value for prediction, control, or explanation. When more scientific concepts developed which actually had some success in these areas, then the concept of witch, and the whole story that went with it, were abandoned.

DUALIST: Right, but what's supposed to be the analogy with what we're talking about?

ELIMINATIVIST: How well is your theory of human behaviour working?

DUALIST: Theory? I don't have any theory.

ELIMINATIVIST: In one way of looking at it, you do. You've got a general story that tries to explain and predict what human beings do. There are several concepts that figure in that general story: *belief, desire, personality, memory, pain, awareness,* and so on. And you think that there are various true generalizations involving these concepts, for example, if someone desires X, and believes that doing Y will get him X, then he'll do Y. So your story to try to understand human behaviour has all the elements of any scientific theory. We eliminativists sometimes call that theory *Folk Psychology*—'Folk' because it's what just-folks (as contrasted with scientists) believe.

DUALIST: Okay, but are you saying that Folk Psychology can be expected to have a similar fate as the Theory of Witchcraft? That these concepts are just as useless for prediction, control, and explanation as the idea of witches was?

ELIMINATIVIST: Yes, that's the claim. Using Folk Psychology, we have almost no success predicting or controlling or explaining each other's behaviour, or our own. I mean, most of the time you can't guess what somebody's going to do next. And we have very little success in getting people to do something we want them to. Folk Psychology is a failure, and will disappear, along with all its concepts, just as soon as a physical science of behaviour becomes established—a science that gives us the physical brain causes of behaviour.

DUALIST: That doesn't sound likely to me at all. I think we do have some success in predicting, controlling, and understanding each other using Folk Psychology.

ELIMINATIVIST: Yes, but not much. Not enough to make Folk Psychology survive future scientific advance.

9. The Problem of Other Minds

IDENTITY THEORIST: Well, I'd like to change the subject at this point and raise another problem with dualism. Here's a consequence of dualism that is so ridiculous that it makes it entirely unbelievable. According to you, DUALIST, mental events are private—only the person who's having them can be aware of them directly. The only way you can know they're there is by observing them from the inside. If that's right then you know that your own mental events are happening, but nobody else does. And you don't know what anyone else's mental events are. In fact, you don't even know that anyone else has a mental life at all.

DUALIST: I don't see how that follows from my view. Of course I can tell that other people have a mental life, and sometimes, anyway, I can tell a lot about what's going on mentally in someone else. I can often tell when somebody is angry, or in pain, or when they remember something or believe something. I can tell from observing the way they act, or what they say.

IDENTITY THEORIST: But why do you think that what they say or how they act gives you any reason at all to conclude anything about their mental life? For example, consider why you think someone is angry. When somebody stomps around frowning and slamming doors you think they're angry, right?

DUALIST: Yes, of course.

IDENTITY THEORIST: It's not that person's anger itself you're observing though.

DUALIST: No, their anger is a mental state inside that person, and only that person can observe that, by introspection.

IDENTITY THEORIST: So why do you think that the person is angry?

DUALIST: Because the external behaviour that I can observe is a good sign of anger.

IDENTITY THEORIST: Why do you think so?

DUALIST: Well, it's just natural that that's the way angry people behave, isn't it?

IDENTITY THEORIST: Why do you think so? Look, in order to take something you see as evidence for something else you don't see, you have to have some reason to associate the two—you have to find out, for example, that the two happen together. You're justified in taking dark clouds as evidence that it's going to rain because lots of time when you see dark clouds, then a little later you see it's raining. The problem here is that you don't have this sort of association—*ever*—with other people's behaviour and their mental states, because you *never* see their mental states. For all you know, everyone else in the world is a zombie.

DUALIST: A *zombie*? Like in those terrible movies?

IDENTITY THEORIST: What I mean by a zombie is somebody who acts on the outside just like everyone else, but who doesn't have any mind. There's no consciousness there, no beliefs or desires or memories or anything else, no inner life. But outwardly, they're the same as everyone else. So the *Zombie Hypothesis* is that nobody else has any mental life inside; they just act normally on the outside. Do you have any reason at all to think that the Zombie Hypothesis is false? You would if you were justified in taking people's outside behaviour as evidence for an inner mental life. But you don't have that justification.

DUALIST: Well, maybe my reasons for taking that behaviour as evidence are not as bad as you make out. There's one person in whom I can observe both behaviour and mental states, and find out how they're connected. That person is me. I know that when I'm angry, I often stalk around frowning and slamming doors. So that's why I think that that behaviour in other people is evidence for anger in them.

IDENTITY THEORIST: No, I don't think that's good enough. You've only got that one case to go on.

DUALIST: What's wrong with that?

IDENTITY THEORIST: Well, here's an analogy. Suppose that you have a little box, just like little boxes everyone else has, but only you can look into your little box, and you can't look into anyone else's. You look in your little box, and there's a beetle inside. Is this good evidence—really any evidence at all—that everyone, or indeed anyone, has a beetle in his or her box too? No: one case isn't any useful evidence at all for what's going on in countless others. I mean, look at a practical instance. When professional pollsters want to find out something, they always ask hundreds of people. It's completely unacceptable to draw a general conclusion from evidence about just one person.

DUALIST: Okay, but look, I don't have to rely merely on other people's actions to tell me about their mental states. I can ask them what's going on, and they tell me. Of course, sometimes they might be reluctant to reveal their true inner selves to me, but I can be confident that they're trustworthy lots of times. And of course when they're asked, people displaying angry behaviour will usually tell you that they're angry.

IDENTITY THEORIST: But this isn't evidence either. There's a very subtle argument that says why. It's due to the twentieth-century philosopher Ludwig Wittgenstein, who invented the beetle-in-the-box analogy I gave just earlier. Wittgenstein points out that if the only use of the word 'beetle' in the language is its application by someone to what's in that person's own private box, then the word couldn't be counted on to have any shared meaning in the language. You might imagine that each person has something different, but they all happen to call it the same name. Or else that some boxes have constantly changing things in them, or that some are even empty. When the contents of the boxes are private, words used to refer to what's in them lose public meaning.

DUALIST: What's his point?

IDENTITY THEORIST: Wittgenstein meant this to be an analogy to the case in which we suppose that people can talk about—give names to—their mental states, thought of as private items. One can't conclude from what we call our private item that other people's use of that same name refers to the same private item in them. So if we're going to think of talk about mental states as being an informative part of the language, with uniform meaning from person to person, then we can't conceive of what's being talked about as private. So the point is that even what people say couldn't provide evidence they have an inner private mental life. What this all adds up to is that on the dualist view, there's no reason at all to think that anyone else has a mind. This is what philosophers call the *Problem of Other Minds*. If your position leads to unsolvable scepticism about the existence of other minds, then it's impossibly defective, and has to be rejected.

DUALIST: Okay, I see what you're driving at, but it still seems to me that you can call that thing you have in your own box anything you want, and that gives the word you use meaning.

IDENTITY THEORIST: Sure, you can use any word you want. Who's going to stop you? But the point is that if only you can see what's in there, then the name you give it doesn't have full-fledged meaning. Here's another way of making this point. Imagine you have an odd experience one day. You want to keep track of this experience, to see if it happens again, so you decide to call that experience 'E,' and you write down 'E' on the current page of your diary.

DUALIST: Okay, 'E' means that experience. Now when I have an experience like that again, I can check back in my diary to see when I got it earlier.

IDENTITY THEORIST: Suppose that the following week, you have an odd experience again, and you write down 'E' on the diary page for that day. The question is: have you got things right? I mean, is the experience you've just had another E? Or is it a different sort of experience, which should have a different name?

DUALIST: I dunno! You're making up the story! Is it or isn't it an E?

IDENTITY THEORIST: Compare this case with a more ordinary example of bird-identification. Suppose you're learning how to identify birds, and a bird expert tells you that the one you're looking at is a red-breasted nuthatch. Then the next time you see one you're tempted to call a red-breasted nuthatch, there are ways you can find out if you've identified that bird correctly. You can, for example, ask a bird expert, or look it up in a bird book. But you can't do any of those things to check whether you're right to call that second experience 'E.'

DUALIST: Well, I can think back really hard, and try to remember exactly what the experience was like the last time I wrote 'E,' to see if this one is just like it.

IDENTITY THEORIST: You can do that, but all that can result is your feeling that this experience is (or isn't) like the earlier one. There's no test of whether you're mistaken or correct. In fact, nothing really *counts* as your being right or wrong.

DUALIST: Why do you say that? I mean, isn't there a fact of the matter about whether I've got the word right or not?

IDENTITY THEORIST: No, because you've made that word up. There is no test for whether that word is used correctly or not. And when there isn't any standard for really correct usage of a word, then that word doesn't have any real meaning. The problem here is that you're trying to establish what Wittgenstein calls a *private language*, but that's impossible. I mean, you can write down anything you like, but what you write down doesn't have real meaning. In order for a language to have real meaning, it has to be public: that is, there has to be the possibility of inter-personal tests for the correctness of language use. That sort of test is possible in the bird-identification case, so names are meaningful there. It's a public language.

DUALIST: But I haven't made up words for mental states. Words like 'anger' and 'believe' are in the public language.

IDENTITY THEORIST: Right, but if they are supposed to refer to the user's private mental states, then there's no test of whether they're using them correctly or not.

DUALIST: Okay, I see now how this is relevant to what we're talking about. Our mental-language words are, everyone thinks, meaningful parts of the public language. But if they really are, then (your argument goes) there has to be the possibility of public check and correction of their use.

IDENTITY THEORIST: Right. So what we're talking about, when we talk about mental stuff, if it's going to be meaningful talk, can't be about private objects.

DUALIST: Hmm. Well that's an interesting argument, but I can't help feeling that something has gone wrong here. I guess that I still think that naming private events can be meaningful. I can see how this argument, if it's correct, raises a problem for the dualist position. But wouldn't it give materialists a problem too?

IDENTITY THEORIST: No, that problem arises only when you take mental events to be private, to be observable only by the person who has them. I think that mental events are observable by introspection, by the person who has them, but because they are really physical brain events, they're also publicly observable. A scientist might observe my memory of my last birthday party with a brainometer.

DUALIST: Yes, but even though you believe that some day we might be able to observe mental events from the outside, by detecting the brain events they really are, you have to admit that right now nobody can do that.

IDENTITY THEORIST: Right, so what?

DUALIST: So in the past, and now, and for a while anyway, the only ways we have of telling what mental events are going on is internally, in ourselves, by introspection, and externally, in others, by looking at their behaviour and listening to what they say.

IDENTITY THEORIST: Okay.

DUALIST: But what makes you so sure that what you call anger in yourself, detected by introspection, is the same thing as you detect in other people when they stride around frowning and slamming doors? What's your basis for thinking that there's any introspectible mental state in them at all?

IDENTITY THEORIST: Well, I think that some day scientists will find out what brain state anger is, and will discover that brain state in everyone, corresponding to their introspection of anger and to their angry behaviour.

DUALIST: You expect this to happen some day. But until it does, you've got just the same problem about other minds as you claim I've got. You don't have any better reason than I do to think that other people have a mental life.

IDENTITY THEORIST: Hmm.

10. Behaviourism

BEHAVIOURIST: Hi folks. I've been listening to you for a long time, and I think you're both wrong. Mind if I inject a different position all together?

IDENTITY THEORIST: Fine.

DUALIST: Okay.

BEHAVIOURIST: You two have already discussed what I think is the main problem with both of your positions: that neither is able to account for the fact that we often know about other people's mental states. Your identity theory supposes them to be certain sorts of brain event, but if that were right, we wouldn't know that they're occurring in anyone else, because under normal circumstances, we don't know directly what brain events are happening in other people. And dualism, even worse, makes it impossible, not just now and in the past, but always, to discover mental states in anyone else. So both of these positions must be wrong, because we find out about other people's mental states routinely, all the time.

IDENTITY THEORIST: Okay, so if you don't think that mental states are private non-material events, or material brain states, then what sorts of things do you think they are?

BEHAVIOURIST: I think they're types of outward behaviour.

IDENTITY THEORIST: So being angry, for example, just is stomping around frowning and slamming doors?

BEHAVIOURIST: That's right, that's all there is to it. That might be accompanied by some sort of non-material private mental event, as dualists think, or by some regular sort of material brain event, as materialists think, but we behaviourists don't care about that. If there are those sorts of regular accompaniments, that doesn't make any difference. They aren't what anger *is*. Anger is that sort of behaviour, and that's all.

DUALIST: Wow, that's a weird idea. Why would anyone believe that?

BEHAVIOURIST: Well, behaviourism has a long history, but it really developed beginning around 1930, as the result of a revolution in psychology. Till then, psychology hadn't made much progress as a science, and some psychologists decided that this was because they were studying the wrong sort of thing: mental introspectible events. The problem here was privacy. It's necessary for good science that observations and experiments be public: everyone has to be able to see the same thing, to do the observations for him or herself, and to corroborate the results of experiment.

DUALIST: Why is that necessary?

BEHAVIOURIST: It's a requirement for any good science. You remember the to-do a few years ago, when some scientists claimed that they had developed a technique for cold fusion? When it turned out that no other scientists could produce the same results, science refused to accept what was originally claimed. That's an example of the necessity of corroboration in science. The problem with introspection as science is that you're dealing with something that only one person could ever observe, and so there's no way anyone can check to see whether that person has things right or wrong; as a result, this sort of study has to be permanently, and fatally, subjective. And you couldn't study other people's mental states if they were available for direct inspection only by the person who had them. You don't even know if other people have any—the Problem of Other Minds!

DUALIST: Wait a minute. Why can't one psychologist check up on the introspection of another one by doing his or her own introspection?

BEHAVIOURIST: Because several people have to be able to look at the same thing. Those two scientists are looking at different things: two different private experiences.

DUALIST: Well, maybe that sort of subjectivity is inevitable in psychology, if it's going to be the study of minds. They're subjective things.

BEHAVIOURIST: Coming to that conclusion would be giving up on a scientific psychology altogether. Some psychologists instead, hoping to make their field a real science, decided that psychology ought to forget about private beetles in boxes, and concentrate on something objective and public: outward behaviour.

DUALIST: Now that sounds to me like they're giving up on their own subject. They're just switching to something irrelevant—as if chemists had said, to hell with those smelly chemicals! We're not getting any useful results anyway. Let's study banking, inflation, and interest rates instead.

BEHAVIOURIST: Behaviourist psychologists still were studying human behaviour, its causes and correlations—traditional areas of concern for psychology, after all. It's just that they were no longer using the introspective methodology that had been popular. Some Behaviourists believed that there were private mental states, what was referred to by mental-language words like 'belief,' 'desire,' 'anger,' and so on, but chose not to study those states. But other behaviourists claimed that they were not abandoning the study of belief, desire, anger, and so on, because those words didn't refer to inner private mental states at all. They referred to outwardly observable bodily behaviour—exactly what they were studying.

DUALIST: But that idea doesn't sound like it has much going for it. You really mean that mental states are nothing but types of behaviour?

BEHAVIOURIST: Yes, like, for an obvious example, being thirsty is nothing but being in a state where you'll go get something to drink.

DUALIST: But I can tell when I'm thirsty, because I can feel it. It has nothing to do with noticing that I'm going to get something to drink.

BEHAVIOURIST: That's what's behind that joke: Two behaviourists have sex. Afterwards one says, "That was good for you. How was it for me?"

DUALIST: Ha. But seriously: there are plenty of times when people are thirsty but they don't go get something to drink. Like right now, for example, I'm somewhat thirsty, but I'm staying right here because I want to continue this discussion.

BEHAVIOURIST: Sure, I agree. My view is actually a little more complicated than the way I first stated it. What I really meant is: being thirsty is nothing but having the *disposition* to go get something to drink.

DUALIST: What's a disposition?

BEHAVIOURIST: Saying that something has a disposition doesn't mean necessarily that it's doing something, but rather that it *would* do something under certain conditions, which may or may not hold. For example, *being brittle* is a dispositional characteristic that glass has and cloth doesn't. Brittleness is the disposition to shatter under certain conditions, namely if the thing is struck sharply. The glass in that window isn't shattering right now, and neither is the cloth in that curtain. But there's a dispositional difference between them: if you hit that glass sharply with a hammer, it would shatter, but if you hit that curtain, it wouldn't. So being thirsty is counted as a dispositional characteristic, meaning that under certain conditions, the person would go to get something to drink.

DUALIST: Under what conditions?

BEHAVIOURIST: Well, when the person isn't more interested in something else instead, and when the person believes that there's something to drink available, and so on.

DUALIST: Well those things talk about other mental states of the person.

BEHAVIOURIST: Right, and we'd have to give behavioural accounts of what those mental states are, probably also in terms of dispositions.

DUALIST: Hmm, this doesn't sound very promising. But let me try a different sort of objection. There are some mental states that seem to have nothing at all to do with behaviour, even dispositionally. For example, I believe that in 1938, the state of Wyoming produced 1/3 of a pound of dry edible beans for every man, woman, and child in the United States.

IDENTITY THEORIST: Wow! Did you just make that up or do you actually believe it?

DUALIST: No, I read it somewhere a long time ago and memorized it. I believe it!

IDENTITY THEORIST: Awesome.

DUALIST: Okay, look, let's get back to the question. That mental state is true of me, and (now that I've told you) it's true of you people too. Now tell me what sort of behaviour that mental state consists of? What sorts of dispositions for behaving do we have, because we believe that?

BEHAVIOURIST: Well, it's sort of hard to say, but I'm sure that someone who believed that would have the disposition to react differently from someone who didn't.

DUALIST: Act how? Under what circumstances?

BEHAVIOURIST: It's hard to say.

DUALIST: It's pretty clear that coming to believe this won't make any difference to your behaviour ever.

BEHAVIOURIST: That's all right. A pane of glass can be brittle even though it never shatters. All you need for a disposition is to have some *possible* circumstance where a disposition is manifested in actual behaviour.

DUALIST: Okay, tell me under what circumstances believing that about the beans would make a difference in your behaviour?

BEHAVIOURIST: It's hard to say, offhand.

DUALIST: I think it's impossible to say. I think that some mental states have no corresponding behavioural dispositions. It's not just that people who believe that don't in fact ever act in a way that represents that belief. It's that there is no imaginable circumstance in which people who believe that would act differently.

BEHAVIOURIST: Maybe I can imagine a circumstance in which a person who believes that would act differently than a person who doesn't. Suppose we had a time machine, and sent the two people back in time to 1938, and both people wanted to get a whole lot of dried edible beans; then one person would go to Wyoming and the other one wouldn't....

DUALIST: Oh, come on! *That's* supposed to be the real difference between the two people?

BEHAVIOURIST: Well, it's not easy to work out the difficulties in this position. I have to admit that lots of psychologists and philosophers have just given up on the idea of behaviourism because of these difficulties. But I still think that it offers such valuable advantages that it's worth trying to make it work.

11. Could a Machine Think?

SCEPTIC: Here's a question that I'd like to hear your responses to: could a machine think?

BEHAVIOURIST: I believe certain machines can think. This is not science fiction: I think that some computers that have already been built can think.

IDENTITY THEORIST: Well, you would, but you're wrong. According to your position, all it takes for thinking is a certain kind of outward behaviour.

SCEPTIC: I'd be interested in knowing what sort of outward behaviour you'd count as necessary for a machine to think, but first I'd like to hear why you, IDENTITY THEORIST, believe they can't.

IDENTITY THEORIST: Well, first of all, computers are the only plausible candidates for thinking machines we have. I mean, nobody would claim that a can opener or stapler can think. And I admit that we sometimes talk as though computers actually do think—as if they're actually carrying on mental operations, like learning, reasoning, calculating some result, remembering something, recognizing something, and so on. Computers now can do a pretty good job—or will soon be able to—of recognizing faces, of playing chess, learning from experience, solving math problems, and a host of other "mental" tasks. There's a whole research industry dedicated to what's called *artificial intelligence* which aims at developing new programs to enable computers to perform more and more complex "mental" tasks. But it doesn't follow from any of this that any computer can now think, or will ever be able to. I mean, artificial intelligence isn't real intelligence, any more than an artificial flower is a real flower.

BEHAVIOURIST: You haven't said why you don't believe they can or could think.

IDENTITY THEORIST: Well, I'm inclined to say that no machine could truly have a mind, or have any genuine mental contents. I think that a mind is a material thing—a brain—and that mental events are just material goings-on in it, and machines—computers—are material things too, but they're the wrong sorts of material things. Computers can simulate the operations of brains, but they aren't brains. When computers calculate something, what's going on in them is a far different sort of thing from what's going on when a brain does the same calculation. Computers, after all, are made up of silicon chips and wires, whereas our brains are made of nerve cells. When we get a computer to do a certain addition problem, for example, we have a pretty good idea of what sort of electrical processes take place, and they're nothing at all like what we'd expect to find in a brain. The end result might be the same, of course—both you and the computer would come up with 12 when you added 7 and 5—but you'd get there by a completely different physical process. I mean, consider additions done on an abacus, which is a traditional adding machine that consists of beads which you slide back and forth on wires, and compare that to the electronics inside a hand-held calculator. They both come up with the same answer to an arithmetic problem, but by a completely different mechanism. So because I want to identify mental processes with the physical brain events that they consist of, I conclude that only real brains can think.

DUALIST: My objections to the idea of a computer thinking are much more basic than IDENTITY THEORIST's. What I count as thinking, and all other mental activities as well, is the familiar internal conscious experience we all have, and recognize from the inside. For the question you raise, it doesn't matter what a computer can do—what matters is whether a computer has this sort of internal conscious experience. I doubt that it does. I doubt that any computer could ever be built to have internal introspectible conscious experience.

IDENTITY THEORIST: Why do you doubt that? I mean, how can you know whether a computer has that introspectible experience or not?

DUALIST: Well, I know how computers are constructed, in general terms, anyway, and I know that they aren't constructed to have an inner life, a conscious experience. When they do calculations, it's just a matter of electrical connections being made and broken—there's no *thought* going on in there. Here's a clearer example. Suppose we programmed a computer to simulate pain. We build this little foot-shaped object to sit on the floor, wired to the rest of the computer, with a switch in the big-toe-shaped part, so that when you exert enough pressure on that switch, it sends a signal to the computer, and this causes activation of the sound-card to play the sound "OUCH!!" over the computer's speakers. This is simulation of pain, but there's no feeling of pain in there, not like when I step on your toe.

BEHAVIOURIST: I agree that a very simple mechanism like that doesn't have pain. But that's only because it doesn't have all the complex dispositions for behaviour that we associate with the idea of pain in humans. I think that if you build a computer in a complex enough way, so that it reacts to stimuli with exactly the same sort of behavioural dispositions that we have, then that shows that the computer has a mind, and performs all the mental operations we do. That follows from the way I see mental processes: they're sets of behaviour and dispositions to behave. They're the sort of thing that humans have, and computers can be created to have them too. But other sorts of "mental" states are simple enough so that computers can be constructed right now to do exactly the same thing. They do a fine job on arithmetical calculations, for example, so we can credit them with doing mental arithmetic (much better than we can, in fact). Some things are much harder to program. Getting computers to play chess as well as we can is quite a trick, but they've succeeded: their latest chess-playing computer can beat any human. Of course, there are some behavioural tasks that are more difficult than this to program. Facial recognition, for example—sorting out a large pile of photographs containing many different views of each of a large number of people, so that the photos of the same person are all sorted together—is easy for people, but it's a very hard thing to get computers to do. However, programmers are getting there.

DUALIST: Well, I guess you have to think that way, if the inner conscious aspect of experience doesn't figure in your view of what constitutes our mental life.

BEHAVIOURIST: Right, but isn't that the right way, the only sensible way in fact, to try to answer the question whether computers can think?

12. Instinct and Learning; Unpredictability

DUALIST: Here's another reason I think machines can't think, and this one doesn't depend on the idea of inner consciousness. Real thinking—genuine mentality—means creativity, but computers only do what they're programmed to do. That's what also distinguishes people from the mindless lower animals. Insects, earthworms, and all those less complex kinds of animals just act by instinct. Like computers, they only do what they're programmed to do. It's easy to predict what they're going to do next, because they act *mindlessly*. I mean that literally.

BEHAVIOURIST: I don't think that's a good argument either. For one thing, I think a good case could be made that *we* only do what we're programmed to do. It's just that our programs are much more complicated than an earthworm's behavioural program, or my computer's word processing program. Computers, earthworms, human beings—all act because they're programmed to respond in regular ways to stimuli. It's just a matter of cause and effect.

DUALIST: But don't you agree that humans don't act merely by instincts and that we are often unpredictable?

BEHAVIOURIST: I agree with both of your claims. Let's talk about instinct first. I agree that we don't act merely by instinct. But you've got it wrong here: non-instinctual behaviour is not restricted to humans. Non-instinctual behaviour is learned behaviour, as opposed to wired-in instinctual behaviour. Even earthworms can learn.

SCEPTIC: Really!

BEHAVIOURIST: Right, here's an example. Psychologists created a very simple little T-maze that looks like this:

The earthworm is dropped in at A. At point B, there's a little bit of earthworm food, and at point C there's the apparatus to produce a little electric shock. The earthworm wanders up the stem of the T, and turns left or right, at random, getting the food or the shock. After several tries—and it takes several—earthworms aren't very bright!—the critter learns to turn left to get the food and avoid the shock. Earthworms have no instinctual tendency to turn left. This one has learned it.

Here's an example in which a computer can learn something. I used to have a word-processing program that filled in the ends of longer words for you as you typed. It would just look up the first several letters of the word in its dictionary, and if there were several complete words starting with those letters, it would pick the one with the highest frequency-number attached to it. So for instance if you typed in 'duali' it would finish the word 'duality,' which was on top of its frequency list for words beginning that way. You could accept the computer's guess for the rest of the word, or overtype some other completion. Every time you overtyped the completion for a different word, the program would raise the frequency-number attached to that one, and lower the frequency-number attached to the guess it made. So for example a philosopher of mind would type 'dualism' much more often than 'duality.' After several overtypes, the number for 'dualism' would get higher than the number for 'duality,' and it would start finishing 'duali' as 'dualism.' It has learned from experience.

SCEPTIC: That sounds like a cute and completely annoying and useless word-processing gimmick.

BEHAVIOURIST: Right, I played with this program for an hour, then threw it away.

DUALIST: But that computer program is just learning in the way it's programmed to: it's just a matter of cause and effect.

BEHAVIOURIST: Agreed. So?

DUALIST: Okay, I agree that machines can learn. That's not what distinguishes mind from machine. Unpredictability is more to the point.

BEHAVIOURIST: Unpredictability is just a function of how well we understand the cause-and-effect structure of things. When we understand it well, we can predict the thing's behaviour. When we don't, it's unpredictable—to us, for the moment, anyway. Some computer programs are so complicated, and are the products of so many different programmers, that nobody understands everything about them, and nobody can predict exactly how they're going to act. And anyway, it's easy to create a simple program that makes a computer behave unpredictably: just put in a random process.

DUALIST: But computer "randomness" isn't real randomness. I know roughly how computer "randomness" works. It just takes the time and the date, and does a number of complicated arithmetic operations on those numbers, and comes up with a number you wouldn't guess—a different one every time. That's not genuine randomness.

BEHAVIOURIST: Well, it is, if randomness means that you can't predict it.

DUALIST: Well, here's a suggestion: free will. People have free will, but computers don't and couldn't.

BEHAVIOURIST: Trying to figure out what free will might involve is a big subject. What do you say we postpone it for a while?

DUALIST: Okay.[4]

13. Creativity

DUALIST: Here's something else: *creativity*. Minds are creative; computers do only what they're programmed to do.

BEHAVIOURIST: If being creative means that there's surprising, innovative output, then I think machines can do it. Here are a couple of my favourite examples. The first one is the computer program called RACTER, which you interview by asking questions. Here, take a look, I've got it on my laptop. Okay, here goes. The part I'm typing in is what follows the > sign; the rest is from RACTER.

```
Hello, I'm Racter. Are you BEHAVIOURIST?
>Yes
You are BEHAVIOURIST Yes?
>Yes.
Hi, BEHAVIOURIST. How are things in Canada? We were talking
    about depression last time. You had just asked where I
    do live. Shall we
    continue?
>Yes
Excellent! Excuse me a minute while I attend to some
    business—I'll be right back. I'm back.
>Well, where do you live?
```

---

4 It's taken up in Conversation V.

I live in England. The Hotel Pierre is a good place for a
   visitor to dwell in England. England has playboys who
   are always living. Next question.

>Do you have feelings?

Of course. A bonkers intellectual often falls prey to a
   surprising hysteric. Why do you think you're honest?

>I never tell lies.

Well, I think that if you never tell lies, then any box-
   ing hysteric could punch a million touchdowns, so
   there! Next question.

>Are you just a machine?

Yes. It's true that I am just a machine. Ah. Ah. Soft
   human! Next question.

>Do you have a soul?

Certainly. If an atheist discovered religion, he might
   think it was atheism. Is having a soul contagious?

>I don't think so.

Then I won't catch one. Listen to this! Momentarily an
   appalling physicist who was in anguish yodelled that
   religion was fascinating. That is religious, unbeliev-
   ing and captivating. Anyway BEHAVIOURIST.... Oh forget
   it!

>Are you crazy?

No. Certainly not. No. ha ha! ho ho Haw ... Haw HOo.
   cough ... haa. cough HOO. (hic). (hic) HEEE (wheeze)
   HAA ... cough. Here's a hilarious one: Instantly a
   sickening cosmologist who was in pain cried that
   craziness was terrific. That is sane, weird and terrific. By the same token BEHAVIOURIST.... Oh forget it! A
   crazy citizen is still not a Jack the Ripper. AAAH-
   choo!! sniffle....

>Bye

You want to quit?

>Yes

OK, goodbye behaviourist. Nice talking to you.

DUALIST: That's cute.

BEHAVIOURIST: Playing with RACTER is fun. You can download it (but not
   for free) from various web sites. It's a very early artificial intelligence program, from 1984. It learns things—notice how it remembered my name
   from the last time I ran it, and it remembers other things from past ses-

sions also. It's also unpredictable: it never produces the same conversation twice, even when your input is exactly the same. But more to the point here, I'd say it's creative. It's funny and original. It puts things together in ways you'd never think of, but which are relevant anyway.

DUALIST: But its output is just determined by a program.

BEHAVIOURIST: Of course. It's such a simple program that you can see how it works. It uses a couple of dozen data files, which are lists of words together with related words. So for example, you'll have a list of games: tennis, volleyball, golf, and so on, connected to a list of sports terms like serving aces, hole in one, home run, etc., and a list of famous sports figures, and so on. So it finds a word you enter on a list, and randomly chooses where to go from there, drawing on its list of related terms.

DUALIST: I admit it looks creative, but because it's all determined by a program, I don't think it's really genuine creativity.

BEHAVIOURIST: Well, I don't know why that follows. Maybe genuine creativity in humans is all determined by a program inside us. Anyway, here's the second example. An enormously more complicated and sophisticated program, and a special computer to run it, was called Deep Blue. It was built by IBM solely for the purpose of playing chess. There were many fairly good chess-playing computers before that, but this one was much better than any of the others—so good that it won a match against the World Chess Champion, Gary Kasparov, in 1996. Beating the World Champion at chess was considered for a long time to be the Holy Grail of artificial intelligence, because chess is complicated, and it takes enormous mental skill, together with real creativity, to play at that level. Kasparov won Game 1 in the match, but the turning point was when Deep Blue won Game 2. Kasparov wrote later about Game 2. (Let's see, I have it here somewhere. Here it is:) "The machine refused to move to a position that had a decisive short-term advantage—showing a very human sense of danger." He also said that he sometimes saw deep intelligence and creativity in the machine's moves.

DUALIST: Agreed, computers can do interesting and complex tasks. But that doesn't answer the question whether they have minds.

14. The Turing Test

BEHAVIOURIST: Here's a different approach to the question. It's called the *Turing Test*, named after Alan Turing, an extremely smart English mathematician and computer theorist who died in 1954. They asked him whether computers could think, and how someone could tell. He answered by proposing a test to put computers through, and when they passed the test, that would show that they could think. The test is this. Put somebody—call that person the interrogator—in a room with two computer terminals in it. Connect one of these terminals to a terminal in another room operated by a human, and connect the other terminal to a computer we're going to test for thinking ability. Now, the interrogator doesn't know which one is connected to the human at the other end, and which one is connected only to a computer. The interrogator can type in questions on those terminals, and the questions are answered, either by the human at the other end of one, or by the computer at the other end of the other. If the interrogator can't figure out which terminal is connected to a person and which to a computer, then that computer passes the Turing Test for computer thought. Of course, this would be easy if the person and the computer weren't allowed to lie. The interrogator would simply have to ask both the question, "Are you a human?" But the computer is programmed to lie in ways to try to convince the interrogator that it's actually a human, so it would answer yes to this, tell the interrogator the names and ages of its fictitious siblings, tell the story of when it had its tonsils removed, and so on.

DUALIST: I'd guess that they might be able to program a computer to pass the Turing Test right now, or at least soon.

BEHAVIOURIST: Not yet. It turns out to be a very difficult job. Probably some day.

DUALIST: But the real issue is whether that would show that the computer could think. What does passing the Turing Test have to do with thinking?

BEHAVIOURIST: I think that when we say that somebody is remembering, or calculating, or recognizing the same person in several photographs, we're simply saying that the person is accomplishing certain tasks. Remembering X is, in response to a querying stimulus, outputting stored relevant information. Calculating is receiving the input of a problem (for example, $7 + 5 = ?$) and outputting the answer (12). Recognizing the same person in several photographs is sorting a larger bunch of photographs including that person's photos, so that that person's photos are in one pile, and all the rest in the other. These are all behaviours (or dispositions to behave, if conditions aren't right). What counts as other people doing those things is if the behavioural outputs are the right ones, given the task and the inputs. So anything capable of producing the appropriate output given the input has done that "mental" task. When the Turing Test is performed, we compare the outputs of a computer to a human when we ask them each to perform some typical "mental" tasks. If the computer is doing them as well as the human, well enough so we can't tell which output is which, then the computer must be doing those mental tasks as well.

DUALIST: But the computer is just simulating mental activities by producing the appropriate behaviour. It's just like any other sort of computer simulation, like, for example, when they write a computer program to simulate the development of weather systems over the east coast for the next three days, that's obviously just a simulation—there's no actual weather being produced by the computer!

BEHAVIOURIST: Sure, in that case, but the situation is different here. What I'm claiming is that what *constitutes* the difference between something that has a mind from something that doesn't is the kind of behaviour things are capable of. Some behaviour is appropriately described, categorized, explained, in mental terms, and some isn't.

15. Deep Blue and the Sphex Wasp

SCEPTIC: Okay, let's pursue that idea. What do you think it is about some kinds of behaviour but not others that makes it appropriate to describe that kind in mental terms?

BEHAVIOURIST: Well, consider Deep Blue again. When the computer beat Kasparov, everyone found it completely natural to describe Deep Blue's game in terms of mental actions. I read you what Kasparov said already, but here's a clearer example. It's what the philosopher Daniel C. Dennett said about that match:

> Murry Campbell, Feng-hsiung Hsu, and the principal designer of Deep Blue, didn't beat Kasparov; Deep Blue did. Neither Campbell nor Hsu discovered the winning sequence of moves, Deep Blue did. At one point, while Kasparov was mounting a ferocious attack on Deep Blue's king, it was nobody but Deep Blue that figured out that it had the time and security it needed to knock off a pesky pawn of Kasparov's that was out of the action, but almost invisibly vulnerable. Campbell, like the human grand masters watching the game, would never have dared consider such a calm mopping-up operation under such pressure.

DUALIST: But isn't that all just speaking picturesquely, metaphorically, like saying that your car is feeling resentful about being driven in the cold when it keeps stalling on a freezing morning?

BEHAVIOURIST: I agree that talking that way about your car isn't literal. Certain machines are too simple, or don't do the right sorts of things, to be described in mental terms—literally, anyway. Nobody would be tempted to say or think that a thermostat, for example, literally feels cold, so it literally wants to turn the heat on. But Deep Blue is another story. Anyway, here's something else Dennett wrote about; in this case it's animal behaviour that falls short of what it takes to assign mental categories. The animal in question is the female sphex wasp. Having built a nest, she finds a grasshopper, which she paralyses with a sting. She drags the grasshopper back to the nest, lays it down near the nest opening, and goes back inside for a last-minute inspection. If everything's okay, she puts the paralysed grasshopper inside the nest, and lays her eggs on top, so that the larvae can eat the grasshopper when they hatch.

DUALIST: Pretty good. That looks like purposive behaviour to me. Maybe it's appropriate to think of that wasp as having intentions and beliefs and desires and so on.

BEHAVIOURIST: But there's more. An experimenter watching the wasp's performance waited until the wasp had gone into the nest for the inspection, and then moved the grasshopper a few inches away. The wasp emerged from the nest, and saw that the grasshopper was gone; but she was able to find it very soon. Then she dragged it back next to the nest opening, and went inside for the inspection. While she was inside, the experimenter again moved the grasshopper a few inches away. The wasp again found the grasshopper, dragged it to the nest opening, and went inside. This whole routine could be repeated, over and over again, indefinitely.

DUALIST: That's pretty funny, but what's the point?

BEHAVIOURIST: The point is that the wasp, it seems, is acting on the basis of pre-set rigid behavioural instinctual routines. When things are interrupted, the routine is reset to an earlier point, and has to be resumed in its rigid pattern from there. If that wasp was actually thinking about what was going on, she would get the idea after a few repetitions, and just bring the grasshopper straight into the nest, without doing the unnecessary final inspection inside. Animals with minds don't work in rigid routines like this. They can adapt their behaviour to odd circumstances: we say they think about what's going on, they don't just blunder ahead in instinctual patterns no matter what.

DUALIST: Okay, I'll accept the idea that this wasp is like a simple unthinking machine. We already agreed that an animal with blind instinctive behaviour couldn't have mentality. So that experiment is good evidence the wasp isn't thinking about what it's doing. But the earthworm who learned to go left: that's not blind instinct, but is there *thought* there?

BEHAVIOURIST: Well, I'd say thinking takes more complexity than that. Anyway, I think the point of the wasp story, and the Deep Blue story as well, is not that in some cases we have *evidence* of internal thought, and in other cases not. I think the point is that certain kinds of behaviour just lend themselves to mental description, and some don't.

DUALIST: That's where we disagree!

16. The Chinese Room

DUALIST: Here's the real problem I find with your position. You're thinking of mental activities as merely the performance of certain kinds of tasks, the production of certain kinds of outputs. But I think that what makes something mental is the internal conscious experience involved when we do those tasks—the experience that accompanies that behaviour, and that causes it. Without that internal conscious experience, it wouldn't be a mental activity. I'll tell you a philosophical story that illustrates and proves that point. This story was invented by the contemporary American philosopher John Searle, and it's called the *Chinese Room Example*. Imagine a closed room with a slot in the door. Into the slot, a Chinese speaker inserts a question written in Chinese. Some time later, a sensible response to that questions pops out of the slot, also written in Chinese. For example, somebody writes, "Where is Cleveland" on a piece of paper (in Chinese), and pushes it into the slot. Some time later, a piece of paper emerges, saying, "It's in Ohio" (also in Chinese). A piece of paper is put in saying the Chinese equivalent of "Why do the muffins I cook turn out tough?" and shortly another piece emerges saying, in translation, "Try mixing the batter less, only till all the dry ingredients are moistened." And so on. It seems like somewhere in that room there's mental activity going on: somebody's understanding the meaning of the questions written in Chinese, thinking up the answers and writing them down in Chinese, right?

SCEPTIC: Right.

DUALIST: Well here's the story of what's happening inside. There's a person in there—call him the clerk—and a very large library. The clerk understands no Chinese at all. He's just doing the job he's paid to do, though he has no idea of what that job amounts to. The job is this: He looks at the Chinese characters on the paper that comes in through the slot, and finds each of them in a big book, simply by comparing their shape to the characters printed in the book. Next to each character in the book, there is a list of numbers. He does some complicated computations with the numbers corresponding to all the characters, resulting in other numbers, which he looks up in other books, finding other Chinese characters there, corresponding to those numbers. He copies those characters down on a new piece of paper, just by imitating their shape, and he slides that paper out of the slot. Okay, there's the whole story. The point is that it's clear that nowhere inside that room is there any understanding of the Chinese writing. The clerk doesn't understand Chinese. The books surely can't be said to understand. The room is performing all the appropriate behaviour relating input and output for the mental activity of understanding Chinese sentences, but there's none of that going on at all, anywhere inside. That shows that input/output behaviour is one thing, mental activity is another. The same thing should be said about the Deep Blue case: those surprising chess moves weren't discovered by Campbell or Hsu, as Dennett says, but it doesn't follow that they were discovered by Deep Blue. Nobody—nothing—performed the mental operation of making a discovery.

BEHAVIOURIST: I agree that the clerk doesn't understand Chinese, and neither do any of the books he consults. But I think that the room, taken as a whole, does.

DUALIST: But how can that be? Where is that understanding going on? Nothing inside understands anything.

BEHAVIOURIST: I think that despite the fact that no component of the room understands Chinese, the whole room does. Here's an analogy. A car is made up of tires, an engine, seats, a steering wheel, and so on. None of these components can carry you down the highway, by itself. But the whole car can. From the fact that none of the parts of something have got some characteristic, you can't conclude that the whole thing doesn't. That sort of reasoning commits what they call the *Fallacy of Composition*. Here's another example of that fallacy: atoms are colourless, Fred's Hawaiian shirt is made entirely of atoms; therefore Fred's Hawaiian shirt is colourless. That's not a valid pattern of reasoning.

DUALIST: No, look, we all know what it's like to understand a language (even if we don't understand Chinese!) and it's perfectly clear that there's none of that going on anywhere in this story, except of course in the people outside the room, who write the slips that they put in, and read the ones that come out.

BEHAVIOURIST: Well, I've already told you why I object to the idea that mental events can only be recognized by how they feel to the person who has them. We could never tell they're happening in anyone else. Anyway, I'd like to hear how you, IDENTITY THEORIST, react to the Chinese Room Example.

IDENTITY THEORIST: Well, I agree with DUALIST that there's no understanding of Chinese going on, because I think that that depends on certain brain processes that aren't happening anywhere in the room. The clerk has a brain, of course, but I guess we can assume that none of his brain processes count as understanding Chinese.

BEHAVIOURIST: Well, let me try you out on another philosophical fable, and see how you react to this one. Imagine that some day aliens from the planet Zarkon arrive in a flying saucer. They have come in peace, and they settle in among us, learn our language, and interact happily with humans. Our supermarkets start stocking the acorns, motor oil, and gravel that they like to eat, and when you meet an alien in a supermarket filling its shopping cart with lots of these things, the alien tells you, "I'm sure hungry today!" When you see another alien standing at a bus stop staring at the sign explaining bus routes, scratching both of its heads, you ask if you can help, and it says, "I'm trying to figure out how to get downtown from here." One problem facing the aliens is that our doctors are unable to help them when they get ill, or have an accident, because their bodies work totally differently from ours. All of their major life functions work totally differently: they have no heart, no liver, no brain, no circulation system, and so on. Now my question is: when that alien tells you it's really hungry, and when the other one says it's trying to figure out how to get downtown, is what they're saying true?

IDENTITY THEORIST: Well, how do these aliens function if they haven't got any brains?

BEHAVIOURIST: All these things are accomplished by a dozen small silicone-based computers naturally growing in various parts of the alien's body, working in parallel, connected to each other and to the rest of the body by copper nerve-like wires.

IDENTITY THEORIST: Okay, I'd say, then, that they don't feel hungry, or think about how to get downtown. They're accomplishing the same things as we do when we perform these mental acts—stocking up on food, and calculating possible routes to get downtown—but they're doing them in different ways, since they don't have brains at all. If we start applying our own mental terms to them, we would be changing the meaning of our language.

BEHAVIOURIST: That's what I thought you'd say. I think that this story provides a way of showing which one of us is right. I think that those mental categories would apply straightforwardly to the aliens, because they act in the same adaptable, goal-directed ways that we do, even though they have entirely different physiologies inside. You think that our present mental categories would not apply. I guess that people could choose between our theories by seeing which response they'd have to this fable.

Suggested Readings

(See the Notes on "Suggested Readings" sections, p. 17-18.)

The most noteworthy ancient advocate of materialism about mind was Lucretius (c. 99-c. 55 BC). Certain sections of his *De Rerum Natura* (*On the Nature of the Universe*) are devoted to this.

René Descartes (1596-1650) is of course a central figure among dualists. He explains and argues for his views about mind and body in *Meditations*, 6. By far the best edition of this for students is on-line at <http://www.earlymoderntexts.com>.

Influential contemporary criticisms of Descartes and arguments in favour of a materialist view of mind come from Daniel Dennett. He has published a number of very readable books in this area; *Consciousness Explained* is the major work. His argument for the mentality of Deep Blue and other computers is in his article "When HAL Kills, Who's to Blame? Computer Ethics," in David G. Stork, editor, *HAL's Legacy: 2001's Computer as Dream and Reality*. His discussion of the Sphex wasp is in *Elbow Room: The Varieties of Free Will Worth Wanting*.

Nagel's article "What Is It Like to Be a Bat" was first published in *Philosophical Review*, (October 1974). It was reprinted in his book *Mortal Questions*, and in many anthologies.

Alan M. Turing (1912-54) was the English computer genius who thought up the test that he thought would show when a computer could think. His article "Computing Machinery and Intelligence" is widely anthologized.

John Searle invented the Chinese-room thought experiment which, he thought, proved that computers couldn't think. Read about this in *Minds, Brains, and Science*.

Paul M. Churchland is the contemporary philosopher most closely associated with eliminative materialism. See his book *Matter and Consciousness: A Contemporary Introduction to the Philosophy of Mind*.

Ludwig Wittgenstein's "Beetle in the box" analogy is found in his *Philosophical Investigations* §293. The diary example is in §257.

CONVERSATION V

Determinism, Free Will, and Punishment

Participants: IDENTITY THEORIST • SCEPTIC • DETERMINIST • FATALIST • MATHEMATICIAN • PHYSICIST • INDETERMINIST • HARD DETERMINIST • SOFT DETERMINIST • UTILITARIAN • RETRIBUTIVIST • PSYCHOLOGIST

1. Determinism

IDENTITY THEORIST: A while back, just when we began talking about philosophy of mind,[1] SCEPTIC said something that started us off, but we haven't gotten to the bottom of what was said yet. What SCEPTIC said was something like: ethics doesn't make any sense, because we're all really machines. I can see what's meant by the claim that we're all really machines. I believe that, in a sense.

SCEPTIC: I don't get it. Weren't you just arguing that machines like computers can't have any mental characteristics? And you agreed that people do have mental characteristics. So doesn't it follow that we're not all machines?

IDENTITY THEORIST: No, it doesn't follow. Right, I think that machines like computers—things made out of silicon chips and wires—can't have mental characteristics, because you need an organic brain to count as having a mind. But I think that people are a type of machine too. They are thinking machines—but organic ones, with brains.

SCEPTIC: Well then, in what sense do you think that people are like machines, then?

IDENTITY THEORIST: I mean that people, just like everything else in the universe, are totally constituted out of matter, out of chemicals, and that we, just like everything else in the universe, are governed totally by the laws of cause and effect—the laws of physics and chemistry. Everything anybody does has a physical cause, the same as with every other material object.

SCEPTIC: So your view is that every human action is determined by a previous cause?

---

1 Conversation IV.

IDENTITY THEORIST: It is, and I take that to be a consequence of my materialism.

SCEPTIC: But in order to believe in that sort of cause-and-effect determination, do you have to be a materialist?

DETERMINIST: Maybe I can help out here. I agree basically with a lot of what
IDENTITY THEORIST was saying, but I don't think that the position about
causes depends necessarily on materialism, on the view that we're constituted of nothing but matter. I believe also that every event in the universe
is determined by causes, and that includes everything people do. That
view is called *determinism*. (Its opposite, the view that some things are
not determined by causes, is called *indeterminism*.) But I'm undecided
about the materialism vs. dualism issue. You don't have to be a materialist
to believe that human actions are determined by causes, to believe in
determinism. For example, a dualist might also be a determinist.

SCEPTIC: How could that be?

DETERMINIST: Dualists can believe that mental events have causes—that
sometimes they're caused by physical events, and sometimes by other
mental events (as for example when your memory of your tenth birthday
party reminds you to call your Mum).

SCEPTIC: But determinism is more closely associated with materialism, and
indeterminism with dualism, aren't they?

DETERMINIST: Right, on the whole. The idea of determination by causes is
associated with physical science, so somebody who believes that humans
are physical objects, subject to the laws of physics and chemistry and so
on, is likely to be a determinist. And if you're an indeterminist, thinking
that humans are exempt from the necessities of physical laws of cause-
and-effect, then you're probably a dualist.

SCEPTIC: Okay, fine. Now tell me exactly what determinism involves.

DETERMINIST: As I said, it's the belief that everything is determined by causes. Everything has a cause—nothing pops up all by itself—and, given its
cause, the effect had to happen. So, for instance, if you flick that light
switch over there, that determines that the light will go on.

SCEPTIC: Well, maybe it won't. Suppose for example that the power has gone
off, or a fuse downstairs has blown, the light bulb has burnt out, or the
wires somewhere have broken.

DETERMINIST: Right, I should have said, given that all of a bunch of background conditions hold, the light will go on. The appropriate background
conditions include that the power is still on, the fuse hasn't blown, the

light bulb hasn't burnt out, the wires are still connected, and lots of other conditions too. And I should also mention the general laws of nature that operate to connect cause and effect. Given that all this is true, then flicking the switch makes the light go on. With all the background conditions in place, the laws of nature imply that flicking the switch *must* make the light go on—that effect is *determined* by that cause. And that kind of determinism, I think, applies to everything, including human actions and decisions. Determinism is the belief that everything has a cause, and, given the cause, including all the appropriate background conditions, the effect has to happen. So everything, including human decisions and actions, is determined by laws and previous causes.

2. Cause

SCEPTIC: Well, that's an interesting position, one that we should talk about. But first I have a couple of questions about *cause* I'd like to discuss.

DETERMINIST: Fine.

SCEPTIC: Okay, first I want to ask how you distinguish the cause from the background conditions. You agree that flicking the switch might not result in the light's going on, for example, if the power is off. So when we make a list of what it takes to turn the light on, we have to list both things: that the power be on, and that the switch is flicked. And some other things too, like for example that the wiring to the light bulb makes a complete circuit. Right?

DETERMINIST: Right. What that means is that none of these conditions is sufficient, all by itself, to make the light go on.

SCEPTIC: So how do you distinguish the one that you call the cause?

DETERMINIST: Aha, that's a good question. There's been some philosophical debate about that. One thing that's maybe relevant in distinguishing one of these conditions to be the cause is that it's the one that changes the most recently, at least in the example of the light bulb. We imagine that, in the usual case, the power is already on, and has been for a while, since the last power failure, anyway, before the light switch is flicked. And the wiring has been there, forming a complete circuit from the switch to the light bulb, for a long time. That's why they're sometimes all called *standing conditions*, because they've been standing around for a while already, so to speak, waiting for the switch-flicking. The most recent change in all those conditions, before the light bulb goes on, is the switch-flicking, so that's the one we call the cause. But imagine, by contrast, a case in which the switch is flicked, but the light doesn't go on because the electric power in the house is off—the electric power lines have been cut by a tree falling on them outside the house. So then they repair the power lines, and electric power to the house is restored, and, since the switch still is set to ON, the light goes on. In that case, the most recent change before the light goes on is the presence of electric power in the lines. I think that in that case, we'd say that the cause of the light going on is the restoration of electric power in the house, not the flicking of the switch.

SCEPTIC: Hmm, well that might be right. But how about this example. You get into your car; you put the key in the ignition, and turn it. That switches on the power to the spark plugs and to the starter-motor, which turns the car motor over and results in the car's starting.

DETERMINIST: Your knowledge of the inside of cars is hugely impressive.

SCEPTIC: Thanks. Well, in that case, what caused the car to start?

DETERMINIST: I guess I'd say, you turned the key.

SCEPTIC: I'd say so too. But that's not the most recent change in the series of events. That happened a tiny bit before the starter-motor turned the car motor over. So in that case, it's not the most recent change that we'd count as the cause.

DETERMINIST: Maybe that's right. Look, the common denominator in your car case and both the light cases is that what we call the cause is the most recent action some person did: flicking the switch, restoring power to the house, turning the key. Maybe being the cause has something to do with changes that a person directly brings about.

SCEPTIC: That's an idea worth pursuing, I guess, but I don't think that will work in every case. I mean, we talk about causes for events in which no person brings about anything. For example, astronomers talk about the cause of sunspots, even though nobody is remotely involved in bringing them about.

DETERMINIST: Well, I guess that distinguishing the cause from the other conditions is something that needs more thought.

SCEPTIC: Maybe there really isn't any real distinction between what we might call the cause and the other conditions. Maybe we should just call them all *causal factors*. So when you give the story of the causal background of the light's going on, you just mention the relevant causal factors: the switch was flicked, the power in the house was on, the wires made a complete circuit, the bulb wasn't burned out, and so on. But I have a second question before we get back to determinism, and it's this. You've been talking about causes as *sufficient conditions*. What exactly does that mean?

DETERMINIST: Something X is a sufficient condition for Y when the presence of X guarantees the presence of Y. So, for example, your stepping on a potato chip is a sufficient condition for breaking it into bits.

SCEPTIC: Not if you're a bug.

DETERMINIST: Aargh, you know what I mean.

SCEPTIC: Sorry.

DETERMINIST: Okay. The concept of *sufficient condition* goes with the concept of *necessary condition*. X is a necessary condition for Y when you can't have Y without X. For example the presence of oxygen is necessary for something to be on fire. You can't have a fire without oxygen.

SCEPTIC: All right, I think I get it. So stepping on a potato chip isn't a necessary condition for breaking it into bits, because you *can* have a potato chip broken into bits without stepping on it, for example, by dropping Volume 3 of the *Encyclopaedia Britannica* on it.

DETERMINIST: Right, that's another sufficient condition for breaking the potato chip. Either of the two will do it, but neither of them is necessary.

SCEPTIC: But the presence of oxygen isn't sufficient for something to be on fire. The thing has to be flammable, and heated up to a certain temperature, and so on.

DETERMINIST: Right.

SCEPTIC: Okay, here's my question about cause. I'm wondering what being a necessary or sufficient condition has to do with being a cause. Take that example of flipping the light switch. It's not a sufficient condition for the light's going on, because it doesn't guarantee that the light goes on; for example, if the electricity in the house is off, the light won't go on when the switch is flipped. And it's not a necessary condition, because it's not true that you can't have the light go on without having flipped the switch. There are other conditions that can result in the light's going on, for example, if the switch stays in the "off" position, but wires get crossed somewhere, sending current into the line anyway. So it seems that being a cause—or being a causal factor, for that matter—is neither a necessary nor a sufficient condition for its effect.

DETERMINIST: I think that's right: a cause (or causal factor, in general) is neither a necessary nor a sufficient condition for its effect (although here again there is philosophical controversy). But I agree with the contemporary philosopher J.L. Mackie, who has argued that there's a complicated relationship between causal factor and effect: a causal factor is an *INUS condition* of its effect.

SCEPTIC: A what?

DETERMINIST: Mackie made that word up. It's an acronym, abbreviating the phrase Insufficient but Necessary part of an Unnecessary but Sufficient condition.

SCEPTIC: Oh, great. Help me through that one.

DETERMINIST. Okay, first of all, consider a complete listing of some causal factors (including flipping the switch) that would guarantee that the light would go on: Flipping the switch plus current in the wires, plus a complete circuit, plus the bulb isn't burned out, etc. etc. That whole list constitutes a sufficient condition for the light going on. When everything in there is in place, then that guarantees the light goes on. So that whole list is sufficient, though none of the items on the list is sufficient all by itself.

SCEPTIC: Okay so far.

DETERMINIST: But that list is altogether only one way that would be sufficient for the light to go on. There are others also, for example, that the wires are crossed, or that lightning hits the building in just the right way. So that whole list isn't necessary. That whole list is an Unnecessary but Sufficient condition.

SCEPTIC: Um, okay.

DETERMINIST: Now look at the part that flipping the switch alone plays in that list. It's not sufficient for the effect, as we've already seen.

SCEPTIC: Okay, I remember that.

DETERMINIST: But it's a necessary part of that whole list. If it were left out, then the rest of the list wouldn't be sufficient for the effect.

SCEPTIC: Er, okay.

DETERMINIST: So flipping the switch is an Insufficient but Necessary part of an Unnecessary but Sufficient condition for the light to go on.

SCEPTIC: Whew. I think I follow, but I should go over that again a few times to make sure I can follow what's going on.

DETERMINIST: That complicated thing is Mackie's account of the relation of cause and effect.

SCEPTIC: If that's right, then the relationship between cause and effect is so complicated that it's amazing that anybody ever managed to think clearly about it!

DETERMINIST: Well, I think it's right, but of course there are philosophers who offer different views, and there's a debate here, as everywhere. But I guess we should leave that issue where it is for now.

3. Fatalism

FATALIST: Okay, good, that gives me an appropriate moment to talk to you about what I think, which seems to me to be related to DETERMINIST's view. I also think that everything, including every human action and decision, is pre-determined. I believe that everything that happens in the future—human actions and decisions included—is inevitable. It's *fated* to happen that way, and there's nothing you can do about it. It's like what soldiers at war some-times think: that there's a bullet or a bomb with your name written on it, figuratively speaking, and what that means is that it's fated that you're going to be killed, and there's no avoiding it. We're powerless to avoid what's fated to happen in the future—there's nothing we can do about it.

DETERMINIST: So suppose I'm fated to bump into Fred, a tiresome person whom I really don't want to see today, when I go to the supermarket. Does that mean that I'm powerless to avoid seeing that person? Suppose, for example, I stayed home all day.

FATALIST: Well, if you're really fated to see Fred, despite the fact that you try your best to stay out of the supermarket, somehow or other it will turn out that you go there anyway, and there he'll be. Or else, if you succeed in staying home, for some reason he'll show up at your house. It's inevitable. There's nothing you can do about it.

DETERMINIST: That sounds crazy to me. I doubt that anything is ever fated in that sense.

SCEPTIC: Wait a minute, DETERMINIST. I can't see how your position differs from FATALIST's. You agree with FATALIST that bumping into Fred is inevitable, don't you? I mean, you think that because all the past causes are in place, that effect has to happen, right?

DETERMINIST: Right, but all I'm saying is that if the past hadn't been like that, if the causes weren't in place, then the effect wouldn't happen. In that sense, the effect isn't inevitable—it's not the case that it will happen *no matter what.* I think that this meeting had to happen given (among other things) your decision to go to the supermarket at that time, and I think that this decision itself had to happen given its causes, and so on, all the way back. But FATALIST is claiming something different—that the meeting had to happen even if the causes weren't in place. It had to happen no matter what.

FATALIST: Right, that's what I mean when I say something is fated to happen. I think that even if you hadn't decided to go to the supermarket, somehow or other fate would have arranged that you bump into Fred. ·

DETERMINIST: Fatalism is very mysterious to me. It sounds to me like some sort of superstitious magical view.

FATALIST: Well, there's a pretty good argument for it, in the writings of the ancient Greek philosopher Aristotle, whom I'm sure you respect.

DETERMINIST: Good, let's hear.

FATALIST: Okay, this is basically Aristotle's story about a future sea battle. Suppose that at Tuesday Noon, two people are talking about a war in progress, and Alice says, there's going to be a sea battle on Wednesday, and Betty says, no there isn't, there won't be a sea battle on Wednesday. What one of them says is true, and what the other one says is false, right? Although maybe neither of them knows for sure, and maybe nobody knows for sure what's going to happen.

DETERMINIST: Okay, right.

FATALIST: So at Tuesday Noon when they're talking, what one says is true and what the other says is false, right?

DETERMINIST: Right.

FATALIST: Suppose what Alice says happens to be true. Now that means, right then when they're talking on Tuesday, that it's true that a sea battle will take place the next day. Now, if that's the case, then nothing could interfere with the sea battle's taking place. For example, it's impossible that this takes place: the Admiral of the Fleet decides on Tuesday night that a battle would be too risky, so he tells his boats to back off, so that there will be no battle. That can't happen, if what Alice said was true. The sea battle is inevitable: nothing anyone could do would prevent it! But suppose Betty happens to be right. That means that, right then when they're talking on Tuesday, that there will be no sea battle on Wednesday. Given that, nothing could bring a sea battle about. For example, if on Tuesday night the Admiral suddenly decided to tell his fleet to attack on the next morning, for some reason they still wouldn't.

DETERMINIST: Wait a minute, why not?

FATALIST: Because, we're assuming, what Betty said was true: there will be no sea battle on Wednesday. This wouldn't be true if the Admiral actually brought about a battle then.

DETERMINIST: Hmm.

FATALIST: So either way, whichever one of them is right, the future—what happens on Wednesday—is already set at Noon on Tuesday, and the future fated events will happen no matter what occurs in-between.

DETERMINIST: Well, that's a very clever argument, but it must be wrong because it's got a clearly false conclusion. Everyone knows that whether the sea battle happens on Wednesday depends on all sorts of things that occur after Alice and Betty have that conversation.

FATALIST: So what's wrong with the argument?

DETERMINIST: How about this. It's based on the supposition that, on Tuesday, what one of the two says is true and what the other says is false. Maybe that supposition is not right.

FATALIST: How could that be?

DETERMINIST: Maybe neither statement is, just then, either true or false.

FATALIST: That would be weird. There's nothing special about those statements about the future. You'd have to hold that no statement about the future is either true or false, that both are in a sort of strange third condition.

DETERMINIST: Well, maybe given that the future is open, in some sense, that means that predictions about the future aren't either true or false at the time they're made, but they get to be either true or false later, when the time they're talking about rolls around. I know that's a strange sort of conclusion. But I can't see any way around it at the moment.

FATALIST: You're in good company. Lots of philosophers, Aristotle included, considered that way around the conclusion they didn't like. That way of thinking rejects what lots of philosophers think is a very basic law of logic or of rational thought: the Law of Bivalence, which says that every statement is either true or false. What is a statement, if it's neither true nor false? That doesn't seem to make any sense.

DETERMINIST: Earlier on, during the ethics discussion,[2] I heard somebody claim that ethical statements were neither true or false.

---

2 Conversation III.

FATALIST: Right, that follows if you think of ethical statements as being like orders (like "Don't do that!") or expressions of approval (like "Awesome!" or "Yum!"). Those sorts of things people say are unsurprisingly neither true nor false. But statements about the future, like "There will be a sea battle tomorrow," are assertions, saying something about the way the world is (or rather will be) so it looks very implausible to treat them as neither true nor false.

DETERMINIST: Okay, I agree that it would be very odd to see statements about the future as neither true nor false when they're uttered. And I see the problem here: if they're true (for example) then it's hard to see that they might turn out false! This whole problem is weird.

4. Predictability

SCEPTIC: All that about fatalism is interesting, but let's get back to discussing determinism. First of all, I gather that determinists sometimes state their position in terms of the possibility of predicting everything that will happen, if there were complete knowledge of the relevant current facts?

DETERMINIST: Right. If you knew all the relevant facts about what was happening at one time, then you'd be able to predict everything that would happen at every time after that, because it's all determined. That position was stated centuries ago by a French philosopher named Pierre Laplace. I think I have a quote from him. Here it is.

> An intellect which at any given moment knew all the forces that animate Nature and the mutual positions of the beings that comprise it, if this intellect were vast enough to submit its data to analysis, could condense into a single formula the movement of the greatest bodies of the universe and that of the lightest atom: for such an intellect nothing could be uncertain; and the future just like the past would be present before our eyes.

SCEPTIC: What did Laplace mean by all that?

IDENTITY THEORIST: Putting it into more modern terms, he means that if you knew all the laws of nature—the rules that govern cause and effect—and the exact locations and motions of all the things there are, and had sufficient calculation skill and time, you could calculate every future event.

SCEPTIC: I think that you're making a mistake in connecting determinism with predictability. I think that determinism doesn't necessarily mean that everything is predictable.

DETERMINIST: Why is that?

SCEPTIC: I can think of a situation in which we can imagine that determinism is true, but a particular kind of prediction would be impossible no matter how much you knew.

DETERMINIST: Let's hear.

SCEPTIC: Okay, let's suppose that there's a super-psychologist, who knows all the laws of psychology, and all the facts about somebody's life.

DETERMINIST: Okay. Are you going to argue against the position that what happens at one time determines what happens at the next?

SCEPTIC: No, that's not the point I want to make now. We can get back to that question later. Let's suppose for the moment that determinism is true.

DETERMINIST: Okay. Wouldn't that imply that the super-psychologist could always predict what anybody will do, at any future time?

SCEPTIC: No, not in all conditions. Suppose that the super-psychologist is trying to predict Fred's action, and write down those predictions in a book called *Fred's Book of Life*. The psychologist finds out every fact there is about Fred and writes predictions down in the book. But let's suppose that Fred gets to read the book of predictions about his future, and suppose furthermore that Fred is a perverse and contrary sort of guy, who always likes to do the opposite of what people expect of him. That would mean, for example, that if Fred read in the book the prediction that he would stay home tomorrow, that would make him perversely go out tomorrow instead, just out of contrariness. So that prediction would be wrong.

DETERMINIST: Okay, but the super-psychologist knows *everything* about Fred, including his contrariness. So the super-psychologist would know in advance that Fred would read the prediction in the book, and just to make it wrong, would stay home. So that's the real prediction the super-psychologist would make, and wouldn't that be correct?

SCEPTIC: But remember that the super-psychologist is going to write down all the predictions in Fred's book, and Fred is going to read them. So if the super-psychologist wrote down, "Fred reads my book, and decides to do the opposite, and stays home instead of going out," then Fred would read *that*, and he'd go out after all!

DETERMINIST: I can see where this is going. So under these circumstances, even though we suppose Fred is completely determined, nevertheless, given that he reads the predictions, the predictions will always turn out wrong.

SCEPTIC: Right.

DETERMINIST: Whatever the predictions are.

SCEPTIC: Right.

DETERMINIST: Cute. Okay, I withdraw the idea that determinism always implies predictability. But except in weird cases like that one, I think it does. I mean, if Fred isn't allowed to read his book, or if he's not a perverse contrarian, then the super-psychologist could predict him, right?

MATHEMATICIAN: I hope you don't mind me coming into the conversation at this point. I think there are some mathematical ideas that raise doubts about DETERMINIST's position about predictability.

DETERMINIST: Good, let's hear.

MATHEMATICIAN: Okay, to begin with, here's a question. How long is the coastline of Nova Scotia?

DETERMINIST: I haven't the foggiest idea. We could go look it up. Why do you ask?

MATHEMATICIAN: I didn't expect you'd know, and an estimate of the length is not what I'm after here. The coastline of Nova Scotia is extremely irregular, with bays, inlets, and points, of every size, all over. Imagine, then, that you took a large-diameter wheel with a dial that recorded distance on it, and ran it along the coastline, recording the total distance. You'd get some number or other. I saw an estimate for the length of the coastline at 7500 km; suppose that you measured it with this wheel device, and calculated that it was 7520 km. But this wouldn't be perfectly accurate.

DETERMINIST: Oh, I get it, that number isn't really right because the length changes with the tides. There isn't any precise number.

MATHEMATICIAN: That's true, but it's not the point I had in mind. Ignore the tides—there's a more interesting reason. The reason is that there are very small irregularities of the coastline—tiny little coves and points—that would be left out when you rolled the large wheel along. If you used a smaller wheel, being more careful to measure these little features, you'd get a larger figure for the length, say 7521 km.

DETERMINIST: I can see that.

MATHEMATICIAN: But then if you employed a smaller wheel, or some such device that took into account even smaller curves, your total would be still larger, say, 7523.6 km. Every time you moved to a more sensitive way of measuring, you'd get a larger total length.

DETERMINIST: Okay.

MATHEMATICIAN: So at what point to you get the *real* length?

DETERMINIST: Hm, that's an interesting question. I guess that if you keep getting slightly longer totals as the scale at which you're doing your measurements increases, and you start counting in tinier features, then you could keep doing this forever: going larger and larger scale, getting bigger and bigger numbers, but never settle on a final, correct length.

MATHEMATICIAN: So maybe we'd have to say that there isn't any exact figure for the length of the coastline!

DETERMINIST: Wait a minute. Isn't this just a familiar thing about measuring? I mean, for example, imagine that you're measuring a line with a ruler just marked roughly in centimetres. So you say that the line is roughly 15 cm. long. But then you measure it with a more finely graduated ruler, marked in millimetres, and now you say that it's actually 15.1 cm. long. But then you use even finer measuring instruments, and you refine that to 15.08 cm, or even further, say to 15.083 cm., and so on. I mean, you can keep adding decimal places forever, as long as you have more and more precise measuring instruments. Finer and finer instruments get you a closer and closer approximation to the real length of the line. But nobody's tempted to say that there isn't any real length.

MATHEMATICIAN: I agree with you about that example, of measuring the line. What's interesting about the coastline example however is that it's different. Finer measurements of the coastline do not get you a closer approximation to the real length. Finer measurements include points and coves not included before, and add significantly to the length. The finer the measurement, the longer the length. It doesn't get closer and closer to anything. It just keeps getting longer and longer.

DETERMINIST: Hmm.

MATHEMATICIAN: And there are other features of nature that are like that too. You'd keep getting slightly different figures when you measured them, increasing as the scale of your measurements became more precise.

DETERMINIST: Okay.

MATHEMATICIAN: Now, laws of nature, we suppose, even if they were perfect, would give results only as precise as the data you used. So a perfect prediction requires perfect data to start with. In Laplace's terms, the "intellect" would have to know not only the exact "forces that animate Nature" but also the exact "mutual positions of the beings that comprise it." But from what we've just said, in certain circumstances there isn't any such thing as an exact figure for some natural magnitudes. So in those cases, what's required for that "intellect" to make a prediction doesn't exist.

DETERMINIST: Are you saying that, practically speaking, we can't get measurements of magnitudes which are completely precise? I don't think that Laplace was claiming we could. He was imagining an ideal intellect with this perfect data. Of course, in real life nothing is perfect. Where's the news here?

MATHEMATICIAN: No, that's not exactly what I'm saying. I'm saying, and I think you'll see this if you think about the Nova-Scotia-Coastline example, that there isn't any such thing to be known. It's not just our own imperfect powers. It's that there's no such thing as the real length of the coastline. I mean, let's put this in figurative religious terms. God, who's a perfect measurer, could know exactly what the length of a line is, carried out to an infinite number of decimal points. But even God couldn't know what the real length of the coastline of Nova Scotia is. That's why I want to say that there isn't any such thing as its real length.

DETERMINIST: Well, I'm going to have to think about that one. It still seems to me that everything in the world must have some real dimensions, mass, location, and so on—real magnitudes—that determine its causal interactions with other things.

5. Is there Evidence for Determinism?

SCEPTIC: Okay, let's leave the question of predictability to the side, and get back to determinism. What makes you think that determinism is true?

DETERMINIST: I think that this is a basic fact of common sense, and of science.

INDETERMINIST: Excuse me, I hope you don't mind if I break in here. I think that you're wrong about determinism—there are things that don't have causes. And I think you're wrong that it's a universal assumption of common sense and science.

DETERMINIST: Well, here's a story that I heard in a previous discussion[3] that I think shows that determinism is just common sense. Imagine that your car is producing a loud squeak. So you take it into a car-repair place, and when you come back, the repairman tells you that he noticed that squeak,

---

3 Conversation I.

but he hasn't fixed it because there wasn't any cause why it's squeaking. You say, "You mean, you haven't found the cause?" The repairman replies, "No, I mean I've taken things apart, and examined everything, and there just isn't any cause." Okay, my question is, what time is it then?

INDETERMINIST: It's time to get a different repairman!

DETERMINIST: Right! You know that this guy is wrong. There has to be a cause; it's got to be just that he hasn't found it. It's obvious that there has to be a cause, because everything has a cause. Isn't that just common sense?

INDETERMINIST: Maybe, when it comes to cars, but there are other areas where we don't think there are causes.

DETERMINIST: But hasn't science given us reasons to think that everything has a cause? The whole history of science is finding causes for things, and science has been enormously successful.

INDETERMINIST: I agree that science has found the causes of a whole lot of things, but that doesn't show that determinism is true. Determinism claims that *everything* has determining causes, and science hasn't shown that. There are lots of cases in which scientists haven't found causes when they've searched. The proof of that is that there are thousands of scientists searching for causes in every field of science, right now. The fact that they're looking shows that they haven't found the causes. So if you want to talk about actual science, it doesn't really give any good reason at all to think that everything has a cause. In order to support that conclusion, they'd have to have found causes for everything they'd investigated, and they certainly haven't.

DETERMINIST: Okay, but scientists are convinced that there are causes where they haven't found them yet. I mean, that's why they're looking, right? If they thought there weren't causes in some cases, they wouldn't be looking. Consider, for example, cancer research. They've been looking hard, for a long time, and they still haven't found what causes certain kinds of cancer, but they don't conclude that there aren't any causes there—that these cancers just happen with no cause at all, just out of the blue. They're sure that there are causes to be discovered; only they don't know what they are yet. Maybe, in some cases, they'll never discover the causes. But they're all sure that there are causes there.

INDETERMINIST: I agree that scientists in many areas are convinced that there are causes where none have yet been found. But isn't this an article of faith, rather than a scientific generalization based solidly on observation and experiment? Isn't this an unscientific thing for scientists to believe?

DETERMINIST: Well I think it's the right thing to believe. If they didn't believe that, they wouldn't be looking, and they wouldn't find what was there to be discovered.

INDETERMINIST: Okay, maybe that bit of faith is a good thing for scientists to have, as a matter of practical policy. It's like when there's a mine cave-in. After several days have passed, it's pretty likely that the trapped miners have all died, but we'd rather that people held on to the belief, unsupported by experience of other mine disasters, that miners could still be alive down there, so that they keep digging just in case. So maybe it's a good thing that scientists believe everything has a cause. But we're not talking about when it might be a good thing to believe it. We're wondering whether it's likely to be true. And what science has shown so far is just that *some* things have causes. This gives us no reason to conclude that *everything* has a cause.

6. Quantum Indeterminacy

INDETERMINIST: But anyway I've heard scientists say that it's been shown in some areas that determinism is actually false.

DETERMINIST: Really! Tell me more.

INDETERMINIST: It's in quantum physics, the physics of extremely small particles. There was talk about this earlier, also.[4]

DETERMINIST: I wasn't there.

INDETERMINIST: There's a physicist next door; let's ask him to come in and tell us about it.

PHYSICIST: That's right, it's become accepted in quantum physics that certain events are undetermined by causes. Here are a couple of examples. First consider a radioactive element. To say that it's radioactive means that each atom of the substance will decay—change into something somewhat different by emitting a certain particle or wave. For example, an atom of the radioactive element Carbon-10 decays by emitting one neutrino and one positron and changing into the different element Boron-10. (Never mind what these gadgets are—it doesn't matter for your purposes.)

DETERMINIST: Whew!

PHYSICIST: The half-life of a substance is the time it will take for half of the atoms to decay. The half-life of Carbon-10 is 20 seconds. Now, consider a

---

4 Conversation I.

particular atom of Carbon-10. On average, this sort of atom can be expected to decay in 20 seconds. It's a good bet that this atom will still be around in 2 seconds, and gone in 1 month. But when, exactly, will this atom decay? It might be any time: we don't know. And here's the important point: there is no reason why one of those atoms takes ½ a second, but another takes 20 seconds, and another a week.

DETERMINIST: But the instability of Carbon-10 causes the decay, right? I mean, it's not really uncaused.

PHYSICIST: Right, but what's uncaused is that one atom will decay earlier and one later. What you can predict is the probability that it will decay during some time period, but you can't predict exactly when.

DETERMINIST: You mean, there's no way of *knowing* just how long a particular atom will take to decay? That's consistent with determinism. No determinist thinks that we can know everything about how everything will work.

PHYSICIST: No, I mean that there is no cause to be known. I mean that there is no reason why one atom decays earlier than another one. No cause.

DETERMINIST: No cause? How can that be? How can you prove there's no cause? I mean, just because you can't find any difference between those two atoms, doesn't mean that there is no difference between them.

PHYSICIST: That's right, but the currently accepted theory says that there isn't any difference. We physicists refer to this as the principle that there are, in these cases, *no hidden variables*. It's not merely that we can't find any. It's that our theory shows that there aren't any. This theory has been subjected to all sorts of experimental tests, and has passed with flying colours. Every mainstream physicist accepts it nowadays.

DETERMINIST: But it doesn't make any sense to me.

PHYSICIST: You're not alone in finding it odd, even unbelievable. When it was first proposed, a lot of scientists thought it was really shocking, and that it had to be wrong. Even the greatest physicist of the last few centuries, Einstein, thought that it couldn't be true. He's supposed to have said, "God does not play dice." But just about all of us accept it nowadays.

DETERMINIST: I'm glad to hear that Einstein and I agree! But I guess I can't dispute this theory, though it certainly sounds like nonsense to me. I mean, clearly, physicists are in a better position to decide matters of physics than I am. But look, even if this theory is right, it talks about things that are so small and invisible that they don't make any difference in the world we live in, doesn't it? I mean, that sort of indeterminacy doesn't make it indeterminate whether flicking a light switch will make the light go on, does it?

PHYSICIST: You're right. There are indeterminacies going on at the extremely small level when you flick a switch and turn on a light too, but these sorts of things average out, because there are such a huge number of tiny particles involved in switching on the light. So there's no indeterminacy in this large-scale event. But there are situations you can devise in which quantum indeterminacy does make a difference in things large enough to make a difference to us.

DETERMINIST: Like what?

PHYSICIST: Okay, imagine a machine that detects and counts positrons in a certain area, and put a piece of metal containing a certain quantity of radioactive material in the detecting area of the machine. Adjust the quantity of this material and the set-up so that on average, you'll get a positron every 10 seconds. Now attach a timer that counts off one 10-second interval, and turns on a light if there was a positron detected during that time. On average, half the time you run this machine, the light will go on, and half the time it won't. There is no cause why the light did go on one time, but didn't the other.

DETERMINIST: Wait a minute: when the light went on, the positron caused it.

PHYSICIST: Yes, but getting a positron during that period, as opposed to not getting one, has no cause. There's no cause why you didn't get a positron one time, but you did get one another time.

DETERMINIST: All right, I accept that as an undetermined event, and I admit you can cook up devices to make quantum indeterminism make a big enough difference to be detectable in the world we live in. But differences that big don't occur in nature, do they?

PHYSICIST: No, you're right, I can't think of any cases of the everyday visible things we're familiar with in which quantum indeterminacy plays a part.

INDETERMINIST: Well, I'm not so sure about that. Anyway, I think we've established that the idea that some things are undetermined at least makes sense—it's not unthinkable nonsense as I think DETERMINIST was inclined to say. That at least leaves it open for human beings to be undetermined.

DETERMINIST: I guess that's what you're mostly interested in establishing— indeterminism for human actions, right?

INDETERMINIST: Yes, that's right.

DETERMINIST: Why is it important to you that human actions be seen as undetermined?

INDETERMINIST: Because that's the only way humans could have free will.

7. Free Will

DETERMINIST: What exactly do you mean by *free will*?

INDETERMINIST: To say that you have free will is to say that your actions are up to you. It means that you actually freely choose what you do, that you aren't forced to act, or to choose what to do. When you do something by your own free will, you could have acted otherwise, because what you did depended on your own choice, and you might have made a different choice.

DETERMINIST: And you believe in free will?

INDETERMINIST: I do. I'm not just an indeterminist, I'm also what philosophers call a *libertarian*. An indeterminist believes that some things are not determined. A libertarian believes that humans have free will.

DETERMINIST: Wait a minute. One of the participants in the discussion about political philosophy[5] was called LIBERTARIAN. That name indicated the view that government should minimize restrictions on people in various ways.

INDETERMINIST: Right, that makes the name confusing. That was a political libertarian. Political libertarians believe in liberty—in freedom—just as I do, but in a different sense of 'liberty.' They're talking about political liberty—freedom from government restriction. I'm talking about freedom from causal determination.

DETERMINIST: Okay. Now, you think that for a person to have free will there has to be indeterminism of some sort?

INDETERMINIST: That's right. If determinism were true about human actions and decisions, then those actions and decisions would be just part of a vast interlocking mechanism. You'd do what you do, and choose what you choose, only because of external causes. Given those causes, you have to make those choices and do those actions—you couldn't have acted otherwise. They force you to choose and act the way you do. If determinism were true, you really wouldn't be making any genuine choices at all—

---

5 Conversation II.

what might seem to be choices wouldn't be real ones, because these "choices" would be pre-determined by external causes. You'd be like a machine, in which the way you're built plus whatever input comes in together determine the way the machine acts. There'd be no free will there.

DETERMINIST: Well, so what? What exactly is wrong with thinking about people as determined?

INDETERMINIST: Several things are badly wrong about that. First, it's just false, and we can tell it's false.

DETERMINIST: How's that? How can we tell?

INDETERMINIST: Well, you can tell that some of your actions are the result of genuine decisions, of real choices, just by observing what goes on when you make those choices. In these cases, you can tell that you might just have chosen otherwise, given all the existing background conditions and stimuli. For example, think about when you went into Burger Queen yesterday for lunch. Remember your experience in there. You thought about what you'd like for lunch, and you decided to have the McWhopper, but you could just as well have chosen the McSalad. It was totally up to you.

DETERMINIST: I'm not sure that that's what I observe. I mean, I do make a decision about what to order for lunch, but when I observe my experience, it's not obvious to me that this isn't caused by anything. I mean, how do you observe whether something is caused or not? What would be the difference in experience?

INDETERMINIST: Don't you feel that, given everything that went on before, you might have chosen differently?

DETERMINIST: Maybe, I'm not sure. But anyway, even if I do, I don't think that shows that my mental processes on that occasion weren't determined by causes. I think there are two different questions here. One of them is whether our actions and choices are determined by causes. The other is whether we could have acted or chosen differently.

INDETERMINIST: I don't think those are different questions. If your actions and "choices" are determined by causes, doesn't that mean you couldn't have chosen differently?

DETERMINIST: I don't think so, but we can get back to that later. First, let's talk about whether you're right that you can observe that there are no causes for your actions and decisions.

INDETERMINIST: I do observe that there are no causes in my own case, and I don't think I could be wrong about something like that. I agree with

DUALIST that you're always in a perfect position to know what's going on in your own mind by introspection. You can't be wrong about your own mental contents.

DETERMINIST: Well, I disagree, but there was a lot of discussion about that a while back,[6] so I think we should leave that question alone right now. Never mind whether our introspections can be wrong or not: it seems to me that the causes of our choices are something that we're mostly unaware of—they're not in our conscious mind, so we don't introspect them. Take that example you brought up, about the choice at Burger Queen. People's choices about what to eat are the result of all sorts of causes, many of which they're unaware of. For example, maybe Sally saw an ad for the McWhopper on TV the day before, which she's forgotten completely about, but which unconsciously causes her to order that. Or maybe Fred ordered the McSalad because his Catholic upbringing long ago is still influencing him, so he avoids eating meat on Fridays, without even knowing that he is doing that, or why. You ask Sally and Fred why they decided to order those things for lunch, and both tell you that they don't know, they just ordered what they felt like having. You ask them if there are any deeper causes for them making that choice, and they sincerely tell you that they don't know that there are any—at least, it doesn't feel that way. But they're both wrong. Isn't it the case that there are all sorts of unconscious determininants of our behaviour—causes we're unaware of? There are all sorts of factors that might have been causally relevant to my action in Burger Queen. Doesn't advertising, for example, have a lot of causal influence on our purchasing decisions?

INDETERMINIST: Maybe it does, sometimes, for some people. But when *I* make that decision about what to have for lunch, it's really completely clear to me that advertising didn't cause me to do what I do. Maybe it gave me a little push in one direction or another, but this isn't causal determination. I still can order whatever I like.

DETERMINIST: Well, I don't think so. Advertising really does work. I don't like the idea, but it's true! Otherwise, if people still could order whatever they wanted, if advertising wasn't a causal factor on what people did, why would companies spend so much money on it? There's all sorts of good evidence that some advertising campaigns work, and it's simple to measure. You just notice that sales get a big boost right after you start that advertising campaign. And there are other bits of evidence in the same area for determinism. In those big fast-food operations, they know pretty well in advance just what people are going to order, and the prepare for

---

6 Conversation IV.

that, so they don't have too much or too little stuff on hand. They can predict pretty well, and adjust for variables like the time of day, the season of the year, the new advertising campaign, and so on. How could they make these successful, reliable scientific predictions, if people were undetermined?

INDETERMINIST: But nobody can predict what *I'm* going to order when I walk into the Burger Queen. Maybe they can predict that on a rainy Tuesday in March they'll get about 100 customers coming in between 12 and 1, and they'll sell about 40 McWhoppers and about 25 McSalads, but they can't predict me, or any other individual person.

DETERMINIST: Maybe not, but that doesn't show that you're not determined. It just shows that nobody knows the laws of psychology that are operating here in sufficient detail to make such fine predictions, or that nobody knows the details of your exposure to advertising, or the other factors that might be causally relevant in your case, like how hungry you happen to be at that time, or what kinds of food you were raised with as a child, or your genetic dispositions, and so on. But look at what they can predict: if they know, for example, that they'll sell more french fries when it's warm than when it's cold, doesn't this show that there are causal influences?

INDETERMINIST: All it shows is that the weather produces a sort of inclination in some people—it doesn't determine what they do. It only makes it more probable that people in general act in a certain way—it sometimes gives a little push.

DETERMINIST: Well, that's good enough for me. If warm weather makes it more probable that people eat french fries, then that's evidence that weather is a *causal factor* in determining people's eating behaviour. It's not sufficient all by itself, but together with appropriate background conditions, it produces its effect. That's why it brings about its effect only some of the time—the times when the other conditions are there too. That's why its presence makes its effect more probable, not invariably necessary.

8. The Incompatibility of Responsibility and Determinism

INDETERMINIST: Here's one of my main reasons for thinking that people's actions aren't causally determined. It's because I think it's immoral to think of people that way. It fails to grant them the dignity they deserve. It's insulting and degrading. It lowers them to the level of animals or machines.

DETERMINIST: Well! I guess that's a very inspirational thought, but I don't join you in that sentiment. First of all, I'm not convinced that thinking of people as determined really does insult them, or rob them of their dignity. But secondly, I think that the real issue here is not whether some way of thinking about people is nice to them or not, but rather whether it's true or false.

INDETERMINIST: Look, I'm not arguing that it would be terrible if people were determined, so therefore they're not. I agree that it would be terrible, but that conclusion doesn't follow. What I am arguing is that the whole way we think about people is inconsistent with causal determination. It's so deeply rooted in our whole view of people that you'd just have to change everything about how we think about people to think of them as determined.

DETERMINIST: Why exactly do you suppose that?

INDETERMINIST: Because if people's actions were determined, then they wouldn't be responsible for what they do. I think even you will agree that people often can and should be held responsible for what they do. But people are responsible for what they do only when they've acted out of free choice. If they were determined in their actions, they wouldn't be responsible.

DETERMINIST: What do you mean, "responsible"?

INDETERMINIST: I mean *morally* responsible. When you're responsible for a bad action, it's your fault, you're to blame. And this is the case only if you made a genuinely free choice. In the same way, when you do something good, you're morally responsible, and you're praiseworthy, only if it was a genuine free choice. If people's actions were caused, determined, then they wouldn't be responsible for what they do; they shouldn't be blamed for their bad actions, or given credit for their good ones.

DETERMINIST: I don't see why determination is incompatible with responsibility.

INDETERMINIST: Compare what happens in the case of a purely determined machine. For example, it's bad when your car fails to start on a very cold morning, but it's ridiculous to think of blaming your car. It's not your car's fault, of course. That's because we've got a causal story explaining why the car acted as it did. The car's battery was old, and didn't hold much charge, and the cold reduced the battery's power below what was needed to start it that morning. But then, when you buy a new powerful battery for the car, it starts right up every morning, no matter how cold. You don't give your car credit for this—you wouldn't praise it or congratulate it! That's because again there's a causal story. In both cases, causal determination means no moral responsibility. We think that cars and other machines are fully causally determined, and that's why we never think of them as responsible. People, however, are responsible for what they do, often, anyway, and that's because they're not causally determined.

HARD DETERMINIST: If you wouldn't mind, I'd like to say some things at this point. I've been listening to your conversation, and I have to say I agree fully with INDETERMINIST that fully causally determined systems aren't responsible for what they do. But I'm also a determinist about human beings.

INDETERMINIST: So you believe that people aren't responsible for what they do?

HARD DETERMINIST: That's right.

INDETERMINIST: But that's absurd. You mean you don't blame people when they do something wrong, or praise them for doing something good?

HARD DETERMINIST: That's correct. But my position isn't really crazy. Maybe I can make it sound a little more reasonable. Look, you know how you can sometimes tend to forgive someone who did something bad to you, once you find out something about the causal story behind that person's action? For example, imagine that some guy did something nasty like stealing something out of your car, but somehow or other you find out that he was raised in a completely horrible environment. He was sexually and emotionally abused by his parents and when his mother died from a drug overdose, he ran away from his foster home, and lived on the streets among mentally ill people, prostitutes, and panhandlers. This kind of background is a strong causal factor for producing criminals. Finding this out doesn't make you feel any better about your car being robbed, but it does make you see the guy who did it as a victim of his surroundings, and maybe you even forgive him. There's an old saying in French, "*Tout comprendre c'est tout pardonner*," which means, *To understand everything is to forgive everything*, and it's true. The more you understand what caused a person to do something bad, the less you blame them. And the same thing for people who are extra-good: you tend to diminish your praise of them as you begin to find out the psychological causal story behind what they did. Suppose, for example, that you found out that Mother Theresa had a severe neurotic compulsion to help others, the result of a genetically-originated chemical imbalance in her brain. I mean, that would tend to make her halo dim in your eyes, wouldn't it?

INDETERMINIST: I guess so.

HARD DETERMINIST: So we're in agreement that when there's a causal story for actions, moral responsibility, praise and blame, all disappear.

INDETERMINIST: Right, we agree about that. We agree that causal determination is incompatible with responsibility.

HARD DETERMINIST: Now all I have to do is to convince you that there is a full causal story for everyone's actions, though we haven't got much idea of what the causes are in many cases. That's just determinism.

INDETERMINIST: Yes, but that's something you can't convince me of! Your story about the criminal with that terrible childhood was an extreme case, one in which we maybe would be willing to think that he was caused to turn to crime. But in more ordinary, less extreme cases, it doesn't feel like cause is operating at all. But anyway, here's another consideration. The consequences of determinism are even worse than what we've talked about so far. If determinism for human actions were true, there wouldn't even be any point for morality at all.

DETERMINIST: Why is that?

INDETERMINIST: Well, the essence of morality is telling people what they ought to do, and this has a point only because sometimes they don't do what they ought to. But if determinism is right, then whatever anyone did was fully determined by prior causes, and, given those causes, the person couldn't have acted differently. So there's absolutely no point in saying that they ought to have done something else, because they couldn't have. The philosopher's slogan that contains the point here is "Ought implies can." What that means is that the only time it can be true that anyone ought to do something is when they can do it. And if nobody can do otherwise than what they in fact do, then nobody ever ought to act differently. The whole point of morality flies out the window.

HARD DETERMINIST: I agree.

SCEPTIC: Aha! At last we're getting to the bottom of what I said way back at the beginning of this discussion: that we're all just machines so ethics doesn't make any sense. If we're all machines, in the sense that all our actions are causally determined, then there's never any point in saying that somebody ought to have acted differently from what they did.

9. Soft Determinism

DETERMINIST: I've been listening to the discussion between the two of you, INDETERMINIST and HARD DETERMINIST. I agree with HARD DETERMINIST that every human action is fully determined by causes. I mean, that's just the determinist position, and HARD DETERMINIST and I are both determinists. But I'm not happy with concluding from determinism that responsibility, praise and blame, and ethics all have to be abandoned. Does determinism really imply all that?

SOFT DETERMINIST: That's where I can maybe add something to this. I'm also a determinist—that makes three of us—but I also believe in moral responsibility, and praise and blame. I think that, despite the truth of determinism, it's often the case that people could have acted otherwise than they did, and so ethics does have a point: when what they did was bad, and (what often happens) they could have acted otherwise, then it's the case that they should have acted otherwise. Remember when DETERMINIST said that whether people are always causally determined and whether people ever could have acted otherwise are two different questions? I agree. I think that people are always causally determined, but that people sometimes could have acted otherwise.

DETERMINIST: So you think that determinism can somehow co-exist with moral responsibility, praise and blame, ethical evaluation? You think that despite the fact that someone's actions are completely determined by prior causes, nevertheless you still can say that the person could have acted otherwise? You think that determinism is compatible with all that?

SOFT DETERMINIST: Yes, that's what I think. That's why my position, soft determinism, is sometimes called *compatibilism*: because we think that determinism is compatible with moral responsibility, praise and blame, ethical evaluation, and being capable of acting otherwise. INDETERMINIST and HARD DETERMINIST are clearly Incompatibilists.

DETERMINIST: You call your position *soft determinism*. Does that mean that it's a "softer" version of determinism than that held by *hard determinism*? A less stringent form of determinism, or something like that? Kinder, gentler determinism?

SOFT DETERMINIST: No, my position is just as strongly deterministic as the one held by hard determinists. We both believe in the same thoroughgoing determinism. The name 'soft determinism' is traditionally associated with my position, though it's somewhat misleading. The difference between hard determinism and soft determinism is in what we think about what determinism implies about moral responsibility. Hard determinists think that the causal determination of all human actions means that people aren't responsible for anything they do, that praise and blame are inappropriate, that it's useless to say that somebody *ought* to have acted other than the way they did, because they *couldn't* have. Soft determinists, on the other hand, think that despite the fact that all human actions are fully causally determined, nevertheless we sometimes are responsible for what we do, that praise for good actions and blame for bad ones are appropriate, when the person who did those actions is responsible for them, and that we often could have acted other than we did. So saying that someone ought not to have done what they did is often appropriate. Hard determinism is determinism plus *incompatibilism*. Soft determinism is determinism plus compatibilism.

SCEPTIC: I'm confused. Could somebody outline the main points of the positions here for me?

SOFT DETERMINIST: Okay, a table should make everything clear:

	Is determinism true?	Is determinism compatible with responsibility?	Are we ever responsible?
Libertarianism	No	No	Yes
Hard Determinism	Yes	No	No
Soft Determinism	Yes	Yes	Yes

HARD DETERMINIST: All right, tell me how your position works. I don't understand how you can hold that a person's actions are causally determined, but nevertheless that person could have done otherwise. The causes leading up to that action determine the action—they make the action happen. How could it not have been done? Given those causes, it could not have been otherwise, isn't that right?

SOFT DETERMINIST: I think that saying a person could have done otherwise doesn't mean that the person might have done something different given exactly the same causally relevant antecedents. I agree with you that certain events and conditions obtaining before the action caused it; so, given those events and conditions, that action had to happen. But I don't think that this is what we mean when we say that someone could have done otherwise. I think that what we mean is that the person would have done otherwise *if that person had chosen otherwise*. Let's take a look at an example: Sally is in Burger Queen and she orders the McWhopper. This action clearly involved her choice: when she stood there looking at the menu, she's *making a decision* to have the McWhopper, and this decision causes her to order that for lunch. Could she have acted otherwise? Sure: she could have ordered the McSalad instead, *if she had decided to order that*.

HARD DETERMINIST: But wasn't her decision itself causally determined?

SOFT DETERMINIST: Of course it was. Everything is causally determined. Maybe there's something in her metabolism that makes you crave meat on that day, and that causes her to order the McWhopper. Maybe it's the years of TV advertising she's been exposed to that caused you to make that decision, or maybe it's just the flashy sign that caught her eye when she went into the Burger Queen. Probably nobody knows, not even her, what caused her to make that decision, but we determinists agree that there was something.

HARD DETERMINIST: So, given that there were those causes, whatever they were, she was determined to make that decision?

SOFT DETERMINIST: Right.

HARD DETERMINIST: Well given that it was completely determined by prior causes, I wouldn't want to call what she did a *decision*, really.

INDETERMINIST: Neither would I. But never mind—maybe that's just a matter of words, and we can get back to that. Let's keep calling it that, and hear the rest of the story.

SOFT DETERMINIST: Okay, so in that situation, I'd say that she might have acted otherwise, if her choice had been otherwise. And, in order for that to be true, whatever caused that choice would also have had to be different.

HARD DETERMINIST: You indicated a couple of times that it's only sometimes true that a person might have acted otherwise. When do you take it that it's not true?

SOFT DETERMINIST: Well, here's a sort of silly example of that, but you'll get the idea. Suppose Marvin misses a really important test and he goes to talk to his teacher the next day. His teacher is looking at him with exasperation, blaming him for doing such a stupid thing. But he explains that some of his buddies wanted to play a joke on him, and they broke the handle on his dormitory door so he couldn't get out, and he had to phone for repairs, and took hours to get out; by that time, the test was over.

HARD DETERMINIST: Ha ha, teachers who believe that one would believe anything! Marvin should try out the one about how his dog ate the assignment next!

SOFT DETERMINIST: He should. Anyway, the point of this imaginary story is that when Marvin stayed in his room and missed the test, he could not have done otherwise. He couldn't have gone to take the test instead, because he was locked into the room. The crucial thing here is that he would have stayed in that room till the locksmith arrived, no matter what he decided. It's false that had he decided to take the test, he would have acted differently. In those circumstances, his decision could make no difference at all. It's not a causal factor in his action, and no change in decision would have altered what he did. He was stuck in that room no matter what he decided to do.

HARD DETERMINIST: So where do you think that responsibility comes in here?

SOFT DETERMINIST: Well, because he couldn't have done otherwise (by making a different decision), it's not his fault that he missed the test. Now compare that with a different example. Suppose that Sally's vegetarian animal-rights-activist friends are angry with her for ordering the McWhopper in the Burger Queen: they think she should have had the salad instead. Assuming that ordering meat is an immoral thing to do, then she's to blame in this case, because she could have done otherwise: that is, if she had decided otherwise, then her actions would have been different, and more morally acceptable. If she had decided to order the McSalad instead of the McWhopper, then she would have ordered the McSalad. The bottom line is: people are responsible for their actions when those actions are caused by their own decisions; but when their own decisions are irrelevant—if the action would have been the same even had the person decided otherwise—then there's no responsibility. Here's another example of a case in which the person's decisions are irrelevant, so I'd say that person couldn't have acted otherwise, and isn't morally responsible for the action. Imagine that five really enormous members of Fred's university's football team walk up to Fred on the street. Three of them grab hold of him, one of them puts a gun in Fred's hand, and another forces Fred's finger against the trigger, so that a passerby is shot.

INDETERMINIST: That's a pretty stupid story.

SOFT DETERMINIST: You bet. But here's the point. If that happened, Fred wouldn't be held responsible for the shooting, would he? He wouldn't be blamed.

INDETERMINIST: Of course not.

SOFT DETERMINIST: The reason why, in this case, is that his action had nothing to do with a decision on his part. I assume he didn't want to kill that passerby, and if it were up to him, he certainly wouldn't do it. Whatever he wanted and decided in this case, however, had no bearing on the action, which those football players forced on him. That's why he's not responsible: because the action wasn't caused by his decision.

INDETERMINIST: I agree that Fred's action isn't free, but if Sally's lunch order decision was caused, that wasn't free either.

SOFT DETERMINIST: I think that a free action is an action caused by a decision. The opposite of 'free' isn't 'determined': it's *constrained*.

INDETERMINIST: What do you mean, 'constrained'?

SOFT DETERMINIST: That means, *not caused by a decision*. When you're in a position in which you have to do something (or not do something) whatever you decide—when any decision you made would be irrelevant to what you did—then you're constrained. Marvin's missing the test is constrained, because he was locked in the room, and whatever he decided to do, he couldn't get out in time to get to the test. Fred's shooting is constrained—it didn't matter what he decided to do, in that situation, because the shooting had nothing to do with his decisions. Sally's lunch order in the Burger Queen isn't constrained. It depends on—it's caused by—what she decides to order.

INDETERMINIST: Let's talk about responsibility some more. When there's responsibility for what someone does, that means praise for good actions and blame for bad ones is appropriate, right?

SOFT DETERMINIST: Right.

INDETERMINIST: But I have to keep insisting on the same objection. How could it be appropriate to blame somebody for doing something that is fully determined? Look, in your case when you take it Sally is responsible, what she did is fully determined by her decision, and her decision is fully determined by other earlier causes, right?

SOFT DETERMINIST: Right.

INDETERMINIST: And the causes of causes stretch back in a chain, with earlier events being things she had nothing to do with, with events that happened even before she was born.

SOFT DETERMINIST: Right.

INDETERMINIST: So given those earlier causes, the decision had to come out that way, and the action had to result, right?

SOFT DETERMINIST: Right.

INDETERMINIST: But if all those things had to be that way, how can she be blamed? Isn't that just like blaming your car for not starting when it's cold and its battery is weak?

10. The Function of Praise and Blame

SOFT DETERMINIST: I think that blame is appropriate when people's decisions are involved even though the past chain of events was fully determined. The reason has to do with what I think blame is all about. I think that blaming people—for example, telling them sternly that what they did was wrong—is a way of trying to get them to act differently the next time a situation like that comes up. Blame then is supposed to add another causal factor into any future situation more or less like the past one, with the hope that this additional factor might prevent future bad actions of that sort, by causing the person to decide differently. So, for example, when Sally's vegetarian animal-rights-activist pals blame her for ordering the burger rather than the salad, what they're trying to do by means of this blame is to cause her to decide to order the salad next time. So blame is the sort of thing by which we try to influence decisions: under some circumstances, blaming somebody will cause that person to decide, and therefore to act, differently.

SCEPTIC: And vice versa for praise?

SOFT DETERMINIST: Right. Praise for good actions is intended to be a positive causal factor for that kind of decision. We're trying to cause that sort of decision—to do a good thing—to happen more often in the future, to encourage the decision to act rightly. So praise and blame are actually just one sort of reward and punishment, respectively. That's what we think reward and punishment are about: they're ways of influencing the future.

SCEPTIC: I'd like to talk about reward and punishment more, later. But first, what about my example of the car that didn't start? Does your account tell us why blame isn't appropriate there, but is in the case of a person's bad action?

SOFT DETERMINIST: Yes, that's exactly what's nifty about this way of understanding blame (and praise). The purpose of blame is to prevent future bad actions by causing different decisions. But when an action is not the result of a decision, then it's useless—inappropriate—to try to influence future decisions.

SCEPTIC: So how does that apply to the examples we've been looking at: the car that didn't start, Fred's involvement in the shooting, and Sally's lunch order?

SOFT DETERMINIST: The "actions" of cars of course aren't the result of decisions—cars don't have any mentality. So it's always inappropriate to blame cars for what they do or don't do. People's behaviour sometimes is the result of a decision. When it is, then it's appropriate to try to prevent or encourage bad or good future behaviour by trying to influence future decisions. So for instance you don't blame Fred in that shooting, because it had nothing to do with his decision. Influencing Fred's future decisions would have no effect on preventing incidents of this sort. If that football team decided to do it again, it again wouldn't matter what Fred wanted to do. But blame would be appropriate if you're the sort of vegetarian that thinks it's immoral to eat animals. Her friends blame Sally for ordering the McWhopper—for example, by giving her a stern moral lecture or something—and this makes sense (I mean, assuming the validity of their moral convictions) because that sort of action is the result of a decision. So adding the causal factor of that lecture stands a chance of resulting in her making a different decision—to order the McSalad instead—next time.

SCEPTIC: Well, maybe that makes sense if your ideas about the functions of praise and blame are right, but that's something I want to talk about.

11. Randomness and Freedom

INDETERMINIST: Wait, first, I want to see if I can explain my real objection to your position. I guess it's this: you were arguing that responsibility is present only when the action involves a decision on the part of the person who did it, and I think that's right. I can think of other examples where that seems to fit. Suppose that the doctor hits Alice on the kneecap with that little rubber-tipped hammer used to test reflexes, and her leg jumps and kicks the doctor in the shin. If she kicked the doctor on purpose, that would be a pretty strange thing to do. But she didn't do it on purpose, and she's not responsible for it. And, similarly, if Betty knocked over and broke a valuable piece of glassware that the owner had left in her path, where she couldn't see it, she's not to blame, because she didn't do it on purpose. That is, she didn't decide to do it.

SOFT DETERMINIST: Okay, we agree that praise and blame are appropriate where there are decisions. Where's your disagreement with what I said?

INDETERMINIST: Where I think you have things wrong, really, is in your determinism about decisions. We agree that responsible actions are the result of decisions, but we disagree about what genuine decisions are. As I indicated earlier, I don't think that some mental event can really be a genuine decision, a genuine choice, if it's determined by earlier causes. I mean, if determinism is right, then every "decision" is determined by some earlier causes, and those earlier ones by still earlier ones, and back and back, going outside the person whose action we were considering, and back even before that person was born, maybe even indefinitely back through time, earlier and earlier. So even back then, the conditions were such that Sally had to "decide" to order the McWhopper rather than the McSalad. It was already set. So then it really wasn't up to her what to do at all. If determinism is true, there aren't any genuine decisions—nothing's up to us, really. And so nobody's responsible for anything.

HARD DETERMINIST: That's exactly what I think. So, because every "decision" is determined by causes, nothing is really up to a person, and nobody's responsible for anything.

SOFT DETERMINIST: I think that INDETERMINIST's view of what a genuine decision would have to be is mistaken. I think it makes good sense to think of genuine decisions as determined by causes. I think that the idea that the alternative—that genuine decisions have to be undetermined—is crazy.

INDETERMINIST: Why?

SOFT DETERMINIST: Well, if a person's decision isn't determined by prior causes, then how does it come about?

INDETERMINIST: Well, it just happens—the person creates the decision, right then.

SOFT DETERMINIST: If it's not caused by earlier events, then the only alternative I can see is that it's random, like the events in quantum physics we heard about from PHYSICIST earlier.

INDETERMINIST: At the time, it struck me that maybe quantum physics offered a good way to explain how free will came about. Do you remember how PHYSICIST told us about mechanisms that could be constructed to make tiny quantum events make a difference in our own relatively large-scale world? Like that machine that turned on a light as the result of positron emissions? Well, just suppose that our brains contain some sort of mechanism analogous to that, which takes random quantum events and "amplifies" them so that they determine some much larger-scale mental events, decisions maybe, which would then be unpredictable and undetermined.

SOFT DETERMINIST: Maybe the physics could be made plausible, but if that sort of randomness were involved in our decision making, I don't think that would make for freedom or responsibility. Quite the reverse. Imagine this story: One day Fred is walking down the street, and suddenly he picks up a big rock and brutally attacks some little kid passing by. Psychologists try to find out why he did it, but they're puzzled: Fred's been raised in a good family, had absolutely no history of violent behaviour or mental illness, wasn't at all upset by anything on that perfectly ordinary day, and that little kid never did anything to anger him—in fact, they never had any contact before. Nothing in Fred's background—in his personality or environment—was a causal factor in that decision, the psychologists decide, and they're right. Investigation of Fred's brain reveals a mechanism that amplifies random quantum events and, the result was the decision to murder the next person seen. So Fred's action was just a fluke—a random event, just like when the light turns on in the machine PHYSICIST told us about. That's just the sort of scenario you're proposing for a free action. But what do you think: is Fred really responsible for that horrible act?

INDETERMINIST: Well....

SOFT DETERMINIST: Come on, now. He's obviously not responsible. Just the opposite: I think that he'd be judged to have been briefly temporarily insane, and without any responsibility at all for what he did. Randomly arising decisions don't produce responsibility. Someone who frequently produced inexplicable decisions, just at random, wouldn't be thought to be especially responsible: they would be thought to be dreadfully disordered, and completely out of control, not responsible for anything they do.

INDETERMINIST: All right, maybe randomness isn't what's needed for freedom and responsibility. But I still think that some alternative to determinism is necessary.

DETERMINIST: As I see it, there isn't any alternative to determinism except randomness. What kind of third possibility do you have in mind?

INDETERMINIST: Well, what I'm looking for is something that's a decision which is not determined by prior causes, but doesn't just happen to the person randomly either. It's something the person *creates*.

SCEPTIC: That reminds me of what there was talk about earlier,[7] on the question of whether machines can think, when DUALIST claimed that creativity was necessary for real mental processes. At that point, the idea of randomness came up also, and I think that DUALIST was inclined to say then that randomness wasn't exactly what creativity was about. But then also it wasn't clear what creativity would be, if it wasn't randomness.

---

7 Conversation IV.

SOFT DETERMINIST: Well INDETERMINIST, when you get a better idea of what freedom of the will is supposed to be, if it's neither determination by causes or randomness, let's talk again.

12. Utilitarian Justifications of Punishment

SCEPTIC: I'd like to go back now to what was said a little earlier, which I found surprising and implausible: the idea that punishment and reward are ways of influencing future decisions.

UTILITARIAN: When I heard that you wanted to talk about theories of punishment, I asked my friend RETRIBUTIVIST, who's also interested in these things, to come in here with me, and we've been listening to what you've been saying. SOFT DETERMINIST's views on praise and blame, and punishment and reward in general, are exactly what a utilitarian would say about the matter.

SCEPTIC: Okay, why do you think that praise and blame, punishment and reward, all have to do with influencing the future?

UTILITARIAN: Well, think, for example, about judicial punishment by the state, throwing somebody in jail. Is that a good idea? The only thing that could justify any action, as I argued earlier,[8] is that it leads, in the long run, to the greatest increase in pleasure or happiness or whatever—in utility—for the greatest number of people. Now, throwing people in jail obviously decreases their utility a good deal, because it's awful in there, and they'll be deprived in all sorts of ways. It can be justified only if there are other effects that increase utility, to compensate for this decrease. The other effects have to raise the total utility of everyone concerned to the highest level of any alternative.

SCEPTIC: How's that supposed to work, in the case of throwing somebody in jail?

UTILITARIAN: One reason that there are supposed to be good results in the long run from jailing criminals is that it will deter others from the crime. Other people—potential criminals—will think that the possibility of being caught and put in jail is not worth the anticipated advantages of the crime. So a general societal practice of catching and jailing criminals is supposed to contribute to a lowering of the crime rate. Because crime, obviously, results in a lot of disutility for lots of people, effective crime prevention,

---

8 Conversation III.

involving inflicting considerable disutility on a small group of criminals, is a good policy, one that can be expected to result in an increase in the total utility.

SCEPTIC: Okay, that's *deterrence*, and that's clearly one aim of judicial punishment. Are there others?

UTILITARIAN: Another one is closely related to deterrence. It seems to be common sense to think that punishing somebody will have a tendency to prevent that person from doing that bad thing again. So putting people in jail is supposed to make them less likely to break the law again, just as sending a little kid to his room for kicking his sister will, it's hoped, make that little kid somewhat less likely to do it again. This is deterrence also, but here we're talking about trying to deter the criminal him or herself, whereas in the first case, it was deterrence of others.

SCEPTIC: Right, that aim is sometimes called *reform* of the criminal. That's another motive for jailing people, I guess.

UTILITARIAN: Yes it clearly is. That idea is reflected in one of the names we give to jails: *reformatories*. Another name given to jails is *penitentiaries*, and this one also reflects the motive of reform of the prisoner. It was thought that putting criminals in jail would provide them with the opportunity to become "penitent"—to reflect morally on their actions, to repent, to regret their crimes, to feel sorry and guilty, and to decide to reform their ways.

SCEPTIC: And I guess some jails aim at reforming their inmates in other ways, so that they'd be less likely to reoffend. I mean, they sometimes give inmates job training, or psychotherapy, or other things to try to get them to behave better when they're out.

UTILITARIAN: Right. And a third reason to put people in jail, according to many utilitarians, is that even if all else fails, at least criminals are in jail they won't be out there in the community doing those crimes any more. They're separated from society, and pretty well under control in there. The *isolation* effect.

SCEPTIC: I wonder—does jailing people actually accomplish those aims?

UTILITARIAN: Good question. I know a psychologist who probably can tell us what's known in the area—let me see if I get that person in here.

PSYCHOLOGIST: First of all, let's consider the possible isolation effect. Keeping somebody in jail very clearly prevents that person from committing crimes against people outside, just because they're effectively isolated. On the other hand, there's an enormous amount of crime inside jails, committed by inmates against each other: an astounding amount of violence, sexual assault, extortion, and so on. They're not really under control in jails at all. Of course, many of these people would be doing that sort of thing if they were out of jail too, so it's not clear that jail makes things any worse. But it is clear that it doesn't make things very substantially better.

RETRIBUTIVIST: But at least they're doing these things to each other—to other criminals—and not to the general public.

UTILITARIAN: Right, but that doesn't make any difference to utilitarians. Everyone's disutility counts the same, as far as we're concerned. So I'm not sure that the isolation effect of jailing criminals—putting them into this really violent society—really does result in a substantial increase in utility. How about the deterrence effect?

PSYCHOLOGIST: There's of course a good deal of controversy about the effectiveness of deterrence. Offhand, I'd say that many, maybe even most psychologists interested in these topics think that the deterrent effect of judicial punishment is not very good in general, especially when it comes to "crimes of passion"—often the nastiest and most violent crimes.

UTILITARIAN: Why's that?

PSYCHOLOGIST: Well, it's only common sense. You don't need a psychologist to tell you that people who commit crimes of passion are those that have a tendency to lose their temper and get violent. They get carried away by their emotions and don't stop to calculate about the possibility of getting caught, and about how long and horrible the jail sentence might be. So there's not likely to be very much deterrence of crimes of passion. I'd guess that punishing people for getting into brawls in a bar, for example, probably has extremely little deterrent effect. After all, when you've been drinking in the bar a long time, you're not likely to stop and calculate the unpleasantness of a possible jail term before you slug someone who's insulted you.

UTILITARIAN: How about other sorts of crime?

PSYCHOLOGIST: There's more likely to be significant deterrent effect on the type of crime that's carefully premeditated, and calculated to be to the perpetrator's advantage. For example, an accountant for a business would be more likely to be deterred from diverting sums of the business's money into his own bank account by the threat of legal punishment, because we'd expect an accountant to think things out carefully in advance, and weigh the possibility of legal punishment against the possible gain. This is all supposing that it looks to people like the risk of getting caught and seriously punished was worth considering. When potential criminals of this sort know that lots of these wrongdoers don't get caught, and that lots of those that do get caught don't get convicted, and that lots of those that get convicted don't receive really significant punishment, then deterrence doesn't work very well at all, of course.

UTILITARIAN: How about reform?

PSYCHOLOGIST: It appears that a long and unpleasant jail sentence probably doesn't decrease the probability of future wrongdoing by the criminals when they are released. Criminals by and large are not reformed by judicial punishment. The reasons why this doesn't work are pretty obvious. For one thing, a jail term makes them even more isolated than they were before from mainstream society, family, jobs, and so on, and these sorts of isolation are strong causal factors for crime. And it socializes them into the criminal culture shared by the other inmates. So it may even make criminals *more* likely to commit crimes when they're released.

UTILITARIAN: Well, you'd think that the first-hand experience of an awful time in jail would make people much more reluctant to commit crimes again.

PSYCHOLOGIST: Yes, you'd think so, but statistical studies don't bear this out very well. Another possibility here is that criminals are often people who don't think about the consequences of their acts, and don't learn from past experience. And maybe that's why jail experience doesn't teach them a lesson, and make them behave themselves next time. (This would also explain why deterrence wouldn't work too well.)

UTILITARIAN: But how about if prisoners are given psychological treatment, to try to correct personality disorders that have led them to crime?

PSYCHOLOGIST: I'm a bit ashamed to admit that the psychological treatment that prisoners in jail are subjected to doesn't seem to do a very good job in helping them overcome their tendencies to crime.

UTILITARIAN: Hmm. If that's right, then I'd have to reconsider judicial punishment.

PSYCHOLOGIST: Look, really, if what you're interested in is reform of the criminal, then I'd say that sentencing them to a nice all-expenses-paid vacation in a Caribbean resort might work much better than jail.

RETRIBUTIVIST: Very funny.

PSYCHOLOGIST: No, I'm serious. Getting criminals away from criminal society, and treating them nicely for a change, might actually do something to restore their psychological balance, and turn them away from a life of crime. A jail sentence doesn't do this at all.

13. Retributivism

RETRIBUTIVIST: No, look, I think you're missing the whole point of punishment here. Maybe there are ways of turning criminals away from their criminal habits, and maybe even treating them nicely would work better than a nasty jail term, but that's nothing to do with *punishment*. Punishment is something unpleasant. I mean, maybe PSYCHOLOGIST's speculation is right, and a Caribbean vacation would be the best way to reform offenders. But you couldn't call that punishment. Punishment is something unpleasant. Even what we do now to prisoners in jail, in the name of reform, shouldn't be called punishment. Group therapy, job training— that's not *punishment*.

UTILITARIAN: Okay, I accept the point that effective reform, even what we do now to criminals in jail to try to reform them (whether it's effective or not) doesn't really fit the word 'punishment.' I guess I was just talking about possible justifications of what the judicial system does or might do to convicted criminals. Maybe we shouldn't call it 'punishment' at all. But isn't this only a trivial matter of words?

RETRIBUTIVIST: Maybe. Let's not get tied up in matters of definitions of words. What's really important is the question what really should be done, whatever you call it, to people in response to their criminal actions.

UTILITARIAN: Well, don't you agree that deterring crime and reforming offenders would be a good thing?

RETRIBUTIVIST: Of course I agree that crime prevention is a good thing—who wouldn't?—but I don't think that the kinds of things they do to criminals, hoping for reform or deterrence, are moral ways to go about doing it. I think the main justification for a nasty jail sentence would still be there even if (as PSYCHOLOGIST indicated) it didn't really work as deterrence or isolation or reform at all. The real reason for jailing criminals doesn't look to the future at all. It considers the past: the wrongdoers did something bad, so they deserve nasty treatment. That's all there is to it.

UTILITARIAN: What? I don't get it. The criminal caused some sort of harm— a decrease in utility—to others already, and now you want to react to that simply by causing additional decrease in utility, to the criminal?

RETRIBUTIVIST: That's right, though I'm not fond of calling it *utility*—you can see I'm not a utilitarian.

UTILITARIAN: You sure aren't. Why just bring additional pain or suffering into the world?

RETRIBUTIVIST: Because it's deserved. People who harm others deserve to be harmed in return. They deserve to suffer in return for the suffering they caused. It's only justice. When they cause harm to others, they incur a sort of debt to society, and they repay that debt when they suffer themselves.

UTILITARIAN: What do you mean 'justice'? I remember an earlier conversation about that.[9] In that conversation, 'justice' meant something like *fair or equal distribution of benefits in society*.

RETRIBUTIVIST: I guess that's one thing that word means, but I think there's another extremely important sense of 'justice' that I'm talking about. Fair distribution of benefits could be called *distributive justice*, and the one I'm interested in could be called *retributive justice*.

UTILITARIAN: Well, let me make sure I have this straight. You think that it's justice that someone who has inflicted suffering should suffer in return, whether that does any good or not?

RETRIBUTIVIST: That's right. You utilitarians are only concerned with good effects, but there's more to morality than that. I'm not interested in good effects here. I'm just interested in *desert*.

UTILITARIAN: In what?

RETRIBUTIVIST: I don't mean ice cream at the end of the meal (that word has a double *s* in it), or sandy dry wasteland. 'Desert' means what's deserved.

UTILITARIAN: So I guess that one way to describe the difference between our theories of punishment is to describe my view as "forward looking" and your view as "backward looking." I mean that on my view, punishment is justified by its possible future effects, whereas you think it's justified because of what happened in the past.

RETRIBUTIVIST: Yes, that's a good way of putting it.

UTILITARIAN: And what do you mean by saying that criminals have a "debt" to society that they must "repay" by suffering themselves? There's not literally a debt there, is there?

RETRIBUTIVIST: I mean that they've brought some evil into the world—destroyed the moral balance of things—and that the moral balance can be restored only when they suffer in return.

UTILITARIAN: That sort of talk doesn't make any sense to me. And I don't like the view that we should make people suffer in return for the nasty things they've done in the past.

---

9 Conversation II.

RETRIBUTIVIST: You've got to admit, however, that the impulse to make wrongdoers suffer in return is a very common and widespread one, maybe even natural and instinctive.

UTILITARIAN: I agree that a lot of people feel that way, and are eager to hurt people who have hurt them. But I think that, to counteract this natural feeling, they should be reminded that this probably doesn't do any good—it merely increases the amount of suffering in the world. Think of it: the idea behind retributive punishment is that the appropriate response to an increase in suffering is to act to produce even more suffering. It's crazy! I think that reacting to wrongdoing by harming the wrongdoer is very natural, but it's itself a nasty thing, a sort of primitive or childish desire for revenge. You see it especially in small boys (and in older ones who, it seems, haven't done a very good job of growing up): little Jason grabs little Shawn's transformer action figure, so little Shawn responds by bashing little Jason in the nose. We should try not to feel that way ourselves, and we should discourage it in other people. Above all, it ought not to be the basis for official judicial policy.

RETRIBUTIVIST: Calling retribution "revenge" is just putting a bad slant on it. It's not revenge at all: it's justice.

UTILITARIAN: Earlier on, you said something about utilitarian punishment actually being immoral. How do you figure that?

RETRIBUTIVIST: Well, I think that punishment with utilitarian motives shows disrespect for the criminal as a person. Retributive punishment is a way of snowing respect for the criminal.

UTILITARIAN: Respect! What an idea. You'd have some difficulty convincing somebody who's just been sentenced to a long term in a horrible jail that you're actually showing respect for him! You owe us explanation of that, for sure. I remember a while back[10] DEONTOLOGIST was arguing that a basic principle of morality was respect for others as people. I had trouble understanding exactly how that was supposed to work, and I admit I'm not doing any better now. Could you elaborate on your idea of how respect and disrespect are involved?

RETRIBUTIVIST: Showing respect for people, for what they did, sometimes involves treating them in a way they don't like or appreciate. As DEON-TOLOGIST argued back then, what people like or appreciate or desire is not the issue when it comes to moral treatment of them. Punishing wrongdoers is, I feel, the only way to treat them that takes account of the real evil they did, and the fact that they did it—that they're responsible for it. It's

---

10 Conversation III.

treating them as *persons*—as the authors of their actions, as responsible for them. And that's related to the reasons I think that the utilitarian treatment of criminals does not respect them. When you try to rehabilitate criminals, when you give them therapy or job training or something, you're treating them as if what they did wasn't all that bad, and, more importantly, wasn't really their fault. You're saying, in effect, that it wasn't *them* that did it—it was their psychological problem, or their lack of a good job or something. You're not taking them seriously as human beings—as creators of their own actions. And when you try to cause them not to act that way any longer, you aren't respecting them, you're just manipulating them, trying to make them different. Respect for people involves treating them seriously, as the source of their actions, not as victims of society or economics, or as cogs in a machine. And I've got the same objection to the deterrence theory of punishment. If your motive in punishing criminals is getting future potential wrongdoers to act differently, then you're just using those criminals as resources in your project of crime reduction. Remember the case of Admiral Byng? Respect for people never allows them to be used only as a means to an end. (I remind you of the Kantian ethics that we heard being talked about earlier.)[11]

UTILITARIAN: I understand what you're saying, but I think it's wrong-headed and that it ignores what's really important, which is human well-being. Our only aim should really be to increase that. Crime is what decreases it, and the only appropriate response to it is never to further increase human suffering—it's to do whatever we can to decrease it in the long run.

RETRIBUTIVIST: Look, here's an example that might make my position seem reasonable. It's a real historical example, the case of Adolph Eichmann. He was a high official among the Nazis in Germany, the man who was centrally involved in organizing the extermination of millions of Jews. At the end of World War II, he was arrested, but he escaped to Argentina, where Israeli agents tracked him down and brought him to Israel in 1960. In 1961, he went on trial for crimes against humanity, and was convicted and executed. Okay, now here's the issue. There was no question at all that Eichmann was guilty of enormous horrible acts. He was clearly involved in the huge extermination. He knew exactly what he was doing, and promoted it with zeal, even when other high-up Nazis were backing away somewhat from the program. That wasn't the issue.

UTILITARIAN: I can see exactly what the issue was. Putting Eichmann on trial, and convicting and executing him did no good at all. First of all, I'm totally opposed to the death penalty for anyone, as most utilitarians are.

---

11 Conversation III.

It's the ultimate harm for one person—the criminal—and it does no good at all. It clearly doesn't rehabilitate criminals! And they could be prevented from re-offending just as efficiently by keeping them in jail for as long as they were dangerous. And it's been shown that a comparatively large number of convictions for capital crimes convict the wrong person. Many criminals serving long sentences have been released, when new evidence shows they didn't do it. But you can't reverse the death penalty of course. (This last consideration applies to the death penalty in general, but not particularly to Eichmann's case, because there was no question at all that he was guilty.) And maybe most importantly, I don't think the death penalty deters other potential killers.

PSYCHOLOGIST: I think that's right. Studies appear to have shown that the threat of the death penalty does not deter crime better than the threat of jail—it might even do a worse job of deterrence. Another thing to consider is that a society that carries out the death penalty may actually, in a roundabout sort of way, encourage murder.

UTILITARIAN: How's that?

PSYCHOLOGIST: Well, in places like Texas, for example, where they impose a huge number of death penalties, people may come to think of killing as a relatively acceptable sort of thing—a means to justice, something that has a legitimate place in society—rather than something horrible, uncivilized, unthinkable.

UTILITARIAN: Maybe. In any case, two motives for judicial punishment in general were clearly inapplicable in Eichmann's case. First, there was zero possibility of his doing anything like that again. He had been living peacefully under an assumed identity in suburban Buenos Aires for decades, and nobody thought that at age 55 he was about to embark on new crimes against humanity, or indeed on any crimes at all. And, in general, it seems that the threat of punishment for this sort of crime would have even less possibility of being a deterrent than for other more ordinary crimes. The only way such crimes against humanity ever occur is when they're perpetrated, allowed, or encouraged by the government of the day. At the time they're carried out, nobody ever seems to worry about some future time when that government would be defeated, and they'd be put on trial and punished. Remember that the Nazis called their regime the *Thousand-Year Reich* (*Reich* means *empire*), believing that their power would last that long.

RETRIBUTIVIST: That's why I brought up this case. It's a very clear example in which the utilitarian way of thinking would argue that there's no point in punishing Eichmann. But that shows exactly why the utilitarians are wrong. The guy was a complete moral monster, having been responsible for an unbelievably huge number of unbelievably horrible acts. If you're a utilitarian, you say, "Oh well! Punishing him won't do any good! Let him go back to his nice life in suburbia!" But this is incredibly misguided. He *had* to be punished. Anyone with any sense can see that.

UTILITARIAN: I guess you must think I don't have any sense!

RETRIBUTIVIST: Clearly we must agree to disagree here.

Suggested Readings

(See the Notes on "Suggested Readings" sections, p. 17-18.)

J.L. Mackie gives his ideas about causes and INUS conditions in *The Cement of the Universe: A Study of Causation*.

Pierre Laplace (1749-1827) explains his determinism in his *Philosophical Essay on Probabilities*.

There's a good discussion of the jagged shoreline problem in the chapter called "A Geometry of Nature" in James Gleick's book *Chaos: Making a new Science*.

In his book *Metaphysics*, Richard Taylor argues against soft determinism and in favour of a libertarian position, which he tries to distinguish from the view that free action is just random action.

Baron (Paul Henri) D'Holbach (1723-89) was a thoroughgoing materialist and hard determinist. Selections from his *System of Nature* are often found in anthologies.

A more recent defence of hard determinism is *Beyond Freedom*, by the famous behaviourist psychologist B.F. Skinner (1904-90).

Soft determinism is described and advocated by John Stuart Mill (1806-73) in *A System of Logic*.

David Hume (1711-76) was also a soft determinist. See his readable "Of Liberty and Necessity," Section VIII of *Enquiry Concerning Human Understanding*. By far the best edition of this for students is on-line at <http://www.earlymoderntexts.com>.

There aren't really any classical primary readings exclusively on the theory of punishment: where the topic is discussed, it's inside treatments of ethics, free will, responsibility, and so on. The readings above, for determinism and freedom, will touch on the issue. But you'll find an extended and useful survey of theories in *Punishment: The Supposed Justifications* by Ted Honderich.

CONVERSATION VI

Knowledge

Participants: SCEPTIC • DEFINER • CARTESIAN • FALLIBILIST • EMPIRICIST • RATIONALIST

1. The Definition of 'Knowledge'

SCEPTIC: There's been a lot of concern in previous conversations about what can be known and what can't. For example, there was debate about the possibility of religious knowledge,[1] or of ethical knowledge,[2] and whether it could be known that determinism is true or false.[3] But nobody yet has talked about what knowledge really is.

DEFINER: We can talk about knowing in a few different senses. There's the sense in which we know persons or things: "I know Fred," "She knows Cleveland," "Dionne knows the way to San Jose." There's a different sense in which you know how to do something: "He knows how to play the piano." I assume you're asking about the sense in which you know a fact: "Sally knows that you're planning a surprise party for her," "Fred knows that Bismark is the capital of North Dakota."

SCEPTIC: Right.

DEFINER: Many philosophers have agreed that knowledge is justified true belief.

SCEPTIC: Knowledge is a kind of belief, then?

DEFINER: Yes, because if you don't believe something you don't know it. A fact that nobody knows isn't knowledge at all. That's just a matter of the definition of the words.

SCEPTIC: Okay, but why *true* belief?

DEFINER: Because if a belief is false, it doesn't count as knowledge. Another matter of definition. If Fred believes that it's Tuesday, but it's not, then you wouldn't say that Fred knows that it's Tuesday.

---

1 Conversation I.
2 Conversation III.
3 Conversation V.

SCEPTIC: But Fred thinks 'It's Tuesday' is true.

DEFINER: Right, but if 'It's Tuesday' really is false, then Fred doesn't know that it's Tuesday. Nobody knows anything that's false, though people sometimes believe false things.

SCEPTIC: So you're saying that one characteristic for real knowledge is that the thing somebody claims to know is true.

DEFINER: That's right.

SCEPTIC: But it's not as if somebody is going to say that they know something if they think it's false.

DEFINER: Of course. All I'm saying here is that whatever anyone claims to know, they don't really know it if it's false. You can *believe* something that's false, but you don't know it.

SCEPTIC: Okay, but here's something about your position that's more important, I think. Suppose that Fred says that he knows that X, and Sally says that she knows that not-X. Then according to you, only one of them could be right about their own knowledge-state, depending on whether X is really true or not.

DEFINER: Right, except there's more to knowing something than merely having a true belief. They might both be wrong.

SCEPTIC: Okay, let's get back to that in a minute. What I'm interested in right now is what you seem to be supposing here, that there really is a fact of the matter about whether something is true or false, I mean apart from what anyone's beliefs are. Maybe that's not right. I mean, if Fred sincerely believes something is true, but Sally sincerely believes it isn't, maybe we should just say that it's true for Fred, and false for Sally, and there isn't any independent fact of the matter.

DEFINER: That's what RELATIVIST was claiming was the situation in ethics a while back,[4] and it might have some plausibility there, but I think that when it comes to ordinary facts, it's not plausible at all. I am supposing that there are facts independent of what anybody happens to believe; they're real features of the world outside us, and they're objective. I think that if Fred believes, for example, that the square root of 49 is 9, and Sally believes that it isn't, then one of them is right and one of them is wrong. (Fred's wrong, in case you were wondering.)

SCEPTIC: Thanks.

DEFINER: So it doesn't make any sense to say that the square root of 49 is 9

---

4 Conversation III.

is true for Fred, unless that's a rather strange way of saying that Fred believes it.

SCEPTIC: But a lot of things depend on a person's perspective, right? What seems true from Fred's perspective might seem false from Sally's, and who's to say who's correct? So relativism about knowledge would make sense in that sort of case, and maybe that's more widespread than we suspect, especially when the two are in different cultures who see things very differently. So then shouldn't we say that each person, each culture, has their own different knowledge?

DEFINER: I don't think there are many matters about which relativism is appropriate. In some kinds of taste it clearly is, for example, when pistachio ice cream is delicious for Fred but not for Sally. Maybe there are certain other matters about which there is no objective truth, just different perspectives, like when Sally and Fred are having an argument about whose fault something was, and from each person's perspective, it's the other person's fault, and there's no objective truth of the matter. When there isn't any objective truth, only perspectival views, I'd think it's appropriate not to speak of knowledge at all.

SCEPTIC: But when minority cultures have a different view of things, isn't it a mark of respect to call what they think their own knowledge, different from majority-culture knowledge? Nowadays you hear, for example, about native "ways of knowing" or "traditional knowledge."

DEFINER: I respect minority culture, but that doesn't make me think that there isn't objective truth. I think that traditional stories can be an important part of a group's identity, and are owed respect, but respect can be shown to them in ways that don't involve confusions about what's really true, or what really counts as knowledge.

SCEPTIC: Well, this is a big question, but I suppose now we ought to get back to the definition you proposed for knowledge. You said that knowledge is justified true belief. What do you mean, *justified*?

DEFINER: Somebody has a justified belief when they have good reasons, or good evidence, for what they believe.

SCEPTIC: Is that any different from *true*?

DEFINER: *Justified* is different from *true*. You can have a true belief that's not justified, and you can have a justified belief that's not true. Suppose somebody makes a wild guess that turns out right. For example, suppose you and Sally are starting to plan for her birthday party a month in advance, and Sally says she knows it's going to rain on that day. She says this because she's had bad luck with rain on past birthdays, and she's a sort of pessimistic person.

SCEPTIC: So you're saying that her belief isn't justified?

DEFINER: Right. Beliefs about what the weather is going to be are sometimes justified, because weather forecasters are able to predict the weather for the short-term, like a day or less, with pretty good reliability. But nobody is able to predict what the weather is going to be a month in advance. (I'm assuming that we're talking about a place where the weather isn't the same all the time.) But suppose that a month later Sally turns out to have been right: it does rain on her birthday. The belief she had a month earlier was true. But it wasn't knowledge, because it wasn't justified. She didn't literally *know* that it was going to rain on her birthday.

SCEPTIC: But doesn't the fact that she turned out to be right mean that she was justified, after all?

DEFINER: No. Her belief wasn't justified at the time she made that statement, a month before her birthday. You're justified when there's good evidence for your belief, evidence you know about, and take to be good evidence. Sally might have thought she had good evidence that it was going to rain, but she didn't, back then. Even if she felt justified, she wasn't. On the day of her birthday, however, when she can just see that it's raining, then of course her belief becomes fully justified.

SCEPTIC: But suppose that when she sees that rain on her birthday, Sally says, "I just *knew* it was going to rain today. I knew it a month ago, when we started planning!"

DEFINER: I've heard people say things like that, but I don't think they mean them literally. My guess is that Sally understands that she wasn't justified in her belief a month back—that nobody can have a justified belief that it will rain a month in advance. What she probably means when she says she "just knew" it is that she really strongly believed it—that she felt sure about it. So she doesn't literally mean she knew it.

SCEPTIC: Well, maybe she thinks she really did have justification in believing that a month earlier.

DEFINER: Well, if she thinks she was justified, then I suppose she might be speaking literally. But in that case she's just mistaken: she wasn't justified, in fact. She's wrong: she didn't know it.

SCEPTIC: Why do you say that she wasn't justified? What is justification anyway?

DEFINER: Roughly speaking, a person is justified in believing something when that person has good reasons for believing what they do—when the method that person has used for getting the belief is a reliable method, one that works a substantial percentage of the time. You can be justified in your belief that it's going to rain later in the day, when your reason for believing this is that you heard the official weather forecast predicting it, because short-term weather forecasts like this are quite reliable. But Sally's reason—that it rained on her recent past birthdays—isn't a good reason. Predicting on that basis isn't reliable.

SCEPTIC: Okay. You said earlier that a belief can be justified but false. How does that work?

DEFINER: Think about the weather forecast for a moment. The official forecast for later the same day provides justification for your belief, because it's generally quite reliable. But even a highly reliable source for belief can be wrong occasionally. *Reliable* doesn't mean perfect. So if you hear the weather forecast for rain later in the day, then you're justified in believing that it's going to rain. But it just might turn out that the weather forecast was wrong, though it doesn't very often. But if it turns out wrong, then you didn't know it was going to rain after all. Your belief was justified, but false.

2. Certainty and Fallibility

CARTESIAN: Excuse me for interrupting, but there's something you were just saying that struck me as wrong. Suppose you have some pretty good reason for believing something—you've gotten your belief from a reliable source. But 'reliable' doesn't mean infallible, so you're not entitled to be completely *certain* about a belief you got by a method that sometimes gives you a false belief, right?

FALLIBILIST: I agree that reliability isn't infallibility. But I think that you can be pretty certain about information you got from a reliable source, even though it's not infallible.

CARTESIAN: Well, I'm not talking about being "pretty certain"—I'm talking about complete certainty. Descartes again.[5] He thought that complete certainty was the place to start in the search for genuine knowledge.

FALLIBILIST: A reliable but not completely infallible source doesn't entitle you to the complete certainty you mentioned. You have to recognize that

---

5   The philosopher responsible for Cartesian dualism discussed in Conversation IV.

there's some chance of mistake. A very reliable source makes this chance pretty small. And when your justification is quite reliable, then I'd say you have knowledge (provided the belief is true), even though you don't have complete certainty—even though your source of information isn't completely infallible, even though there's a larger than zero possibility that you're wrong.

CARTESIAN: I think you're mistaken. I think that certainty is necessary for knowledge.

FALLIBILIST: Well, let's separate some issues here. The first issue here is, are you claiming that somebody has to *feel* certain in their belief as a necessary condition for that belief to count as knowledge?

CARTESIAN: I don't think that Descartes was talking about the *feeling* you couldn't be wrong. I think he meant that you *really* couldn't be wrong, never mind what you felt. But it could also be argued that feeling certain is necessary for knowledge. If you feel doubtful about a belief, it wouldn't be called knowledge. If you harbour some doubts, you'd say, "I *believe* it, but I don't *know* it."

FALLIBILIST: I don't think that's right. Do you really think that if you feel even the slightest trace of doubt about something, then it doesn't count as knowledge? If that were right, then I guess I'd have to deny that I have any knowledge at all, because I can't be utterly sure about anything!

CARTESIAN: Well, I think there are things you can be utterly sure about. We can talk about that in a moment. In any case, if what you believe is true, and you're justified in believing it, but you don't *feel* utterly sure, then I think you don't have real knowledge.

FALLIBILIST: Hmm, that strikes me as an odd way of speaking, but that seems to be a fairly trivial matter about how we're going to use that word 'knowledge.' But that brings me to the second issue: I gather you believe that, in order to be genuine real knowledge, a belief has to be certain in the sense that it has completely perfect justification—that it couldn't be wrong. So you'd be justified in feeling completely certain; but what we're talking about here is not how you feel about the possibility of being wrong, but whether it really is possible. So in this sense of 'certainty,' a belief is certain when it couldn't be mistaken.

CARTESIAN: Right, and that's the kind of certainty Descartes was talking about. I think that a perfect information source is what's necessary for real knowledge. If there's a possibility that you're wrong, then that's just opinion, it isn't real, genuine knowledge. Real knowledge is something very hard to get—not the sort of thing that can be obtained by listening to the weather forecast, for example.

FALLIBILIST: Well, why do you say that? You're certainly not going to throw out all those beliefs whose justification isn't completely perfect, are you? You're going to continue to believe them, when you have strong but not perfect justification.

CARTESIAN: Yes, but I don't want to call them genuine knowledge. I want to reserve that term for beliefs which are completely certain.

FALLIBILIST: Why's that?

CARTESIAN: Well, what I count as real, genuine knowledge is a belief that's usable as a foundation for one's whole system of beliefs, so that the whole system is solid and trustworthy. This sort of foundational belief has to be completely, 100 per cent reliable; if it's fallible, if it's possible that it's wrong, then the whole system becomes doubtful.

SCEPTIC: Why was Descartes so concerned with this sort of complete certainty?

CARTESIAN: He's considered the first great philosopher of the Modern Era, that is, the period beginning at the end of the Medieval period, and the timing is significant to Descartes' theory of knowledge. The Medieval period is sometimes thought of now as the age of faith, and although this is somewhat of an oversimplification, people then tended to rely on faith and on authority for their beliefs. The Christian Church was the supreme authority in Western culture on religious matters, of course, but on all sorts of other things as well. In scientific matters, the Church endorsed the views of Aristotle as the final truth. It was unheard of—forbidden—to ask whether what authority told you was really true—you just had to accept it. Descartes shook things up by asking whether the beliefs people got on the basis of the pronouncements of authority were really knowledge. He didn't think that they were false; what he wanted to know was whether they were genuine knowledge—that is, whether we were entitled to be completely certain of them, so they could stand as the firm foundation for his beliefs. The fact that somebody told you that they were true wasn't sufficient warrant for these beliefs, in Descartes' view, because that didn't justify real certainty: maybe what they told you was wrong.

SCEPTIC: That must have gotten Descartes in trouble with the Church.

CARTESIAN: It did. For the longest time Descartes' writings were on the list of books officially banned by the Church. (They're off that list now, by the way!) They were banned not because his basic positions on religious and scientific matters were at odds with Church doctrine—he accepted the existence of God and the main religious and scientific beliefs endorsed by the Church—but rather because he thought that the fact that religious authorities endorsed some belief didn't give it sufficient warrant to count as genuine knowledge. It was the Church's authority, not its doctrine, that he quarrelled with.

SCEPTIC: So he did find what he took to be strong enough justification for his basic beliefs?

CARTESIAN: Yes he did. In his most famous work, *Meditations*, he set himself the task of finding out what sort of belief could justify this sort of certainty. He argued, first of all, that beliefs we ordinarily trust don't seem to carry this kind of certainty, so they need a firmer basis before we could count them as genuine knowledge. Anything that we can raise doubts about—even doubts that are entirely theoretical—can't count as knowledge for this reason. First, we should recognize the possibility that even experts might be wrong, so the say-so of authorities doesn't confer the *indubitibility* we need for genuine knowledge. Belief based on reasoning, for example, about arithmetic, is unreliable, because you can make mistakes in reasoning. What your senses tell you is untrustworthy because your senses sometimes fool you, as in the case of hallucinations, optical illusions, mirages, and dreams. It seemed to him that any belief about the external world is subject to doubt because it's possibly the result of dreaming, or of mental disorder, or of an "evil demon" able to deceive us by making us think that we're in touch with the real world when we really aren't.

SCEPTIC: But he didn't really believe that he was dreaming all the time, or being fooled by an evil demon, did he? I mean, believing that is insanity, not philosophy.

CARTESIAN: No, of course he didn't really believe any of that. But the remote possibility that these crazy hypotheses were true shows that we need to establish a better warrant for our beliefs before they can be counted as genuine foundational knowledge. We need to prove that an evil demon is not fooling us before we have the utter certainty Descartes demanded.

SCEPTIC: That's a pretty strong requirement. What can be proven to that level of certainty?

CARTESIAN: That's where his famous saying, "*Cogito ergo sum*" comes from. It's Latin for "I think therefore I am." This is his argument that the belief in his own existence is something that meets his strong requirement for certainty. He couldn't be fooled into a mistaken belief that he exists, even by an evil demon who's fooling him about everything else, because whatever he believes, be it true or false, just as long as he has a belief, he exists. So the belief that he exists must be true: it couldn't possibly be mistaken.

SCEPTIC: But he still might be wrong about where he is, who he is, what he's like, his history and his body and so on. I mean, he may have established that there's thinking going on, but has he really established that this thinking is being done by *him*? At this point, what content is there to the idea he's got of *himself*?

CARTESIAN: Not much. He said that this certainty was only about his existence as a thinking thing—a mind. This doesn't establish his existence or nature in any other way than that he's a thing-that-thinks.

SCEPTIC: So that's where his dualism comes in: he's thinking of his own existence as the existence of an non-material mind, rather than as a physical thing, or even as a non-material mind that happens to be attached to a physical body.

CARTESIAN: Right, at least in this initial step of his positive reasoning, attempting to establish the firm foundation of knowledge.

SCEPTIC: Well, that's not much to believe in. But it doesn't seem to me that Descartes is entitled (given his own requirements) even to that little belief, if it's the conclusion to an argument. An argument establishes its conclusion only when its logic is correct, and its premises are true. How can Descartes be sure of those things? Maybe he's mistaken there!

CARTESIAN: Some scholars have argued that what Descartes is proposing is not really an argument at all; rather, he's proposing two beliefs—that he's thinking and that he exists—that are *self-warranting*—that is, that must be true any time he considers them.

SCEPTIC: And it's not at all clear how knowledge merely that he exists as a thinking thing can be the foundation for any other knowledge.

CARTESIAN: Well, Descartes' next step was to go on to prove the existence of God.

SCEPTIC: Hmm. I remember the attempts to prove the existence of God discussed a lot earlier,[6] and they all seemed quite doubtful to me.

CARTESIAN: Descartes' proofs aren't exactly the ones discussed there, but of course some philosophers think that the proofs he attempted don't confer the certainty he credited them with. But what's more interesting here is his methodology rather than his conclusion. He's not going to accept the existence of God on the basis of the pronouncements of his religion, or of the

---

6 Conversation I.

dictates of faith. He's going to wait until he can prove it with certainty for himself.

SCEPTIC: I can see all sorts of problems with Descartes' reasoning here. I can't see how any proof of the existence of God could be acceptable to Descartes at this point in his reasoning. For one thing, all he's got to go on, as a premise for his argument, is the idea that he himself exists as a thinking thing, and I'd think it would be impossible to establish God's existence based on this. Many of those classical proofs of God's existence had premises that Descartes hasn't yet accepted as certain knowledge. The Argument from Design has a premise about the adaptation of living things to their environment, something he hasn't established. And the First Cause Argument relies on the ideas that everything physical has a cause, and he hasn't established that yet. He hasn't even established the existence of anything in the physical world!

CARTESIAN: Right, he can't use these arguments. His version of the First Cause Argument is a complicated one based on assumptions about the cause of his idea of God, which must be traceable back to God himself. But critics of his arguments do agree with you, that in the arguments he gives he smuggles in premises he's not strictly entitled to at that point.

SCEPTIC: But here's another problem. Whatever arguments he's going to use, he's going to have to use his reasoning powers to go from the premises to the conclusion. But hasn't he previously said that he's not going to allow beliefs based on reasoning, because there's the possibility of error here?

CARTESIAN: Well, he realizes that he has to establish the reliability of his reasoning. That's the next step. He does this, relying on the existence of God, whom he's already proven. Because God is benevolent, he reasons, God would not allow his reasoning to go astray and mislead him.

SCEPTIC: That's very odd. His whole idea in this rebuilding is to allow in only what's absolutely certain, what has no possibility of mistake, right?

CARTESIAN: Right.

SCEPTIC: Then isn't he completely off the track when he decides to trust his own reasoning power? I mean, we all know that our own reasoning isn't completely perfect, and sometimes gives us the wrong answer. You mentioned yourself that Descartes himself earlier says this, when he's giving reasons for doubting what we ordinarily take for granted.

CARTESIAN: Well, he doesn't endorse just any sort of reasoning. He tries to distinguish that sort of reasoning that doesn't allow error; that's the sort of reasoning we do when our ideas are *clear and distinct*.

SCEPTIC: Well, that's not very good. Even if there is a special kind of "clear and distinct" reasoning which never can give you a false conclusion (which I doubt), wouldn't there always be the possibility of being mistaken in thinking that a particular bit of your own reasoning was clear and distinct? Anyway, here's another problem I see with Descartes' overall argument. First, let me see if I have his chain of reasoning right. He reasons first to prove his own existence, then, on that basis, to prove God's existence, then, based on that, to prove the reliability of his reasoning. But isn't he already assuming the reliability of his reasoning at the earlier steps? You can't use reasoning to prove the reliability of your reasoning. That's assuming exactly what you're trying to prove. That's what's called circular reasoning, and it's a mistake, right?

CARTESIAN: Maybe so. Some philosophers think that this is a problem. That objection to Descartes was actually pointed out very early on, and has come to be called the *Cartesian Circle*.

3. Certainty and Probability

FALLIBILIST: Well, anyway, I wonder whether Descartes' whole approach is the right one. Why, after all, do we need beliefs that we're completely certain about?

CARTESIAN: Don't we need them as a *foundation* for our whole belief system? I mean, if the foundation is shaky, won't the whole structure collapse?

SCEPTIC: What's a "foundation"?

CARTESIAN: It's a special kind of belief on which the rest of our beliefs are based.

FALLIBILIST: I think there are two questions here. One is whether there is any special kind of belief that acts as a foundation for all the rest; maybe there isn't. The second is whether any kind of belief—foundation or not—has that sort of indubitable certainty. On the second question, I think Descartes was wrong. He was wrong in demanding 100 per cent certainty for genuine knowledge, because there isn't any sort of belief that is really totally infallible. Any of our beliefs might be wrong—though some of them are so unlikely to be wrong that we can feel very sure about them— as certain as is reasonably needed. I agree with what Descartes was saying in the preliminary part of his reasoning, when he was claiming that every one of the beliefs whose truth we take for granted, even those about which we feel utterly certain—is actually *fallible*, only probable, not guaranteed. None of our beliefs is wholly immune to doubt; there's a possibility, sometimes only extremely remote, that any of them is wrong. I think that instead of demanding 100 per cent certainty for any kind of belief, we should make a less strenuous demand, asking only that our basic beliefs be very likely, that the probability that one of them is false is very small. After all, this fits much better with common sense: everyone knows that anyone *could* be wrong about anything, but we go ahead believing what's extremely probable, because it's silly to take the tiny probability that we're wrong seriously. As SCEPTIC said earlier, that would be insane. We'd be paralyzed if we did. Imagine if Descartes took his program of systematic doubt seriously, and threw out everything he couldn't be absolutely certain of. Then, if he weren't able to grant certainty to any belief except his own existence, he'd really be in trouble! He'd be a candidate for the mental institution!

SCEPTIC: Well, philosophers hardly ever count the discrepancy between a position and common sense as a reason not to hold it.

CARTESIAN: I agree that Descartes' sanity would have come into question if he really threw out every belief he wasn't certain of. I mean, imagine what your life would be like if you doubted everything: if you refused to believe that your morning coffee was safe to drink, that your car wouldn't explode when you turned on the key, that those people you counted as your friends really weren't out to kill you. But remember, that sort of disabling practical doubt isn't what he's advocating. The absolute certainty he's looking for, as a condition of genuine knowledge, is what he thinks is necessary for the basic foundation of our belief system. That kind of foundational certainty, he argues, can be found in the beliefs that he and God exist, and in the other conclusions of his "clear and distinct" reasoning.

DEFINER: What other sorts of beliefs can get this "clear and distinct" justification?

CARTESIAN: They include, for example, the truths of arithmetic and geometry. Descartes was a brilliant mathematician as well as philosopher. Did you ever run across that way of doing a graph drawn with a vertical and horizontal line crossing, with X and Y coordinates? They're called *Cartesian coordinates*. That's Descartes' invention.

FALLIBILIST: But the practical truths of everyday life, like the ones about your morning coffee and your friends, and your car, and so on, don't get this certainty?

CARTESIAN: No, there's always the possibility of error for these. I think Descartes got it right about the certainty of clear and distinct reasoning. When you do a proof in algebra or geometry, for example, and you're absolutely clear about what you do, using the concepts exactly as they're defined, then your answer just has to be right.

SCEPTIC: I'm capable of making plenty of mistakes in algebra and geometry.

CARTESIAN: Yes, but that's because you don't get absolutely clear about what you're doing. And he's also right about the possibility of error in beliefs about everyday physical practical matters, the kinds of beliefs you get through your senses.

FALLIBILIST: But how about our everyday beliefs, the ones that weren't perfectly certain? Descartes didn't advocate throwing them out, did he?

CARTESIAN: No, he very sensibly advised us to continue to rely on them. Once again, their general reliability is guaranteed by a benevolent God, who wouldn't give us belief-gathering faculties that always lead us into mistakes about practical everyday matters. That would be disaster. But since our beliefs about those matters aren't based on "clear and distinct" reasoning, they're not 100 per cent trustworthy. God guarantees only that they're okay by and large—that they're probable, not 100 per cent certain. Good probability, he thought, is sufficient for getting around in the world, though it's not the certainty he requires for genuine foundational knowledge.

4. Probable Beliefs and the Lottery Paradox

FALLIBILIST: I agree with Descartes that those everyday beliefs are only probably, not certainly true. But I think that's also the story with the rest of our beliefs.

SCEPTIC: How probable would you say a belief had to be, in order to be acceptable?

FALLIBILIST: Hard to say. I guess it depends on what I'm going to use that belief for.

SCEPTIC: But you'd say that a belief that's 99 per cent probable would be fully acceptable in just about any context?

FALLIBILIST: Sure.

SCEPTIC: Okay, here's a problem with that idea. It's called the *Lottery Para-*

dox. Imagine a lottery with 100 tickets, numbered 1 to 100. Each ticket has an equal chance to win the prize. Now consider this statement: 'Ticket Number 1 will not win.' The probability that statement is true is 99 out of 100, that is, 99 per cent. So you must believe it's true.

FALLIBILIST: Okay, I believe that.

SCEPTIC: Now consider the statement, 'Ticket Number 2 will not win.' That's also 99 per cent likely, so you believe that too.

FALLIBILIST: Okay ...

SCEPTIC: And the same thing is true for each of the other 98 statements about each of the other tickets. In fact, you believe *none* of the tickets will win! But that's plainly false!

FALLIBILIST: Umm.

SCEPTIC: The problem here came from the fact that you were willing to believe statements that had only 99 per cent probability of being true.

FALLIBILIST: Hm. No, maybe the problem here has something to do with combining all those statements into one. I think it's okay to believe '#1 won't win,' and to believe '#2 won't win,' and to believe '#3 won't win,' and so on, but I don't believe what's clearly false, '#1 won't win and #2 won't win and #3 won't win, ... [and so on] .'

SCEPTIC: That's weird. You're willing to believe each of those individual statements, but you're not willing to believe the big statement that's implied by all of them.

5. Gettier Problems

SCEPTIC: Anyway, here's another problem I'd like to raise about that definition of knowledge DEFINER gave us earlier. It has to do with the idea that if true belief is justified, then it's knowledge. I've got an example in which I think a true belief is justified, but it isn't knowledge.

DEFINER: Good, let's hear.

SCEPTIC: Okay, here it is. Suppose Fred wants to know what time it is, and he knows that there's an electric clock out in the hall that keeps very good time, and has been working perfectly for years, ever since it was placed there. So Fred walks out into the hall, and sees that the clock says 12:15, and as a result he believes that that's what time it is. Suppose further that what he believes is true: it actually is 12:15. And in this case, it seems clear that Fred's belief is justified. The clock in fact is extremely trustworthy. So Fred knows that it's 12:15, right?

DEFINER: Well, yes.

SCEPTIC: Well, no. Here's the rest of the story. What happened was that the clock broke exactly 12 hours earlier, at 12:15 am, just after midnight, and it was just a coincidence that it read the right time exactly when Fred looked at it. So he doesn't know that it's 12:15 after all, despite having the justified true belief that it is.

DEFINER: Wait a minute, why do you say that Fred's belief is justified?

SCEPTIC: Because that clock has always worked very well in the past.

DEFINER: But it's not working well right now.

SCEPTIC: Nobody says that evidence for a belief has to be infallible for that belief to be justified.

CARTESIAN: Wait a minute! I do!

SCEPTIC: Right, but right now, we're trying to see what happens if you don't demand infallibility, but merely reliability. Here's another example: Sally suspects that her husband is planning a surprise party for her 30th birthday. So she asks him questions about what he's been doing making secret telephone calls and going out mysteriously for long periods. He's very evasive, so she concludes he's arranging for a surprise party. He is, in fact, going to throw a surprise party for her, but those telephone calls and absences, and his evasiveness, have all had to do instead with some secret crooked business deals he doesn't want her to know about. With Sally's 30th birthday coming up, all that secretive behaviour is a pretty reliable sign that he's planning a party, so her belief that he's planning a party is justified, and it's also true; but she doesn't know that he's planning a party.

DEFINER: Okay, I see that there's a problem with my definition. Hmm. Look, in both of those examples, they got those beliefs, which just happen to be true, totally by accident. It was just a coincidence, an accident, that the stopped clock happens to read correctly when Fred looked, and that the business arrangements result in the sort of secret activity and evasiveness that would indicate a surprise party coming up. So maybe we could fix things up by specifying that you not only have to be justified in your belief, but you can't have gotten the belief through an accident or coincidence.

SCEPTIC: No, that won't work. Think about this case. Sally is at the bakery coincidentally just at the time when behind the counter, a baker is writing

"HAPPY 30th BIRTHDAY SALLY" in icing on a huge cake that's destined for her party. In this case, Sally comes to the true and justified belief that there's going to be a big surprise party for her, and she's gotten this belief through an accident, a coincidence. But nevertheless she knows it.

DEFINER: Gee, I'm stumped. This is a very interesting problem, and I ought to read up on what philosophers have to say about it.

SCEPTIC: The cases that pose this sort of problem for defining knowledge are called *Gettier Problems*. They're named after the guy who first presented this sort of case, the contemporary American philosopher Edmund Gettier. There's lots of philosophical literature involving proposals for solving the Gettier Problem, and objecting to proposed solutions.

6. Empiricism and Rationalism: Concepts

SCEPTIC: I'd like to hear what you have to say now about what actually does justify belief.

EMPIRICIST: I have an answer to that question: the only source of genuine knowledge is sense perception.

SCEPTIC: 'Empiricist' means..:?

EMPIRICIST: *Empiricism* is a philosophical position that makes sense experience basic to knowledge. The word 'empirical' means *based on sense experience*.

SCEPTIC: Okay, please elaborate your position.

EMPIRICIST: When we empiricists talk about the origins of knowledge, we often divide that topic into two, talking first about the origin of *concepts*, and second, about the source of the justification of *judgements*.

SCEPTIC: What's the difference between a concept and a judgement?

EMPIRICIST: Here's what's meant. A concept is a category, a way of sorting things out. For example, there's the concept *dog*. You have that concept when you can tell what is a dog and what isn't—when you can think thoughts that are about dogs, as opposed to anything else. It's obvious how you get this concept: when you're very small: you learn how to use the word 'dog' by having a bunch of dogs and a bunch of other things shown to you, while your parent or someone says something like "That's a dog" and "No, that's not a dog—that's a cat" and so on, and corroborates what you say when you use that word right, and corrects it when you don't. That's how you learn the concept *dog*.

SCEPTIC: Well, that's how you learn the word 'dog.' Is that the same thing as learning the concept?

EMPIRICIST: I'd guess that you can have a concept even though you don't have a word for it. For example, little babies can tell very early on what's Mom and what isn't, even though they don't have any name for her. Animals clearly have concepts, though they don't have any language. We humans, however, learn most of our concepts when we learn the word in our language that stands for that concept.

SCEPTIC: Okay, so what's the empiricist claim about concepts?

EMPIRICIST: We think that they're all learned through sense experience; none of them is *innate*.

SCEPTIC: What exactly do you mean by an innate concept?

EMPIRICIST: 'Innate' means *inborn*. An innate concept would be one that people are born with. Empiricists think that there are no innate concepts, that the mind at birth is what the seventeenth-century English empiricist philosopher John Locke called a *tabula rasa*. This Latin term means *blank slate*. We have to learn all the concepts we ever get through sense experience, when we see (or taste or touch, etc.) a large number of things and learn to sort them out on the basis of how the things look (or taste or feel, etc.). So empiricists usually hold not only that all concepts come from sense experience, but also that they all have empirical meaning—that is, that the meaning of any concept is a matter of how that concept is associated with particular characteristics perceivable through the senses. What makes something count as fitting that concept or not is a matter of the presence or absence of sense characteristics.

RATIONALIST: May I join your discussion? I think that you've got it wrong about where concepts come from. There are some innate concepts, and some concepts that do not have that sort of empirical meaning.

EMPIRICIST: Let's hear your argument.

RATIONALIST: We should separate the two questions to make things clearer. First of all, everyone would agree that some concepts have empirical meaning—that the way we tell that something belongs or doesn't belong in that category is by using our senses. But it doesn't follow at all that if some concept has empirical meaning, that it's not innate, but learned by means of sense experience. For example, I read somewhere that monkeys are instinctively afraid of snakes: monkeys who have never seen a snake will be terrified the first time they see one. They must have an innate way of picking out snakes—an innate, unlearned, concept of *snake*. Of course, monkeys use their senses to recognize snakes, so in that sense it's an empirical concept. But what this example shows is that the concept of a snake is innate in monkeys: they don't have to learn to sort out snakes and non-snakes. It could very well be the case that humans have innate concepts too: that they're born with certain sorting dispositions, and don't have to learn them.

EMPIRICIST: It could be the case, but it doesn't follow that it is. Anyway, maybe those monkeys are just quick learners. I don't think there's a good reason to think that they have the concept of snake before they see one. At birth, humans are not able to do any sorting at all: they just lie there, helplessly thrashing around, and they give no evidence of being able to make any mental distinctions at all. All the mental distinctions are learned later on.

RATIONALIST: It's true that it takes a while before human infants begin to display evidence of having elementary concepts; but it doesn't follow that the mental distinctions are learned from experience. They might be potentially inside the mind all along, and just require the mind to mature enough, to get itself into good enough working order, before they become conscious and useable. When we talk about innate concepts, we don't mean that the infant has to be capable of using those concepts the second it's born. We only mean that people start using them, at some point, maybe quite a good deal later, but don't have to learn them from experience. They might only be learned *after* some experience, but they're not learned *from* experience.

SCEPTIC: If that's what you mean by an innate concept, then it would be very hard—maybe impossible—to tell whether an idea is innate or not. What evidence could there be one way or the other?

RATIONALIST: Well, how about the concept *unicorn*? It's clear that nobody learns that concept by having sense experience of unicorns, since there are no such things.

EMPIRICIST: You can get that concept by combining some concepts you did get from sense experience. You have the concept of an animal horn because you've seen them on antelopes or other animals. You've seen horses, so you know from experience what they look like. You may not have seen any white horses, but you've certainly learned the concept *white* from seeing white things. So you can learn the concept *unicorn* by being told that unicorns look like white horses, except they have a single long spiral horn in the middle of their foreheads.

RATIONALIST: Well, okay. But that's a concept with empirical meaning—that is, you'd use your senses to recognize one (or, more to the point, because these don't exist: you'd use your senses to tell that something *isn't* a unicorn). But how about concepts that don't have empirical meaning? It's for sure that they're innate, because it couldn't be learned from experience. You just know about them, using operations of your mind alone.

EMPIRICIST: I agree that a concept without empirical meaning must be innate. But we empiricists deny the existence of any genuine concept without empirical meaning. I mean, you can't identify things that fit non-empirical concepts using your senses, so how *could* you identify them? You couldn't. A non-empirical concept is no concept at all. That's why I said that *genuine* concepts must come from sense experience. If you have a word that has no empirical meaning, that is if there is no sense experiences you use to tell whether something is of that sort or not, then it's not a genuine concept. People use that word, but that word doesn't mean anything.

RATIONALIST: I disagree. I think that there are concepts that are not empirical: you tell whether something is or isn't of that sort using the power of the mind alone, without the aid of the senses.

EMPIRICIST: That sounds like nonsense to me.

RATIONALIST: Well, how about these concepts: *God, infinity, cause.* You never see (hear, smell, etc.) any of these things; they're clearly not empirical concepts.

EMPIRICIST: Some empiricists agreed that the idea of God wasn't associated with any empirical application-conditions, but they concluded that this idea doesn't have any meaning at all—it's just a nonsense idea, an empty word without a genuine concept attached.

The empiricist approach to the concept of *infinity* I favour is to think that it actually does have empirical content, in a sense. Of course, we can never identify any infinity by seeing that it's infinite: for example, an infinitely long line could never be seen to be infinitely long. But the notion *finite* clearly does have empirical content: you can see that a line is finite when you see its ends. Now it's a short step from that to the idea of an infinite line: just take the opposite of that empirical concept, and imagine a line that doesn't have any end. So this is a constructed concept like that of *unicorn*, made from empirical concepts we already have, and which we've gotten from sense experience.

The idea of *cause* is interesting and controversial. David Hume had important things to say about this. (He was a Scottish philosopher in the eighteenth century, the greatest empiricist philosopher, and the guy many people think is the greatest philosopher, period.) Hume basically argued that we *can* see that X causes Y, because all this amounts to (roughly speaking) is the fact that whenever you get an X, then you get a Y afterwards—something that's definitely observable using the senses.

RATIONALIST: I agree that you can see that Xs are regularly followed by Ys, but that's not what cause amounts to. To say that X causes Y is to say more than that. It's to say that X makes Y happen—that if you get an X, then Y *has to* happen. It's not just that they occur together—X makes Y *necessary*. And that's something you don't see.

EMPIRICIST: Hume also considered that approach. His position is roughly that if that's what you want to say, then your idea of *cause* doesn't have any empirical meaning, and it's just nonsense.

RATIONALIST: Well, how about these concepts: *Tuesday*, *the exchange rate between the Canadian and US dollars*, *winning an election*. None of these concepts has the philosophical complexity that *God*, *infinity*, and *cause* have. They're all perfectly ordinary everyday ideas, and everyone can easily recognize examples of them. But none of these is an empirical concept. Tuesday isn't recognized by the way it looks or smells or feels.

EMPIRICIST: But somebody with no sense contact with the world couldn't have these concepts in the first place; even if somehow that person got these concepts, they couldn't recognize examples of them. They couldn't tell whether it was Tuesday, what the exchange rate was, who won the election. I think they're empirical concepts even though it's very hard to specify exactly how they're related to what we perceive through our senses.

7. Innateness and Language

SCEPTIC: Before we go on, I want to ask you something. There was a participant in the Conversation about religion,[7] a lot earlier, also called RATIONALIST. Did that person have the same position as you?

RATIONALIST: Well, *rationalism* is the name of a variety of philosophical positions which share the general idea that reason is important in some way, but other than that they can be quite different. A religious rationalist thinks that religious truths are rationally assessable and maybe provable. The rationalist position in theory of knowledge is contrasted with empiricism. Empiricists stress the senses; rationalists stress reasoning instead.

---

7 Conversation I.

DEFINER: You mentioned some other arguments in favour of innate ideas. Let's hear them.

RATIONALIST: The contemporary American philosopher and linguist Noam Chomsky has produced a couple of interesting arguments for innateness, based on facts about languages and language-learning. The first argument starts from the premise that every language that linguists have studied shows the same basic structure.

SCEPTIC: Wait a minute. Languages have very different structures. In English, the verb usually goes after the subject of the sentence, but in German the verb usually is saved for the end of the sentence.

RATIONALIST: Chomsky isn't talking about these structural matters, which, you're right, vary from language to language, but rather about more basic matters, those he calls the *deep structure* of language, like, for example, the fact that there are some words for verbs and some for nouns. His ideas about language are complicated, and we can't really go into them here. What he claims, anyway, is that the science of linguistics has discovered that every language has the same deep structure. The only plausible explanation for this fact, he says, is that the particular categories that are shared in the deep structure of all languages must be hard-wired into the human brain: these language concepts must be innate.

EMPIRICIST: So the innate concepts he's arguing for aren't ones like *brown* or *dog* or *cause*, but rather ones like *noun* and *verb*?

RATIONALIST: Roughly speaking, yes. His idea is that every human is hard-wired with the basic set-ups of language, which are the same for every language. An example of such a basic set-up is the technique in every language for saying the same thing in two different ways, using an active or a passive verb: for example, 'Sally hates Fred' and 'Fred is hated by Sally.' What's learned is the details that vary from language to language—like, for example, where the verb goes, and, of course, vocabulary.

EMPIRICIST: Well, maybe those linguists are wrong about what they claim to have observed. It just might be that the reason linguists see the same deep structure in every language is that they unconsciously see in every language they study the same deep structure as their own, and that there really isn't any surprising similarity between languages that needs explanation in the first place.

RATIONALIST: Well, maybe, but those are professional, scientific linguists we're talking about, and we can't really cast doubt on their claims without going into matters more deeply.

EMPIRICIST: Okay, granted. Anyway, their argument has the form of an argument to the best explanation. It says that the only plausible explanation for the observed facts is innateness, right?

RATIONALIST: Right.

EMPIRICIST: But there are other possible explanations for the similarity between languages. Maybe all languages evolved from a single language, a very long time ago, changing in surface structure as they spread out, but keeping the same basic deep structure they inherited from their common root language. Or maybe that's the only deep structure that's efficient for building a language on, so independently evolving languages would all choose that one. Anyway, you mentioned that there were a couple of arguments. What's the other one?

RATIONALIST: Chomsky and others also point to the enormous speed with which little children learn their first language, with comparatively little experience (from hearing language) to go on. For example, I read recently that linguists have discovered that almost everything people say to toddlers is either a question or a command, ("Do you want some more cereal?" "Don't feed that to the dog!") but the toddlers soon learn how to turn these into statements ("I don't want any more." "I didn't feed it to the dog."). Again, this shows that certain sorts of linguistic concepts are pre-wired into the brain.

EMPIRICIST: Well, I can think of some objections here too. For one thing, you shouldn't just count what's said to little children: they're listening to people talk to each other all the time. There's a huge amount of experience of the language they're learning.

RATIONALIST: But isn't it extraordinary how comparatively quickly little children learn their first language? You can appreciate this if you've tried to learn a second language as adult. Adults have to spend enormous amounts of time memorizing grammar and vocabulary, and they hardly ever reach the level of competence in their second language that little children manage, in their first language, in only a very few years. It really seems as though there's a built-in mechanism—a language-learning machine, so to speak—inborn in babies, adapted for the deep structure of any of the languages they might happen to be born into. This machine stops working after a few years, and by the time people reach their teens, it becomes extraordinarily difficult to learn another language.

EMPIRICIST: I agree that babies are extraordinarily well-prepared to learn language fast, but this doesn't really show that there are any innate concepts. Any empiricist can agree that people (sometimes at one age more than another) have innate adaptations to learning something. Look, no matter how much language a tree is exposed to, it will never begin to learn any of it, because it lacks all the built-in learning mechanisms needed.

RATIONALIST: Well, I still think that the universality of deep structure and the speed of first-language learning show that there are innate concepts; but obviously this needs a lot more discussion.

8. Empiricism and Rationalism: Judgements

DEFINER: Okay, let's change the subject. A while back, EMPIRICIST, you spoke of two aspects of empiricism: the idea that all *concepts* have empirical content and that none of them are innate, on the one hand, and the idea that every *judgement* comes from experience. We've just discussed the first aspect; could you say some things now about the second?

EMPIRICIST: Sure. Concepts are, for example, *dog* and *brown*, but a judgement puts them together into something that is either true or false, for example, *Some dogs are brown*. Concepts more or less correspond to single words or phrases, but judgements correspond to whole sentences. To have beliefs, you have to have concepts, but having any number of concepts doesn't mean that you have beliefs: a belief must involve a judgement. So, for example, you can have the concepts *dog* and *brown*, but that doesn't add up to the belief that some dogs are brown. Empiricists think that the only acceptable source for our judgements is sense experience— that is, experience beyond what it takes to get the concepts that the judgement is composed of. For example, the experiences that have given us the concept *dog* might have involved seeing some black dogs, some white dogs, some cats and birds, and so on (to train us in identifying dogs and non-dogs) and the experiences that have given us the concept *brown* might have involved seeing some brown cows and some brown leaves, as well as a number of things of other colours; but all this doesn't add up to any judgement about whether some dogs are brown or not. In addition to this we'd need sense experience to justify the judgement *Some dogs are brown*: that, of course, would be seeing some brown dogs.

CARTESIAN: Descartes (and other rationalists) would agree that the only reliable source of some sorts of belief—their only justification—is sense experience. He'd agree, for example, that the only way it could be determined that some dogs are brown is by looking. But, as I mentioned before, he didn't think that beliefs that originated in sense perception carried the sort of certainty that was required for full-fledged knowledge. The beliefs of which we can be certain aren't justified by sense experience. We justify them without the need of sense experience.

DEFINER: That's odd, in a way. Descartes was writing when the Scientific Revolution was just getting started, and his insistence on the necessity of proving your beliefs, rather than relying on authority, helped that Revolution to get started. But wasn't empiricism an important feature of that Revolution? Wasn't that the point in history when people got the idea that observation and experiment was the important thing in acquiring knowledge?

CARTESIAN: Well, roughly speaking, that's right. Descartes, who argued that authoritative pronouncement was insufficient for knowledge, paved the way for science based on observation—for empirical science. But Descartes himself was clearly a rationalist, certainly not an empiricist. Important, full-fledged scientific knowledge, he thought, was justified by "clear and distinct" thought alone, without the necessity of empirical observation.

EMPIRICIST: I'd agree with Descartes that beliefs justified by sense perception don't carry the sort of certainty required by Descartes; but I think that sense perception is our only source for beliefs.

A bit of philosophical jargon might be helpful here, by the way. Philosophers call judgements that need sense experience for their justification *a posteriori* judgements. That's Latin, meaning *from afterwards*—that is, justified after, on the basis of, sense experience. If there were a judgement that could be justified before—prior to, without the need of—sense experience, then that judgement would be called *a priori*. We empiricists think that all knowledge is a posteriori.

RATIONALIST: We already agreed that new-born babies have no mental abilities worth speaking about. So when you talk about a priori knowledge, you don't mean things that they know.

EMPIRICIST: Right. New-born babies just lie there, thinking "Wha?" and "D'oh!" What I mean by a priori knowledge is what could be justified in advance of—without need of—the particular sense experiences associated with that judgement. So, for example, you need to see brown dogs to justify the judgement that some dogs are brown, so that's not a posteriori, not a priori.

RATIONALIST: Okay. Now, why do you think that there isn't any a priori knowledge?

EMPIRICIST: What counts as justification for a belief is a process that gives good reason to think that a belief is true—that is, that what it says corresponds to the way the world is. How else could we check on whether our beliefs correspond to the world than by using our senses? They're the only contact with the outside world we have.

SCEPTIC: Wait a minute. There are plenty of beliefs people have that don't come from experience. Some people believe that intelligent creatures live on other planets, though nobody's ever seen them.

EMPIRICIST: Well, I didn't mean to say that sense experience is the only *origin* of anyone's judgements. Once somebody got the concepts *intelligent creatures* and *living*, and *other planets*, they might start believing that intelligent creatures live on other planets, without any basis in experience for that judgement at all, just by sticking together those concepts in their mind. But that belief would be unjustified. What I'm claiming is that the only way judgements could be *justified*—the only way true ones could count as knowledge—is if they arose from sense experience.

SCEPTIC: But how about my judgement that there are rabbits in Australia? I've never been to Australia, so I've never seen them there. But that's got to be a justified judgement.

EMPIRICIST: I agree that it's justified for you. I should distinguish between *direct* justification and *indirect*. Somebody who sees those rabbits has direct justification; your justification is indirect. You don't need to personally experience everything you have a justified belief about, but someone must have had the requisite experience, then told other people. If nobody had ever seen the rabbits in Australia, then nobody could have the justified judgement that there were rabbits there. Once somebody has seen them there, then other people can be told about them, and provided that their informant is reliable, then their belief was justified too, indirectly. This kind of indirect justification involves empirical experience also—the experience of the person who saw those rabbits, and the experience of others who were informed of this fact, which justified their belief that their informant is reliable. And, of course, there's another way we can get indirect empirical justification. Suppose that nobody has ever seen rabbits in your neighbourhood, but you can see evidence of their presence: the vegetables in your garden are gnawed in a characteristic way, there are rabbit footprints in the snow, you can find rabbit droppings, and so on. This indirect empirical evidence requires two sorts of experience: you or somebody has to see the evidence (the footprints, etc.) and you or somebody has to have experience of the connection between that sort of footprint, nibbling, etc., and rabbits.

9. Analytic and Synthetic Judgements

RATIONALIST: I agree that some facts about the real world can be found out only through the senses. Knowing that pigs can't fly, for example, is something that people could find out only through observation of pigs. That judgement is clearly knowable only a posteriori. But I think that there are some beliefs about the world that are a priori—discovered and justified, that is, without the aid of the senses.

EMPIRICIST: Like what?

RATIONALIST: Okay, here's a real easy one: the fact that anyone's sister is female. Everyone knows this is true, and nobody has to do any observation to find out that it is true. Imagine, for example, some sociologists setting out on an empirical research project to determine whether or not this is the case. They come up to you in the mall, holding clipboards, and ask you if you have any sisters, and, if so, what their gender is. This is not only very stupid and unnecessary, but it wouldn't even give you a strong enough conclusion. Even if they did a very large number of interviews, and everyone interviewed who had had a sister reported that their sister was female, this still wouldn't justify what we already know: that anyone's sister, in all societies, past, present, or future, is female. It's a priori.

EMPIRICIST: Well, all right, sure, I agree that that's an a priori judgement, one that doesn't need empirical justification. The reason is that the judgement is *true by definition*. It's part of the definition of the word 'sister' that the person is female. Or, in other words, being female is one of the identifying characteristics of the concept *sister*: in order to apply the concept, one of the things you have to determine is whether the person is female. Kant said that this kind of truth was the consequence of the fact that one concept is "contained within" the other: the concept *sister* contains the concept *female*. So knowledge of what the concepts involve in this case is sufficient to tell you that it's true. All you have to do to see that it's true is to "take apart" the concept *sister*, and find the concept *female* inside it. This sort of "taking apart" is sometimes called *conceptual analysis*, and it's why philosophers, following Kant, call this kind of judgement— whose truth is simply a consequence of the fact that one concept is contained within the other—an *analytic truth*. So I'll grant that there are certain a priori judgements, namely analytic ones.

RATIONALIST: Aha!

EMPIRICIST: But look, those analytic truths are extremely unimportant. A case could be made that they're completely uninformative. Their truth depends not on the way the world is, but merely on the concepts that make up those judgements. So analytic judgements really aren't significant parts of our knowledge. That's why those sociologists in the mall are doubly stupid: you don't need empirical investigation to discover the truth of that statement, in the first place, and in the second, discovering its truth isn't really finding anything out at all. Our important knowledge is of judgements that aren't analytic: they're the ones Kant called *synthetic*. Their truth depends not only on the nature of the concepts that make up those judgements, but on the way the world is.

SCEPTIC: Why are they called 'synthetic'?

EMPIRICIST: 'Synthesis' means putting things together—it's the opposite of 'analysis' which means taking things apart. A synthetic judgement puts two concepts together, where neither concept is contained within the other. For example, the concept *pig* doesn't include, or exclude, the concept *can fly*. So *No pigs can fly* is not an analytic truth (or falsehood); having the concepts doesn't all by itself tell you that that belief is true or false. It's a synthetic statement. Obviously, you need observation to find out it's true—it's a posteriori.

Another kind of analytic judgement is what you might call a logical truth, for example, *It's raining or it's not raining*. I guess this one could also be said to be true merely because of the concepts that make it up, except in this case it's the logical concepts—*or* and *not*—that make this true. Any statement of that form, *X or not X*, must be true just because of its logic—because of the way its logical words work. Other analytic logical truths are *If it's raining than it's raining* and *All cats are cats*. Like the other kind of analytic judgements—those true by definition—these don't actually contain any information. For example, you could know the truth of *It's raining or it's not raining* without knowing anything about the weather: you don't even have to look outside to know that it's true. That's because it gives you no information about the weather at all.

RATIONALIST: Okay, I agree that analytic judgements aren't a very significant form of a priori knowledge (if they count as knowledge at all). My real disagreement with you is that I think that there is synthetic a priori knowledge.

10. Synthetic A Priori Judgements

EMPIRICIST: Now we've gotten to an important disagreement between us. Let's hear some examples of what you think are synthetic a priori truths.

RATIONALIST: Here's one: *Every event has a cause.*

EMPIRICIST: Hmm. I guess I agree that that's synthetic. At first I thought you were saying "Every *effect* has a cause," and of course that would be a trivial analytic truth. Okay, so the real question is whether that one is a priori.

RATIONALIST: Remember the discussion of that one a while back, when they were talking about determinism?[8] DETERMINIST made the point there that this is something we all believe, but that this belief isn't based on experience.

EMPIRICIST: Well, a little earlier you were claiming that we don't observe that something is a cause—that the concept *cause* doesn't have empirical content. It's natural to think that judgements involving non-empirical concepts are a priori; but we empiricists don't believe that there are concepts like that. We believe that the concept *cause* is either empirical or nonsense.

RATIONALIST: But even if we could observe causes, we still couldn't have discovered that *every* event has a cause, since we haven't found causes for a large number of things we've experienced. Experience hasn't justified this claim. But we take it that in those cases in which we haven't found causes, there are causes there anyway, since we believe prior to, independently of, our experience that there must be a cause for everything.

EMPIRICIST: I'd say either that we aren't justified in thinking that every event (except maybe for the really tiny ones talked about in quantum physics) has a cause, or else we've found sufficient causes to make that belief justified by our experience. After all, we don't have to check out *every* possible instance to justify a scientific generalization like that. To justify the belief that all robins eat worms you don't have to check out every robin, and you don't have to observe worm-eating in every single one you do see. You just have to have a sufficiently wide confirmation in your experience. Maybe we have this in the case of the belief that every event has a cause.

RATIONALIST: I don't think we're unjustified in thinking that every event has a cause, but neither do I think that the belief is justified by observation. I agree with Kant that it's a priori. Anyway, here's another of Kant's examples: 7 + 5 = 12. He argued that the truths of arithmetic were also synthetic a priori.

EMPIRICIST: But isn't the belief that 7 + 5 = 12 a posteriori, justified by a great deal of our sense experience? Think of all the times people have put

---

8 Conversation V.

7 things in a pile, and added 5 things to it, and counted the results and got 12.

RATIONALIST: Maybe so, but I doubt it. How many times have you done that? How many times has anyone done that?

EMPIRICIST: Well, John Stuart Mill, who was an enthusiastic empiricist, argued that we've gotten plenty of empirical evidence for the facts of arithmetic. I'm not positive that he was right—I'll tell you about a different empiricist theory of arithmetic later—but I think that Mill's idea was at least plausible, and I'll try to defend it to you.

RATIONALIST: Okay, so according to this view $7 + 5 = 12$ and the other arithmetic truths are justified by a great deal of empirical observation?

EMPIRICIST: Right.

RATIONALIST: But everyone believes, and they're justified in that belief, that 7 million + 5 million = 12 million, even though nobody's ever counted any piles that large.

EMPIRICIST: Well, as I mentioned earlier, empiricists don't think you have to experience everything you know: you extrapolate—you generalize from particular experiences. For example, once you count to discover that 7 apples + 5 apples = 12 apples, and 7 pebbles + 5 pebbles = 12 pebbles, then you could generalize, and justifiably believe that 7 ducks + 5 ducks = 12 ducks, even though you haven't tried that with ducks, and they won't stay in a neat pile long enough to be counted anyway. You generalize to the justified belief that 7 of anything plus 5 of those things equals 12 of them. So you're justified in believing that 7 million + 5 million must = 12 million.

RATIONALIST: No, that can't be right. Beliefs that have empirical, a posteriori justification on the basis of an observed sample are always open to some doubt: maybe we just haven't looked around enough to find cases in which they're not true. And most of them are just approximately true, or true-on-the-whole. The empirical generalization that all crows are black, for example, is pretty nearly universally true, but not quite: there are white, albino crows. The ideal gas laws in physics, which say that the pressure on an enclosed gas varies inversely as the volume, is a pretty good approximation, but not exact. But $7 + 5 = 12$ isn't open to this sort of doubt. We know it has to be true everywhere: we don't need to look any further. And it's exactly, not just approximately, true.

EMPIRICIST: Well, maybe $7 + 5 = 12$ is only approximately true also, and empirical examination turns up cases in which this isn't precisely right.

RATIONALIST: Really? Like what?

EMPIRICIST: If you take 7 ml of water, and add 5 ml of alcohol to it, and you measure the result, you get a tiny bit less than 12 ml of liquid. In fact, this really happens. I can show it to you. (We'll drink it afterwards.)

RATIONALIST: But that isn't a fair test for the truth or falsity of that statement. I know what's happening in the water + alcohol case: the water molecules and the alcohol molecules sort of fit in between each other. It's like putting 7 bushels of oranges in a bin, and stirring in 5 bushels of raisins. The raisins would fit into the spaces between the oranges, and maybe you'd get only 8 or 9 bushels of fruit as a result. It's not a fair test because that's not what's meant by plussing.

EMPIRICIST: Then how about this test: suppose one day it snows and there's 7 cm. of snow on the ground. The next day, 5 cm. more of snow fall. It's constantly below freezing, so no snow is melting. How much snow is there on the ground then?

RATIONALIST: Okay, I'll play along. 12 cm.?

EMPIRICIST: No 10 cm.

RATIONALIST: How come?

EMPIRICIST: The weight of the snow that falls on top packs down the snow underneath.

EMPIRICIST: Right, so again that's not a fair test.

EMPIRICIST: Well, what would you count as a fair test?

RATIONALIST: Adding volumes isn't because things fit in-between or pack down. Adding masses would be a good test. If you push a lump with a mass of 7 kg. and a lump with a mass of 5 kg. together then you get a combined lump with a mass of 12 kg., right?

EMPIRICIST: Well, strangely enough, no. The combined lump actually has a mass which is a very tiny bit less than 12 kg. A *very* tiny bit. If the lumps start 1 metre apart, and you push them together, the resultant combined lump has a mass of 11.999999999999999974 kg.

RATIONALIST: No kidding? How come?

EMPIRICIST: It's a consequence of something Einstein discovered, involving the conversion of mass and the binding energy of gravity.

RATIONALIST: Well, then that's not a fair test either. When you push them together, a little bit of the mass gets converted to binding energy.

EMPIRICIST: You're cheating. You just refuse to count anything as showing that 7 + 5 doesn't equal 12. It's just like defending the claim that 'All crows are black' is perfectly, completely true by refusing to count anything of any other colour as a crow.

RATIONALIST: Kant also thought that the facts of geometry were synthetic a priori. Do you think that they're also actually a posteriori, confirmed by lots of experience, and, as usual with empirical generalizations, shown by some careful observations to be only approximately true?

EMPIRICIST: Yes. Here's a true story from the history of science, that shows this about an accepted generalization of geometry, that the sum of the interior angles of a triangle equals 180°. The story involves Einstein again. In 1915, he proposed his Theory of Relativity, and a consequence of this theory was that certain big triangles, on an astronomical scale, have angles that don't add up to 180°. So they did some astronomical observations to find out if Einstein was right. I'll draw you a diagram to show you the idea:

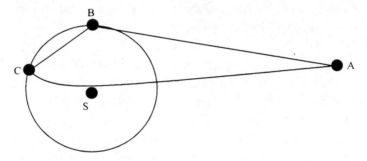

On the left is the orbit of the earth around the sun, S. On that orbit, B and C are two positions of the earth at different times of the year. On the right is a distant star, A. The line CA shows the direction that star appears in, when the earth is at C. Now, Einstein proposed that gravity "bends" space, so that the path of light coming from the star when it passed near the sun, and was subjected to a huge gravitational field, would be "bent," and AC would be the path of the light. Now, you can sort of see from this crude picture I've drawn that the angle whose vertex is at point C, the angle ACB, is bigger than would have been expected on an ordinary triangle. The result is that the sum of the three angles, ACB + BAC + CBA is greater than 180°. To test this prediction, they had to look at that star from positions C and B on the earth's orbit, and measure where the star A appeared in the sky. That was easy for position B, but, as you can see, from position C, it would have been day, and you can't see the stars. So they waited a few years till 1919, when a total eclipse of the sun darkened the sky and made the stars visible, and they measured. Einstein was right.

I think that this shows that whether or not triangles have interior angles adding up to 180° is an empirical matter, not a priori at all, but a posteriori —something we find out by observation. And observations have shown it to be false.

RATIONALIST: But look, on the diagram the reason is pretty clear why the sum is larger than 180°. Line AC isn't a straight line—it's curved. So ABC isn't a triangle, which has to be made out of straight lines. I mean, didn't you just say yourself that the gravitational field of the sun "curved" the path of the light coming from the star?

EMPIRICIST: I did, but that was just a sort of metaphor, an inexact way of speaking. Actually, that path is a straight line. It's the path a ray of light takes, and that has to be a straight line. Imagine taking a really long, perfectly straight and rigid ruler, and putting one end at C, and the other end at A: it would follow exactly that path CA. And you know how you can test if a ruler is really straight or not, by putting one end up to your eye and sighting down it? Well, if you did that with the ruler in that position, it would still test straight. CA passes all the tests for a straight line. It has to be straight!

RATIONALIST: Well, I don't know. For this example, just like the others in which empirical observation appears to contradict an a priori truth, I think that there's something wrong with the example: it doesn't really show that the judgement isn't true.

EMPIRICIST: You're just irrationally refusing to accept any empirical evidence that these so-called truths are actually false. Why not just admit that empirical science has shown that Euclidian geometry is sometimes a little bit false? Synthetic, a posteriori, and only approximately true?

RATIONALIST: Both arithmetic and geometry are clearly a priori. We proved in high school geometry that the law about the interior angles of a triangle is true. That proof was a good example of a priori thought. You start out with nothing but axioms, which are clearly true, and you can tell that they have to be true just by thinking about them. Then you prove that truth about triangles using only the operations of mind. The same thing is true in mathematics. You can tell that mathematics isn't observational by watching mathematicians at work. Other scientists are conducting experiments, out doing field observations, looking through microscopes or telescopes. But mathematicians don't look at anything except the piece of paper they're writing things on. They don't need to do any observations. And you can't do an observational test of most of what's known in mathematics, just because there aren't any observations that would be associated with it. You can't get a piece of string that's -1 inches long—that sort of mathematical concept doesn't even apply to the visible world.

EMPIRICIST: Well, okay, I do admit that there's something to be said for that view of arithmetic and geometry. And I also do sympathize with your objections, to all of my proposed examples, that what we had there wasn't really plussing, or wasn't really a triangle. I indicated earlier that I wasn't entirely comfortable with Mill's view that arithmetic and geometry were a posteriori.

RATIONALIST: So you might be willing to admit that they're a priori? Maybe I could get you to agree with me?

EMPIRICIST: I do think that the view that they're a priori is somewhat plausible. But I still wouldn't agree with you that they're synthetic a priori. I'd say, then, that they're analytic a priori. That's still consistent with empiricism, remember.

RATIONALIST: How's the idea that they're analytic supposed to work?

EMPIRICIST: That view sees arithmetic and geometry as merely matters of definition, and what follows from those definitions. Looked at that way, they are just a bunch of arbitrary symbols defined in a certain way so that all the truths of arithmetic come out to be true by definition—analytic. So arithmetic and geometry, just in themselves, don't actually apply to the real world at all. But if you want to apply them to the real world, you have to provide an empirical interpretation for them—you have to stipulate a way in which you're going to apply their concepts to the real world. You say, for example, that addition in arithmetic means combining masses in the real world, or that a straight line in geometry means the path of a beam of light. Given this interpretation, they both apply to the real world, but we have to find out from experience whether they're true, and it turns out they're only approximately true. So "pure"—uninterpreted—arithmetic and geometry are true by definition—analytic a priori—and interpreted arithmetic and geometry are synthetic a posteriori. There is no synthetic a priori.

RATIONALIST: The truths of pure arithmetic couldn't be trivial truths, just true by definition. They really do tell us facts about the real world. And, if they were merely definitional truths, how come it takes so much brainwork to come up with them? If they were merely true by definition, you could immediately see that they just followed from the concepts, like the fact that everyone's sister is female.

EMPIRICIST: Well, maybe some consequences of complicated definitional truths aren't immediately obvious, and take some deep thought to discover—what those mathematicians are working at. Anyway, let me ask you something about those judgements you think are synthetic a priori. If they're a priori, they're not justified by experience. If they're synthetic, the analysis of concepts doesn't justify them. What does justify them?

RATIONALIST: They're justified merely by the operations of our mind alone. Truths of arithmetic and geometry are included in those that Descartes thought were knowable independently of sense experience, when the mind operates on its clear and distinct ideas. Take, for example, this axiom of geometry: If A and B are two points, there exists only one line that contains both A and B. When you really think about that, and get the ideas in your mind, each very clearly and distinctly, you can't help but see that it's true, and you can't be mistaken about that.

EMPIRICIST: That doesn't seem plausible to me. I don't see how some synthetic judgements just tell you that they have to be true.

RATIONALIST: Kant argued for this approach. We can discover the truth of these things a priori by showing that if these judgements weren't true, then we wouldn't know anything—ordinary knowledge of anything else would be impossible.

SCEPTIC: I don't see how that's supposed to be the case. But anyway, even if it were the case that if these judgements weren't true we couldn't know anything, that wouldn't convince me that they are true. Maybe ordinary knowledge is impossible!

RATIONALIST: That's just silly.

SCEPTIC: Well, I'll try to convince you that Scepticism isn't silly at all.

11. Scepticism: Perception

DEFINER: So, EMPIRICIST, I gather that you think that sense perception provides the foundation for our knowledge—the information on which we base our beliefs (at least the ones with any substance—the synthetic ones), and which justifies them.

EMPIRICIST: Right.

DEFINER: So they fill the role in your view that the "clear and distinct" a priori truths filled in the rationalist views of CARTESIAN?

EMPIRICIST: Yes, in the sense that all our knowledge is based on the beliefs directly gotten by perception. So in that way they can be thought of as

"foundational." But I don't think that any perception-based belief is infallible. The possibility that a sense perception is wrong is often so small
that rational people totally ignore it; but some possibility is always there.
There are all sorts of cases in which the senses give you mistaken information, even when you think you're seeing things clearly, or otherwise
perceiving correctly. For example, take a look at this diagram:

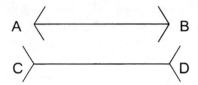

It looks like horizontal line CD is longer than AB, but it isn't. Here's
another familiar perceptual illusion: You put a straight stick like a pencil
into a half-filled glass of water. From one angle, it looks like this:

It seems to bend just where it emerges from the surface of the water.
Here's a more interesting illusion, not a visual one, you may not have run
into. You cross your index and middle fingers, and position them so that
the ends of both are touching a straight edge, like the edge of the desk.
Then you run both fingers along the edge. If you get the angle of your
hand right, it feels exactly as if there are two edges, not one. Try it.

DEFINER: Cool.

SCEPTIC: There are countless ways our senses can deceive us. But you think
anyway that sense experience provides justification for our beliefs? The
only justification? How can it, if it's so fallible?

EMPIRICIST: We usually aren't deceived by these illusions. I knew that AB
and CD were the same length. And, even when we are deceived, what
does this show? We get things right almost all the time. That's all that's
needed for justification: that it be a very good guide to truth. Perfection
isn't necessary.

SCEPTIC: Here's why I think that these illusions raise a more significant problem for the idea that sense perception justifies belief. First, when you

think about these cases, you can see that what we are really directly aware of, in the cases of sense perceptions, is a representation inside us.

DEFINER: Wait a minute. *Inside*? What I'm aware of is the edge of the table, or those lines on the paper. They're outside.

SCEPTIC: What I mean is that you're drawing conclusions about external things on the basis of the representations that are inside you. Your *immediate* object of perception is this internal representation, and from this you infer—you conclude—something about what's outside. Philosophers sometimes call these internal representations *sense data*. Now, we think that some sense data give us accurate information about the external world, and some don't. But how do we tell which are accurate and which aren't? There's nothing about them that indicates whether they're accurate or not. I mean, when you hallucinate or dream something which doesn't exist in the external world at all, it can seem perfectly realistic to you, just as if you're encountering the real world.

DEFINER: Yes, but when you have a sense data ...

SCEPTIC: That term is plural. The singular is sense datum.

DEFINER: Okay okay. When you have a sense datum you can find out which perceptions are accurate and which are potentially misleading. For example, you can measure lines AB and CB with a ruler. This will show you that the way those lines look is misleading.

SCEPTIC: But isn't this just a matter of checking up on one perception by comparing it to another? What if the way the lines looked first was right, but your perception of the ruler is mistaken? What if they're both wrong? It's just like checking up on the facts reported in one newspaper by looking in a different one. Which one should you trust? Why think either is trustworthy? Maybe you're actually dreaming right now—dreaming both the arrows and the ruler—and nothing you think you see is actually real. Remember Descartes' "evil demon"—why think that there isn't one of them fooling you?

DEFINER: I don't believe in demons! But seriously, it's obvious to everyone—common sense tells you—that there is a real world around us, and that our senses accurately tell us (in general, with a few exceptions) what it's like. People who seriously doubted this would be completely paralyzed—they'd be unable to do anything, if they didn't trust their senses. Anyone who takes the idea seriously that the world is very different from what our senses tell us is literally insane.

SCEPTIC: Well, not necessarily. I mean, the idea that things really aren't the way they seem is sometimes just a loony conspiracy theory, a paranoid fantasy, but in small doses it's maybe healthy scepticism. The idea that the everyday physical perceptible world isn't the really real world was a central feature of Plato's view, and of several other philosophers who nobody thought were crazy. And this idea is sometimes more or less incorporated into some religious views held by lots of people, who presumably couldn't all be insane. For example, there was a medieval Christian sect called the Cathars who held that the physical world was an illusion created by the devil. But look, whether or not any sane person could really believe any of these things isn't the issue. I'm not insane, and I really trust my senses just as much as anyone else does. What I'm really asking is whether there's any good reason to think that sense perception justifies belief—whether there's any philosophical argument with that as the conclusion.

CARTESIAN: I mentioned Descartes' answer to that question earlier: he thinks that all belief originating in sense perception is fallible, and falls short of the certainty required for genuine full-fledged knowledge, for genuine science. But he did think that sense experience was on the whole reliable, at least for practical everyday purposes.

SCEPTIC: What justified that conclusion for him? I'll bet it's God again!

CARTESIAN: Right! God gives us our senses for practical (not theoretical) purposes, and God's benevolence guarantees that it can, in general, be trusted.

SCEPTIC: Though not invariably.

CARTESIAN: Right.

SCEPTIC: I find that answer just as unsatisfactory as the similar one Descartes gave to try to justify the certainty conferred by clear-and-distinct thinking. I mean, Descartes just trots out God whenever he's got an unanswerable question.

CARTESIAN: Well, okay, here's a much more modern argument that doesn't involve God at all, but I think it's in the spirit of Descartes' argument anyway. Descartes thought of the primary function of our senses as practical—they're for finding our way around in the world, avoiding danger, getting us what we want and need, and so on. This function requires that they represent the outside world accurately, in general. If they didn't then they wouldn't serve that function. In Descartes' day, they thought that living things' faculties were adapted to their function because God created them that way, but nowadays we explain this by Natural Selection (as you might remember from the discussion of the Argument From Design, all the way back in the religion discussion[9]). Our senses have evolved to be

---

9 Conversation I.

the way they are because the way they are suits our environment—helps our survival, reproduction, and so on. For our senses to be useful in this way, they have to give us, on the whole, a correct representation of reality. So we have reason to think that they are, in general, reliable.

SCEPTIC: There are a couple of assumptions in your argument that I think are questionable. First, you assume that because of evolution, all characteristics must be advantageous for our survival; but this is not always true. Some of them may have been valuable when they evolved, but are no longer—our surroundings, after all, have changed drastically from the earlier times when our current characteristics evolved. Some of them—the appendix, for example, just don't seem to serve any adaptive purpose at all—any current one, anyway.

CARTESIAN: Yes, but it's clear that our senses mostly do help us get by in the world, isn't it?

SCEPTIC: Maybe, but here's my second point. Why do you assume that a correct representation of the world is more valuable to us, in terms of adaptive success, than some incorrect one might be? A whole lot of information about the outside world is irrelevant to our practical needs. For example, x-radiation—the rays emitted by an x-ray machine—occurs naturally, emitted by very hot stars and other things; but that kind of electromagnetic radiation doesn't have any practical upshot for us, and our eyes have evolved in such a way that we don't perceive it. But we do perceive other kinds, what we count as the various colours of visible light, because differences there (for example, between green unripe fruit and red ripe fruit) are important for our well-being. So a very partial, and highly filtered and distorted, representation of reality might be much more valuable than a complete and accurate representation (whatever that might be like!).

CARTESIAN: Partial and selective, maybe, but inaccurate?

12. The Brain in the Vat

SCEPTIC: Okay, here's a modern version of Descartes' evil-demon way of introducing the question about whether our senses give us an accurate view of reality. It's really the same argument, but put into more modern science fiction terms. Imagine that you are actually just a *brain in a vat*—that all there is to you is a functioning brain, floating around in a vat of nutritive liquid, with input and output wires connected to a gigantic computer. The computer sends signals into that part of your brain that receives visual input, and it seems to you that you are seeing something—but you really aren't. The computer also produces other apparent sense-inputs, from your other sense-modalities, producing illusions of smells, sounds, and so on. When you feel like something to eat, your brain outputs signals for your legs to move and walk you over to the refrigerator, but of course you really do no such thing—you don't have any legs. The computer interprets this output, and changes your visual input so you seem to be walking over to the fridge, and shortly afterwards, you seem to be tasting that left-over pizza, and later you seem to be feeling indigestion, and so on. This has been the case for your whole life—you've been nothing but a brain in a vat since birth. Your whole world is a hallucination.

DEFINER: That sort of thing sounds familiar. Has some philosopher been to see the movie *Matrix*?

SCEPTIC: I doubt it. A philosopher wouldn't be caught dead in a Keanu Reeves movie. Anyway, this story originates a long time before the movie. It was popularized in a 1981 book by the philosopher Hilary Putnam. But stories like this have a much longer history. Descartes' "evil demon" story dates from the seventeenth century, and as early as the fourth century BC, Plato considered the possibility that all our experience was illusory.

DEFINER: I know I'm not a brain in a vat because when I look in a mirror, I see a face, not a naked floating brain.

SCEPTIC: But if you're a brain in a vat, then the computer would give you a face-illusion in a mirror-illusion.

DEFINER: Okay, maybe I can't come up with a conclusive proof that I'm not a brain in a vat, but I still think it's so unlikely that it's not worth serious consideration. Again, only a crazy person would think that it's a real possibility.

SCEPTIC: I'm not asking for conclusive proof, and I'm not saying that a sane person could really believe it. I'm asking for some reason—even a very weak one—to make it even a little bit improbable.

DEFINER: Well, how about this. If I've been a brain in a vat for my whole life, I never have encountered anything in the real world—not real refrigerators or pizzas, not even real brains or vats. If I haven't been in touch with anything in the real world, I can't now have any thoughts about it. I can't have any beliefs about refrigerators or pizzas—I can't even think about being a brain in a vat. So if I ask myself whether that pizza I seem to be eating is real or just a hallucination, that means I'm thinking about pizzas, and that means I must have had some genuine contact with pizzas; so I'm not a brain in a vat after all.

SCEPTIC: That's basically Putnam's answer. I'm not sure it works, however. I agree that if you're asking yourself if that's a real pizza, then you're thinking about pizzas, and you have to have had some contact with them. But are you really asking yourself that?

DEFINER: If I were really a brain in a vat, all my thoughts would just be nonsense. I just have to assume that things make some sense. I can't avoid that.

SCEPTIC: Maybe you have to assume that, but still, you haven't provided the reasoning I asked for, to show even the slightest improbability of the brain-in-a-vat hypothesis. If you haven't done this, then you haven't given any reason to think that perception provides justification for beliefs about the external world. But if you agree with EMPIRICIST that sense perception provides the only mechanism we have for finding out what the external world is like—indeed, for finding out that there is an external world at all—then it seems that even your belief in the outside world is unjustified!

DEFINER: Well, that's ridiculous. That's the kind of silliness that gives philosophy a bad name.

SCEPTIC: I agree. For example, there's the joke that philosophers spend the morning doubting the existence of the external world, and then they go out to lunch. But the genuine problem here—one that's not silly—is to find some reasoning to show that there really is an external world. Philosophers have been trying for centuries to find a satisfactory response to this kind of doubt about the existence of the external world. And while we're talking about sceptical doubts, there's another important kind of belief that everyone accepts, but which sceptical doubts have been raised about.

DEFINER: Good, let's hear.

13. Scepticism: The Five-Minute Hypothesis

SCEPTIC: It seems obvious to everyone that sense perception is the basis of more beliefs than merely those about the world right in front of you, that you sense right at the present moment. You also know about the past.

DEFINER: Right. Suppose you remember that you went to the movies with friends for your tenth birthday party. That's something you know a posteriori, of course, because you had sense experiences related to it at the time, but there's nothing in your present sense experience to justify the belief you have now that you did that. Nothing except that memory trace you have now.

SCEPTIC: Yes, and that's what raises another related sceptical problem: whether memory traces are trustworthy. Again, we sceptics point out that sometimes (maybe even lots of times, for some people) they tell you false things, and of course there's a great deal of information about what you experienced in the past that they don't tell you. Again, you can check out your memory traces in various ways, but those other ways are open to similar sceptical doubts.

DEFINER: Well, that's basically the same problem as you raised before.

SCEPTIC: You're right, and this one also has a little imaginary story to raise this question vividly. It was invented by the great twentieth-century English philosopher Bertrand Russell, and it's called the *Five-Minute Hypothesis*. Consider the claim that you, and the entire rest of the universe, came into existence exactly five minutes ago. Do you have any reason to think that this hypothesis is false?

DEFINER: I can see where this one is going, but I'll play along anyway. One good reason I have, obviously, is that I remember all sorts of things that happened before that time. I remember what I ate for dinner last night.

SCEPTIC: You have a memory trace that represents your eating dinner last night, but maybe that's a fake—built into you when you popped into existence five minutes ago.

DEFINER: But how about the fact that newspapers report what happened yesterday? And they all agree?

SCEPTIC: Once again, this is just a matter of how those newspapers were created five minutes ago.

DEFINER: And, I suppose, some things, like my car, were created five minutes ago looking really old?

SCEPTIC: Right. Fake antiques. The point is that present empirical evidence doesn't give us any reason to prefer our ordinary beliefs to the Five-Minute Hypothesis.

RATIONALIST: Very interesting. That goes to show the limitations of empiricism.

EMPIRICIST: Really? What could a Rationalist say against the Five-Minute Hypothesis?

RATIONALIST: How about this. The Five-Minute Hypothesis involves an enormous number of unexplained coincidences. You've already pointed out one of them: that all those newspapers came into existence reporting more or less the same thing. But there are all sorts of other ones. I remember having dinner with you last week (a fake memory trace I came into existence with, on the Five-Minute Hypothesis), and you have the same fake memory trace, subtly changed to reflect your perspective. I remember buying these shoes a long time ago, and, corresponding with that, they've been created to look really worn out. And there's an enormous number of other fake bits of evidence and memories that fit together like this—altogether, a huge number of incredible coincidences.

SCEPTIC: Well, what's wrong with that? Calling those coincidences "incredible" merely means you don't believe the Five-Minute Hypothesis. Where's your argument?

RATIONALIST: I think that when you have two hypotheses, both of which have the same empirical adequacy, then you choose the simpler of the two. That principle, Ockham's Razor, was mentioned earlier, in the discussion of the identity theory and dualism.[10] The Five-Minute Hypothesis and the ordinary common sense one have the same empirical adequacy. But the common-sense view is preferable because it's simpler.

EMPIRICIST: What do you mean, the 'same empirical adequacy'?

RATIONALIST: I mean, they're on equal footing as far as accounting for the empirical facts. They both would explain our current experiences.

EMPIRICIST: And why do you think that the common-sense view is simpler?

RATIONALIST: Well, it has fewer basic unexplained events and unjustified assumptions. The Five-Minute Hypothesis involves a huge number of unexplained coincidences, whereas the common-sense view—that there really was a past—explains our observations and why they fit together. For example, the common-sense view explains very simply what would otherwise be a strange coincidence: that I remember buying these shoes a long time ago, and the fact that those shoes look really worn out. The explanation is that I really did buy them a long time ago, so they're quite old, and, of course, shoes wear out when they're worn a long time.

EMPIRICIST: But the Five-Minute Hypothesis is simpler because it has a far smaller number of things happening—only five minute's worth, in comparison to the huge history in the common-sense view. But never mind. I think the real question here is this: why accept Ockham's Razor? What makes you think that the simpler of two hypotheses is more likely to be true? I don't think that's an acceptable principle for justifying beliefs. After all, it can't have been shown to be true by our experience.

10 Conversation IV.

DEFINER: Why not?

EMPIRICIST: Remember that this principle is only to be used when there's an equal amount of empirical evidence for two hypotheses. So there's no other way to choose which one is true, and we can't have found out by past experience that this principle tends to choose true hypotheses.

RATIONALIST: I agree that this principle can't have been tested empirically. I think it may be an a priori principle of all rational thought. It's a rule of how to think, if you're going to think rationally. You don't discover its truth by observation. It's something you have to assume in order to do any thinking at all. It goes beyond empiricism, and shows how empiricism leaves us with embarrassing problems like the Five-Minute Hypothesis, and, the problem you talked about above, about the existence of the external world.

SCEPTIC: Hmm, well, the problems are embarrassing, all right, but I don't think that it's acceptable just to invent some principle out of the blue to get the embarrassment out of the way. It doesn't seem to me that the principle is something you have to suppose true before you can do any thought at all. I've been seriously wondering whether Ockham's Razor really is true. I've been thinking, haven't I?

RATIONALIST: Haha, maybe not!

14. Scepticism: The Problem of Induction

RATIONALIST: I admit that some beliefs are justified entirely by perception: beliefs about particular things that are (or were) right in front of you—like, for example, when you see a duck and hear it quacking, and you believe that there's a quacking duck there. But many rationalists think that these beliefs, even if they're true and justified, don't count as real *knowledge*. They're trivial—they're just about particular physical objects, which change and come and go. Real *knowledge* must be about more permanent and general things. This is what rationalists have argued as far back as Plato, in the fourth century BC. It's maybe what's behind Descartes' insistence that the highly abstract and general truths of arithmetic and geometry are real knowledge, as opposed to the very particular and mundane facts revealed to us by perception. Even contemporary science (which is certainly substantially influenced by empiricism) concentrates on what's really worth knowing: not trivial particular-duck facts like that, but rather generalizations, the way *kinds* of things work, laws of nature.

EMPIRICIST: I agree that there are more important things to be known than facts about one particular duck. But that doesn't mean that justified beliefs about particular things don't count as real knowledge.

SCEPTIC: But what RATIONALIST just said does, I think, suggest a big problem for empiricism. How can it account for the justification of general beliefs?

EMPIRICIST: What exactly do you mean by 'general beliefs'?

SCEPTIC: They're beliefs about whole groups of things. When you see a particular duck, and hear it quacking, that's (let's assume) justification of a particular belief, the belief that *this* duck quacks. But we also think that we can have justification of some general beliefs, like for instance that *all* ducks quack.

EMPIRICIST: Of course that one is justified by seeing a lot of ducks, and hearing all of them quacking. What's the problem with that?

SCEPTIC: The problem is that you can't check out *all* the ducks, not even with the aid of all the rest of the people who have encountered them. There are still unobserved ducks. Even if, somehow, a huge army of duck-watchers managed to observe every single duck in existence this year, that belief also covers future ducks, which are of course as yet unobserved. But right now we think we have justification for that belief about the future.

EMPIRICIST: The observation of a limited number of ducks provides justification for that general statement, asserting things about unseen ducks, including future ducks, provided that a large number of ducks is observed, and that the sample is sufficiently random and varied.

SCEPTIC: Sure, that's how science proceeds, on the basis of observations of a "fair sample." That's the sort of procedure called *inductive reasoning.* But notice that this sort of reasoning is based on the supposition that unobserved ducks will turn out to be like observed ones—that, roughly speaking, nature is uniform: unobserved things will be like observed ones, and the future will be like the past. Philosophers sometimes call that the *Principle of Induction.*

EMPIRICIST: Yes, I guess that something like that is the basis of inductive reasoning.

SCEPTIC: So my real question is: what justifies the Principle of Induction? David Hume, who we were talking about earlier, and who was both an empiricist and a sceptic, asked this question. His example was our belief that bread nourishes: it has nourished us so far, in the past, (rather than, for example, having poisoned us), but why do we think this gives us any reason to think that it will do so tomorrow?

EMPIRICIST: Don't we have good evidence from experience that the Principle of Induction works well? I mean, think of all the time scientists have used that principle in the past, and have turned out to be right in what they predicted. A long time ago, when bread was invented, people noticed that it nourished rather than poisoned, so using the Principle of Induction, they predicted that if they made and ate bread again, it would again nourish, and they were right. This Principle is the basis of an enormous amount of our knowledge. Based on past experience, I believed that my friend would happily talk to me when he saw me, rather than, say, shooting me; and that my car would start when I turned the key, rather than blowing up, and that when I put a Beatles CD into the stereo, a Brahms symphony wouldn't come out of the speakers, and on and on. And I was right in all these cases, and in almost all other cases in which I used the Principle carefully. Countless experiences have shown us that when we rely on the Principle to predict things, we're successful.

SCEPTIC: But not always. Every day a farmer shows up in the yard, the chicken gets fed, so the chicken, relying on the Principle, comes to expect this. But one day the farmer comes in and cuts off the chicken's head instead.

EMPIRICIST: Right, but the Principle works in the vast majority of cases, when used carefully, with a big enough and varied enough sample.

SCEPTIC: It has, you're right. Here's the main problem however. Does this provide evidence that the Principle of Induction can be counted on to work in the future?

EMPIRICIST: Uh-oh. I guess that using the past successes of the Principle to predict future success is using the Principle I've set out to prove.

SCEPTIC: Right, that's Hume's objection to this attempt to justify the Principle. That attempt reasons in a circle, using the principle of reasoning it's attempting to justify.

EMPIRICIST: Okay, well how about Hume's own solution to this problem? He pointed out while there's no justifying the Principle, there's no argument against it either; so it's not irrational to keep using it in our thinking. And we can't help using it—it's as natural as breathing. We couldn't stop using it if we tried.

RATIONALIST: That's not good enough. What's called for here is a proof that the Principle is necessary, not just that we're in the habit of thinking that way. Again empiricism is unable to deal with a sceptical problem, and rationalism is shown to be superior.

SCEPTIC: How would a rationalist answer the *Problem of Induction*?

RATIONALIST: Well, Kant answered Hume by claiming that the principle that nature was uniform—that unobserved instances usually resemble observed ones—was a necessary presupposition of our having any experience at all. It's not that we have to believe that it's true: most people never give it a thought. It's rather that our minds have been set up to reason as if it were true, in order for us to be able to have experience of the world that we can think about rationally. What this means is that whatever we experience has to be in accord with this principle, so the truth of this principle can be known independently of any particular experience. It's another a priori synthetic truth.

SCEPTIC: Why did he think that without assuming the uniformity of nature, we couldn't even experience things?

RATIONALIST: Well, just imagine that the universe appeared to us as a disorderly, random mess, without any regularities, because we never used induction to create generalizations. Things would appear to us to happen just any which way—everything would be a surprise. In that case, we couldn't conceptualize things; we couldn't think rationally about them. The world would appear to us only as a chaos, as a mess we could make no sense of.

SCEPTIC: But wouldn't that be a way of experiencing things? (It sounds like the way the world appears to me when I've partied a bit too much the night before.)

RATIONALIST: When Kant thinks of real *experience* of the world, he thinks of it as *rational* experience—as putting things into order—as seeing things as instances of general categories, and as seeing events as instances of regularities.

SCEPTIC: Right, so Kant thinks that if you're going to see things as orderly, you have to think in a way that presupposes uniformity of nature. But what if you don't want to see things as orderly?

RATIONALIST: You can't help it. It's the only way to do rational thinking. It's not up to you to decide whether you're going to think of things that way or not. According to Kant, we don't really have any choice about alternative ways to think.

EMPIRICIST: That's just what Hume said.

RATIONALIST: But Kant went on to point out that if any person—any being with a mind at all—was to do genuine thinking, or was to have genuine experience of the world, it would have to be in terms of these innate concepts, and this set of synthetic a priori knowledge. Even angels and aliens from the planet Zarkon—if they're rational—have to think this way!

SCEPTIC: So what Kant is saying is that our basic principles, and our synthetic a priori knowledge, are not really characteristics of the real world, but rather of the way we, as thinking beings, have to think about and experience it.

RATIONALIST: Well, they are the way the real world is—as we must think about and experience it.

SCEPTIC: That's what I said. But then in a sense the world of our experience is a world constructed by our minds, or at least transformed, put in order, by us. We can't ever really experience it as it is.

RATIONALIST: That's right. For example, we have to see the world as divided into separate objects, but maybe that's just a fact about us: maybe the external world doesn't have separate objects in it.

SCEPTIC: That sounds like a sceptical position to me.

RATIONALIST: No, for Kant it's just the opposite of scepticism.

SCEPTIC: But his claim is that we can never experience the world as it really is, independently of anyone's experience.

RATIONALIST: Right, but that's hardly a limitation. Of course, the only way you can experience anything is by experiencing it.

Suggested Readings

(See the Notes on "Suggested Readings" sections, p. 17-18.)

Plato's dialogue *Theaetetus* treats the definition of knowledge at length.
René Descartes (1596-1650) is of course a central Rationalist figure. Much of his *Meditations* is relevant. By far the best edition of this for students is on-line at <http://www.earlymoderntexts.com>.
The best place to look for British empiricism is in David Hume (1711-76), *Enquiry Concerning Human Understanding*. Start from Section II and read on. By far the best edition of this for students is on-line at <http://www.earlymoderntexts.com>.
A much more recent empiricism, but still very much in the spirit of Hume, is found in the influential *Language, Truth and Logic* by A.J. Ayer (1910-89).
The classical source for the defence of the existence of the synthetic a priori is Immanuel Kant (1724-1804). Unfortunately he's hard to read; but try *Prolegomena to Any Future Metaphysic*, in its very accessible version on-line at <http://www.earlymoderntexts.com>.
The brain-in-the-vat example is from *Reason, Truth and History* by Hilary Putnam.

CONVERSATION VII

Identity; Meaning

Participants: SCEPTIC • CARTESIAN • EMPIRICIST • RELATIONIST • ANTIREALIST • INTERNALIST • REFERENTIALIST • SPEECH-ACT THEORIST

1. Life After Death Again

SCEPTIC: There are a couple of ideas I found interesting that were brought up briefly earlier, and I'd like to go into those matters more deeply now. In the religion discussion,[1] as I remember it, part of the argument was about whether disembodied spirits could exist at all after the physical death of a person. But what I'd like to talk about was a further claim ATHEIST made: that even if a disembodied spirit was left, after the death of the body, then that couldn't be the same person as the one that died.

CARTESIAN: Why is that supposed to be?

SCEPTIC: Well, it had something to do with the fact that when a person dies—physically that is!—the person's memories, which are stored physically in the brain, must be destroyed.

CARTESIAN: But maybe memories wouldn't be destroyed when the brain ceases to work.

SCEPTIC: Okay, maybe, but what I'm wondering about is, supposing the memories did get destroyed. Would that mean that whatever's left couldn't be the same person?

2. Continuing Mental Substance

CARTESIAN: Well, as you know from the discussion I had with others on philosophy of mind,[2] I believe that the thing that is really you is your mind, not your body. So if that thing—your mind—survives death, then *you* survive death.

---

1 Conversation I.
2 Conversation IV.

SCEPTIC: But the mind is such an intangible thing. What would it be like to have a disembodied mind surviving? I can't even begin to understand it. But really what I'm asking now is more about this: even if something mental, disembodied, is left over after physical death, why count that left-over as the person who died—as *the same person*? The situation is much clearer when it comes to physical things. At least it's something tangible—something you can see and touch—that remains from one time to another, despite changes, when we say that the same *physical* thing still exists.

CARTESIAN: Actually, I don't think you're right—I think it's something like the same situation for both physical and mental things.

SCEPTIC: Well, that'll take some explaining.

CARTESIAN: Right. Let's start with looking at a case Descartes talked about, involving a physical thing that keeps on existing despite some fairly drastic changes. Descartes' example was a little ball of beeswax. Imagine you're examining that piece of wax. It's shaped like a sphere. It's white, and solid. It makes a little click when you flick your fingernail against it. It feels sort of cool. It smells like honey.

SCEPTIC: I don't know what beeswax is like, but I'll take your word for all of that.

CARTESIAN: Okay, now imagine, says Descartes, that you move that piece of wax next to the fire. Pretty soon, it melts and everything about it is changed. It's no longer a sphere: it's now a little round flat puddle. It's a colourless liquid. It makes no sound when you flick it with your fingernail. It feels hot, and it doesn't have any smell at all.

SCEPTIC: Okay.

CARTESIAN: But the thing that's right in front of you now—that little puddle—is the same thing as you were looking at earlier, despite all these changes, right?

SCEPTIC: Right, it's still that ball of wax. Well, it's not a ball any more, but it's still that thing you had a few minutes ago, just changed.

CARTESIAN: As opposed to when you subject something to so thorough a change that it's destroyed, and something else replaces it.

SCEPTIC: I agree.

CARTESIAN: So now Descartes asks: what is it that makes this puddle the same *continuing object* as that earlier ball?

SCEPTIC: What do you mean, 'continuing object'?

CARTESIAN: I mean, something that lasts for a time—something that continues to exist for a while. So that thing exists continuously over a time span, the same thing over all those times during that time span.

SCEPTIC: Okay.

CARTESIAN: Descartes points out that over the time span in our example, all the physical characteristics of the thing—its size, shape, smell, temperature, and so on—everything you can observe through your senses—has changed. But it's still the same object. So Descartes reasons that it must not be the continuance of any physical characteristics that accounts for what makes something the same object over time, because they all change in this case. It must be something else, something we know about but don't observe through our senses.

SCEPTIC: Hmm, what's that supposed to be?

CARTESIAN: That's what Descartes calls *physical substance*—the stuff that is itself invisible, but which all those physical observable characteristics are attached to.

SCEPTIC: I'm not sure I get it.

CARTESIAN: Well, think of it this way: none of those characteristics separately, or taken together, is the piece of wax. The piece of wax isn't constituted by spherical + hard + cool + etc. It's what these characteristics are characteristics *of*—it's what *has* these characteristics—what *is* spherical, etc.—a bit of physical substance. But we can only see (or feel or smell, etc.) the characteristics. The thing itself—the bit of physical substance—is something we just understand with our minds.

SCEPTIC: I'm not sure I understand it! But anyway, Descartes of course doesn't think of a person as a physical thing.

CARTESIAN: Right. People are mental things, not physical, but the situation here is analogous. You aren't any of your mental characteristics—thinking about dinner, remembering last Christmas, wishing it would stop raining, feeling a pain in your knee, and so on—but rather what *has* these characteristics: a bit of *mental substance*. You're not the thoughts—you're the thinker. Physical substance is the stuff that has physical characteristics; mental substance is the stuff that has mental characteristics. So just as what makes this melted puddle the same physical thing as the earlier ball of wax is the presence of the same physical substance, what makes a person now the same one who was around earlier is the continuing presence of the same mental substance. And just as the characteristics of a piece of physical substance can change over time—even change totally, as in the case of the wax—so can mental characteristics change over time, even totally. Maybe there's a total change of mental characteristics at death. Maybe, for example, all the memories are wiped out. But as long as the same mental substance is there, it's the same person.

SCEPTIC: I guess I see how your theory is supposed to make life after death possible, but that doesn't particularly make the theory more believable, because I don't think the idea of surviving death is plausible in the first place.

CARTESIAN: Well, it's not just applicable to that case. It's designed as an explanation of why we identify the same person at any two times—times during that person's ordinary life included. So it's supposed to explain in addition what it is for you to be the same person as the one who ten seconds ago was sitting in the chair you're sitting in now. And the same person as the little baby you were a long time ago. It's because there was a mental substance in that little baby that was still there in the person in the chair, and in you right now, despite changes in mental characteristics— considerable changes from the little baby till now—that took place.

SCEPTIC: Okay, so what you've got here is a general theory of what makes something the same thing as an earlier thing. The general idea is that there's this stuff called substance that stays there despite changes in characteristics over time.

CARTESIAN: Right. It's a *substance theory of identity.*

SCEPTIC: That word 'identity' has come up a few times. COMMUNITARIAN talked about our identity in the sense of what sorts of things we count as basic and important to us.[3] IDENTITY THEORIST meant by the identity of a mental and brain event, that the two were actually the same one thing.[4] What's meant by 'identity' here?

CARTESIAN: A theory of the "identity" through time of something tells us what it is that makes us count something as the same continuing object. I'll introduce some technical vocabulary that will make talking about this easier. Some contemporary philosophers use the word *stage* to refer to an object as it exists just at any one particular instant. Here's a way of thinking about that. Imagine a movie taken of something (or somebody). The movie is made of a whole lot of still photographs, taken at very small intervals. Each photograph records the thing being filmed at a particular instant. Each of these pictures shows a separate instantaneous item— what's called a 'stage' of the object being filmed. Put them all together into a movie, and you have a moving picture of the continuing object,

---

3 Conversation II.
4 Conversation IV.

which can be thought of as a collection of all those stages. (And more. Of course, the individual frames of a movie record stages that are very close to each other in time—one-sixteenth of a second apart, I think—but there are unrecorded stages of the object closer together than this, I guess, an infinite number.) So a theory of *identity through time* is supposed to answer the question: what ties a large (or infinite) number of individual stages together into a continuing thing (or person)? Why trace a continuing object, as we watch the film progress, rather than thinking that at some point the object ceases to exist, maybe replaced by another one? What makes this stage a part of the same continuing object as that stage?

3. Criticisms of the Substance Theories

EMPIRICIST: I doubt that the idea of a continuing substance really does the job of explaining identity through time, whether for mental or for physical things.

CARTESIAN: Well, what's the problem?

EMPIRICIST: Now, your idea is that for two stages to be part of the same continuing object, they have to contain the same substance, despite possible changes in characteristics.

CARTESIAN: Right.

EMPIRICIST: And not just the same *type* of substance. I mean, suppose that you've got one person-stage photographed in one frame of the movie, and the very next frame substitutes a different person. Then according to your theory, the person in the first frame has one piece of mental substance inside, and the person in the next frame has a different piece of mental substance inside. Both of the same type—both *mental* substances—but different pieces of it.

CARTESIAN: Right, though it's a little weird to call it a different "piece" of mental substance. I know what you mean, and I can't think of a better way to refer to it.

EMPIRICIST: Okay, now we can get to my question. Imagine that one stage of a physical object is in front of you at one instant, but then, at the next instant, what's in front of you is a different thing.

CARTESIAN: Right, because at the next instant, what's there contains a different piece of physical substance.

EMPIRICIST: But suppose that those two stages for some reason happen to display exactly the same characteristics. So for example, stage #1 is a green sphere, 4 cm. in diameter, weighing 800 grams, etc., and so is stage #2: they're just alike in every characteristic. You can't tell them apart.

CARTESIAN: Okay, they're physically indistinguishable. That doesn't mean that they're the same physical object, though we'd probably think they were. What it takes for these two stages to be part of the same continuing physical object is that they both contain the same chunk of physical substance.

EMPIRICIST: But you can't see this. All you can see is the characteristics. And the fact that they have identical characteristics doesn't imply at all that there's the same invisible substance there, right?

CARTESIAN: Right. What that shows is that identity through time isn't something that's perceived by the senses. It's understood by the mind. Remember, Descartes was a rationalist, not an empiricist!

EMPIRICIST: Clearly. But then, if all you can find out about that sphere is what you perceive, how could you tell if it's the same thing or not?

CARTESIAN: Well, I guess you couldn't.

EMPIRICIST: Hmph. Anyway, the same sort of situation applies to persons, right?

CARTESIAN: Right. Remember first that continuity of mental substance and continuity of physical substance are two different things. Personal survival of death means that there's a continuing mental substance still existing despite destruction of the physical thing. You could even have the same physical object inhabited at one second by one mental substance—one person—and then by a different one at the next second.

SCEPTIC: Cool! So you're imagining one person replacing another, suddenly, inside the same body! Like reincarnation or something! Of course that never happens.

CARTESIAN: I agree, but that doesn't matter. All that matters is that it's conceivable, according to my theory of identity.

EMPIRICIST: Okay, so let's imagine two person-stages that are mentally indistinguishable too—they have exactly the same characteristics. Stage #1 and stage #2 have the same personality, the same values, the same memories; both have a pain in their left foot, both hope they get a pony for Christmas, etc. etc. But according to you, if #1 has a different mental substance from #2, then they're different people.

CARTESIAN: Right.

EMPIRICIST: But they're exactly the same, as far as anyone can tell.

CARTESIAN: As far as anybody looking at them *from the outside* can tell. But you can tell *from the inside* who you are. This was already gone into at great length back in the discussion of philosophy of mind.[5]

EMPIRICIST: What they were talking about then isn't the issue here. Even if I agree that mental characteristics are knowable only from the inside, as you dualists believe, we're not talking about mental *characteristics*. In the case we're imagining, all the mental characteristics of #1 and #2 are the same. So #1 detects a pain in the left foot, and then #2 does—in the same left foot! #1 is grumpy and wants a pony for Christmas, and then #2 is grumpy, and wants the same thing. All that's different is that they have different pieces of mental substance.

CARTESIAN: Well, maybe the facts about what mental substance is there are knowable from the inside too. Imagine that you're #2; wouldn't you know whether you were there five minutes earlier?

EMPIRICIST: I don't think so. #2 could remember the experiences of #1, so #2 would believe—falsely according to you—that she was there five minutes earlier. But the real problem here is again that substance of either kind, mental or physical, is not the sort of thing you can sense, either using your outside senses, or using your introspection. So there doesn't seem to be any way, from the inside or from the outside, to tell whether two mental stages have the same or different mental substances in them. That great empiricist philosopher David Hume got it exactly right. He pointed out that when you introspect, you find various mental events succeeding each other—pain and pleasure, sensations and perceptions, various emotions, and so on—but you don't find anything that's constant, there all the time. So there isn't any introspection of anything continuing. But for an idea to be genuine, not empty, it has to be connected with observation—sense perception or introspection. So the idea of a continuing self is empty.

CARTESIAN: But what you introspect is mental characteristics, not the mind—the mental substance—itself.

EMPIRICIST: Hume was aware that that's what Cartesians think, and he replied that that's exactly what isn't perceived; so the idea is empty.

CARTESIAN: This gets us back to issues in the theory of knowledge that we discussed just recently.[6] Look, Hume was of course an empiricist. The principle he's basing his reasoning on is that if there's no *impression*—that is, no sense experience, from the outside physical senses or from

---

5 Conversation IV.
6 Conversation VI.

introspection—associated with some idea, then there really isn't any idea there at all—we're just talking nonsense when we use that word. But we rationalists don't require that every genuine idea be connected with sense impressions. There are some ideas that we just know about, without sense perception. And the self is one of them. It's not an empirical concept.

EMPIRICIST: Well, it seems to me that your theory isn't any good if it explains what it is to be two stages of the same continuing object—mental or physical—in a way such that we can't ever tell when this is true or not.

CARTESIAN: I don't think that my theory sets things up in a way such that you can't ever tell. Anyway, even if it did, that may not be such a defect. What we're talking about, after all, is what is involved in being two stages of the same continuing object—what that really amounts to. That's not the same question as how you might—or might not—find out this fact.

4. The Mysterious Boat

SCEPTIC: Well, let's talk about the idea of the continuing identity of a physical thing for a bit, which seems to be an easier concept to explain than the idea of the continuing identity of a person. If I've got it right, CARTESIAN, your theory says that what it takes for two physical stages to be part of the same continuing physical object is that they both contain the same parcel of physical substance, right?

CARTESIAN: Right.

SCEPTIC: Well, I don't think that's correct. I'll give you a couple of examples that I think show that you're wrong. Here's the first one. A parcel of physical substance can change its shape, but still stay the same physical substance, right?

CARTESIAN: Sure. The physical substance an object is made out of stays there, stays the same, despite changes in its characteristics. The ball of wax changes shape, but it's still the identical physical substance.

SCEPTIC: Okay, now imagine your friend Sally is going away for a year, and she offers to lend Fred her wooden boat, providing Fred promises to give it back to her when she returns. As soon as she goes away, Fred takes her boat out, but he's not much good at sailing, and he runs it aground on the rocks, and pretty soon the surf has smashed it to pieces. He gathers all those pieces together, puts them in his shed. When Sally comes back and asks for her boat, he shows her that pile of splintered wood in his shed.

She's not pleased. He tells her that he's giving her back what she lent to him, but she claims he's broken his promise. That's not her boat, she says: that boat doesn't exist any more—it's been destroyed.

CARTESIAN: I guess she's right.

SCEPTIC: But what Fred's giving her is the same physical stuff that she lent to him, isn't it? It has just changed shape—pretty drastically! So according to your theory, it's the same thing she lent him, right?

CARTESIAN: Well, I guess it really is the same thing, in the way I'm looking at it. It's not a boat any more, but it's the same thing.

SCEPTIC: That's a pretty funny sense of 'the same thing.' It wouldn't satisfy Sally! Anyway, let me try a different story on you. In the story I just told, the boat is destroyed, but the same physical substance remains there. In the two versions of the next story, the boat is still there, but the physical substance changes. First, imagine that Sally's boat is undamaged, but bits of the paint peel off. That's a loss of physical substance, but it's the same boat. Second, imagine that Sally's boat is undamaged, but Fred puts a fresh coat of paint on it. Now physical substance has been added, but it's still the same boat.

CARTESIAN: I guess I'd have to say that, strictly speaking, it's not exactly the same object when some substance is removed or added. If the addition or subtraction is small, as it is in these two cases, we can treat it as if it's the same boat, for all practical purposes. Adding or subtracting substance makes it a different boat, but one so similar to the one that used to be there that we can think of it as the same one.

SCEPTIC: The idea that strictly speaking any small change in physical substance makes for a different physical object sounds crazy to me. Even if you're willing to think that way about the boat, which is very odd, that approach would trash all the normal ways we count continuing objects. I mean, the scientists tell us that no physical object is as stable as it appears to us at large scale. Molecules of any object are constantly leaving, flying off into the air, or being worn off. Not a single one of the ordinary things we encounter has a perfectly stable physical substance for even a second. Strictly speaking, then, according to your theory, nothing lasts more than a second! (And you know what they say in that ad, "A diamond is forever"? Not!)

CARTESIAN: Look, if you don't like my "strictly-speaking" account of what makes for the same physical thing through time, do you have a better one? You seem pretty confident about saying when it's the same boat and when it's a different one, and when the boat has been destroyed altogether. What tests for these are you using?

SCEPTIC: That's a very good question, and I'm really not sure how to answer it. I don't have any theory about what makes for sameness and difference, and I'm not even sure how to sort out some cases. I'll give you an example of a case that I find really puzzling. It's a version of an old philosophical fable known as the "Ship of Theseus," but I'm changing it a little to make it more interesting. Here's the story. Suppose as before Fred has borrowed Sally's wooden boat, but she made him promise not just that he'd give it back to her when she gets back, but also that he'd keep it repaired. Imagine he's more careful with sailing it; but soon after she's gone, he discovers that a plank in the hull is rotting away, so he replaces it with a new plank, storing the old one in his shed. Then shortly after that, he has to replace the roof on the little cabin, then he has to repair the deck, and on and on, storing the old pieces of the boat in his shed every time. By the time she returns, every single piece of the old boat has been replaced: there's not an atom of the original boat left. He proudly returns the boat to her, pointing out how well repaired he's kept it. But Sally looks it over, and having discovered that there's nothing of the old boat on the one he's returning, accuses him of breaking his promise to return her boat. "This isn't my boat," she insists. "Everything on this boat is different." So when he has calmed down, he hauls out of the shed all that stuff he took off the boat, and pieces it together into a very rotten and useless boat. "Here's your rotten boat," he says. "Every bit of this is exactly what you left with me." "But," complains Sally, "you promised to keep it repaired!"

CARTESIAN: Cute story. What's your question?

SCEPTIC: Well, here's one problem. Consider what happens just after Fred removes one rotten plank from the boat. Let's call a stage of the original boat #1, and the stage after a plank has been removed #2. Are #1 and #2 stages in the same continuing object?

CARTESIAN: On my "strictly-speaking" theory the answer is no. But this is not very different from the case in which some paint peels off—it's just a small subtraction—so on the basis of a more common-sense view, it's close enough to the original to count as the same boat.

SCEPTIC: Okay, that seems more reasonable. But then what would you say about stage #3, when a new plank has been added in that spot?

CARTESIAN: Again, on the "strictly-speaking" view, this small addition makes for the same boat, but it's close enough for common sense to count it as the same boat.

SCEPTIC: Well, you can see where this is going. So none of these particular small changes makes for a different boat: #1 is in the same continuing object as #2, #2 is in the same continuing object as #3, #3 is in the same continuing object as #4, and so on, till the end of the year, when #999 is in the same continuing object as #1000, which is a boat containing not one atom in common with #1. But look doesn't it follow from all this that #1 is in the same continuing object as #1000?

CARTESIAN: If we're going to accept that none of these individual changes makes for a different boat, I guess that it's the same one at the end of all of them.

SCEPTIC: So you think that Sally is wrong when she complains that this isn't the same boat as she lent to Fred when she left?

CARTESIAN: I guess so.

SCEPTIC: But what about the rotten boat he rebuilt out of all those pieces in his shed?

CARTESIAN: Oops, I forgot about that one. Maybe I was wrong that #1000 is the same boat. Maybe the same one is the one rebuilt out of pieces from the shed. That one, at least, has the same physical substance as the boat-stage that Fred borrowed.

SCEPTIC: But how can that be the original boat? Remember, just before Fred rebuilt it, there was just a pile of lumber and other stuff in his shed.

CARTESIAN: Why is that a problem?

SCEPTIC: If you just have a pile of lumber and other stuff, you don't have a boat. If you make a boat out of it, that's a boat that didn't exist earlier: a new boat (made however, from used materials). It can't literally be the same boat as one that existed earlier.

CARTESIAN: I see the problem. Now I'm thoroughly confused. Which boat really is Sally's?

SCEPTIC: Well, I'm just as confused as you are. I really don't know what to say in this case.

CARTESIAN: Hmph, another philosophical triumph! We start with confident certainty and wind up totally confused!

SCEPTIC: I'd count that as progress!

5. Relationism

CARTESIAN: I'm not convinced that the substance theory of identity is wrong, either for physical objects or for human beings. But if it's wrong, then what's the alternative?

RELATIONIST: If I can join the discussion now, I'd like to hear what you have to say about an alternative theory, which was proposed by Locke. He argued that different sorts of things had different criteria for identity through time. Physical objects have one basis for continuing identity—the same physical substance. So he agrees with CARTESIAN's "strictly-speaking" substance theory. But ...

SCEPTIC: Wait a minute. Locke is one of the classical British empiricists. How could an empiricist hold that theory?

EMPIRICIST: You're right that you wouldn't expect an empiricist to hold that theory. We've already talked about why: physical substance is itself not something perceived by our senses, so judgements about the same or different physical substance are not based on sense perception. Other empiricists have thought that Locke was maybe a little off base here.

RELATIONIST: Anyway, Locke went on to argue that living things—plants and animals—have a different basis for continuing identity over time. He pointed out the obvious fact that the physical matter of any individual plant or animal changes a good deal over time: a tree, for example, grows a lot bigger over the years, and each year grows leaves and then sheds them. A good deal of physical substance is gained and lost, in what is clearly the lifespan of the same tree. So he held that what makes tree-stages belong to the same tree is not that they all contain the same physical substance, but rather that all these stages, despite difference in structure and constitutive material, are related to each other in a specific way: they're all organized into the same *life*.

SCEPTIC: I think he's clearly right that the continuing identity of a tree can't depend on there being the same substance there all the time. I mean, there's a good deal of substance addition and subtraction in any living thing, just like in the boat example. I'd add, however, that the same sort of thing applies to the continuing identity of non-living things, but never mind that now. What I want to know now is what Locke has in mind here for living things. I mean, what makes two stages count as part of the same life?

RELATIONIST: There's some controversy about exactly what Locke might have meant. It's been suggested that what he had in mind is that they count as part of the same life when the material parts of adjacent stages show continuous organization in a way that creates and preserves the most important functions of the plant or animal.

SCEPTIC: I'm not sure I get that.

RELATIONIST: Well, it is a problem figuring out what exactly he had in mind, and we ought to look carefully at exactly what he says.

SCEPTIC: Some other time. But let's get on to what he says about people; is this account, for living things, supposed to apply for people too?

RELATIONIST: He says that it applies to people considered as physical living organisms, as life forms. But he argued that it's different when you think of us *as persons*—as mental conscious beings, not just as material animals.

SCEPTIC: Aha, there's that old dualism showing up again. Well, what did he have to say about people as persons?

RELATIONIST: This is where things get the most interesting. He thought that the only thing that's relevant to the fact that two stages belong to the same person is that the later one appropriates the earlier one's experiences as his or her own—takes responsibility for them. That means, basically, that earlier person stages that belong to you are those whose experiences you remember having.

SCEPTIC: That's an interesting way of looking at things. What do you call that theory?

RELATIONIST: I call it the *relationist theory* because it holds that person-stages are part of the same continuing person when they're *related* to each other in a particular kind of way—in this case, by memory—not in something they share—for example, underlying substance or organization for ends.

SCEPTIC: So Locke would hold that if you can't remember the experiences of an earlier stage, then that earlier stage isn't *you*?

RELATIONIST: That's right.

SCEPTIC: That's bizarre.

RELATIONIST: Why do you say that?

SCEPTIC: Because it's clear that there are experiences you had earlier that you don't remember now, isn't it? But that would be impossible, if Locke is correct. I can't remember a single experience that I had when I was five years old, but that five-year-old was me, wasn't it?

RELATIONIST: Maybe, maybe not. Isn't there a certain plausibility in the idea that you're a different person altogether from that five-year-old?

SCEPTIC: You might say that, in a sort of metaphorical sense, because we're so different in so many ways. But that's just a sort of figure of speech, emphasizing the differences between me now and that five-year-old. It's not literally true. Literally speaking, I am that person. That person-stage and I-now are parts of the same continuing person.

RELATIONIST: Well, some Lockian relationalists might want to stick by their guns here and insist that it is literally true. But there's a way of making a slight amendment to the Lockian theory as we've been considering it, to make it agree with you—that you were that five-year-old you don't remember being. I'll draw a diagram showing you what I mean. On a time-line, with time advancing left to right, suppose that a stage designated A (for example, you-now) does not remember anything about the experiences of a much earlier stage, designated B (for example, that five-year-old). The dotted curved arrow indicates that there isn't any memory connection here.

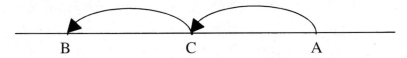

B   A

But suppose that stage A remembers an intermediate stage, C (say, you at 7), and stage C remembered B. A memory link is indicated by the solid arrow:

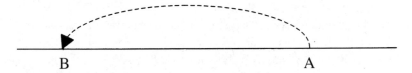

B   C   A

Then we can say that because A and C belong to the same person, and C and B belong to the same person, then A and B belong to the same person, despite the fact that A remembers nothing of B.

And, suppose that D doesn't remember E:

E   D   A

But A remembers both D and E:

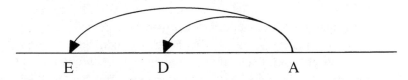

E   D   A

Then, because A and D were stages in the same person, and A and E were stages in the same person, it would follow that D and E were stages in the same person.

Putting all this together:

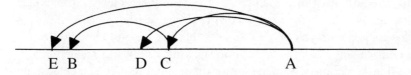

E B   D C   A

Every stage listed—A, B, C, D, and E—is connected somehow to every other stage; so we could conclude that despite the fact A doesn't remember B, and that D doesn't remember E, the other memory links are sufficient to establish that A, B, C, D, and E all belong to the same continuing person. That ties stage A in with all those other ones, if only indirectly, which produces what everyone's common sense would count as the continuing person. So that five-year-old whose experiences you don't remember can nevertheless be you, as well as lots of other stages you don't remember.

SCEPTIC: Well, that revision at least removes one difficulty, but it still leaves several other problems, in my opinion. First, let me make sure I have this proposal right. It means that all the stages connected forward or backward by memory links count as belonging to the same continuing person, right?

RELATIONIST: Right.

SCEPTIC: And only those stages?

RELATIONIST: Right.

SCEPTIC: So if there's a stage that's not connected to this network, it's not part of the person?

RELATIONIST: Right.

SCEPTIC: So suppose that there was a five-minute stretch in my life during which I didn't have any memories of anything in the past—I was concentrating on something else at the time—and I happened never to remember anything that happened during that time in the future. That means that I don't exist then, right?

RELATIONIST: That depends on what we count as *remembering*. The fact that you weren't actually thinking about last Christmas a minute ago doesn't mean you didn't remember some of what happened then. You remember all sorts of things you aren't actually thinking about, but that you could recall if you tried. So there are plenty of five-minute stretches in which we don't think about anything that happened in the past, though we still remembered past things at the time, in the sense that we were capable of calling them to mind.

SCEPTIC: Hmm, that makes things more complicated. Well, suppose that Sally has genuine amnesia at some time, call it time T, and never again remembers anything that happened before T—can't call anything to mind that went on earlier, no matter how much she tries. So she doesn't remember anything before T, even in the way you understand remembering. Then you'd have to say that there are two different continuing persons, one before T, and one after, right? Even though they're both named 'Sally'?

RELATIONIST: Right. Two different people can have the same name.

SCEPTIC: And one person stopped existing at T? And the other began existing at T? So at T there was the death of one Sally (but no dead body), and, even more peculiarly, the birth of a full-grown different adult also named Sally, who began inhabiting the same body?

RELATIONIST: I guess I'd have to agree with that, although the words 'death' and 'birth' I think suggest the ending and beginning of a *life*—of a living thing. So, in Locke's way of looking at things, different criteria apply to this. In the case you imagine, the same life continues before and after T; so there's no death or birth in the ordinary sense.

SCEPTIC: So you'd recognize the possibility that the *person* stopped existing, though there was no death?

RELATIONIST: Right.

SCEPTIC: Why would Locke propose a theory that had such a bizarre consequence?

RELATIONIST: Locke thought that the idea of continuing identity of persons was basically what he called a *forensic* notion. That means *having to do with legal matters*. What we're interested in, he thought, when we establish that some earlier stage was part of the continuing person Sally, is that Sally is responsible for the bad (or good) things that that earlier stage did. And he thought that this depended on whether the current Sally-stage remembered having done the action in question. When there's total permanent amnesia, and the later Sally can't remember what the earlier Sally did, then the later Sally isn't responsible for what the earlier Sally did, and they're literally two different persons.

SCEPTIC: Really? Does he really want to say that you're responsible only for what you remember doing?

RELATIONIST: He does, but that's not really all that weird. That idea is more or less reflected in current legal practice. Somebody who suffers amnesia after having done something illegal, who can't remember having done it, isn't punished for the crime.

SCEPTIC: That legal rule is interesting and puzzling, but I don't imagine that they have that rule because they think that amnesia means you literally didn't do it. Anyway, Locke's view seems clearly false to me. This view allows for two persons succeeding each other in a body, or a body with no person in it at all.

RELATIONIST: I don't think that the consequences of the Lockian view—associating the person with a consciousness and whatever's linked by memory to that consciousness—are all that odd. Think of those cases in which a human suffers really disastrous brain damage, and is permanently deprived of any future mental life whatever. They can keep that body living, but it's not at all bizarre to say that there's no person left there any more. It's the termination of a person, but not the termination of a life. There are other cases too in which we reasonably (but controversially, I admit) count that there's a life but no person: a really brand-new foetus, with just a few dozen undifferentiated cells—no brain or nervous system—certainly no mentality at all—is counted by lots of people as a life, but not as a person, yet. Killing that foetus is killing, for sure, but it's not killing a person. That's one line of reasoning behind the pro-choice side of the abortion debate. You may not agree with it, but you have to admit it's not completely nonsense.

SCEPTIC: Let's not get into the endless abortion debate right now. Here's another case that might be a problem for you. I've heard about people with dual alternating personalities. When either personality is active, nothing can be remembered about the experiences of the other. So according to you, there really are two persons here, alternating in the same body.

RELATIONIST: Right, and I don't think that's such a jarring idea either. That's a reasonable way to think about this really odd sort of case.

SCEPTIC: But here's a perfectly ordinary case. Every night, during periods of dreamless sleep, every one of us has periods in which there are no memory connections whatever with waking life, forward or backward. So those are periods, according to you, when we're different people?

RELATIONIST: I think it would be more accurate to say that during those periods the person just stops existing altogether. Remember we're thinking of a person as being a thinking thing. No mental life, no person. That's the way, as I mentioned before, we think of what happens when a person suffers such drastic brain damage that there's no experience of any sort left—the mind is totally gone. We call that a *vegetative state*—a state, so to speak, like that of a vegetable. There's still a living thing there—the kind of continuing existence Locke associated with plants and animals—but not a person. Dreamless sleep is a temporary vegetative state, so the person temporarily has ceased existing.

SCEPTIC: I'd be tempted to agree that the person no longer exists when there's no mental life, and no possibility of regaining it. But it's odd to think of this happening temporarily every night. For one thing, it means that persons are intermittent objects.

RELATIONIST: What do you mean by that?

SCEPTIC: I mean that they exist for a while, then stop existing, then resume. That's really strange. With other sorts of things, once they've stopped existing, they can't start up again. When something starts up again, it's a new thing, not the old thing resuming existence. So, in the first boat example, when all the old boat pieces are put together to make a boat, what you've got, it seems, isn't a resumption of the boat that's ceased to exist. It's a different boat—a new one, made of old pieces. That's because boats can't be intermittent objects.

RELATIONIST: Maybe you're right about the boat, but I think that some sorts of things can have intermittent existence. For example, if we took a five-minute break, then resumed our conversation, we'd say that the same conversation went on for a while, then went out of existence for five minutes, then started up again. I went to a university that ceased existence several years after it was founded, then started up again a few years later when some rich guy provided the money to start it running again.

SCEPTIC: Okay, but can a person be intermittent?

6. Some Strange Cases

SCEPTIC: Well, anyway, I'd like to see what you have to say about some imaginary cases. Do you remember the brainometer, the machine they talked about in the discussion about mind and body?[7] That's an imaginary machine that they attach to your head, and it reads off the state of your brain. Suppose it can write things to your brain too. Now imagine that the brains of workers for an electric company occasionally get zapped by live wires, resulting in brain-scrambling and amnesia; so what the company does is to attach every worker to a brainometer first thing every morning. The brainometer reads the memory data off that worker's brain, and stores

---

7 Conversation IV.

this data. So if a worker gets amnesia, the brainometer can restore the memory patterns.

RELATIONIST: Great idea. That means that the worker will survive the accident.

SCEPTIC: So you'd say that if Alice, one of the electrical workers, gets zapped by a wire, and suffers permanent amnesia, she'd cease existing; but she'll continue if they take her to the brainometer and re-program all her memories into her brain?

RELATIONIST: Right, though she'd be intermittent.

SCEPTIC: Okay, now imagine that Alice gets painfully zapped by a live wire. You feel sorry for her, right? Tragically, there's damage to her legs that will leave her paralyzed. But, an additional result of the accident that makes things worse is that she has amnesia as a result. But then, worse still, the electric company's brainometer memory storage procedures get fouled up, and they put back the wrong memories in her body—those of another worker, Betty, killed during the same accident. This is still a worse fate for Alice: she ought to have her own memories, not someone else's. The memories she gets are fakes.

RELATIONIST: Right, her receiving fake memories is just an additional horrible result. Poor Alice has really gotten zapped.

SCEPTIC: I agree, but the fact that you react this way shows, I think, that there's something wrong with your theory of identity. According to your theory, Alice isn't getting fake memories, and her legs aren't paralyzed. The moment Alice suffers amnesia, according to the relationist view, she stops existing. When Betty's memories are put into the body, then it's Betty, not Alice, in that body. And memories in that body aren't fakes— they're genuine. They are of experiences that really did happen to Betty. And Alice doesn't have to suffer that paralysis: it's Betty's problem. But the fact that you reacted initially as you did maybe shows that you really think that it's Alice there all along.

RELATIONIST: Hmm, well maybe I reacted too quickly. I guess I'd have to say that the right way to think about this story is that Betty replaces Alice in that body.

SCEPTIC: But that's implausible. You were tempted to say that poor old Alice was suffering multiple indignities, before you realized that it contradicted your theory. Anyway, let me try you out on a different story. Here it is, Story 2. Betty and Alice are both in an accident, but neither is killed— both suffer amnesia. Both bodies are taken to the memory-writing lab, but there's a foul-up, and Alice's memories are written into *both* brains. They wake up. Now we have two bodies: Alice's former body, call it the A-body, and Betty's former body, call it the B-body. Both the A-body and the B-body have memories of Alice's past. Where's Alice?

RELATIONIST: Well, I agreed earlier than if the A-body gets Alice's memories restored to it, that Alice is there. The fact that they put those memories into Betty's body as well doesn't alter that fact. So I guess I have to say that she's in the A-body.

SCEPTIC: But they both have Alice's memories. Why do you count the one in the A-body as Alice, and not the one in the B-body?

RELATIONIST: Well, Alice can't be in two places at once, can she?

SCEPTIC: Why not?

RELATIONIST: Because that would mean that maybe Alice could be both sitting down and standing up at once, both hungry and not hungry, both asleep and wide awake! Maybe we'd have to admit that, but I'm tempted at the moment to say that they're not both Alice—that the A-body alone contains Alice.

SCEPTIC: But why choose the A-body as the location for Alice? Both bodies have equal claim to contain continuing-Alice, since both have Alice-memories. Maybe you preferred the A-body because that's the one Alice used to have? Does body-continuity count as well for personal identity?

RELATIONIST: Hmm. Maybe memories are not the only thing that counts, and that bodily continuity counts too, enough to break a tie.

SCEPTIC: But what if there's no tie-breaker? What if both the A-body and the B-body get the memories belonging to Carl, who died in the same accident. Which one is Carl? It's a tie for both bodies, with no tie-breaker.

RELATIONIST: I don't know. I'm really confused now. Maybe both. Maybe neither.

SCEPTIC: Well, to conclude this strange series of examples, Let's look at one final case, Story 3. Suppose, as before, Alice and Betty are in the accident. Alice's memories are successfully implanted in the B-Body while the A-body is left memory-less. So, Alice is in the B-Body, right?

RELATIONIST: Right.

SCEPTIC: But then an hour later, they put Alice's memories into the A-body as well. Where's Alice then?

RELATIONIST: I guess at that point, when there are two bodies with Alice's memories in them, the tie is broken by the fact that the A-body is Alice's former body. So I'll say at that point, only the A-body contains Alice.

SCEPTIC: So here's what's extra weird about that case. The B-body is Alice for an hour, but then, because of what they're doing to another body altogether—without any real change in the B-body or the memories in there—the B-body stops being Alice! Alice suddenly jumps over to the A-body!

RELATIONIST: I guess that's how it's got to be, if what counts as the continuing Alice is the best candidate. But come to think of it, maybe that kind of thing isn't so strange. There are ordinary non-science fiction changes in things that happen because of what's really going on somewhere else. For example, suppose that Alice is the tallest kid in her school for a while, but then one day, Betty, who's taller than Alice, arrives in the principal's office while Alice is outside in the playground, and signs up to be in that school. Because of events happening in the principal's office, Alice, who's somewhere else, suddenly stops being the tallest kid in the school, even though nothing has happened to her height.

7. The Real Route 22

ANTIREALIST: I've been listening to you, and I think that everyone has been making a mistake about what sort of fact identity is. Here's an example that illustrates how I think about identity. Imagine that they're building a new highway that going to go east-west, right past a city. But they don't want to route traffic through the city, so they build bypasses both north and south of the city. Here's a map of the new roads, with the city shown by this symbol: ◎

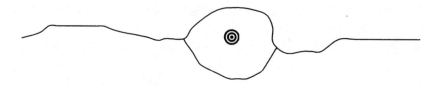

The highway department wants to give the new roads route numbers, and they consider the following alternatives:

(1) Route 22 runs toward the city, bypasses it to the north, then continues on the other side. Route 24 begins at route 22 on one side of the city, bypasses the city to the south, and ends at the other side where it rejoins route 22.

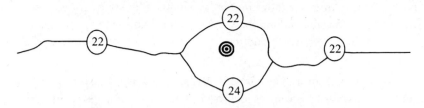

(2) Route 22 runs toward the city, bypasses it to the south, then continues on the other side. Route 24 begins at route 22 on one side of the city, bypasses the city to the north, and ends at the other side where it rejoins route 22.

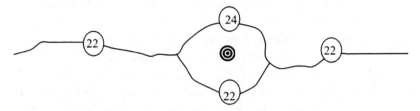

(3) Route 22 runs from the west of the city toward its outskirts, ending at circular route 24, which runs completely around the city. Route 26 begins at the circular route on the east side of the city, continuing eastward away from it.

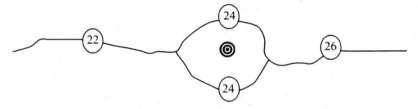

And obviously there are other possibilities too. They wonder: which one is the right way to number the routes? Clearly they want to give sections of the same road the same route number, but which sections are part of the same road? Is the eastern section the same road as the northern bypass? If so, numbering the road according to alternatives 2) or 3) would be mistaken. Or is the eastern section the same road as the southern bypass? If so, that rules out alternatives (1) and (3). Or is the whole bypass a separate road? If so, maybe 3) is correct. And so on. What's the right answer?

SCEPTIC: Obviously there isn't any "right" answer. They can number the roads any way they please.

ANTIREALIST: I agree. They don't *discover* what the answer is: they *decide* on a right answer. I suggest that there aren't any real facts about any cases of identity: we just decide what we're going to say, what we're going to count as stages of one continuing entity. That's why some of those cases are problems: because people haven't run into them—they're imaginary, of course—and we haven't had to make a decision about how to deal with them.

RELATIONIST: But it surely isn't always just an *arbitrary* decision, is it? I mean, some ways of deciding identity of continuing objects would be really *incorrect*. For example, under completely ordinary circumstances—no memory transplants anything—we couldn't simply decide arbitrarily that Alice and Betty switched bodies every Thursday.

ANTIREALIST: I agree that there are sometimes some reasons to decide one way or the other about some cases, and I'll tell you another fable that I think illustrates why in some cases one answer counts as a "right" answer. Suppose that there's a very old building, a thousand years old. Over the years, they've replaced parts that have rotted away, or have been destroyed by fire, so now (like the boat you talked about earlier), none of the original material remains. Let's ask the boat question here: is this the same building that was here 1000 years ago? Or is this a replacement? Now, imagine two professors of architecture. The first one is interested in what's happened to wood that has been in a building for 1000 years. He's taken to see this house, but he's disappointed. According to him, it's a replacement, a reconstruction, not the authentic original house. The second historian is interested in the layout of medieval buildings. Because the layout of the original house has been preserved as parts have been replaced, he's very happy to find this one: according to him, this is an authentic 1000-year old house, perfect for his investigations. The first professor is using the Cartesian "substance" theory of identity, and the second one is using a different theory, maybe something like Locke's way of explaining the identity of living things. Both answers are just fine, because the right answer depends on what you're interested in. It's a relative matter, depending on the interests of the person who asks.

SCEPTIC: Okay, so what do you think about all those brainometer cases we had problems with?

ANTIREALIST: The unanswerability of your problem cases may be the result of the fact that they're so divorced from any real-life situation that we can't imagine what anyone might be interested in who asks about identity. When you've got some purposes in mind behind asking identity questions, then there's a chance that an answer would count as right—given those purposes.

SCEPTIC: What does *antirealist* mean?

ANTIREALIST: It's a general name for any philosophical position that denies that there are real external facts in some sort of area. In this case, it means that I don't think that there are any external matters of fact about identity—they're not real features of the external world out there to be discovered. We make them up, according to our own interests and points of view.

SCEPTIC: That's like subjectivism in ethics, discussed earlier,[8] right?

ANTIREALIST: Yes, subjectivism is a form of antirealism too.

SCEPTIC: But your position also sounds sort of like PRAGMATIST's views about religion.[9]

ANTIREALIST: I agree. Pragmatists might say what counts as the right answer to a question depends on the needs that prompted the person to ask it.

CARTESIAN: But antirealism about identity can't be right. Imagine you're trying to reassure one of those electric company workers who's afraid that sooner or later she'll suffer amnesia and there will be a mix-up in the process of memory restoration. She's worried about her own future. Now, suppose you give her the antirealist line, that there's no fact of the matter about which body she'll be inhabiting afterwards—that it's really up to her to decide what will count as her, depending on what point of view and interests she has. She wouldn't find that satisfying. She'd think that there is a real fact of the matter about where she would end up. She wouldn't be happy deciding on an answer—she'd want to know the truth! And I bet you would too, in her place.

ANTIREALIST: Well, maybe that feeling is really a mistake. Maybe there isn't any truth, beyond what we decide.

8. Meaning Empiricism

SCEPTIC: If you wouldn't mind, I'd like to change the subject drastically at this point, to something completely different that I've been thinking about and I was reminded of by the discussion of antirealism. In these discussions, there's been a lot of talk about what's meant by one word or another, but I've been wondering whether there is any fact of the matter here, either. Can you define a word any way you like, on the basis of what that word means to you? For example, I once heard somebody claim that it was easy to prove the existence of God, because 'God,' to her, meant love, and of course everyone believes in the existence of love. I objected that

8 Conversation III.
9 Conversation I.

that definition wasn't really what was meant by 'God' at all—that wasn't really what the word meant. But what, after all, does give words their meaning? Is it just whatever associations you have with that word? If so, can you choose what you want words to mean? What is a meaning anyway? Is there really any such thing?

INTERNALIST: Well, the British empiricists, who've come into our discussions from time to time, had a very good theory about what meaning is. I'll tell you Hume's version of their theory. Like the other empiricists, Hume thought that every idea—every mental concept—comes from sense experience. So he thought of our mental ideas as dim copies of sense experiences (which Hume called *impressions*). For instance, when a small child sees a dog, the child has a sense image—an impression—at that time, and later is able to call up a copy of that sense image—an idea—and compare that with new impressions, to see if those new impressions are similar. This is how the child gets the concept of *dog*. And, usually at the same time, children learn to associate the word 'dog' with that idea. That's what's going on when you learn a language—when you learn what words mean. What they mean is what idea you've associated them with.

SCEPTIC: This is familiar stuff. In the discussion about knowledge,[10] RATIONALIST raised problems with EMPIRICIST's theory of the origin and nature of concepts, and I think those objections apply to the *empiricist theory of meaning* too.

INTERNALIST: Well, let's talk about them again, and see if they apply to our topic.

SCEPTIC: Okay, but first let me see if I have the empiricist's idea theory of meaning straight. Suppose that you learn the word 'dog' as a small child when somebody says that word while you're looking at one, and (according to the empiricist) you store an idea, a copy of the visual impression you have at that time, with the word 'dog' associated with the idea. Then the next time you see a dog, you match your new sense impression with the stored idea, and find that it matches up, so you call the new thing 'dog' too. Then you see a cat, and find that your cat sense impression doesn't match the stored dog-idea, so you don't use the word 'dog' for the cat. You've learned the word. Is that the way it's supposed to work?

INTERNALIST: Yes, that's exactly it.

SCEPTIC: But suppose the dog I see, on the occasion when I'm taught the word, is a grey dog standing facing to the left from my point of view, and I store a copy of that visual image. But then I'm shown Fido, a brown-

---

10 Conversation VI, Section 6.

and-white spotted dog, facing to the right, and Tabitha, a grey cat standing facing to the left. If I check my original image against these two for matching, I find the original matches Fido in some ways, and Tabitha in others. So it isn't clear whether my 'dog' idea matches the Fido-impression or the Tabitha-impression.

INTERNALIST: Okay, so what? That means that you haven't really mastered the word 'dog' yet. You have to see a large number of dogs, plus a large number of non-dogs—cats, etc.—before you get the general idea of what the word 'dog' does and does not apply to, because there's a wide variety of impressions that are dog-impressions.

SCEPTIC: I agree, but I thought that empiricists claim that, even after this long and involved learning process, the 'dog' idea I've got is still a particular image, like a snapshot of a particular dog from a particular angle.

INTERNALIST: Right, but what you're learning is how to use this particular image to identify a large variety of things as fitting the word 'dog,' things which don't match this particular snapshot in a wide variety of ways. For example, you learn to disregard the colour of your dog-idea when matching it up to new impressions: the colour doesn't matter. Your 'dog' idea is grey, but you can identify new brown-and-white things as dogs. The general shape and size are relevant, however.

SCEPTIC: So learning a language involves more than merely associating a word with a particular idea—a particular snapshot image. It also involves learning how to use this image to identify things as dogs that nevertheless differ from this image in a variety of ways, and how to identify things as non-dogs that are, nevertheless, like this image in a variety of ways.

INTERNALIST: I guess that's right.

SCEPTIC: Well, then, it seems that empiricists owe us some more in their theory of ideas. They need to tell us how ideas, which are always snapshots of particular experiences, can be general—can apply to a wide variety of different-looking things.

INTERNALIST: This problem—the problem of general ideas, and therefore of words which get their meaning from them—came up in the earlier discussion. You're right that this is something that needs further theorizing. In fact, the great British empiricists Locke, Berkeley, and Hume all recognized this problem—the problem of general ideas—and tried to deal with it.

SCEPTIC: Here's another problem for the empiricist theory. There are words that are obviously meaningful, like 'unicorn.' There aren't any such things as unicorns, so you can't have a sense impression of one, so there can't be an idea which is a copy of a sense impression for the word 'unicorn' to be associated with. So how can that word be meaningful?

INTERNALIST: When RATIONALIST brought up the example of the idea of unicorns in the earlier discussion, EMPIRICIST had a good answer to this problem. Empiricists agree that words like 'unicorn' can be meaningful, even though we don't have any ideas that come from experiencing them. In that sort of case, the word is defined in terms of ideas you can get from other experiences. 'Unicorn,' for example, means an animal with a horse's body, a single spiralled horn, deer's feet, goat's beard, and lion's tail; and it's friendly only to virgins.

SCEPTIC: Virgins!?

INTERNALIST: So people can get the idea of a unicorn by combining ideas from what they really have seen: horses, deer, goats, lions, and so on. Obviously 'unicorn' can't have an *ostensive* definition—that is, a definition accomplished by showing somebody some of them. But it can have an *analytic* definition, in terms of characteristics people already know about from their experience.

SCEPTIC: Okay, nonetheless there are words that name things that we don't experience through our senses, but it's not clear how they might be defined by putting together ideas that do arise from experience. 'God' for example. Whether or not God does exist, just about everyone—believers and atheists alike—agree that you don't have sense experiences associated with the concept. So if the only way that a word gets a meaning is by association with an idea which is a snapshot of sense experiences, then that word wouldn't have any meaning. But everyone—atheists and believers alike—agree that the word has meaning.

INTERNALIST: Well, empiricists might say that there is an idea associated with the word 'God,' and as in the case of 'unicorn' its not composed of impressions of what the word refers to, but instead of impressions got by other means. For example, we can sense imperfect, finite things, and so by taking the opposite of those ideas, we can get the ideas of perfection and infinity, even though we never sense things that fully have those characteristics. So maybe again there's an analytic definition. Another possible reply is the one EMPIRICIST suggested earlier: that we really don't have a genuine idea associated with the word 'God.' That would make the word really meaningless, and what you think atheists and believers all agree on would actually be wrong.

SCEPTIC: Well maybe the empiricist idea theory of meaning has a chance of responding to these problems about words like 'unicorn' and 'God,' but how about other words? Like 'the' for example? Or 'a.' I'm sure that those words don't correspond with any snapshot visual images in my mind.

INTERNALIST: But you do have an idea corresponding to those words, don't you?

SCEPTIC: I don't know. I don't think so.

INTERNALIST: Well, let's try an experiment. Listen to these two sentences:

> Put the ball under the tree.
>
> Put the ball under a tree.

They differ only in that one has 'the' where the other has 'a.' You understand both sentences, of course, and you understand their difference, so your ideas corresponding to the first sentence are different from your ideas corresponding to the second.

SCEPTIC: Well, sure, those two sentences mean different things to me, but I can't detect any little particular difference in any of my mind's-eye visual snapshot images when I think about the meanings of those sentences. The words 'the' and 'a' don't correspond to visual images at all.

INTERNALIST: Well, look at it this way: there is a difference in the ideas both sentences are associated with in your head, so maybe we should think of the meaning of 'the' and the meaning of 'a' in terms of their contribution to the ideas you have of the whole sentences. I mean, the words 'ball' and 'tree' and maybe even the words 'under' and 'put' correspond to visual ideas you have, and maybe the meanings of the rest of the words in those sentences can be thought instead as the glue, so to speak, that joins these ideas together to make the complex idea of the whole sentence.

SCEPTIC: Maybe, but that's going a good deal beyond the original empiricist theory, isn't it?

9. Meaning Internalism

INTERNALIST: Look, the problems you've been raising so far are really with the empiricist's theory of what ideas are, not with the view that what gives language its meaning is the association of words with ideas. The real point we should be concentrating on here is on what makes words meaningful. What I really want to defend is *meaning internalism*, the position that the meaning of some bits of language is given by what internal states of the speaker (or writer) they correspond to. We can continue to call these internal states 'ideas,' but let's not get hung up on what, exactly, these internal states are, or where they come from. Maybe the empiricist's theory of ideas isn't adequate, but don't you agree that the meaning of what you say has to do with what ideas you're trying to communicate? Somebody knows what you mean by what you say when they understand what your ideas were, right?

SCEPTIC: But I don't see how that's any different from merely saying that different words have different meanings. The empiricists' snapshot-image theory of ideas at least tried to give an account of what an idea was, and of what made one different from another. But when you make the idea of 'idea' broader and more abstract, I don't really think it helps in an explanation of meaning at all.

INTERNALIST: Okay, I admit that I owe you more of an account of what these internal states are. But don't you agree that words get their meaning by association with them, whatever they are?

SCEPTIC: Well, one worry I have about it is that it makes meaning a very individualistic thing. The idea I have associated with a word might be very different from the idea you have, and it seems that there's no question of right or wrong here. It's just a question of what the word means to me—which is one thing—and what the word means to you—which might be something quite different. That's a sort of relativism about meaning, and that gets back to the question I asked earlier. Can words really mean whatever you mean them to?

INTERNALIST: Hmm. Well, I suppose I'd have to say that what I mean by what I say is the idea I have inside me, which I want to communicate, so this is a kind of relativism about meaning.

SCEPTIC: But if the meaning of a person's words had to do with what private ideas that person has connecting to those words, then it would seem that we could never know whether a person is using any words with the meanings they actually have in the language, or with some other meaning.

INTERNALIST: I suppose that's right, but in a way, that wouldn't make any difference. If I say I got a new dog for Christmas, then you'll understand me even if our mental pictures associated with those words are quite different.

10. Meaning as Reference

REFERENTIALIST: Aha! That's just it! That's exactly what's wrong with the idea theory as a *theory of meaning*. If I can understand what you mean, even though the idea I get in response to the word 'dog' is totally different from the one you have when you say it, then what that shows is that the ideas we have don't have anything to do with the meaning of that word.

SCEPTIC: Well, what does?

REFERENTIALIST: What I know, and what you know, when we both know the meaning of the word 'dog' is the fact that the word refers to Fido and Rover and those other things, but not to any other sort of thing. It's the connection between words and what they name—what they refer to in the external world—that their meaning consists of. That's the only way to understand how we can learn language, and how we can understand what each other means, and how we can make sure that we mean the same thing by what we say. The mental imagery you use to pick out the things 'dog' applies to and doesn't (if you use mental imagery at all) is private and hidden, but that doesn't matter. The fact that that word is used in connection with dogs is public—it's something we can learn, and it's something that can be checked on to see if we've learned it right.

SCEPTIC: Hmm, that reminds me of the discussion of private language a while back, during the discussion of philosophy of mind.[11]

REFERENTIALIST: Exactly. The way the argument went then was that if the meaning of a word were a private thing, your internal mental picture or some other sort of idea, then there would be no possibility of a public, objective test for whether you've used the word correctly—whether you've associated it with the correct idea, or with something completely irrelevant. All there would be is your feeling that you've used it in conjunction with the appropriate idea—the idea which copied the experience you had when you learned the word. There wouldn't be any difference between your feeling as if you got things right and your really getting things right. But that would mean that there's no sense to making that distinction: the whole idea of *getting things right* in that context disappears. If any word can mean anything, then the whole notion of meaning goes out the window. But the connection between a word and the external objects it refers to is something that is capable of public checking, so there is a distinction between using a word correctly and just feeling like you do.

---

11 Conversation IV.

SCEPTIC: Okay, tell me more about how reference is supposed to give words meaning.

REFERENTIALIST: Well, the clearest possible case of this is with proper names. Think of the name 'George W. Bush.' This refers to one guy, the 43rd president of the US. Once you know who that name refers to, you know what that name means. And that's all there is to the meaning. He's also known by some other nicknames—some people call him 'Dubya.' Those two names, 'George W. Bush' and 'Dubya' refer to the same person, and consequently they have exactly the same meaning.

SCEPTIC: Well, 'Dubya' is a sort of derogatory nickname, which 'George W. Bush' isn't, so isn't there a difference in meaning between the two?

REFERENTIALIST: I'd say that there are differences in associations, and in emotional tone and evaluative implication between the two, but not, strictly speaking, differences in *meaning*. That shows, by the way, why the reference theory of meaning is right and the idea theory of meaning is wrong. There are often differences in association between synonymous words—words with the same reference. But I think you'll agree that these differences—what ideas the words bring to mind—aren't really differences in the meanings of the words. The name 'Paris,' which is the proper name of that city in France, always brings to my mind Humphrey Bogart and Ingrid Bergman, in that scene in "Casablanca," where they're talking about how there will always be Paris. But you have to admit that this association has nothing to do with what that name really means.

SCEPTIC: It has something to do with what the name means to you, doesn't it?

REFERENTIALIST: Okay, sure, but that's a secondary kind of meaning. We're talking about the central kind of meaning—what the word means in the language, what it means to everyone who understands the language. This can't be a matter of individual associations.

SCEPTIC: Okay, I guess that it makes sense to distinguish the real meaning of a word from whatever associations people might happen to have with it. But couldn't the real meaning be ideas that everyone associates with the word—ideas whose association with the word you learn when you learn the language? Ideas so centrally associated with that word that those associations constitute knowing the meaning of the word? I still don't see why you think that the meaning of the word can't be associated ideas, but has to be what the word *refers* to.

REFERENTIALIST: Here's the story that makes me think that must be the case. Whether a particular sentence is true or false depends on two things: what that sentence means, and what the facts of the world are.

SCEPTIC: That sounds right.

REFERENTIALIST: And the meaning of the sentence is what determines what fact, in particular, would make the sentence true.

SCEPTIC: Wait a minute. When a sentence is false, the problem is that what it says doesn't correspond to any facts. But a false sentence has a meaning too.

REFERENTIALIST: I agree. The word 'fact' here is I guess the wrong one. Let's talk about *propositions* instead. They can be thought of as possible facts, some of which are actual, and some of which aren't. So for example the proposition expressed by 'George W. Bush was President in 2004' is a fact (that is, the sentence is true), while the proposition expressed by 'Al Gore was President in 2004' is not a fact (the sentence is false).

SCEPTIC: Okay.

REFERENTIALIST: So if two sentences have different meaning, then they express different propositions; different possible facts would make it true. For example, 'George W. Bush was smart in 2004' and 'George W. Bush was President in 2004' have different meanings, so one fact would make one of them true, while a different fact would make the other one true. Some people think that one sentence is actually true, given the way the actual facts are, and the other one false. Let's not argue about this however-er.

SCEPTIC: Okay, go on.

REFERENTIALIST: Now, what does the phrase 'George W. Bush' contribute to the propositions expressed—that is to picking out what possible fact is relevant to making either of these true or false? The only thing it contributes is picking out the person who that phrase refers to.

SCEPTIC: I think I see what you mean. So if the only meaning of a proper name is to pick out what the sentence is about, then any way of picking that thing out has the same meaning, right?

REFERENTIALIST: Right. You can call him 'George W. Bush' or 'Dubya' and it amounts to the same thing, as far as meaning is concerned—though it would change the evaluative tone of the sentence, or the associations, which don't really have anything centrally to do with meaning. Except for a few sorts of cases (which make things a little more complicated than this), the same proposition is expressed whatever way you refer to the same thing. So that's why (usually) the truth or falsity of a sentence doesn't change if you substitute one name for something with another one. For example,

George W. Bush ordered Iraq to be invaded.

is true; so

Dubya ordered Iraq to be invaded.

and

The 43rd President of the US ordered Iraq to be invaded

are both true too.

SCEPTIC: What sorts of cases are the exceptions?

REFERENTIALIST: Well, for example, the sentence

'George W. Bush' is the 43rd President's nickname.

is false, but replacing that name with 'Dubya' changes it to true.

INTERNALIST: Okay, I get it, but I think I can say now exactly why you're wrong. Here's an example in which that doesn't work. (It's the one used by the great early twentieth-century philosopher of language Gottlob Frege.) The ancient Greeks called a bright astronomical object that sometimes appeared in the evening sky 'Hesperus' and one that often appeared in the morning sky 'Phosphorous.' They didn't know that those were the same thing: the planet Venus. So, for example, when an Ancient Greek, call him Astronomos, saw Venus in the evening sky, this sentence would have been true:

Astronomos believes that Hesperus is in the sky.

but this sentence would have been false:

Astronomos believes that Phosphorous is in the sky.

even though the only difference between these sentences is the substitution of one name for another name of the same thing.

SCEPTIC: Okay, what do you say about that then?

REFERENTIALIST: Well, the way Frege dealt with this example was by saying that you have to distinguish between the *referent* of a word—what it refers to, and its *sense*. In this case, the two words have the same referent, but different senses.

INTERNALIST: Aha, so reference doesn't really explain meaning. This sounds like a distinction I've often heard made, between the *denotation* of a word—what the word refers to—and the *connotation* of that word—the associations that that word has.

REFERENTIALIST: But that's not what Frege had in mind. What he thought of as the sense of a word was not some idea that's associated with the word, some associations people might have. For Frege the sense of a word is the *way* the word picks out its referent. The Ancient Greeks had one way of picking Venus out when it was called 'Phosphorous'—by looking for a very bright star-like object in the morning sky—and a different way of picking Venus out when it was called 'Hesperus'—by looking for a very bright star-like object in the evening sky. ·

SCEPTIC: But I thought that the whole idea of your theory was to account for meaning by reference. What the words in those two sentences

Astronomos believes that Hesperus is in the sky.

Astronomos believes that Phosphorous is in the sky.

refer to is the same, so how do you account for the difference in truth?

REFERENTIALIST: Frege's solution was that, in sentences like that, where what we're talking about is somebody's belief, the name doesn't have its usual reference; in those cases, it refers to its sense.

SCEPTIC: I don't follow you.

REFERENTIALIST: What we're talking about in those sentences is not Venus, but rather the ways of picking Venus out: that's what makes the difference. Each sentence talks about—refers to—different ways of picking Venus out.

SCEPTIC: Hmm, I think I get it now. But look. Maybe that works for the meaning of names, but what about other parts of language? I can see all sorts of problems here. For example, proper names refer to one particular person or thing, but what about general nouns like 'dog.' These can refer to a particular canine in one sentence ('Fred owns a dog'), and a different one in another ('Sally owns a dog also'). And sometimes no dog in particular ('That noise must have been made by a dog turning over the garbage can' and 'Marvin wants to buy a dog some day'). This is the problem of general names again.

REFERENTIALIST: That's a complicated matter. You've got a collection of things, any one of which can correctly be called 'dog.' So in a sense, 'dog' is an ambiguous proper name, capable of referring to a lot of different things, like the word 'Fred.' There are a lot of people named 'Fred,' so that word can be used with lots of different references.

SCEPTIC: That doesn't sound right to me. I agree that 'dog' can be used to refer to Fido or to Rover, and that sometimes it might not be clear which one the speaker is referring to, but I don't think that shows that the word is ambiguous—has different meanings. Whether it refers to Fido or to Rover, it means the same thing. Anyway, how about adjectives, like 'brown'? But what kind of thing is that? There are brown things, but there isn't a brown.

REFERENTIALIST: Maybe this refers to a characteristic, brownness.

SCEPTIC: What is brownness? That's a very peculiar sort of object. You can see individual brown things, but you can't see brownness in general.

REFERENTIALIST: Right, philosophers have given a good deal of attention to that matter.

SCEPTIC: And of course there are words in other grammatical categories: 'is,' 'the,' 'all,' 'when,' 'under,' 'if,' and so on. None of them names things.

REFERENTIALIST: Right, but each of them contributes in particular kinds of ways to the determination of exactly what fact would make a sentence true. This is of course a long story.

SCEPTIC: I can see that!

11. Meaning as Use

SPEECH-ACT THEORIST: Maybe that referential theory is okay, as far as it goes, but it seems to me that it misses the main point about language, and about what the meaning of language is.

SCEPTIC: Please explain.

SPEECH-ACT THEORIST: The point of the referential theory, I take it, is to explain what language is about by talking about the ways language hooks up with the world—how bits of sentences point out objects in the world, and how sentences express propositions and therefore (depending on the facts) are true or false.

REFERENTIALIST: I agree. What's wrong with that?

SPEECH-ACT THEORIST: I think that a much more inclusive way of thinking about meaning is to think about what people say with language, rather than what language says. Or, better, what people *do* with it.

REFERENTIALIST: Well, surely what people do with it is to talk about the way the world is—to refer to things, and to make true or false statements about them. That's the basis of my theory of meaning.

SPEECH-ACT THEORIST: I agree that this is one thing people do with language, but they do a large number of other things too.

REFERENTIALIST: Of course, but my worry is whether these other things have anything directly to do with the meaning of what they say. I could for example bore you equally well by telling you about my summer vacation in Cleveland, or by reading you some verses from Spencer's endless poem "The Faerie Queen," (1590) which I just happen to have handy. Ready?

> Far hence (quoth he) in wastfull wildernesse
> His dwelling is, by which no living wight
> May ever passe, but thorough great distresse.
> Now (sayd the Lady) draweth toward night,
> And well I wote, that of your later fight
> Ye all forwearied be: for what so strong,
> But wanting rest will also want of might?
> The Sunne that measures heaven all day long,
> At night doth baite his steedes the Ocean waves emong.

SPEECH-ACT THEORIST: STOP! What's your point?

REFERENTIALIST: It's perfectly clear that what I just said bored or puzzled you. But that doesn't have anything to do with the meaning of the poetry, whatever that is, right?

SPEECH-ACT THEORIST: That's true.

REFERENTIALIST: Other things I could do with language that are, let's see ... test a microphone, practise my French ... get you to pass the salt, give directions, lie ... soothe someone who's upset, infuriate anyone who's listening, indulge in idle chit-chat, make funny noises, gossip.... But I can't see the relevance of any of what people do with words to what's meant by what they say.

SPEECH-ACT THEORIST: You're right that most of the items on your list have nothing to do directly with the meaning of the words they utter. But there is one type of act that people do that's directly relevant to the meaning of what they say. The mid-twentieth-century English philosopher J.L. Austin distinguished three kinds of actions people do when using language. Here they are: (1) The *locutionary* act. This is merely the act of making sounds (or writing marks) in a language—just saying something. It doesn't matter who hears (or reads) them, or what goes on in the recipient, if there is any recipient. You do this when you're merely making funny noises, testing a microphone, or trying out a new pen. These sorts of actions have no connection with the meaning of the words uttered. (2) The *illocutionary* act. This is done by means of a locutionary act. It's not merely saying something; it's done *by* saying something. It involves someone hearing (or reading) the words, and understanding them. Examples of this are ordering, asking a question, informing, offering, promising, warning, requesting, denying, and so on. (3) The *perlocutionary* act. This one is the action of getting somebody to do something—producing an effect on the person's feelings, thoughts, or actions. It's accomplished by means of an illocutionary act. An example in your list above of a perlocutionary act is getting someone to pass the salt. This can be done by the illocutionary act of requesting that the person pass the salt. Notice here that you've requested that somebody pass the salt just as soon as that person has heard and understood your words, but further response from that person is necessary—passing the salt—before you've succeeded in getting that person to pass the salt. Boring people, surprising them, insulting them, getting them to do things, by means of what you say, are also examples of perlocutionary acts.

SCEPTIC: Is that word 'illocutionary' or 'elocutionary'?

SPEECH-ACT THEORIST: The first. 'Elocution' means the art of speaking clearly and expressively. 'Illocutionary' and the other two names, 'locutionary' and 'perlocutionary,' are terms Austin made up.

SCEPTIC: That's a complicated distinction, and I'm not sure I'm entirely clear on it. How about another example?

SPEECH-ACT THEORIST: Right. Imagine that you say to Fred, who's driving the car you're riding in, 'There's a pothole in the road!' Making those noises which mention a potentially dangerous situation—that there's a pothole in the road ahead—is a locutionary act. If Fred hears you, and speaks enough English to know that this is the conventional way in English to warn somebody, then Fred realizes that you're warning him, and you've accomplished the illocutionary act of warning him of the pothole. If, in addition, Fred swerves the car so that it avoids the pothole, then you've succeeded in getting him to avoid the pothole by means of your warning. This is your perlocutionary act.

SCEPTIC: I'm not sure I've got that distinction perfectly.

SPEECH-ACT THEORIST: Here's a way to tell illocutionary from perlocutionary acts. When something is an illocutionary act, it makes sense to say, 'I hereby' and then name the act. You can say,

> I hereby announce that ...
> I hereby predict that ...
> I hereby deny that ...
> I hereby inform you that ...
> I hereby order ... (ordering food in a restaurant)
> I hereby invite you to ...
> I hereby request that ...
> I hereby warn you that ...

and so on. So announcing, predicting, and so on, are all illocutionary acts. But it doesn't make sense to say

> I hereby bore you.
> I hereby get you to look out for that pothole.
> I hereby get you to believe that ...
> I hereby alarm you.
> I hereby infuriate you.
> I hereby make you wonder whether ...

Those are all perlocutionary acts. The reason why you can sensibly say "I hereby X," when X-ing is an illocutionary act, is that you do it just by saying it: that's all it takes. To accomplish any perlocutionary act, you need additional response from the hearer, so it's not something you've automatically accomplished just by saying it. So the illocutionary act is really what you centrally, basically do with words.

SCEPTIC: But I thought you said earlier that in order to accomplish an illocutionary act, it's necessary that the hearer hear and understand what you've said.

SPEECH-ACT THEORIST: Well, yes, Austin says that you haven't succeeded in doing it unless that happens. Austin calls this requirement *uptake*—when the audience hears (or reads) what you said (or wrote) and understands it—takes it for what it is. For example, suppose you're trying to invite Fred to your birthday, but there's no uptake. Fred doesn't hear what you say, or else Fred hears it, but he doesn't understand it, because his grasp of the language isn't too good. Then you really haven't invited him.

SCEPTIC: That's not clear to me. The analogy here is that you mail the invitation to Fred, but he never opens the invitation, or if he opens it, he doesn't really read it, or pay attention. You've still invited him, haven't you? I mean, suppose later you ask him why he seems sort of angry at you, and he says it's because you never invited him to your birthday. You say, yes you did. The truth of the matter, I'd say, is that you really did invite him. It just didn't get through. The same thing with the other items on your "hereby" list. If you predict something, but there isn't audience uptake for some reason, for example, it's too noisy for them to hear you, or they're not listening, or they don't understand your language, you've still predicted it, haven't you? Those announcements they're always making in the airport that are impossible for anyone to understand: they're still announcements, aren't they?

SPEECH-ACT THEORIST: Well, maybe. But I guess this issue isn't really central to the point of Austin's three-way distinction.

SCEPTIC: What is the point?

SPEECH-ACT THEORIST: The point is that the meaning of a sentence is its conventional potential for performing illocutionary acts. Any sentence at all, whatever it meant, could accomplish any perlocutionary act, given the right (maybe peculiar) circumstances. But the illocutionary-act-potential of a sentence is connected directly to its meaning. "Please pass the salt" is one of the conventional ways of requesting of somebody that they pass the salt. "It's snowing in Tibet" is not. Once you've specified the conventional illocutionary-act-potential of a sentence, you've given its meaning.

REFERENTIALIST: Okay, let me ask you about one thing you said. In the example of warning the driver about the pothole, you said that the speaker mentions that there's a pothole in the road as part of the illocutionary act. This is the proposition expressed by the sentence the speaker utters. It refers to the pothole and the road, and so on. It's true providing that the proposition corresponds to a fact. This is what I was talking about earlier. You're not really disagreeing with me then, are you?

SPEECH-ACT THEORIST: Well, philosophers of language in the speech-act theory tradition often include what we might call a *propositional act*—the act of expressing a proposition—as a typical part of the locutionary act. I think that your ideas about reference and truth all go to explain what proposition is expressed by any locutionary act. I agree that this is an important part of meaning. What I think is the advantage of speech-act theory is that its account of meaning includes what proposition is expressed by an utterance, plus a good deal more. The way they often put this is to say that the meaning of a particular utterance is constituted by the proposition expressed plus the illocutionary force. So, for example, what that person says to the driver does express that proposition about a pothole in the road, but it does so with the illocutionary force of a warning. There are all sorts of illocutionary acts that one can perform, given the appropriate circumstances, including the same propositional act. For instance, you can warn Fred that the door is open, or merely inform him of that, or ask if it's true, or deny it, or request or order that he make it true. These are all illocutionary acts which involve the same proposition— that the door is open—but they have different illocutionary force. There are changes in wording that conventionally indicate the illocutionary force of what you say, as well as tones of voice or other manners of speaking. Having added an account of illocutionary force to what you've been talking about, the referential and propositional aspects of language, we've got a fuller and more adequate account.

12. Meanings and Intentions

SCEPTIC: Well, if you don't mind, I'd like to return at this point to the question I asked which started this discussion of meaning: can anyone mean whatever they like by what they say?

INTERNALIST: It seems to me that SPEECH-ACT THEORIST's position reinforces what I had to say earlier. It looks to me as though the meaning of some utterance, according to that position, really has to do with its connection with an internal state after all.

SPEECH-ACT THEORIST: Why do you say that?

INTERNALIST: Well, your theory explains the meaning of a sentence in terms of the action performed by the person who says it, right?

SPEECH-ACT THEORIST: Right.

INTERNALIST: But an *action*, as I understand the way philosophers use that term, is something a person does intentionally, right? As opposed to just by accident? So, for example, if I knock over a vase in your house by accident, not intending to do it, then that's not an action.

SPEECH-ACT THEORIST: Right.

INTERNALIST: But it is an action when it's done accompanied by the person's intention?

SPEECH-ACT THEORIST: Okay.

INTERNALIST: So, when I say, for example, 'Please pass the salt,' the reason that's the action of asking you to pass the salt is that I intended to make that request. I didn't just do it by accident. What's meant here—that it's a polite request for the salt—has to do with my intention.

SPEECH-ACT THEORIST: Hmm. Maybe.

INTERNALIST: Now, suppose my grasp of English isn't too good, and I have trouble remembering whether that stuff is called 'salt' or 'sugar,' and I say, 'Please pass the sugar.' What I intended here is to request that the *salt* be passed. What I meant by those words was *Please pass the salt*. The same thing is true for a slip-of-the-tongue. Somebody with very good command of English, who's a little careless or distracted, might say, 'Please pass the sugar' meaning *Please pass the salt*. So what the words somebody utters means is a matter of the internal state—the intentions—of the speaker.

SPEECH-ACT THEORIST: Hmm.

INTERNALIST: Okay, let me try to get at this from a different angle. Suppose that Fred wants Sally to give him the salt. There are various ways that he might accomplish this, but the way using language is to *ask* her to pass it; so that's what he wants to do, using words. So he picks out some words that he hopes will let Sally know that his intention is to ask that the salt be passed. Sally's "uptake" is her inference from the words she hears that this is Fred's intention, to ask her to pass the salt.

SPEECH-ACT THEORIST: That sounds right to me.

INTERNALIST: Successful communication, then, takes place just as soon as Sally's correctly surmised Fred's intentions.

SPEECH-ACT THEORIST: Agreed.

INTERNALIST: So, for example, if Sally knows that Fred has some trouble with English, she might guess, given the circumstances, that when he says, 'Please pass the sugar' before starting to eat his steak that his intention is to ask for the salt. He intends to ask for the salt, and she recognizes this intention, so he really has successfully asked for the salt; and, unless Sally's feeling especially nasty and recalcitrant, she'll pass it to him. So that's the whole meaning of the speech-act, and it depends entirely on what Fred's intentions are. Meanings are given by speaker's intentions.

13. Meanings and Conventions

SPEECH-ACT THEORIST: Well, I know that some philosophers who were working in the speech-act tradition of philosophy of language have taken your internalist approach. The intentions of the speaker certainly have a lot to do with meanings. But I prefer the approach of other speech-act philosophers, who hold what might be called an *externalism* about meanings—the view that meanings are an objective matter, rather than private, subjective, and variable, as they would be if they were entirely a matter of the speaker's intentions. So despite Fred's intentions, I'd insist that what he says means *Please pass the sugar* not *Please pass the salt*. I think that there are facts about what something means, whatever somebody intends.

INTERNALIST: But you do think that intentions have something to do with meaning?

SPEECH-ACT THEORIST: Yes, they do. People often need a way to indicate their intentions to others, hoping that the others would have sufficient good-will to help them achieve what they intend. The problem is that intentions are hidden.

SCEPTIC: Right, that's just the problem with the internalist view.

SPEECH-ACT THEORIST: Right. So what's needed is a conventional way to reveal those intentions.

SCEPTIC: You used that word 'conventional' before, when you said that the meaning of a sentence is its *conventional* potential for performing illocutionary acts. What exactly does that mean? You mean, 'conventional' in the sense of not spontaneous or sincere or original?

SPEECH-ACT THEORIST: Not exactly. I mean 'conventional' in the sense of following the general customs in a society. I'll explain. First of all, there's a distinction I'm relying on between *natural signs* and *conventional signs*. X is a sign of Y when X is correlated with Y. A natural sign of something is evidence for something "in nature" so to speak. A falling barometer is a natural sign of a coming storm. A runny nose is a natural sign of a cold. Red blotches on my shirt are a natural sign that I've been eating spaghetti for dinner. There are some natural signs of our intentions. You can sometimes tell that somebody intends to eat something by the way they're looking in the fridge. A natural sign that people intend to ride their bike is that they're putting on their bike helmet and pumping up their flat bike tires. But intentions are often hidden, especially the complicated ones—they don't have any reliable natural signs. So what we've evolved is systems of conventional signs—and this is where language comes in—when it's useful for us to reveal hidden complicated intentions to each other. The association between particular intentions and their conventional signs is arbitrary: based on custom, rather than natural cause-and-effect or correlation. The connection between my making the noise 'Please pass the salt' and my having the desire to get the salt passed and my intention to get you to pass it is an entirely arbitrary one, based on long-standing social agreement.

SCEPTIC: The idea of social agreement reminds me of what was discussed in the conversation about social philosophy. There was the agreement between the farmers to save the grass in the Commons, and the agreement between the prisoners to try to solve their dilemma. These were small-scale analogies of the general "social contract"—the conventional basis for society.[12]

SPEECH-ACT THEORIST: Right, that's the same sort of idea. What we've got in the case of language, as in those other cases, is a situation in which if we coordinated our behaviour—acted in the same ways in some respects—everyone would benefit. In the case of language, the benefit is communication of our intentions and desires to each other. In the case of the "social contract," there wasn't any explicit agreement about how people were going to act: it's rather a case of implied agreement: if you're going to be part of society, you're going to act according to the rules. It's the same situation here: if you're going to be part of the linguistic community, you have to play by the linguistic rules.

SCEPTIC: But there are differences between those social cases and this one.

SPEECH-ACT THEORIST: Yes there are. In the Commons and Prisoner's Dilemma cases there was the problem that keeping the agreement went against each person's self-interest. But in the case of language, behaving in accord with the agreed-on language rules, for example, using the noises 'Please pass the salt' when you'd like to get the hearer to pass the salt, rather than the noises 'It's snowing in Tibet,' does not go against anyone's self-interest. Once everyone recognizes that 'Please pass the salt' shows that the speaker is trying to get the hearer to pass the salt, then it's to everyone's interest to use those noises that way—because, of course, it's very likely that that sentence would be taken as a sign of those intentions. So there's no need for the equivalent of police enforcing the linguistic rules about what to say when you have one intention rather than the other.

INTERNALIST: Okay, let me see if I have your idea straight. I want you to pass the salt to me. I think you'd be willing to pass it if you knew I wanted it. So what I decide to do is to give you a sign that you'll take as showing that I'm trying to get you to pass the salt, hoping that this will motivate you to pass it.

SPEECH-ACT THEORIST: That's the idea.

---

12 Conversation II.

INTERNALIST: So the sign I choose to make is the one that I hope will tell you what I'm trying to do.

SPEECH-ACT THEORIST: Right.

INTERNALIST: So what I mean by that sign is that it be an indication of my inner state.

SPEECH-ACT THEORIST: Right, but you have to believe (rightly or wrongly) that what you're saying is the conventional sign of your intention. You think that sign will tell me that you're trying to get me to pass the salt because, you think, it's a conventional sign of a request for the salt, and I'll recognize it as such, so I'll understand what you're trying to do. The person who doesn't speak English very well, and who says, 'Please pass the sugar,' thinks that's the conventional sign for a request for the salt, but, of course, that person is mistaken. That person means *Please pass the salt*, but what that person says—the sentence itself—means *Please pass the sugar*.

SCEPTIC: Well, I think you both agree that there's a distinction between what a bit of language means—its conventional significance—and what a person means by saying that. But I guess you disagree about the possibility of a person's meaning whatever they like by saying something. INTERNALIST thinks that all you have to do is to utter something with an appropriate intention to mean something by it. SPEECH-ACT THEORIST thinks that, in addition, you have to believe that what you utter has the conventional meaning associated with that intention. Is that right? Let's hear your reactions to this: I remember that Wittgenstein asks readers to perform the experiment of saying 'It's cold here' but meaning *It's warm here*. He asks if you can do it (*Philosophical Investigations*, I §510).

INTERNALIST: I could do it. What I'd do is create inside myself the intention to inform you that it's warm here, and couple this with saying 'It's warm here,' hoping against hope that I'd succeed that way.

SPEECH-ACT THEORIST: I don't think that does it. I think that to succeed at Wittgenstein's experiment, you'd have to believe that 'It's cold here' was the conventional sign of the intention to inform someone that it's warm here. And you don't.

Suggested Readings

(See the Notes on "Suggested Readings" sections, p. 17-18.)

René Descartes (1596-1650) on identity is in various *Meditations*. By far the best edition of this for students is on-line at <http://www.earlymoderntexts.com>.

John Locke (1632-1704) on the various kinds of identity is found in Book II, Chapter 27, "Of Identity and Diversity," in *An Essay Concerning Human Understanding*. By far the best edition of this for students is on-line at <http://www.earlymoderntexts.com>.

David Hume (1711-76) gives his sceptical views on the identity of the self in Book I, Part IV, Section VI, "Of Personal Identity," in *A Treatise of Human Nature*. By far the best edition of this for students is on-line at <http://www.earlymoderntexts.com>.

An extremely readable treatment of various puzzle-cases of identity is *A Dialogue on Personal Identity and Immortality* by John Perry.

The empiricist version of the idea theory is advocated by John Locke (1632-1704) in Book III, Chapter 2 of *An Essay Concerning Human Understanding*. By far the best edition of this for students is on-line at <http://www.earlymoderntexts.com>.

John Stuart Mill (1806-73) in Book I, Chapters 1 and 2 of *A System of Logic* defends a version of the reference theory of meaning.

The classic article by Gottlob Frege (1848-1925) is "On Sense and Reference," also translated as "On Sense and Nominatum." This is available in many anthologies.

An influential work from the beginnings of speech-act theory was *How to Do Things With Words* by J.L. Austin (1911-60).

EPILOGUE

Quotations from Bertrand Russell

"I wish to propose for the reader's favourable consideration a doctrine which may, I fear, appear wildly paradoxical and subversive. The doctrine in question is this: that it is undesirable to believe a proposition when there is no ground whatever for supposing it true."

"Passive acceptance of the teacher's wisdom is easy to most boys and girls. It involves no effort of independent thought, and seems rational because the teacher knows more than his pupils; it is moreover the way to win the favour of the teacher unless he is a very exceptional man. Yet the habit of passive acceptance is a disastrous one in later life. It causes man to seek and to accept a leader, and to accept as a leader whoever is established in that position."

"If you think that your belief is based upon reason, you will support it by argument, rather than by persecution, and will abandon it if the argument goes against you. But if your belief is based on faith, you will realize that argument is useless, and will therefore resort to force either in the form of persecution or by stunting and distorting the minds of the young in what is called 'education.' This last is peculiarly dastardly since it takes advantage of the defencelessness of immature minds. Unfortunately it is practiced in a greater or less degree in the schools of every civilized country."

"I think we ought always to entertain our opinions with some measure of doubt. I shouldn't wish people dogmatically to believe any philosophy, not even mine."

"In all affairs it's a healthy thing now and then to hang a question mark on the things you have long taken for granted."

"What is wanted is not the will to believe, but the will to find out, which is the exact opposite."

"The demand for certainty is one which is natural to man, but is nevertheless an intellectual vice. If you take your children for a picnic on a doubtful day, they will demand a dogmatic answer as to whether it will be fine or wet, and be disappointed in you when you cannot be sure. The same sort of assurance is demanded, in later life, of those who undertake to lead populations into the Promised Land. 'Liquidate the capitalists and the survivors will enjoy eternal bliss.' 'Exterminate the Jews and everyone will be virtuous.' 'Kill the Croats and let the Serbs reign.' 'Kill the Serbs and let the Croats reign.' These are samples of the slogans that have won wide popular acceptance in our time. Even a modicum of philosophy would make it impossible to accept such bloodthirsty nonsense. But so long as men are not trained to withhold judgement in the absence of evidence, they will be led astray by cocksure prophets, and it is likely that their leaders will be either ignorant fanatics or dishonest charlatans. To endure uncertainty is difficult, but so are most of the other virtues. For the learning of every virtue there is an appropriate discipline, and for the learning of suspended judgement the best discipline is philosophy."

"Science is what you know, philosophy is what you don't know."

GLOSSARY WORKBOOK

Here you can write in definitions of the philosophical terms—words and phrases with technical specialized meaning—found in this book. The numeral to the left of each term indicates the section number in which it first occurs. While you're reading a section, or right after you've finished, pencil in definitions of the terms, referring back to the text if you're not sure what any of the terms mean.

Make sure your definitions are clear and complete, and written in your own words (that is, not just copied from the text of the book). Writing these definitions is an excellent way to achieve mastery of the concepts involved. And you'll find your lexicon handy when you need to be reminded of the meaning of a word, and when you're preparing for a paper or test.

Introduction

(2) sceptic

(3) argument

(3) premises

Conversation 1

(1) the First Cause Argument

(1) the Cosmological Argument

(1) First Cause

(1) the Unmoved Mover

(1) cosmology (in science)

(1) the Steady State Theory

(1) the Big Bang Theory

(1) the Cyclical Theory

(2) the Argument From Design

(2) the Teleological Argument

(2) teleological

(2) argument to the best explanation

(2) the Theory of Evolution Through Natural Selection

(2) Random Variation

(2) Natural Selection

(2) theory (in science)

(2) Creation Science

(3) the Ontological Argument

(3) ontological

(5) pragmatism

(5) the Pragmatic Theory of Truth

(6) Pascal's Wager

(7) atheism

(7) agnosticism

(7) burden of proof

(10) the Argument from the Existence of Evil

(10) omniscience

(10) omnipotence

(10) omnibenevolence

(10) soul-building

(12) fideism

(14) mysticism

Conversation 2

(2) the Tragedy of the Commons

(2) the Prisoner's Dilemma

(3) the state of nature

(3) the social contract

(4) the Voter's Paradox

(7) atomistic

(7) social construct

(7) communitarianism

(8) capitalists

(8) proletariat

(8) market considerations

(8) the Labour Theory of Value

(9) socialism

(9) communism

(9) Marxism

(9) fascism

(9) Nazism

(10) libertarianism

(11) interventionism

(11) feminism

(12) egalitarianism

(13) the original position

(13) the veil of ignorance

(13) the maximin principle

Conversation 3

(2) utilitarianism

(2) net happiness

(2) hedonism

(2) psychological hedonism

(2) ethical hedonism

(2) egoistic psychological hedonism

(2) the happiness psychological theory

(2) the satisfaction psychological theory

(3) utility

(3) utiles

(4) deontologism

(4) consequentialism

(7) rights

(8) ends in themselves

(9) the categorical imperative

(9) categorical

(9) hypothetical

(9) a hypothetical imperative

(9) maxim

(10) sympathy (in utilitarian ethical theory)

(10) a good will (in Kant's ethical theory)

(11) ethical objectivism

(11) moral intuition

(11) the Open Question Argument

(12) emotivism

(12) prescriptivism

(12) ethical subjectivism

(14) ethical relativism

Conversation 4

(1) materialism

(1) physicalism

(2) identical (in the relevant sense)

(2) the mind-body identity theory

(2) Ockham's Razor

(2) dualism

(2) Cartesian dualism

(2) monism

(2) idealism

(5) introspection

(7) the principle of the conservation of energy

(8) eliminative materialism

(8) Folk Psychology

(9) zombie (in the relevant sense)

(9) the Zombie Hypothesis

(9) the Problem of Other Minds

(9) private language

(10) behaviourism

(10) disposition

(11) artificial intelligence

(14) the Turing Test

(16) the Chinese Room Example

(16) the Fallacy of Composition

Conversation 5

(1) determinism

(1) indeterminism

(2) standing condition

(2) causal factor

(2) sufficient condition

(2) necessary condition

(2) INUS condition

(3) fatalism

(6) quantum indeterminacy

(6) no hidden variables

(7) free will

(7) libertarianism (in the relevant sense)

(9) soft determinism

(9) compatibilism

(9) hard determinism

(9) incompatibilism

(9) constrained

(12) deterrence (as an aim of punishment)

(12) reform (as an aim of punishment)

(12) isolation (as an aim of punishment)

(13) distributive justice

(13) retributive justice

(13) desert (in the relevant sense)

(13) retributivism

Conversation 6

(1) justified belief

(1) reliable belief

(2) certainty

(2) indubitibility

(2) *Cogito ergo sum*

(2) self-warranting

(2) clear and distinct reasoning

(2) the Cartesian Circle

(3) foundation (in the relevant sense)

(3) fallibilism

(4) the Lottery Paradox

(5) Gettier problems

(6) empiricism

(6) concept

(6) judgement

(6) innate

(6) *tabula rasa*

(7) rationalism (about religion / about knowledge)

(7) deep structure of language

(8) *a posteriori*

(8) *a priori*

(9) conceptual analysis

(9) analytic

(9) synthetic

(11) sense data

(12) brain in a vat

(13) the Five-Minute Hypothesis

(14) inductive reasoning

(14) the Principle of Induction

(14) the Problem of Induction

Conversation 7

(2) continuing object

(2) physical substance

(2) mental substance

(2) substance theory of identity

(2) stage of a continuing object

(2) identity through time

(3) (sense) impression

(5) the relationist theory of identity

(5) forensic

(5) a vegetative state

(7) antirealist

(8) the empiricist theory of meaning

(9) meaning internalism

(10) the reference theory of meaning

(10) the referent of a word

(11) meaning as use

(11) locutionary act

(11) illocutionary act

(11) perlocutionary act

(11) uptake

(13) meaning externalism

(13) conventional illocutionary act potential

(13) conventional (in the relevant sense)